The Crossing
of Two Roads

American Catholic Identities
A Documentary History
Christopher J. Kauffman, General Editor

American Catholic Identities is a nine-volume series that makes available to the general reader, the student, and the scholar seminal documents in the history of American Catholicism. Subjects are wide-ranging and topically ordered within periods to encounter the richly textured experiences of American Catholics from the earliest years to the present day. The twenty-six editors of these volumes reveal a command of trends in historiography since the publication of John Tracy Ellis's three-volume work, *Documents of American Catholic History*. Hence the American Catholic Identities series shows developments in our understanding of social history — the significance of gender, race, regionalism, ethnicity, and spirituality, as well as Catholic thought and practice before and since the Second Vatican Council.

The series elucidates myriad meanings of the American Catholic experience by working with the marker of religious identity. It brings into relief the historical formations of religious self-understandings of a wide variety of Catholics in a society characterized by the principles of religious liberty, separation of church and state, religious pluralism, and voluntarism.

American Catholic Identities is united by such dominant factors in American history as waves of immigration, nativism, anti-Catholicism, racism, sexism, and several other social and ideological trends. Other aspects of unity are derived from American Catholic history: styles of episcopal leadership, multiple and various types of Catholic institutions, and the dynamic intellectual interaction between the United States and various national centers of Catholic thought. Woven into the themes of this documentary history are the protean meanings of what constitutes being American and Catholic in relation to the formations of religious identities.

A workshop for the editors of the books in this series was entirely funded by a generous grant from the Louisville Institute.

American Catholic Identities
A Documentary History
Christopher J. Kauffman, General Editor

The Crossing of Two Roads

Being Catholic and Native in the United States

Marie Therese Archambault, O.S.F.

Mark G. Thiel

Christopher Vecsey

Editors

ORBIS BOOKS

Maryknoll, New York 10545

Founded in 1970, Orbis Books endeavors to publish works that enlighten the mind, nourish the spirit, and challenge the conscience. The publishing arm of the Maryknoll Fathers and Brothers, Orbis seeks to explore the global dimensions of the Christian faith and mission, to invite dialogue with diverse cultures and religious traditions, and to serve the cause of reconciliation and peace. The books published reflect the opinions of their authors and are not meant to represent the official position of the Maryknoll Society. To obtain more information about Maryknoll and Orbis Books, please visit our website at www.maryknoll.org.

Library of Congress Cataloging-in-Publication Data

The crossing of two roads : being Catholic and Native in the United States / Christopher Vecsey, Mark G. Thiel, Marie Therese Archambault, editors.

     p. cm. – (American Catholic identities)

    Includes index.

    ISBN 1-57075-503-5 (cloth) – ISBN 1-57075-352-0 (paper)

    1. Indians of North America – Religion. 2. Indian Catholics – North America – History – Sources. 3. Indians of North America – Missions. 4. Missions – North America – History – Sources. 5. Racism – Religious aspects – Christianity. I. Vecsey, Christopher. II. Thiel, Mark G. III. Archambault, Marie Therese. IV. Series.

E98.R3C76 2003

282′.73′08997 – dc21

2003011537

CONTENTS

Part 2
THE FRENCH HERITAGE

Part 3
LEADERSHIP, URBAN MINISTRY, AND INCULTURATION

FOREWORD

Christopher J. Kauffman

The editors of this documentary study of Native American Catholics in the United States and Canada reveal rich experience in archives and a strong command of an enormous amount of secondary works in several spheres of specialization. Because of the wide diversity of native people and because there is a large pool of documents available, the editors' achievement of a comprehensive study is a splendid testimony to their professionalism and commitment.

Contemporary American Catholic historiography has been shaped by trends of the 1960s in the academy, church, and society: the emphasis on social history in the academy; the emergence of a new model of ecclesiology in the church; and the recognition of the legitimate voices of protest uttered by African Americans, Native Americans, Latinos, and women in society. Historians of American Catholic life and thought published articles and books reflecting the view from below of social history, a people of God ecclesiology flowing from the documents of Vatican II, and the voices of the marginated uttered from below.

Marie Therese Archambault, O.S.F., is a Lakota woman-religious theologian, teacher, and scholar who is responsive to the voices of protest and committed to the ecclesiology, spirituality, and anthropology flowing in the currents of renewal and reform from Vatican II. Her book, *A Retreat with Black Elk: Living in the Sacred Hoop*, illustrates a synthesis of theology and history. The imprint of her experience is to be seen in documents on the controversy of the religious identity of Black Elk. The very subtitle of this book, *Being Catholic and Native in the United States*, also corresponds to the religious and ethnic identity of Sister Archambault. Mark Thiel, who is committed to the preservation and popularization of written, oral, and visual documents of Native Catholic people, published a detailed finding aid for the massive collection of such documents at Marquette University Archives, where he is an archivist. Among his publications is an impressive article on the Catholic Sodalities among the Sioux during the late nineteenth and early twentieth centuries (*U.S. Catholic Historian*, spring 1998; this issue also includes articles by Sister Archambault and Christopher Vecsey). Many documents published in this book are from the archives at Marquette. Several documents are oral interviews by Mark Thiel. Christopher Vecsey's magisterial three-volume study of Native-American Catholics in every region of the country will not be surpassed for many years, if ever. Professor of religion and Native American studies at Colgate University in Hamilton, New York, Vecsey is at ease in a multidisciplinary methodology; he evinces a command of history, anthropology, sociology, and religion. Over the years he has collected many documents related to numerous tribes in the Spanish, French, and English spheres of interest. The three editors were committed to selecting documents that feature four centuries of complex relations between Native American and Catholic identity, relations that resulted in several patterns of Catholic identity formation. As Vecsey mentions in the introduction, the need for balance and the limited number of documents depicting the experience from below necessitated including many documents in the book from the missionaries' and other non-Indians' points of view.

The tripartite structure of the book is based upon chronology in each part, but the documents are configured along topical lines, such as the story of the Pueblo people that encompasses the periods from colonial times to the post–Vatican II period. Because long periods of resistance by Pueblo peoples were followed by conversion initiated from officials in the church, and an accommodation to the Pueblo peoples' traditional ceremonies, which were scheduled on the calendar of Christian feasts, the story represents a development of "compartmentalism" with the traditional and the Catholic in separate compartments. A severe polarization between the Church and Pueblo people occurred that was characterized by the Sante Fe bishops' intolerance of the traditional dances, a conflict that lasted for many years in the middle third of the twentieth century and was not resolved until after Vatican II. This book's configuration according to topics is modeled on the methodological design of Vecsey's three-volume study. The documentary story of the Pueblo people is longer than the other topical renderings, but it will appeal to the general reader as groups of documents represent several phases in the formation of Catholic identities. The documented "stories" of the first part on the Spanish sphere offer a fascinating background for comparative understanding with the French in Canada and portions of the northern tier of the United States.

The third part is organized on religious themes of leadership, ministries, and the theological implications of the recent way Native American leaders have revived their religious traditions and have found receptive Catholic leaders eager to fuse native religiosity with the good news of the gospel for the mutual vitality of a distinctive Native American Catholicity. This latter process of inculturation entails an ongoing dialogue, one that is based upon openness and trust with the intention of creating new forms of Native Catholic practice. In the leadership section there are several letters from Native American priests and sisters of the mid-nineteenth through the twentieth century. There are also documents related to the Tekakwitha Conference that originated in 1939 as a support group for missionary priests. Over the last twenty-five years it has been transformed with the participation of Native American lay leaders. There are documents from the National Conference of Catholic Bishops and responses from the lay leaders. This reflects the convergence of the ecclesiology that generates a sensitivity to the voices of legitimate protest from below, neatly captured by the editors' selection of documents grounded in a commitment to the cultural and social history from below.

The configuration of the documents into topics and subtopics guarantees that this book will be very useful in the classroom of both undergraduate and graduate courses in American and Catholic history, anthropology, and religious studies. Indeed, professors could design new courses based upon this book and companion books and articles by the three editors of this very distinctive documentary history of Native American Catholic identities. This work is a singular contribution to a genre abundant with significance and is suitable for a wide variety of readers.

ACKNOWLEDGMENTS

We offer thanks to the following persons and institutions: Sister Louise La-Coste, C.S.J., and Msgr. Stephen H. Callahan, Archivists, Diocese of San Diego; Dr. R. Bruce Harley, Archivist, Diocese of San Bernardino; Msgr. Francis J. Weber, Archivist and Historian, Archdiocese of Los Angeles; Marina Ochoa, Archivist, Archdiocese of Santa Fe; Msgr. Roland J. Boudreaux, Archivist, Diocese of Houma-Thibodaux; Sister Therese Pelletier, S.C.I.M., Archivist, Diocese of Portland, Maine; John LeDoux, Archivist, Diocese of Green Bay; David Kingma, Archivist, Oregon Province of the Society of Jesus; Isabelle Contant, Archivist, Province of French Canada of the Society of Jesus; Nancy Merz, Archivist, Missouri Province of the Society of Jesus; Denise Thuston, Archivist, Province of the Sacred Heart Franciscan Friars; Reverend Melvin A. Jurisich, O.F.M., Secretary, Province of Santa Barbara Franciscan Friars; Sister Jolyce Guteman, F.S.P.A., Archivist, Franciscan Sisters of Perpetual Adoration; Sister M. Celine Erk, O.S.B., Archivist, Diocese of Rapid City; Sister Kateri Mitchell, S.S.A., Executive Director, Tekakwitha Conference; Vi Hilbert, Archivist, Lushootseed Research Archives; Msgr. David W. Stinebrickner, Archivist, Diocese of Ogdensburg; Reverend Leo Cooper, Archivist, Archdiocese of Kansas City in Kansas; Sharon Sumpter, Archivist, the University of Notre Dame; Christine Taylor, Archivist, Archdiocese of Seattle; Most Reverend Rembert G. Weakland, O.S.B., Archdiocese of Milwaukee; Msgr. Paul A. Lenz, Executive Director, Bureau of Catholic Indian Missions; Sister Geraldine Clifford, O.S.F.; Reverend Kevin Gordon; Anita Hamley; Susana LaBelle-Boyd; Tony Machukay; Freeman A. Mesteth; Reverend Louis J. Renner, S.J.; Joan Staples; Sister Margaret Troy, S.S.M.; Reverend Theodore F. Zuern, S.J.; Joseph W. Thomas; Sister Anthony Davis, O.S.B.S.; Marvin Clifford; Joe Pecos; Juana Pecos; Mark J. Cheresposey; Thomas W. Foley; Prof. Clara Sue Kidwell; Reverend Michael F. Steltenkamp, S.J.; Anne M. Scheurman; Sister Mary Ewens, O.P.; Prof. Steve Jacobson; the Archdiocese of Oklahoma City; The American Philosophical Society; Ballena Press; Fordham University Press; Indiana Historical Society; St. Anthony Messenger; Florida State Archives; University of Arizona Press; University of California Press; University of Chicago Press; University of New Mexico Press.

MARIE THERESE ARCHAMBAULT, O.S.F.
MARK G. THIEL
CHRISTOPHER VECSEY

PREFACE

How have we chosen the following documents? What rules have we followed in reproducing them? And whose voices are missing?

At first my two colleagues and I considered a book made up wholly of American Indian Catholic texts and testimonies. So much that has been written about Catholicism among Native Americans has emphasized the activity of non-Indian missionaries; we hoped for a corrective volume that would feature only Indian viewpoints in all their variety. This plan did not prove feasible. Although this volume does contain many and mostly Native testimonies, we realized that certain non-Indian (and especially clerical) statements were necessary for a balanced history of Indian Catholicism.

We have included sources from the sixteenth to the twenty-first century, almost every one produced within the boundaries of the present-day United States. In Native American history the thresholds between the United States and its two immediate neighbors to the north and south are somewhat arbitrary impositions; therefore, we have selected several documents from the borderlands, for example, regarding two pilgrimage sites — one in Canada and the other in Mexico — frequented by U.S. Indian Catholics.

We chose written documents, including transcripts of interviews, speeches and dialogues, handwritten letters, and other informal material, sometimes composed in a language (e.g., English) that was not the first tongue of the speaker or writer. As a result, the texts contained numerous irregularities in spelling, grammar, and punctuation. We decided not to correct grammar; however, we have made changes in spelling and punctuation, and when doing so, we have placed the change in brackets. For instance, in document 7 the reader will find "[Guadalupe]," which was misspelled in the original letter. We have tried not to alter the meaning and tone of the originals; we hope that we have succeeded.

We are acutely aware that the documents available to us represent only the smallest sample of significant expressions made by or about American Indian Catholics over a half-millennium. In this frame of time most Indians have been nonliterate, so unless some writer quoted (or misquoted) them, their expressed ideas have been lost. Thus, we are compelled to rely on the reporting of Euroamericans — most prominently the French colonial *Jesuit Relations* — with no means, ultimately, of verifying their accuracy.

It is disappointing to be refused permission to reproduce valid primary documents. We have been fortunate in receiving the generous agreement of many authors and archivists; however, on several occasions our requests have been denied. Diocesan administrators are sometimes embarrassed by their predecessors' insensitivity toward traditional Indian religious practices. Tribal officials sometimes would prefer not to dwell upon their past battles with the Church. An individual sometimes has changed her mind, or fears the contemporary consequences of her past words, and no longer wishes to see her praise or criticism quoted publicly in a collection of historical documents. When faced with these lacunae, we have summarized from the missing testimonies in our narrative overviews.

The American Philosophical Society, the Cushwa Center for the Study of American Catholicism, and Colgate University (through the Division of Humanities and the Faculty Research Council) have provided generous grants of money to defray research costs. Colgate's Case Library staff and faculty, particularly Emily Hutton and Judy DeMuro, have been very helpful to my study. So have my former students Kenneth B. Mello and Shannon Thompson. Beth MacKinnon, administrative assistant, Colgate's Division of Humanities, has produced considerable portions of the book manuscript, and Christopher G. Vecsey has aided in the proofreading. Pat Poskie-Thiel has provided most gracious hospitality. Above all I thank my two remarkable colleagues, Sister Marie Therese Archambault, O.S.F., and Mark G. Thiel, archivist, Marquette University John P. Raynor, S.J., Memorial Library, Department of Special Collections.

CHRISTOPHER VECSEY

GENERAL INTRODUCTION
Christopher Vecsey

Having written three heavy tomes on the history of American Indian Catholicism in North America, I may be excused for having little else to say on the matter. Readers who want a thorough narrative investigation of Catholic Indians' histories over five centuries should peruse *On the Padres' Trail* (1996), *The Paths of Kateri's Kin* (1997), and *Where the Two Roads Meet* (1999), all published by the University of Notre Dame Press.

Our present book of documents follows the structure of these three volumes. Part 1 traces the relationship between Roman Catholicism and Native American peoples within the borders of what was once colonial New Spain and what is now the southern region of the United States. We begin at the crossing of the two roads with a catechetical device — a 1613 *confesionario* (doc. 1) — used as a template throughout New Spain, in this case specially adapted for the Timicuas of Florida. The *confesionario* expressed the Catholic goal to convert Indians *from* their traditional culture and *toward* a Christian way of life, an attempt from the outset of Christian missions in the New World to remove Indians from their Native road and place them on the path of Catholicism.

The next set of documents depicts the spiritual conquest, resistance, transformation, and accommodation of the Pueblo Indians in present-day New Mexico. The Spaniards reached this area in the late sixteenth century, insisting upon the Natives' "obedience and vassalage," and punishing acts of rebellion with military might, for example at Acoma (doc. 2). The Franciscan padres who oversaw the religious pacification of the Pueblos wrote (doc. 3) of the progress being made in at least the outward signs of Catholic faith. Baptized Indians attended Mass, said their prayers, sang their hymns, and observed various Catholic devotions under the Franciscans' watchful gaze.

In 1680, however, the Pueblo Indians staged a revolution against the Spanish Church and state, killing more than a score of priests and driving soldiers and administrators from their district. In the course of the reconquest the Spaniards heard testimony (doc. 4) from Indians that explained the revolt. For all their outward piety, the Natives would no longer permit the Franciscans' repression of traditional religious practices. As a result the Spaniards reentered the Pueblo homeland under a tacit arrangement: the Indians would engage in Catholic sacramental acts but without leaving behind their kivas, kachinas, and caciques. By the second half of the eighteenth century it was clear to episcopal (doc. 5) and Franciscan (doc. 6) observers that the Pueblo peoples possessed dual loyalties — to their aboriginal religion and to Catholicism. It was not so clear to the outsiders how deep the latter loyalty ran. This ambiguity persisted throughout the nineteenth century, even when the United States seized the northern rim of Hispanic Christendom from Mexico in the 1840s and took over the administration of the Pueblos. Franciscan friars continued to visit the missions of New Mexico. The Indians received them but continued to practice their ancient ways.

Some Puebloans bound themselves more firmly to the Church, especially in the communities that escaped with the Spaniards in 1680 to the area around what is now El Paso, Texas. These Indians established their own villages under the spiritual guidance of Our Lady of Guadalupe — the Marian appearance among the Mexican populace. By the early twentieth century, for example, the Tortugas Indians had a longstanding Catholic identity under the aegis of Guadalupe. Their concern, expressed (doc. 7) to the Bureau of Catholic Indian Missions (BCIM, founded in 1874), was to maintain their autonomy in the face of non-Indian encroachment into their local church.

Other Pueblo Indians of the first half of the twentieth century melded Christian and Native beliefs, molding the story of Jesus' nativity, for instance, into a traditional Laguna folk narrative (doc. 8); or at Zuni (doc. 9), adopting characters of American Christian folklore, like Santa Claus, into their devotional worldview. Christmas became an important part of the Pueblos' liturgical calendar, replete with obeisance toward the Christ child, shared with the Franciscan fathers at Jemez (doc. 10).

Authorities in the Archdiocese of Santa Fe appreciated the Puebloans' religiousness; however, the clerics worried about the degree to which the Indians were participating in two different religious traditions — Catholic and Native. The documents from the 1930s to the 1960s (docs. 11–18) reveal the struggle between Church and Pueblo hierarchies over the spiritual life of Catholic Indians. How far would or could the Church go in enforcing its sacramental hegemony or in forbidding traditional ceremonialism?

At Santo Domingo, San Felipe, and Isleta, the Indian authorities questioned the archbishops' prerogatives in controlling the whole of their people's religious lives. The Indians maintained their right to persist in dual religious loyalties, following the accommodation established as far back as the 1690s. At Santo Domingo and Isleta the archbishops were willing to shut down the local churches and refuse the sacraments to the Indians. In both cases the Indian communities experienced internal disagreements; nonetheless, their determination to walk *both* religious paths outlasted the episcopal interdictions. In the 1970s the Santa Fe archbishop was eager to improve relations between Puebloans and Hispanics in the archdiocese (docs. 19–20). The issue of dual religious identity seemed to have quieted without explicit resolution.

If Pueblo peoples came to practice their Indian and Catholic faiths separately from one another, the Yaqui Indians of northwestern Mexico created their own brand of indigenous Catholicism under colonial Jesuit instigation. When some of these Indians emigrated to Arizona in the late nineteenth century, they brought their semiautonomous Yaqui Catholicism with them, including a christianized mythology (doc. 21), a local religious leadership, and a ceremonial system focused upon the cosmic drama during Easter week (doc. 22), a rich ritualism that continues today.

From the late 1600s the O'odham (Papagos and Pimas) of southern Arizona received instruction from Jesuit (and then Franciscan) missionaries, and in the mid–twentieth century these Indians were still making pilgrimages to Magdalena in the Sonoran Desert of Mexico to solidify their Catholic identity (doc. 23). To the present day the O'odham have perceived similarities between their traditional and Catholic spiritual ways, regarding them as part of a single, blessed way of life (doc. 24).

For at least one Navajo sister (doc. 25), Catholicism has upheld the values of her people's old-time culture. And for at least one Apache (doc. 26), the Catholic boarding school was an ideal institution for inculcating American Catholic values, thereby helping Indians of the American Southwest to adapt to mainstream culture without losing Indian identity. Other Native American Catholics in recent years have strongly criticized the mission boarding schools for their destruction of the Indian family and their imposition of foreign cultural values and authority on the reservation population. One Catholic Indian educator has called the effect of boarding schools a "genocide of the spirit."

In California the Franciscans of New Spain and their soldierly sponsors commenced the process of baptizing Indians in 1769 (doc. 27). The Spanish built missions and presidios along the coast and expected the christened neophytes to relocate to the missions and live under priestly rule in order to effect long-term conversions. Some Indians bridled under the hard labor and corporal punishments within the missions and designed to escape to their homes (doc. 28). Others grew up as Mission Indians, as it was the only life they knew, and they regarded the founding Franciscan padres with appreciation and affection. One Luiseño lad in the nineteenth century entered a school in Rome with an eye toward the priesthood. Before his early death he penned a telling description of California mission life (doc. 29).

When Mexico gained its independence from Spain in 1821, the pressure began to "secularize" the California missions and make their neophytes into citizens (doc. 30). "Secularization" meant separating Catholic Indians not only from their ecclesiastical overseers but also from their Indian identity. Mission Indians who maintained sacramental contact with the Church, for example, the Cupeños (doc. 31), upheld both Native and Catholic identities into the twentieth century. Some descendants of the Mission Indians conducted their own services—especially at funerals (doc. 32)—combining traditional and Christian forms. One California Indian tribe thanked the Catholic bishop (doc. 33) for allowing its members to practice their two modes of spirituality. Some Catholic Indians (doc. 34) looked upon the Franciscans as their special apostles and petitioned the pope to keep the friars in the California Indian ministry. Considering the sharp criticism of the Franciscans in secular historiography (e.g., Costo and Costo 1987) and among Indian proponents (doc. 95) in the late twentieth century, documents from earlier years evidenced admiration for the padres.

Part 2 begins where part 1 left off, with a sanguine reflection in the early twentieth century (doc. 35) upon several hundred years of Catholic evangelization — this time in the northeastern corner of the United States. In the early 1600s French missionaries reached out to the Algonkian peoples of Acadia, including the Passamaquoddy and Penobscot Indians of present-day Maine. Three hundred years later *The Indian Sentinel* celebrated the French Catholic heritage among these peoples, calling them "the happiest people in the world." Toward the end of the twentieth century a bishop in Maine (doc. 36) tried to comprehend the societal dysfunctions and anti-Church resentments of these same Catholic Indians.

Document 37 returns us to the beginnings of Catholic outreach on the east coast of North America, between the Spanish missions of Florida and the spiritual expansion of New France. In 1639 English Jesuits initiated short-lived but effective contact with the Piscataway people of Maryland.

Far-flung evangelization throughout New France was memorialized in the voluminous *Jesuit Relations* (Thwaites 1896–1901). From these colonial Jesuit missions grew an archipelago of apostolic expansion that eventually reached the Gulf of Mexico and the Pacific Ocean. Documents 38 to 43 recount from the *Jesuit Relations* the progress of Catholicism among the Iroquoians in the seventeenth century, providing vignettes from the lives of prominent converts and martyrs among the Hurons, many of whom were incorporated into Iroquois communities; and of Iroquois themselves, in particular the Mohawk convert Kateri Tekakwitha (doc. 43), who lived and died according to a saintly asceticism. Sites associated with her in the United States and Canada have become loci for pilgrimages among Indian and non-Indian Catholics. So has Sainte-Anne-de-Beaupré in Quebec, first visited by a Huron delegation in the seventeenth century (doc. 40).

Iroquois territory became a testing ground for the Christian faith in the colonial era, with Indians pulled toward English Protestantism as well as French Catholicism (doc. 44). In the nineteenth and twentieth centuries many Iroquois groups abandoned their Christian allegiances and adopted the Longhouse Religion of the Seneca prophet Handsome Lake. By the 1960s even an indigenous Mohawk priest (doc. 45) had great difficulty in convincing many of his Native flock to remain faithful to Catholicism, as the tug of Indian nationalism grew ever stronger.

Documents 46 to 48 tell of the Jesuit experience among the peoples of the western Great Lakes: Ojibwa, Potawatomi, Ottawa, and Menominee Indians. The priests made clear the obstacles they faced in attracting these Algonkian peoples to Christianity, not the least of which was a deeply entrenched spirituality that was grounded in visionary experiences. When faced with devastating diseases (spread by European presence), however, the Indians were apt to turn their habitual spiritual energies toward baptism, especially under the direction of the Jesuits, who spoke of the curative and salvific powers of the sacraments.

The French missionary efforts waned in the eighteenth century; nonetheless, aspects of Catholic identity persisted among some Great Lakes Natives. In

1830 a delegation of Potawatomis approached the bishop of Detroit, seeking a regular ministry (doc. 49). These Michigan stalwarts of the faith survived attempts by the United States to remove them from their homes, and they left a record of Catholic deathbed devotionalism (doc. 50).

In the late 1800s in Wisconsin, Ojibwas relied on Catholic agencies such as the BCIM to support them against their Protestant and pagan relatives and to protect them from U.S. governmental policies (doc. 51). Ojibwas in Minnesota looked to the BCIM to furnish churches for the growing Native Catholic population (doc. 52). A century later Menominees in Wisconsin celebrated a "Ghost Dinner" to honor their ancestors on All Souls Day in a manner that reflected both their Native and Catholic spiritual heritage (doc. 53).

Throughout the nineteenth century Great Lakes Indians moved westward onto the prairies, intermarrying with fur traders with whom they were employed. From these contacts emerged a people called the Métis, based in Manitoba: part-Indian, part-white, largely influenced by French culture, strongly Catholic, and wholly opposed to the creation of Canada as a nation-state. Louis Riel, once a seminarian and eventually a twice-failed revolutionary, took refuge in Montana, where he urged his followers (doc. 54) toward the ill-fated second Métis rebellion of 1885.

In the territory of Louisiana, French, Indian, Spanish, and African populations combined to produce the Catholic Houmas, "free people of color" — mixed-heritage Muskogean American Indians without federal recognition — whose lineages were recorded in church records (doc. 55). In neighboring Mississippi the Choctaws received rudimentary instruction from the colonial French; hosted sustained evangelization in the 1880s; solidified their Catholicism in Oklahoma; and then returned to Mississippi upon receiving federal recognition. Their correspondence (doc. 56) revealed their spiritual and political ties to their BCIM mentor.

Francophone fur-trading voyagers brought Catholicism to the Rocky Mountains in the early nineteenth century, particularly Quebecois Iroquois who settled among the Flatheads in what is now Montana. In the 1830s representatives of these Iroquois and Flatheads journeyed to St. Louis, where they attracted the attention of Catholic authorities, and thus began missionary efforts, from the prairies and plains to the Pacific Northwest. The beginnings of these efforts were recalled in *The Indian Sentinel* (doc. 57).

As the United States conquered the plains and created reservations, federal policy after 1869 entrusted local Indian administration to Christian missionary agencies. Although the government favored Protestants to Catholics, some Indians, for example, three Osages in Indian Territory (now Oklahoma), felt differently and were not ashamed to say so (doc. 58). Nor were three Lakota Sioux leaders, who requested Catholic priests when they met with the president of the United States (doc. 59). Responding to these requests, Catholic missions spread through the West and with them interdenominational rivalries.

Catholic missionaries in western Canada and the United States employed several pictorial catechisms in their religious instructions. The most widely used was the Two Roads Picture Catechism, which presented Indians with a visual choice between the way of the Church and the path to hell (doc. 60). As dioceses were formed in the West, for example in South Dakota, Church authorities tried to provide moral guidance (doc. 61) to the Catholic Indians under their jurisdiction. Jesuits among the Lakotas created sodalities for Catholic Indian men and women in order to serve as models of Christian virtue (doc. 62). Although some Siouian Catholics resisted the authority of non-Indian priests and favored their Native catechists (doc. 63), the South Dakota missions fostered tractable devotees whose lives and deaths were marked with sanctity (doc. 64). Lakotas tried to adjust their habits regarding marriage to the canons of Catholicism (doc. 65) and bowed to the will of their priestly chiefs. Each summer the missionaries of North and South Dakota gathered thousands of the Native faithful in Catholic Sioux Congresses (doc. 66), where they renewed both their religious and kinship obligations, helping to create a culture that bound Catholic and Indian relations in a single knot.

Perhaps the most well known Lakota of the twentieth century was Nicholas Black Elk: famous to the world for his words of Native spirituality in *Black Elk Speaks* (Neihardt 1932), but also esteemed among his people as a Catholic catechist. Document 67 includes correspondence from his years as a zealous convert and peripatetic evangelist, to the years immediately following the publication of *Black Elk Speaks,* when he was required to disavow the book.

In the same year as Black Elk's recantation, 1934, hundreds of Lakotas from Black Elk's reservation of Pine Ridge signed a petition (doc. 68) to the U.S. president's wife, protesting the threat of the Indian New Deal to their local Catholic boarding school's federally administered trust funding. Yet a generation later a Lakota educator decried the effects of such boarding schools that imposed foreign cultural values and authority on Indian communities, thus exacerbating the disintegration of Native family life. The state of this disintegration is indicated in document 69: the violence, the substance abuse, but also the heartfelt thanks given to Catholic priests for their ministry.

In some locales Indian Catholicism was able to develop on large reservations in relative isolation. In other areas, for example, around Seattle in Washington state, non-Indian populations overran Native communities — Suquamish, Swinomish, Skagit, Lummi, and other Coast Salish people — taking over their parishes and alienating Indian Catholics from the churches they thought of as their own (doc. 70). Following Vatican II a shortage of priests led to the closing of several Indian missions near Seattle, and the Indians were expected to assimilate into non-Indian parishes, much to the dismay of Indian congregants (doc. 71).

Still, many Coast Salish remained attached to the Catholic faith brought to them in the nineteenth century. At the same time, a post–Vatican II relativistic ethos allowed some of them to consider Catholic and aboriginal religions to be two manifestations of the same basic spirituality (doc. 72). One Swinomish woman encouraged the Church to develop the more celebrative aspects of Native American spirituality in its Indian ministry, instead of emphasizing sinfulness and penance (doc. 73).

In 1987 the archbishop of Seattle joined other Christian denominational leaders in apologizing to Indian and Inuit (Eskimo) communities of the northwest coast for a history of scorn for Native culture (doc. 74). The document affirmed the rights of Natives to engage in traditional religious practices. The same archbishop established an urban ministry for Native American Catholics, in response to a plea from local Indians (doc. 75). In 1992, five hundred years after the first contact between Christians and Native Americans, a Swinomish Eucharistic minister joked publicly about the ambiguities of Indian conversion to Catholicism (doc. 76).

Parts 1 and 2 have delineated the development of American Indian Catholicism in its variety, drawing primarily upon the heritage of Spanish and French missionary efforts. Part 3 examines three salient features of Indian Catholicism, particularly over the last century or so.

The first concerns Native leadership within the Church. We have already made reference in this introduction to Indian catechists, prayer leaders, Eucharistic ministers, community organizers, and exemplars of virtue, even a Native priest. In personages such as Kateri Tekakwitha we have seen the galvanizing religious influence of a single person with no official title or position beyond her own saintliness.

In the mid-1800s the first American Indian from the United States — a Delaware-Comanche of French ancestry, James Chrysostom Bouchard — was ordained a Catholic priest. His interior life reflected the visionary heritage of his tribes, although with a Jesuitical content. Once ordained, he wished to serve his Delaware people or at least take up an Indian ministry. His Jesuit superiors refused him his desire and he was forced to comply with their directive or leave the order. He acquiesced under the advice of a renowned Belgian Jesuit and enjoyed a long priestly career in California (doc. 77).

Other Indian men felt the call to the priesthood (doc. 78); however, it was not until the first decade of the twentieth century that the first full-blood Indian priest, the Potawatomi Albert Negahnquet, was ordained. Negahnquet's letters from Rome (doc. 79) revealed his spiritual calling and his fascination with rough and tumble life in the seminary and about Rome, but also his struggle with alcoholism, which troubled his priestly years.

Philip B. Gordon's priesthood was no less fraught with difficulty. Of mostly Ojibwa and some French ancestry, he wished nothing more than to minister to his natal community in Wisconsin. Assignments took him to the Haskell Institute in Kansas, where he feuded with the Protestant authorities at the federally run Indian school, now a college. Returning to Wisconsin, he found himself embroiled in ecclesiastical and political controversies, and much to his regret, he was removed from Indian service and was compelled to devote the remainder of his long tenure to non-Indian parishes (doc. 80). Fathers Bouchard, Negahnquet, and Gordon were priestly pioneers. More recent Indian priests have experienced some of the same turmoils, especially in their competing loyalties to their peoples and their Church.

American Indian sisters have also had their callings and their tribulations. Although a few Indian women had taken their vows over the centuries, the first attempt to create a Catholic sisterhood explicitly for Native Americans occurred in 1891 with the Congregation of American Sisters. Document 81 comprises letters from several of the Lakota women who joined the order, describing their vocations, their vows, and the obstacles — including what they perceived as institutional racism — hindering their spiritual goals. Other Indian women found less complicated fulfillment in attaining the sisterhood and served as models to other girls of their tribes (doc. 82). Some have experienced daily life in convents under the authority of priests (doc. 83). Some have enjoyed long, fruitful careers with enduring support from their orders, making it possible to express their Native spirituality and commit themselves to their reservation communities (doc. 84). Some have found a home in large, multiethnic orders; others have joined the Oblate Sisters of the Blessed Sacrament, founded in 1935 for American Indian women (doc. 85).

After Vatican II, the Church began to encourage lay leadership in Indian congregations, especially through the ordination of men as permanent deacons. In Alaska the diaconate of Inuit (Eskimo) men has been noteworthy for its success (doc. 86) in finding men with unbroken roots in both their Native circles and the Church to serve as mediators between the two.

At the end of the Second World War, thousands of Indians in the United States began to leave their reservations in search of jobs. Encouraged by U.S. Relocation and Termination policies in the 1950s and beyond, they migrated to urban areas throughout the country, so that today more than two-thirds of Native Americans live in cities. Tens of thousands of these urban Indians are Roman Catholics, and the Church has had to meet the challenge of ministering to them apart from their reservation milieu. In many cities Catholic Indians felt alienated from the Church and the non-Indian Catholic populace. Church authorities assayed this situation as early as the 1950s (doc. 87). At first the thought was to integrate Indians into mainstream urban parishes. Much later the Church attempted to organize an urban ministry directed to Native Catholic needs.

One of the most successful urban ministries has taken place in Milwaukee. The Indian parish — the Congregation of the Great Spirit — derived from the initiative of Indian Catholics themselves (doc. 88), the support of the archbishop, whose partial Indian ancestry was made known in the process (doc. 89), and the organizational prowess and cooperation of the board of directors, including both Indians and non-Indians (doc. 91). Along the way the members of the Milwaukee Indian Catholic group expressed divergent views regarding the inclusion of Native ritual elements in Catholic liturgy (doc. 90). Some wanted to combine Indian and Catholic ceremonialism; others felt that Catholics should eschew all non-Catholic forms. Document 92 indicates how thoroughly intertwined are Native and Catholic spiritual convictions among contemporary Milwaukee Indians, especially in regard to the dead. So closely fused are Indian and Catholic ways that they seem to constitute one experiential whole.

Catholic missionaries have often entertained the idea of comparable functions between Indian religious phenomena and their own. Indian Catholics have frequently combined Native and Catholic religious elements — a process sometimes referred to as syncretism. Or they have participated in the two religious systems, however, keeping them separate from each other, at least in practice — which is called compartmentalization. Both syncretism and compartmentalization constitute ways in which Indian Catholics have tried to relate Catholicism to their Native culture, making the Church their own. This process of identifying Catholicism through and in Native culture is often referred to as inculturation, and since Vatican II the Church has made this one of its major projects.

One way toward inculturation is through dialogue. In the 1970s a group of Jesuits met regularly with Lakota religious leaders — including traditionalists as well as Catholics on the Rosebud Reservation in South Dakota. The transcripts of these bi-weekly dialogues (doc. 93) displayed the thoroughgoing theological interchange that took place, leading to the conclusion that Catholicism and American Indian religion were comparable systems of spirituality.

Since the late 1970s the National Tekakwitha Conference has provided a forum for Native American Catholic dialogue and inculturation. Named for Kateri Tekakwitha, the organization grew from a small missionary support group founded in 1939 to an assembly for American Indian Catholics with membership in the thousands and participation at national, regional, and local levels. As many as fifty thousand Indians in the United States and Canada are involved in the Tekakwitha movement in general — praying in their local Kateri Circles, supporting the drive for Kateri's canonization, attending regional liturgies and catechetical workshops, and receiving encouragement for inculturative initiatives. At annual meetings Indian Catholics (numbering about two thousand each year) gather from all across North America with occasional participants from Latin America, notably Mexico and Guatemala. The *Tekakwitha Conference Newsletter* has published essays by Catholic Indian leaders, addressing the aims of inculturation (doc. 94). Sometimes the Native Catholic leadership — including bishops, priests, sisters, and laymen — has criticized the Church for the triumphalist and sometimes coercive character of its missionary endeavors (doc. 95). Sometimes an Indian Catholic spokesman has suggested that Roman Catholicism could be improved in its spirituality by learning more about Native American religious practice (doc. 96).

The Tekakwitha Conference has set forth its goals in a public "Vision Statement" (doc. 97). Inculturation has been primary and all-inclusive, but also important has been the need to promote social and economic justice. In 1992 the *Tekakwitha Conference Newsletter* printed the entire text (doc. 98) of a pastoral statement authored by the National Conference of Catholic Bishops. At the moment of the Columbian Quincentenary, the statement recognized the need for reconciliation between American Indian peoples and the Church, and it acknowledged the validity of Indian grievances regarding Catholicism's record of undermining Native culture in the Americas. In the same year at the annual Tekakwitha meeting, the Association of Native Religious and Clergy (ANRC, founded in 1971) distributed a broadside (doc. 99) highly critical of the Catholic Church and the National Tekakwitha Conference itself.

For all its dissension from the Church, the ANRC circular maintained its reverence toward Kateri Tekakwitha. For thousands of American Indian Catholics, Kateri has remained (or become) the touchstone for their devotional lives. Lakota (doc. 100), Pueblo (docs. 101–2), and Mohawk (doc. 102) peoples, among others, have felt the force of inculturation in the person of Kateri Tekakwitha. At her shrine, in her presence, they have uttered a Native Catholic profession of faith (doc. 104). In her they have experienced the meeting of two roads, Native and Catholic.

The Crossing
of Two Roads

Part 1

THE SPANISH HERITAGE

1. *Confesionario* of Fray Francisco Pareja, O.F.M., 1613

Spanish evangelism in Florida began in the sixteenth century, first with Domini-
cans, Jesuits, and then Franciscans, as well as diocesan priests. Their missions
stretched from St. Augustine to the northern reaches of Florida and into the
present state of Georgia, among Timicua, Choctaw, Creek, Apalachee, and
Apalachicola peoples. Fray Francisco Pareja's 1613 Confesionario, *composed in*
Timicua and Spanish and based on earlier versions used by Franciscans through-
out New Spain, expressed the catechetical goals of Catholic expansion. Priests
were to uncover and subvert the bases of aboriginal American Indian religious
life: belief in the spirits and their manifestations in nature, dreams, omens, and
so on. The Church regarded these spirits as devilish powers and traditional In-
dian behavior as sinful. The Confesionario *directed the confessor to inquire*
about and condemn all manner of acts in defiance of the Ten Commandments,
particularly those of un-Christian worship and sexuality.

[Questions on the First Commandment]

Ceremonies, Omens, and Superstitions That Are Still Used by Some

When someone is possessed, have you believed in what he said?

Have you believed that when the blue jay or another bird sings and the body
is trembling, that it is a signal that people are coming or that something
important is about to happen?

Have you believed that lighting a new separate fire will cure illness?

Being ill, have you had to light a separate fire so that your meal can be cooked,
because if you don't, you will die, have you believed this?

When some woman has given birth, have you avoided coming near the fire,
have you considered this sinning?

Have you consented to be cured by some herbalist by praying with words to
the Devil?

Toward this end, have you offered in the door of the house maize to the Devil
as you used to?

1

The ceremony of the laurel that is made to the Devil, have you made it?

When collecting acorns or other fruits, did you consider it a sin to eat the first fruits that were cut?

In the clearing or field of maize, when lightning strikes them, have you considered it a sin to eat it or advised that no one else eats it, considering it a sin?

Have you considered it a sin to eat the first maize from a new clearing?

The first fish that enters the new fish traps, have you said not to put them in hot water, otherwise no more will be caught?

The first fish that enters the new fish trap, have you put it near the trap, saying that it will bring plenty of better fish?

Placing a new fish trap, have you desired that the prayers pray to it, believing that many more fish would enter?...

When the owl or barn owl sings, have you believed it to be a prognostication and omen of evil?...

Have you held your dreams to be true, believing them?

Document and Advice

Son, as one thinks during the day, thus he dreams at night; if he thinks good things then he will dream good things, and if bad, these will also be represented in his dreams; if the dream is about good things he should try to put them into practice, and if bad, don't pay any attention to them because the Devil is the stoker and cause of bad dreams and no matter what form they take, never give any credit to those dreams.

Having had intercourse with a woman, have you said and believed that if you enter the fish trap, no more fish or eels will enter?...

During your menses have you made a separate fire?

Have you consented that when someone is sick in your house they pray for the counsel of the Devil?

When some relative has died, have you cut your hair?

Have you buried someone with something placed inside of the shroud?

After having been to the burial of someone, have you washed or for some time have you refrained from eating fish?

Having walked in some village of infidels, have you neared where they make some ceremonies with the intention of learning them, or some prayer, or something else that is made to the Devil?...

For Chiefs and Leaders

Before going hunting, have you first made a prayer using tobacco?...

And arriving at the forest, have you had all the arrows gathered and had an old man say a prayer over them for your use?

The first deer that they kill, have you said that it be given to the above mentioned old sorcerer?

To fish in the lake, have you said that they pray to the lake first?

In the same manner, have you said that these fish that you have caught, in order to eat them, that they were prayed to by the sorcerer and one half of them should go to him?

The first fish that is caught, have you said that they be prayed to and then barbecued?

In order to begin the digging of a field, have you prayed the ancient ceremony to the prayer?

The first maize from this digging, have you held it to be a sin not to pray to it?

The first time that the storehouse is opened, have you made flour, and once you made it, in order to eat it, have you prayed to it?

To gather the nuts and palm berries, have you made with the laurel [and] praying that ceremony that you used to do?

Have you said that you will not eat the fruit of the forest without praying?

Any other fruit that has been prayed to, have you desired to eat it?...

Hunters...

In none of these things should you believe nor trust that with the prayers of the Devil you will get the prey; instead pray the things of God, and He being served, with His will you will hunt them, having left the prayer of the Devil you can hunt and trust yourself to God.

Having had the doctor cure you and already convalescing, did you make cakes or pap or something else, and did you invite the doctor that cured you, believing that if you did not act in this manner that your illness would return?

Have you said that no one should go up to the maize storehouse without first praying to the Devil?

In order to seek and take the turtle, did you pray?

Crossing with the canoe some sandbar or obstacle, and there being a choppy area, have you whistled to it, believing that you would not turn over?

Have you whistled to the storm believing that it would stop?

When you are in such distress, you will say the holy name of Jesus so that he will help you....

Sorcerers

Have you prayed to the new maize?

Have you looked with the Devil's arts to see if war approaches?

In what way or with which herb did you do this?

Have you searched for something lost with the art of the Devil?

Son, these things that you do to make the things you lost appear and say that it is in this or that place or that such person stole, this the Devil tells you in order to take your soul; do not believe it, abandon it, this is a grave sin.

Have you made rain?

If God does not wish it, no matter what you do it will not rain, abandon this which is a grave sin.

Questions for Women

During your menses have you held it to be a sin to eat fish or deer?

Having given birth recently have you considered eating these things as sinful?

To this end, have you made a new fire or did you make it during your menses?

[Anointing] the head with bear grease, have you considered it a sin to eat fish for a certain number of months?

Have you eaten charcoal, or dirt, or bits of pottery, or fleas, or lice?

Don't eat charcoal, or dirt, nor bits of pottery, they make a person sick, and because of the harm they do to you, it is a sin.

Your husband having left you, did you bathe with certain herbs, believing that with this he will return to you?

Have you said perfume [with incense] the *guano* with certain herb and he will not leave me?

And thus perfuming, have you put on the dress skirt?

Have you believed that perfuming *guano* with this intention, that someone will take a liking to you?

Have you fasted with this intention?

And thus with someone did you go on to the night, and in order to eat and drink, did you make the ceremony?

All these abuses and ceremonies and many more which are not included because they have left them already and because in some villages there are some of them; these here are so that the confessor will be forewarned so that when he hears them he will understand them; and in each province they have different ceremonies that because of their tediousness are left out....

For Sorcerers

Are you a sorcerer?

Have you bewitched someone?

Have you taken the herb with the intent of bewitching someone?

Have you given the spell to another in order to do evil to him?

Have you advised someone else so that they could bewitch?

Did the spell work?

Did the spell that you gave to the other person take effect?

If he has bewitched someone, it should be said to him to take the antidote and cure him in order to undo the evil done, and when he is cured, to return any he will be absolved, etc.

And if he has given the spell to another or advised that they do it or given instructions for it, the following is to be said to him:

Have you conjured a rain storm or a thunder storm with superstitions?

Thundering, have you blown toward the heavens in order to stop the clouds or water with your evil prayers?

Have you made the ceremony of rain?

Son, don't make this ceremony any more, for do what you will, be aware that it will not rain unless God our Lord is served.

In order to begin to take out the food out of the storehouse, have you prayed?

Have you taken the skin of the poisonous snake or of the black snake and with black *guano* and other herbs have you tried to bewitch someone or have you bewitched them or wished to do so?

And to do the above, have you considered it a sin to eat fish and to paint yourself and to sleep with your wife; but once the person is dead, have you begun to do the things that you were abstaining from, after a bath?

The bewitched person not having died from that evil spell, did you say that then I must die?

And in order to do a similar thing [another ceremony for causing death], have you gone to question the other, and taking water and moss and other things, have you made this evil spell?

Have you told them that they must give you something, otherwise you will kill all of them, and with this fear did they give you something?

Have you made the marriage ceremony, praying over them? And if they did not pay you, did you do something evil?

Have you taken a woman out of her house by singing your charms?

Have you put some herb in the mouth of some woman so that she will love you a lot?

Have you injured anyone with herbs?

Have you ruptured someone?...

On the Sixth Commandment

Have you delighted in past sins, remembering about them and even taking the liberty to tell them to others?

Have you physically fondled another person or have you embraced or kissed or held hands with evil intent?

Have you shown some part of your body to arouse in some person desires of lust or to excite them?

Sleeping two in a bed or taking a bath, have you touched your sexual organs, saying that in this manner you will do it, and etc?

Have you consented in your house or in another part that some kinsman or other person meet to have intercourse?

Have you desired to do some lewd thing with yourself or with another person?

Have you desired someone carnally?

For how much time?

How many times have your desires occurred?

Have you delighted in some lewd signal or afterwards procured or desired to put it into practice?

Have you been a procurer or procuress?...

For All

Within the church have you had intercourse?

Have you had intercourse with some infidel person?

Have you said suggestive words?

Have you delighted in exhibiting the forbidden parts?

Have you desired to have to do some lewd act with some man or woman or kin?

The other degrees of consanguinity, affinity, or relationship, or of godparenthood can be looked up in the big Confessional.

Questions for Married and Single Women

Did you desire someone?

Did you desire some of your kin?

Or some kin of your husband?

Have you consented that some of them kiss you?

Have you decorated yourself with evil intent so that someone desires you and has you?

Have you had intercourse with someone?

Was he married?

Or was he single?

How many single?

With each one how many times?

Did you have intercourse with some of your kin?

In what manner are you related?

Have you gone around with two brothers?

Have you gone around with your brother-in-law?

With some kin of your husband have you mixed?

Has someone that has had your younger sister had a duet with you?

Have you mixed with your godfather?

By chance, have you had intercourse as if you were a man?

Have you had intercourse with father and son?

Have you mixed with some infidel?

Have you taken some herb so that you would not become pregnant?

Have you taken some herb in order to become sterile?

Do you eat meat on a day of abstinence?

Do you consent that another eat it in your house?

For Sodomites

Have you had intercourse with another man?

Or have you gone around trying out or making fun in order to do that?

For Boys That Are in the Custom of Doing This

Has someone been investigating you from behind?

Did you consum[m]ate the act?

Jerald T. Milanich and William C. Sturtevant, eds., *Francisco Pareja's 1613 Confessionario: A Documentary Source for Timucuan Ethnography*. Tallahassee: Division of Archives, History, and Records Management, Florida Department of State, 1972, 23–32, 36–39. Printed by permission.

2. Don Juan de Oñate Describes the Acoma Indians' First Contacts with Christianity, 1598

Following several unsuccessful expeditions north of the Rio Grande, Spanish conquistadors determined to expand the northern reaches of New Spain into the territory of the Pueblo Indians in what is today New Mexico. In 1598 Don Juan de Oñate lay the foundation for permanent Christian rule among the Indians through formal and theatrical actions of possession: claiming the land and its inhabitants for the dominion of Christendom and the Spanish Crown and reenacting scenes from Hernan Cortés's conquest of the Aztecs. At the Indian village of Acoma in 1598, Oñate read a theological justification of the conquest and received from the Indians an act of obedience and vassalage. Despite their seeming acquiescence, the Indians rebelled against the invaders several months later. The Spaniards killed some eight hundred Acomans and captured close to six hundred. After a trial the Indians received their sentence: servitude and (for the men) amputation of a limb. Such force effected the conquest but did not facilitate early conversion to Christian allegiance and faith.

ACT OF OBEDIENCE AND VASSALAGE BY THE INDIANS
OF ACOMA, 1598

In the name of the most holy trinity...: Be it known and manifest to all who may see or in any way hear about this instrument of loyalty and vassalage that Don Juan de Oñate...at the foot of a very large rock, on top of which is situated the pueblo of Acoma, accompanied by the most reverend father, Fray Alonso Martínez, apostolic commissary of his Holiness, the friars of the order of Saint Francis, and many captains and soldiers, and there being present also numerous natives, including chieftains, leaders, and common people, and among them three Indians named Coomo, Chaamo, and Ancua, who said that they were chiefs of the pueblo of Acoma, all of whom had been assembled there by the governor; in his presence and before me, Juan Velarde, secretary, with the aid of the reverend father, Fray Alonso Martínez, apostolic commissary, and Don Tomás, Indian interpreter, the governor explained to the chieftains and the other Indians the object of his coming and what it was fitting for them to do.

He told them that he had come to their country to bring them to the knowledge of God and the king our lord, on which depended the salvation of their souls and their living securely and undisturbed in their nations, maintained in justice and order, safe in their homes, protected from their enemies, and free from all harm. Wherefore they should know that there is only one true God Almighty, creator of heaven and earth, rewarder of the good and punisher of the wicked, who has a heaven for the bliss of the former, and a hell for the punishment of the latter. This God and master of all had two servants on earth through whom He governed. The one who ruled in spiritual matters was the pope, Roman pontiff, high priest and head of the church, whose representative in this country was the most reverend father commissary, whom they saw in their midst, and they should respect and venerate him and all the priests wearing the habit, as ministers of God and men of His church. The other, who governed the world in temporal matters, was the most Christian king, Don Philip, our lord, sole defender of the church, king of Spain and the Indies, whose representative in this land was his lordship, the governor, and therefore they should respect and obey him in everything. And it was fitting that they render obedience and vassalage to God and the king, and in their places to the reverend father commissary in spiritual matters and to the governor in temporal affairs and in the government of their nations, as they were free people and owed allegiance to no one. It was to their advantage, moreover, to place themselves of their own free will under the authority of the king, Don Philip, our lord, great monarch and ruler, who would maintain them in peace and justice and defend them against their enemies, and employ them in positions and occupations in political and economic affairs, as would be explained to them in more detail later. Therefore, they should consider whether they wished to render obedience to God and the king.

The chieftains, having heard and understood the above and conferred among themselves about the matter, replied with spontaneous signs of pleasure and accord that they wished to become vassals of the most Christian king our lord, and, as his vassals, they desired to render at once obedience and vassalage for themselves and in the name of their nations. The governor reminded them that they should realize that by rendering obedience and vassalage to the king our lord they would become subject to his will and laws, and that if they failed to observe them they would be punished as transgressors of the orders of their king and natural master. Therefore they should consider what they desired to do and what answer to give. To this they replied that they wished to render the said obedience and vassalage, as they had stated before, both in their own name and in the name of the people of their nations.

The governor said that since this was the case, they should rise, as a sign of obedience, for during all this time they had remained seated, and embrace the father commissary and his lordship and kiss their hands. The said three captains rose and did as they had been directed, as a sign of obedience and vassalage.

The governor ordered me to make a record of these proceedings for him and pointed out that as far as was known and could be learned, the governments and nations in this land were all autonomous and free, not subject to any particular monarch or ruler. They, of their own free will, as has been set forth, wished to have Don Philip, our lord, as their king, and to render obedience and vassalage to him voluntarily, without compulsion from anyone. As I recognized that this was the truth, I made a written record of it for the greater peace and comfort of the royal conscience and in order that the governor's zeal and diligence in the royal service might be manifest to everyone. I gave it to him, with my name and seal affixed. It was likewise signed by the governor and stamped with the great seal of his office. Done at the pueblo of Acoma, October 27, 1598. The witnesses were Don Cristóbal de Oñate, Captain Gregorio Céssar, Alférez Bartolomé Romero, Antonio Conte de Herrera, Cristóbal de Herrera, and Francisco Vido, servants of his lordship. DON JUAN DE OÑATE.

TRIAL OF THE INDIANS OF ACOMA, 1598

Sentence

In the criminal case between the royal court and the Indians of the pueblo and fortress of Acoma, represented by Captain Alonso Gómez Montesinos, their defender, accused of having wantonly killed Don Juan de Zaldívar Oñate, maese de campo general of this expedition, and Captains Felipe de Escalante and Diego Núñez, eight soldiers, and two servants, and of other crimes; and in addition to this, after Vicente de Zaldívar Mendoza, my sargento mayor, whom I sent for this purpose in my place, had repeatedly called upon them to accept peace, not only did they refuse to do so, but actually received him with hostility, wherefore, taking into account the merits of the case and the guilt resulting therefrom, I must and do sentence all of the Indian men and women from the said pueblo under arrest, as follows:

The males who are over twenty-five years of age I sentence to have one foot cut off and to twenty years of personal servitude.

The males between the ages of twelve and twenty-five I sentence likewise to twenty years of personal servitude.

The women over twelve years of age I sentence likewise to twenty years of personal servitude.

Two Indians from the province of Moqui who were present at the pueblo of Acoma and who fought and were apprehended, I sentence to have the right hand cut off and to be set free in order that they may convey to their land the news of this punishment.

All of the children under twelve years of age I declare free and innocent of the grave offense for which I punish their parents. And because of my duty to aid, support, and protect both the boys and girls under twelve years of age, I place the girls under the care of our father commissary, Fray Alonso Martínez, in order that he, as a Christian and qualified person, may distribute them in this kingdom or elsewhere in monasteries or other places where he thinks that they may attain the knowledge of God and the salvation of their souls.

The boys under twelve years of age I entrust to Vicente de Zaldívar Mendoza, my sargento mayor, in order that they may attain the same goal.

The old men and women, disabled in the war, I order freed and entrusted to the Indians of the province of the Querechos that they may support them and may not allow them to leave their pueblos.

I order that all of the Indian men and women who have been sentenced to personal servitude shall be distributed among my captains and soldiers in the manner which I will prescribe and who may hold and keep them as their slaves for the said term of twenty years and no more.

This being a definite and final sentence, I so decree and order, DON JUAN DE OÑATE.

George P. Hammond and Agapito Rey, eds., *Don Juan de Oñate: Colonizer of New Mexico 1595–1628*. Albuquerque: University of New Mexico Press, 1953, 354–56, 477–78. Printed by permission.

3. Revised Memorial of Fray Alonso de Benavides, O.F.M., 1634

In the view of Fray Alonso de Benavides, the rule of Spanish Catholicism was beginning to take hold in New Mexico by the 1630s. Each of the Indian pueblos was under the spiritual direction of the Franciscan padres, who served as agents of occupation and kept the peace. Although the pueblos were nominally semiautonomous, the Franciscans held the authority to suppress traditional religious practices and appoint Native officials loyal to Church and state. Benavides's Memorial of 1634 convinced the Crown to support missionary expansion; its portrayal of successful conversion was probably too sanguine.

THE INDIANS, AFTER BAPTISM, OBSERVE OUR HOLY CATHOLIC FAITH WELL

These are, in short, the nations of New Mexico, where these countless people had lived in the darkness of their idolatry from the time of the Flood until the present most felicitous pontificate of your Holiness; in that land, through the preaching and ministry of the seraphic sons of Saint Francis, more than 500,000 souls are now converted, to the honor and glory of God, our Lord. Once the Indians have received holy baptism, they become so domestic that they live with great propriety. Hardly do they hear the bell calling to mass before they hasten to the church with all the cleanliness and neatness they can. Before mass, they pray together as a group, with all devotion, the entire Christian doctrine in their own tongue. They attend mass and hear the sermon with great reverence. They are very scrupulous not to miss, on Saturdays, the mass of our Lady, whom they venerate highly. When they come to confession they bring their sins, well studied, on a knotted string, indicating the sins by the knots; and, in all humility, they submit to the penances imposed on them. During Lent they all come with much humility to the processions, which are held on Monday, Wednesday, and Friday. On these days of meeting with the friars, they perform penances in the churches. During Holy Week they flagellate themselves in most solemn processions. They take particular care in bringing their children to be baptized. When they fall sick, they at once hasten to confess, and they have great faith and confidence in the priest merely laying his hands upon their heads. They are very subservient to him. When the bell tolls for the *Ave María* and the praying for the dead, they all come out either in their corridors or in the fields wherever the call reaches them, and in a loud voice they pray *Ave Marías,* and for the dead the *Paternoster* and *Ave María.*

They all assist in a body in the building of the churches with all good will, as can be seen by the many we have built, all spacious and neat. The first of their fruits they offer to the church in all reverence and good will. Lastly, they are all very happy and recognize the blindness of idolatry from which they have emerged and the blessings they enjoy in being the children of the church. This they often admit....

In every pueblo where a friar resides, he has schools for the teaching of praying, singing, playing musical instruments, and other interesting things. Promptly at dawn, one of the Indian singers, whose turn it is that week, goes to ring the bell for the Prime, at the sound of which those who go to school assemble and sweep the rooms thoroughly. The singers chant the Prime in the choir. The friar must be present at all of this and takes note of those who have failed to perform this duty, in order to reprimand them later. When everything is neat and clean, they again ring the bell and each one goes to learn his particular specialty; the friar oversees it all, in order that these students may be mindful of what they are doing. At this time those who plan to get married come and notify him, so that he may prepare and instruct them according to our holy council; if there are any, either sick or healthy persons, who wish to confess in order to receive communion at mass, or who wish anything else, they come to tell him. After they have been occupied in this manner for an hour and a half, the bell is rung for mass. All go into the church, and the friar says mass and administers the sacraments. Mass over, they gather in their different groups, examine the lists, and take note of those who are absent in order to reprimand them later. After taking the roll, all kneel down by the church door and sing the *Salve* in their own tongue. This concluded, the friar says: "Praised be the most holy Sacrament," and dismisses them, warning them first of the circumspection with which they should go about their daily business.

At mealtime, the poor people in the pueblo who are not ill come to the porter's lodge, where the cooks of the convent have sufficient food ready, which is served to them by the friar; food for the sick is sent to their homes. After mealtime, it always happens that the friar has to go to some neighboring pueblo to hear a confession or to see if they are careless in the boys' school, where they learn to pray and assist at mass, for this is the responsibility of the sextons and it is their duty always to have a dozen boys for the service of the [sacristy] and to teach them how to help at mass and how to pray.

In the evening they toll the bell for vespers, which are chanted by the singers who are on duty for the week, and, according to the importance of the feast, they celebrate it with organ chants, as they do for mass. Again the friar supervises and looks after everything, the same as in the morning.

On feast days, he says mass in the pueblo very early, and administers the sacraments, and preaches. Then he goes to say a second mass in another pueblo, whose turn it is, where he observes the same procedure, and then he returns to his convent. These two masses are attended by the people of the tribe, according to their proximity to the pueblo where they are celebrated.

One of the week days which is not so busy is devoted to baptism, and all those who are to be baptized come to the church on that day, unless some urgent matter should intervene; in that case, it is performed at any time. With great care, their names are inscribed in a book; in another, those who are married; and in another, the dead.

Frederick Webb Hodge, George P. Hammond, and Agapito Rey, eds., *Fray Alonso de Benavides' Revised Memorial of 1634.* Albuquerque: University of New Mexico Press, 1945, 99–102. Printed by permission.

4. Declaration of Pedro Naranjo on the Pueblo Indians' Revolt, 1681

In 1680 the Pueblo Indians under the leadership of a San Juan Tewa named Popé staged a revolt against Spanish rule and in particular against the Franciscans for their repression of Native religious practice. In the following year during the course of an attempted reconquest, Antonio de Otermín interviewed Pedro Naranjo, a Keres Indian from San Felipe Pueblo, who described the inspiration and regimen of the revolution, and he vowed loyalty to the Spaniards and their priests. Not until the 1690s were the soldiers able to regain the Pueblo area for their own, but then without the strict Franciscan hegemony of the decades before Popé's revolt.

Declaration of Pedro Naranjo of the Queres Nation. [Place of the Río del Norte, December 19, 1681.]

In the said plaza de armas on the said day, month, and year, for the prosecution of the judicial proceedings of this case his lordship caused to appear before him an Indian prisoner named Pedro Naranjo, a native of the pueblo of San Felipe, of the Queres nation, who was captured in the advance and attack upon the pueblo of La Isleta. He makes himself understood very well in the Castilian language and speaks his mother tongue and the Tegua. He took the oath in due legal form in the name of God, our Lord, and a sign of the cross, under charge of which he promised to tell the truth concerning what he knows and as he might be questioned, and having understood the seriousness of the oath and so signified through the interpreters, he spoke as indicated by the contents of the *autos.*

Asked whether he knows the reason or motives which the Indians of this kingdom had for rebelling, forsaking the law of God and obedience to his Majesty, and committing such grave and atrocious crimes, and who were the leaders and principal movers, and by whom and how it was ordered; and why they burned the images, temples, crosses, rosaries, and things of divine worship, committing such atrocities as killing priests, Spaniards, women, and children, and the rest that he might know touching the question, he said that since the government of Señor General Hernando Ugarte y la Concha they have planned to rebel on various occasions through conspiracies of the Indian sorcerers, and that although in some pueblos the messages were accepted, in other parts they would not agree to it; and that it is true that during the government of the said señor general seven or eight Indians were hanged for this same cause, where-upon the unrest subsided. Some time thereafter they [the conspirators] sent from the pueblo of Los Taos through the pueblos of the custodia two deerskins with some pictures on them signifying conspiracy after their manner, in order to convoke the people to a new rebellion, and the said deerskins passed to the province of Moqui, where they refused to accept them. The pact which they had been forming ceased for the time being, but they always kept in their hearts the desire to carry it out, so as to live as they are living to-day. Finally, in the past years, at the summons of an Indian named Popé who is said to have communica-tion with the devil, it happened that in an estufa of the pueblo of Los Taos there appeared to the said Popé three figures of Indians who never came out of the est-ufa. They gave the said Popé to understand that they were going underground to the lake of Copala. He saw these figures emit fire from all the extremities of their bodies, and that one of them was called Caudi, another Tilini, and the other Tleume; and these three beings spoke to the said Popé, who was in hiding from the secretary, Francisco Xavier, who wished to punish him as a sorcerer. They told him to make a cord of maguey fiber and tie some knots in it which would signify the number of days that they must wait before the rebellion. He said that the cord was passed through all the pueblos of the kingdom so that the ones which agreed to it [the rebellion] might untie one knot in sign of obe-dience, and by the other knots they would know the days which were lacking; and this was to be done on pain of death to those who refused to agree to it. As a sign of agreement and notice of having concurred in the treason and per-fidy they were to send up smoke signals to that effect in each one of the pueblos singly. The said cord was taken from pueblo to pueblo by the swiftest youths under the penalty of death if they revealed the secret. Everything being thus ar-ranged, two days before the time set for its execution, because his lordship had learned of it and had imprisoned two Indian accomplices from the pueblo of Tesuque, it was carried out prematurely that night, because it seemed to them that they were now discovered; and they killed religious, Spaniards, women, and children. This being done, it was proclaimed in all the pueblos that everyone in common should obey the commands of their father whom they did not know, which would be given through El Caydi or El Popé. This was heard by Alonso Catití, who came to the pueblo of this declarant to say that everyone must unite to go to the villa to kill the governor and the Spaniards who had remained with him, and that he who did not obey would, on their return, be beheaded; and in fear of this they agreed to it. Finally the señor governor and those who were with him escaped from the siege, and later this declarant saw that as soon as the Spaniards had left the kingdom an order came from the said Indian, Popé, in

which he commanded all the Indians to break the lands and enlarge their culti-
vated fields, saying that now they were as they had been in ancient times, free
from the labor they had performed for the religious and the Spaniards, who
could not now be alive. He said that this is the legitimate cause and the reason
they had for rebelling, because they had always desired to live as they had when
they came out of the lake of Copala. Thus he replies to the question.

Asked for what reason they so blindly burned the images, temples, crosses,
and other things of divine worship, he stated that the said Indian, Popé, came
down in person, and with him El Saca and El Chato from the pueblo of Los
Taos, and other captains and leaders and many people who were in his train,
and he ordered in all the pueblos through which he passed that they instantly
break up and burn the images of the holy Christ, the Virgin Mary and the other
saints, the crosses, and everything pertaining to Christianity, and that they burn
the temples, break up the bells, and separate from the wives whom God had
given them in marriage and take those whom they desired. In order to take
away their baptismal names, the water, and the holy oils, they were to plunge
into the rivers and wash themselves with amole, which is a root native to the
country, washing even their clothing, with the understanding that there would
thus be taken from them the character of the holy sacraments. They did this,
and also many other things which he does not recall, given to understand that
this mandate had come from the Caydi and the other two who emitted fire from
their extremities in the said estufa of Taos, and that they thereby returned to the
state of their antiquity, as when they came from the lake of Copala; that this
was the better life and the one they desired, because the God of the Spaniards
was worth nothing and theirs was very strong, the Spaniard's God being rotten
wood. These things were observed and obeyed by all except some who, moved
by the zeal of Christians, opposed it, and such persons the said Popé caused
to be killed immediately. He saw to it that they at once erected and rebuilt
their houses of idolatry which they call estufas, and made very ugly masks in
imitation of the devil in order to dance the dance of the cacina; and he said
likewise that the devil had given them to understand that living thus in accordance with the law of their ancestors, they would harvest a great deal of maize,
many beans, a great abundance of cotton, calabashes, and very large watermel-
ons and cantaloupes; and that they could erect their houses and enjoy abundant
health and leisure. As he has said, the people were very much pleased, living
at their ease in this life of their antiquity, which was the chief cause of their
falling into such laxity. Following what has already been stated, in order to ter-
rorize them further and cause them to observe the diabolical commands, there
came to them a pronouncement from the three demons already described, and
from El Popé, to the effect that he who might still keep in his heart a regard
for the priests, the governor, and the Spaniards would be known from his un-
clean face and clothes, and would be punished. And he stated that the said four
persons stopped at nothing to have their commands obeyed. Thus he replies to
the question.

Asked what arrangements and plans they had made for the contingency of
the Spaniards' return, he said that what he knows concerning the question is

that they were always saying they would have to fight to the death, for they do not wish to live in any other way than they are living at present; and the demons in the estufa of Taos had given them to understand that as soon as the Spaniards began to move toward this kingdom they would warn them so that they might unite, and none of them would be caught. He having been questioned further and repeatedly touching the case, he said that he has nothing more to say except that they should be always on the alert, because the said Indians were continually planning to follow the Spaniards and fight with them by night, in order to drive off the horses and catch them afoot, although they might have to follow them for many leagues. What he has said is the truth, and what happened, on the word of a Christian who confesses his guilt. He said that he has come to the pueblos through fear to lead in idolatrous dances, in which he greatly fears in his heart that he may have offended God, and that now having been absolved and returned to the fold of the church, he has spoken the truth in everything he has been asked. His declaration being read to him, he affirmed and ratified all of it. He declared himself to be eighty years of age, and he signed it with his lordship and the interpreters and assisting witnesses, before me, the secretary. ANTONIO DE OTERMÍN (rubric); PEDRO NARANJO; NICOLÁS RODRÍGUEZ REY (rubric); JUAN LUCERO DE GODOY (rubric); JUAN RUIZ DE CASARES (rubric); PEDRO DE LEIVA (rubric); SEBASTIÁN DE HERRERA (rubric); JUAN DE NORIEGA GARCÍA (rubric); LUIS DE GRANILLO (rubric); JUAN DE LUNA Y PADILLA (rubric). Before me, FRANCISCO XAVIER, secretary of government and war (rubric).

Charles Wilson Hackett and Charmion Clair Shelby, eds. and trans., *Revolt of the Pueblo Indians of New Mexico and Otermín's Attempted Reconquest 1680–1682*. Albuquerque: University of New Mexico Press, 1942, 245–49. Printed by permission.

5. Bishop Tamarón's Visitation of New Mexico, 1760

In 1760 the bishop of Durango, Pedro Tamarón y Romeral, conducted a tour of the Franciscan missions of New Mexico in order to investigate the state of the padres' zeal and the condition of the Pueblos' faith. Both were said to be lacking. The bishop was pleased by the reception he received; however, he was unconvinced that the Indians' commitment to Christianity ran much deeper than superficial assent. Several months after his stay in Pecos, a Native carpenter named Agustín Guichí held a parody of the episcopal visitation, including a mock Mass. Puebloan imitation of Catholic ritualism functioned as both a resistance and an adaptation to the Spaniards' religion.

Extraordinary Happening in Pecos

On May 29, 1760, I went to the pueblo of the Pecos Indians. They received me with demonstrations of rejoicing. They come out on horseback; they perform many tilts to show how skillful and practiced they are in riding.

I inspected that church, and I confirmed them. An escort of soldiers and the Father Custos accompanied me. Among my family I took with me a Spanish-speaking and civilized negro as my body servant. He is corpulent and has a good presence, and he must have excited the imagination of the Indians.

I finished my visitation of that kingdom and I left for the outside world in July. During the month of September those Indians of Pecos arranged a function similar to my reception and to other ceremonies I celebrated there. The originator of this performance was one of the Indian principal men of that pueblo, called Agustin Guichí, a carpenter by trade. He made himself bishop, and, in order to present himself to his people as such, he designed and cut pontifical vestments. Making the mitre of parchment, he stained it with white earth. Out of a cloak (*tilma*), he made a cape like the cope used at confirmations, and he fashioned the rochet out of another cloak. He made a sort of pastoral crosier from a reed.

The aforesaid Agustín donned all this, mounted an ass, and two other Indians got themselves up to accompany him in the capacity of assistants. One took the part of the Father Custos. They put a garment like the Franciscan habit on him, and they painted the other black to represent my man. These two also rode on similar mounts, and, after all the Indian population had assembled along with others who were not Indians, to the accompaniment of a muffled drum and loud huzzas, the whole crew, followed by the three mounted men with Agustín, the make-believe bishop garbed as such in his fashion, in the middle, departed for the pueblo. They entered it at one o'clock on the fourteenth day of September, 1760. They went straight to the plaza, where the Indian women were kneeling in two rows. And Agustín, the make-believe bishop, went between them distributing blessings. In this manner they proceeded to the place where they had prepared a great arbor with two seats in it. Agustín, who was playing the part of the bishop, occupied the chief one, and Mateo Cru, who was acting the Custos, the other.

And the latter immediately rose and informed the crowd in a loud voice that the bishop ordered them to approach to be confirmed. They promptly obeyed, and Agustín, garbed as a bishop, used the following method of confirming each one who came to him: He made a cross on his forehead with water, and when he gave him a buffet, that one left and the next one came forward. In this occupation he spent all the time necessary to dispatch his people, and after the confirmations were over, the meal which had been prepared for the occasion was served. Then the dance with which they completed the afternoon followed. On the next day the diversion and festivities continued, beginning with a mass which Bishop Agustín pretended to say in the same arbor. During it he distributed pieces of tortillas made of wheat flour in imitation of communion. And the rest of the day the amusement was dancing, and the same continued on the third day which brought those disorders and entertainments to an end.

On the fourth day, when the memorable Agustín no longer found occupation in the mockery of his burlesque pastimes as bishop, he went about the business of looking after his property. He went to visit his milpa, or corn field, which was half a league away near the river. Then he sat down at the foot of a cedar tree opposite the maize. He was still there very late in the afternoon when night was drawing in, and a bear attacked him from behind, so fiercely that, clawing his head, he tore the skin from the place over which the mitre must have rested. He proceeded to the right hand and tore it to pieces, gave him other bites on the breast, and went away to the sierra.

The wounded man's brother, José Churune, states that after his brother was wounded, he came to see what had happened to him and that Agustín received him, saying, "Brother, God has already punished me." Agustín Turifundi, Agustín Guichí's son, relates in his statement that after his father was wounded and when he had been taken to his house, he summoned him and ordered him to shut the door. And when they were alone he gave him the following admonition: "Son, I have committed a great sin, and God is punishing me for it. And so I order you that you and your brothers are not to do likewise. Counsel them every day and every hour." This was the exhortation he made before he died.

The fiscal of the pueblo, Juan Domingo Tarizari, testifies that he went to examine the bear's track and that he followed its prints and saw that when the bear came down from the sierra, he did not go to the milpas, but that he made the whole journey until he wounded Agustín Guichí and returned to the sierra immediately thereafter without eating maize. The fiscal says this and also that bears do not attack men except when the latter chase them. And the other witnesses confirmed his deposition.

Agustín Guichí confessed with the aid of an interpreter, who, at Pecos, is an Indian named Lorenzo. This man relates in his statement that Father Fray Joaquín Xerez, missionary of that pueblo, summoned him to be present as interpreter at the confession, and that he gave him the holy oil of Extreme Unction afterwards. The same mission father certifies that he interred the body of Agustín Guichí, carpenter, in that church on the twenty-first day of September, 1760.

A formal investigation and report and a juridical indictment with regard to all the foregoing circumstances were drawn up by virtue of a decree I issued, granting a commission for this purpose to Don Santiago Roibal, vicar and ecclesiastical judge of the villa of Santa Fe and its district. He examined nine witnesses, three of them Spanish soldiers attached to that royal presidio who were in Pecos on escort duty and were present at the festivities and burlesque function, and who testify as eyewitnesses. Another was neither soldier nor Indian. He is called Juan Gallegos, and he was present.

The Most High Lord of Heaven and Earth willed this very exemplary happening so that it should serve as a warning to those remote tribes and so that they might show due respect for the functions of His Holy Church and her ministers, and so that we might all be more careful to venerate holy and sacred things; for the punishment that befell does not permit its noteworthy circumstances to be attributed to worldly coincidences....

In the year 1759 a rumor spread that the Indians were going to rise on the day of Corpus Christi. The governor was alarmed; he took precautions and made inquiries, but he was unable to clarify the matter. When I was there the following year, they remembered this and told me about it.

Although I made inquiries throughout my visitation, I was unable to discover any use or practice of formal idolatry, nor was any denunciation made before me. I continued to have my suspicions. I asked questions and was not told of any defection on the basis of which I could judge this matter, to which the Indians are usually prone, as experience has shown in other regions. In New Mexico I did not approve of the so-called estufa, which they maintain in the pueblos I went to inspect, after I was informed about it and its nature. Digging three or four varas deep in the earth a circle about five varas in diameter, they build a wall about a vara and a half high all around it above ground, and they roof it like a terrace. The entrance is through the roof and looks like the hatch of a ship, with its small ladder. There is no other door or window. Outside it has the shape of the crown of a hat. There they say they hold their dances, conventicles, and meetings, and receive Indians of other places there. I did not find proof of anything evil, but I ordered them [the friars] to keep their eyes open. They argued the difficulty of depriving them of that dark and strange receptacle, which is also a temptation to evil....

Eleanor B. Adams, ed. and trans., *Bishop Tamarón's Visitation of New Mexico, 1760*. Albuquerque: University of New Mexico Press, 1954, 50–53, 73–74. Printed by permission.

6. Fray Francisco Atansio Dominguez's Description of the Missions of New Mexico, 1776

In 1776 Francisco Atansio Dominguez, O.F.M., described the missions of New Mexico. He found that the Pueblo Indians were persisting in the practice of their traditional religion, even as they participated in the life of the Church. Almost a century since Popé's rebellion and the reconquest, the baptized Indians were little more than neophytes (in his view), attracted more by ornaments than by the substance of the Catholic faith. The friar mentions the continuing importance of kivas (which he calls estufas) among the Puebloans.

INDIANS

Even at the end of so many years since their reconquest, the specious title or name of neophytes is still applied to them. This is the reason their condition now is almost the same as it was in the beginning, for generally speaking they have preserved some very indecent, and perhaps superstitious, customs. Of these, I mention the following: As Christians, a saint's name is given them in holy baptism as is the custom in our Holy Mother the Church, but they value it so much that they do not mention it among themselves nor are they known by it, but rather by appellations according to the custom handed down from their ancestors.

They use these to such an extent that most of them do not know their saints' names and those who know them do not use them, and when we call them by their saints' names they usually have their joke among themselves, repeating the saint's name to each other as if in ridicule....

Their repugnance and resistance to most Christian acts is evident, for they perform the duties pertaining to the Church under compulsion, and there are usually many omissions. They are not in the habit of praying or crossing themselves when they rise or go to bed, and consequently they have no devotion for certain saints as is customary among us. And if they sometimes invoke God and His saints or pray or pay for Masses, it is in a confused manner or to comply in their confusion with what the fathers teach and explain. For example, they pay the father for a Mass, and he asks them what the intention is in terms adjusted to their understanding, and they reply: *You know, that saint what more good, more big, him you make Mass. I not know, maybe him Virgin, maybe St. Anthony*, etc., not to weary ourselves by more. And the father applies it with a good direct intention, as he knows that he must do.

They do not confess annually. If the fathers find some who know how to make a proper confession, and there are few, there is rarely anyone capable of receiving communion. When in danger of death they do indeed confess, most of them through an interpreter....

They are exceedingly fond of pretty reliquaries, medals, crosses, and rosaries, but this does not arise from Christian devoutness (except in a few cases) but from love of ornament. And these objects are always kept for special occasions, and only when the friars admonish them for not wearing them all the time do they wear them until that little scolding has been forgotten. Then they put them away again until another reproof, and so it goes....

They use estufas, of which some pueblos have more, others less. There are sometimes nine in one pueblo, as at Pecos, and one in others, as at Nambe. Some of them are underground, and others are above ground with walls like a little house, and of them all, some are round while others are rectangular. But the entrance is always through a *coi*, or trap door on the roof, as has already been said some time ago. These estufas are the chapter, or council, rooms, and the Indians meet in them, sometimes to discuss matters of their government for the coming year, their planting, arrangements for work to be done, or to elect new community officials, or to rehearse their dances, or sometimes for other things....

Eleanor B. Adams and Fray Angelico Chavez, eds. and trans., *The Missions of New Mexico, 1776. A Description by Fray Francisco Atansio Dominguez with Other Contemporary Documents*. Albuquerque: University of New Mexico Press, 1956, 254–56. Printed by permission.

7. Eugene Van Patten, President of the Tortugas Indians [Los Indios de Nuestra Señora de Guadalupe], to Reverend William H. Ketcham, May 12, 1919

In the Pueblo revolt of 1680 various Indians (Tiwas, Piros, and Mansos) remained loyal to the Spanish and accompanied the soldiers to El Paso, where they established an indigenous community, now in New Mexico. Known as the Tortugas, or the San Juan de Guadalupe Tribe, they maintained devotion to Our Lady of Guadalupe like other Hispanicized Native Americans, and in 1914 they built a church in her name. In a letter to Reverend William H. Ketcham of the Bureau of Catholic Indian Missions in 1919, the president of the Tortugas, Eugene Van Patten, expressed his desire for autonomy over the church and his fear of encroachment from their non-Indian neighbors.

My Esteemed and Reverend Father[,]

I have the honor and pleasure to inform you — that after our [leaving]...the Town of Guadalupe yesterday, the Indians of the corporation of "Los Indigenes de Nuestra Señora de [Guadalupe"] — held their meeting as I requested them to do, and they agreed to support a priest for...their Church at that place — having called in the Commissioners of our adjoining Town of "San Migel" (Tortugas) who were present; and heard and saw all proceedings and they agreed to call a meeting this Evening, the 12th and they would do likewise — and that between them to raise a suffic[i]ent sum; to make...the new appointed parish priest comfortable only they would not [accept] the present Father Juan Melitelo, and for me to ask you in their name to assist them in [retaining] their old [customs], and especially on their having the mass and feast on the 12th day of December as it has [always]...been customary, and that they be allowed to have the *Valorio* as [always] has been customary, and was taught them by the Missionary Fathers[.]

This means an all night prayer meeting at the caciques hall and taking their patron Virgin in procession to the church for mass on the 12th which has been [customary] since their conversion to the Catholic Apostolic Roman church up to the last nine or ten years as I told you yesterday when we removed the head quarters to town of [Guadalupe]. The suit was [brought] before...the then Bishop [of] [Arizona, who] was in charge here. He sent Rev. Father Mizeon of this place to settle it up which he did. I called a meeting — he being present asked what we wished. I answered him only what it was. I stated to him first our right to use our old customs from the Spaniards down to the present which had never been intercepted until now to have our annual feast and mass of our patron Saint, Our Lady of Guadalupe, which comes on the 12 day of December com[m]encing on the 8th of Dec. but for several years the mass would be set for the 20th and other dates. Now this mass it has been our [custom] to pay for separately. We have always paid as high a[s] $26 to $30.00 bill never less than [$] 22.50 even while paying by special contract wages, but we said nothing about it but did object to cha[ng]ing of the date, as we entertained many people who...came from afar to comply with vows or promises to do so and so. And many people cam[e] hundreds of miles on foot to comply with their promises to Our Lady of Guadalupe and on that day we kept an open house and fed and took care of them not only Indians but Mexicans and any Nationality.

This was our principal complaint then: The service of the prayer meeting, the [procession], our dancing before our church, religious service in order, then the right to our property which we built ourselves and owned, but it is a Catholic church free to all Cat[h]olics of the world without any [expense] to them. As you saw about the Key, that night the church has been closed to us for nearly two months, and to the San Juan People for over three weeks. You saw the trouble you had to get into the church yourself, and this is one of your own Indian churches as the Indians built it and paid for everything belonging to it. Now we had a private [cemetery] and we were allowed by the Bishop of [Arizona] to keep it to our own people but the church [authorities] used it for the other [townspeople].

Now I will make an explanation. We have held this property for [some] 40 years. Now the town of San Juan and surroundings are 65 years old, and during all that time never has had so small a population as [today], but the town of San Juan in all that time has never had a small chapel. Nor has it ever had a [graveyard]. They would bury their dead, baptize their children and marry in surrounding parishes. Until we built our church, they never had a priest. Now they want to make us furnish every improvement and even keep our Key. I must say it is aggravating. I do not wonder the Indians are getting angry but our older heads hold them down and will, and now that you came in the nick of time I think we will be able to settle this soon. I will write you a letter to Washington in a few days and give all the information I can. There [is] a Mexican priest at La Mesilla helping Rev. Juan at that place who would be pleased to take the place and is well liked by all our people. And many Fathers all speak very highly of him and if we could get him I think things would change for the better. The Indians and towns people after their Junta Passed a Vote of thanks to you for your kindness in Visiting them and Kindly giving them their first mass for four Sundays. Also your Kindly advice and from me I wish to state you will have a friend for the balance of days in saying good [bye]. We are brothers in blood [nationality], and as Indians all of America, and hope we may be brothers in faith. God preserve you and be with us all forever more.

Eugene Van Patten
President of Guadalupe Corporation

Marquette University, Bureau of Catholic Indian Missions Records. Printed by permission.

8. Nativity Myth at Laguna, Recorded by Elsie Clews Parsons, 1918

Elsie Clews Parsons was an anthropologist who studied Pueblo religious life as thoroughly as any non-Indian observer. In 1918 she recorded a narrative about Jesus told by a Laguna Catholic. The story indicates the way in which Indians made Christian mythology their own.

During a visit to Laguna in February, 1918, I had noticed in the church a model in miniature of the Nativity group. Jesus, Mary and Joseph, the ox and the mule, were represented, and there was a large flock of sheep. José or Tsiwema or Tsipehus, the "sextana," was one of my Laguna informants, and, on asking him the meaning of the crib, he narrated as follows: —

The baby (*uwak*) José Crito, god's child (*hus² ka iach,* "god his child") was brought from a far country by his father José and his mother Mari. They took the journey about the time he was going to be born. He was born in a stable. A big fire, a big star, came down from the sky. There was an ox in the stable. When he was born, the ox came there. He blew on the baby. A little after a shepherd (*shtura*) came. That is the reason the priest put the sheep there. That was the way he was born. He went from there to another town, to the king's house (*re gama*), his mother and father and himself, on a horse. He grew up at the king's house. After he had grown up, the others, the Jews (*Uriu*), were not satisfied with him. They were going to kill him. There were three brothers, three children of god; but this one born in the stable was the leader. They were hunting everywhere for him to kill him. One of the Jews asked the middle (*tsunatseiche*) brother which was Jesus. The Jew said, "Which one is it?" He said, "I am not going to tell you." They said, "Yes, you must tell us." So they bribed him. So another party of Jews came into his house. They were all sitting at the table, and still they kept asking which one was it. He was sitting in the north direction. "That's he." So they took him. "Wait a little," he said. "Wait a little, my brothers [*tiumu temishe*]! Which one of you has been given some money?" — "None of us." The one sitting at the east end of the table was the one that had been bribed. "You are the one, you have been paid some money. Now I am going away. I am going up to Konamats ['place of being thankful']." So they took him out of the room. They stood up a cross (*shukasetse*). He was a spirit (*kokimun*). So it took some time for them to get ready. When god's child made everything ready, they nailed him to the cross through the middle of his hands. There was one who could not see. There was another who was lame, so his brother carried him on his back. They pierced him through the heart. "Now all is ready," said the Jews. They made the blind man and the lame man pierce his heart. When they pierced him, the blood spurted everywhere. In this way (that is the reason why) from the spattered blood all living beings came, horses and mules and all creatures. The man that was lame got up and walked, and the blind man could see, because they had been spattered with the blood. So at last they dug a hole and stood up the cross. They dug the hole so deep, that the cross could never be taken up. They buried him in this deep hole; they threw dirt and rocks on him, some of the rocks so big that they could hardly lift them; still they threw them in. They buried him. The first day, the second day, he was still buried; the third day he was to leave his grave. He went up to Konamats, back to his father, God. The Jews kept shooting upwards. His father was glad he came back up, so they would live there together in Konamats. The season when he was treated so mean is coming back again. Tomorrow is the first day of mass (*misa*). For seven weeks (*domik*) I have to ring the bell. On the sixth (seventh?) Sunday (*domiku*) it will be *kuitishi*. On the seventh Sunday it is coming back to the same time he went up to heaven. On the Wednesday before *kuitishi* will be the covering (*kaitamishe*). All the people come in to take a turn watching. It is covered Wednesday (*tsuna kaiich*), Thursday (*shuwewise*), Friday (*hienis*). On Saturday (*sauwawu*) it is uncovered. He goes back to his father. It will be *kucheachsi* [end or breaking of taboo]. That is all *(hemetsa).*

Elsie Clews Parsons, "Nativity Myth at Laguna and Zuñi," *Journal of American Folklore* 31, no. 120 (April-June 1918): 256–57. Printed by permission.

9. Letter to Santa Claus by Esther Naktewa (Zuni), St. Anthony Indian School, October 18, 1937

A letter from a Zuni girl to Santa Claus in 1937 reveals the way in which Pueblo Indians adopted the religious culture of American Catholicism through the agency of Catholic schools. Esther Naktewa wrote of midnight Mass, Christmas trees, and the hope to receive Santa's gifts.

I am a Zuni Indian girl and go to St. Anthony Indian School; my name is Esther. I thought it would please you if I would tell you about our Merry Christmas at the Mission. The celebration in church is very solemn and a large crowd of Indians come for midnight Mass. The church is decorated very beautifully. The altar is surrounded by stately cedar trees and the lights shining thru the branches look like glittering stars. The crib is very pretty and many people pray devoutly before the Holy Infant. The boys and girls who have gone to St. Anthony's School receive Holy Communion with us children. The pupils of our class are the choir members and all are happy to sing the "Guardian Angel Mass" which we have practiced for this occasion. We children and all the Zuni people like the Christmas celebration in church very much.

Then, dear Santa Claus, Christmas in school is certainly a surprise for us children. We often wonder when you come to our school. Of course, when we see the shades pulled down then we surmise that you must have been there. We are always very anxious to find out what you have brought to us. Some of the boys try to peep thru the transom before we are allowed to enter the classroom. [When] Sister opens the door [everybody] looks with big eyes at the desk and begins to smile and joyously shouts, "Santa has been here," seeing a pretty handkerchief or a toy, an apple and an orange you so kindly have brought to each one of us. Yes, dear Santa, we are always very happy on Christmas. But, you should see the little ones. They think themselves little queens and kings with their presents from you.

Dear Santa Claus, I would like to have a merry Christmas for my father and mother, my brothers and sisters. My brother Walter will get a Christmas tree from the woods; and when at night everybody is at sleep I shall put the tree in the room. Sister will let us make Christmas decorations from tinfoil during our industrial period at school. But I would like to have some presents to put on the table. May I kindly ask you for a handkerchief for my parents? My brother Willie sings in the choir and Sister says that he has a sweet voice. He will be happy with a mouth harp. Aggie has big black eyes and I think she would like a pink dress. Emilia is the baby girl and she would sing a Zuni lulla-bye to a little doll. Harold is my baby brother and he likes to play with a little dog.

Dear Santa, I know that you are very busy now reading the letters from boys and girls the world over. But I assure you that I very gratefully shall appreciate your kindness in helping me to make a "Merry Christmas" to my dear ones.

Your Indian friend

Esther Naktewa

Marquette University, Bureau of Catholic Indian Missions Records. Printed by permission.

10. Reverend Regis Darpel, O.F.M., Writes of the Jemez Hosts to the Christ Child, 1949

Reverend Regis Darpel, O.F.M., depicted the devotional celebration of Christmas among the Jemez Pueblo people in 1949.

HOSTS TO THE CHRIST CHILD

The chapel is already filled, well filled. It is almost midnight, Christmas eve. A pair of altar boys, black eyes sparkling and copper faces glowing, return to the sacristy with candle-lighters trailing wisps of smoke, as though to report their first important function satisfactorily performed. I glance out at the altar. Merry bits of flame are dancing on the tips of the stately candles that stand among the somber evergreens.

Now a line of silent, blanketed Indians solemnly file into the sacristy. They are the officers and elders of the pueblo, the governor, his assistant, the war chief, the fiscal, and the councillors. "Juan," I nod to the big altar boy, "you may carry the processional cross." "Jose, you take the censer and boat."

The cross bearer leads our little procession out of the chapel into the night. On each side of the road leading into the center of Jemez Pueblo flaming bonfires light up our way. We hasten, for a bitter, piercing wind is pouring out of the north. Nervous horses sniff and snort as we pass the corrals. A prowling dog barks. But it is only a few minutes walk from the mission to Ambrosio Toya's house. It would be easy to find. His is the only lighted window in the village.

The door opened as we approached. There against the wall of the large living room stood a shrine — a low table, draped with an Indian rug and covered with an embroidered cloth upon which rested a figure of the Infant Jesus, lying upon a crib under a large arch, rainbow in shape and in coloring, and surrounded by small statues and lighted candles. Slender cedars flanked it, and brightly figured Navaho blankets hung from the walls behind it. Ambrosio and his wife, Estella, chosen to be the *padrinos* or sponsors of the Christ Child this Christmas season, have made Him at home, in Indian fashion, in their house.

We all knelt down before the shrine and said a silent prayer. Then I incensed the statue and the altar. We rose. Estella took the statue of the Infant and wrapped it tenderly in her shawl; Ambrosio took up the figure of His mother. The by-standers formed a guard of honor. Now we all marched in procession to the church, and up the middle aisle to the sanctuary.

Ambrosius and Estella Toya (Jemez) with Reverend Regis Darpel, O.F.M., sitting before a personal shrine and Christmas crib in their home, Jemez Reservation, Jemez, New Mexico, 1949. Credit: Photographer unknown. Marquette University, Bureau of Catholic Indian Missions Records. Reproduced by permission.

I vested and began the midnight Mass. Ambrosio and his wife had the privilege of sitting in the sanctuary near the Crib. At the Gospel, when I faced the congregation to tell them again the never-old story of the Nativity, the sight was one that would have gratified any pastor, almost everyone of his people gathered before the altar to pay their homage to their Lord and Master on this blessed day. It was a scene that would have intrigued an artist. On a gala occasion like this, the Jemez Indians don all their traditional finery, bright-colored shirts and waists and shawls and headbands and strings of turquoise and silver ornaments. Here they were, men on one side of the church, women on the other. A white Catholic would have been thrilled at being in the midst of one of the still surviving groups of Indians and witnessing what devout Catholics they are.

At Communion time two hundred and seventy Indians approached the altar rail. After Mass Ambrosio and Estella stood there, holding the statues of the Child and of the Blessed Virgin for men, women, and children to admire and kiss. After all the congregation had thus paid their reverences, the *padrinos* carried the statues back to their home, followed by a long procession. The midnight Mass and its attendant ceremonies were over.

Christmas day was a wintry day, but not just another wintry day. True, snow-bearing clouds sailed across the sky as usual, casting moving shadows on the red and saffron bluffs which rim our valley. The dull fields studded with withered stalks had the same lonely, cheerless look as yesterday. Puffs of blue-gray smoke rose from the chimney pot of every house; everyone was at home.

Yet one would see a couple of men or women, or a mother, father, and children, entering or leaving Ambrosio Toya's house from time to time during the day. I myself called that afternoon. I found several Indians there admiring the Christmas shrine. A large table, crowded with plates, and cups, and bowls, and heaps of bread and cakes, was prominent in another part of the room. Ambrosio and Estella urged us to sit down and eat. One could not refuse. The padre is always an honored guest in an Indian home. So, too, are all visitors welcome on occasions like this.

Relatives, friends, and neighbors came and went all day. These visits, in fact, continued all of Christmas week.

Everyone in the pueblo came at least once, some repeatedly, and everyone was invited to eat. This hospitality must have been costly to the good hosts. So I remarked to Ambrosio later. He admitted it, but added quickly that they were glad even so to be *padrinos*, because they considered it a great privilege to be hosts to the Savior of the world and to His visitors.

> Reverend Regis Darpel, O.F.M., "Hosts to the Christ Child," *The Indian Sentinel* 29, no. 10 (December 1949): 147–48. Printed by permission.

11. Archbishop Rudolph A. Gerken's Declaration to the Governor, Officials, and People of the Santo Domingo Pueblo, July 16, 1935

When Rudolph A. Gerken became archbishop of Santa Fe in 1933, he was concerned that the Puebloans in his archdiocese had retained too many aspects of their traditional religion, even as they received baptism and other sacraments. He wished to establish his priests and sisters as permanent residents in the pueblos, for example at Santo Domingo, where village authorities kept all outsiders at bay. In order to maintain ritual secrecy, they forbade outsiders from viewing their Native ceremonies, and they prevented tribal members from making confessions. They guarded their sovereignty, and when the archbishop insisted that a priest and sisters be allowed to live in the village, the Indian leaders refused. In 1935 Archbishop Gerken put pressure on the people of Santo Domingo Pueblo by withdrawing priestly visitations. There would be no more regular baptisms, Masses, or marriages until the officials bent to the will of the Church.

TO THE GOVERNOR, OFFICIALS AND PEOPLE OF THE [SANTO] DOMINGO PUEBLO, JULY 16, 1935:

I, the undersigned, Rudolph A. Gerken, Archbishop of the Archdiocese of Santa Fe; having been officially appointed by the highest authority under god of the Holy Roman Catholic Church, as his representative to be the head of this Archdiocese and being therefore obligated to rule the church and to safeguard the spiritual interests of the faithful as well as the integrity of the teachings of the Church; feel in duty bound before God to solemnly make this official proclamation and publish its nature through the Priest appointed in charge of [Santo] Domingo.

On Monday, July 15th, a date agreed upon, I together with Father Jerome, your former Priest, met with the officials of the Pueblo here in [Santo] Domingo for the purpose of arranging to station in this Pueblo a Priest and also Missionary Sisters, who should teach Religion to the children and others in the Pueblo, and who should carry on activities such as sewing clubs, visit the sick and in general be agents of mercy in your midst. I fully explained that our only object was to do for the faithful of [Santo] Domingo what is being done by the Church in every part of the world to all peoples and races. The officials of the Pueblo denied us this right to do for the Catholics and the children of the Church what is our duty as the head of this Archdiocese. I fully explained that the people and children must be better instructed in their Religion in order to be good Catholics.

I furthermore requested that the officials of the Pueblo would not interfere with the rights of the people by forbidding them to receive the Sacrament of Penance in Confession and receive Holy Communion. The officials said that this was not necessary to be good Catholics. I pleaded with the officials to reconsider this matter and explained to them that I do not interfere with the authority of the Pueblo, which is only and purely civil, and further explained that my authority is over the spiritual and religious life of the people, and that the people have no duty to obey the officials of the Pueblo in things purely spiritual, and that the people have a right before God, a right which God has given them, to do what is necessary to save their immortal souls so that they may hope to go to Heaven when death takes them from this world. The officials, however, told me that their decision was final and they stubbornly refused to reconsider the matter.

WHEREAS, therefore, the officials of the Pueblo refuse to respect the authority of the Church, which I represent, even to the extent that they would forbid the people to receive the Sacraments of Confession and Holy Communion, which is necessary and essential if we want to save our souls, and,

WHEREAS, they refuse us freedom to instruct the children and the people as we see fit and as is our duty, we are no longer permitted to Baptize the children, because it is made impossible for them to become good and practical Catholics, since the officials do not permit us to instruct the children and to administer to them the Sacrament of Penance in Confession and Holy Communion, and,

WHEREAS, the officials of the Pueblo are so disrespectful and disobedient to the authority of the Church that they deny us the right to station a Priest and Missionary Sisters in the Pueblo, which is permitted by all other peoples over the whole world, we by our authority given to us by the Supreme Pontiff, the Pope of the Church, the Vicar of Christ, herewith now solemnly proclaim and declare: that the Priest shall no longer visit the Pueblo of [Santo] Domingo: that the Priest shall not come to Baptize the children excepting only when they are very sick and in danger of death: that the Priest shall not say Holy Mass in the Pueblo of [Santo] Domingo, and that the Priest shall not unite in Marriage any of your young people in the Pueblo as long as the present officials hold office in the Pueblo, and this shall not be changed until these present officials or their successors in office will grant us the liberty to carry out the work of the Church, as it is our duty to do.

You good Catholics, who may be here and who are sincere in your faith are exhorted and urged to pray Almighty God, that He will not permit the people of this Pueblo to be punished by Him, because your representatives in the Pueblo, the officials, will not permit God's Church to do the work for its members and children, which is the Will of God. We also exhort you to do everything in your power to see to it that these officials will not be permitted to rule over you as tyrants in matters over which they have no right. Before God, every individual has a right to practice His Religion not only in part but as the Church prescribes. We will hold you in our prayers and together with you storm Heaven that God will see fit to enlighten those, who are in authority in this Pueblo, so that they will see their mistake and submit to the Laws of God and His Church and be obedient and respectful to those, who are appointed by Divine Law to rule the Church.

I hereby officially appoint Father Remigius to read this proclamation to you, as he is doing, on this 21st day of July, 1935, in both the English and Spanish language, and affix my name and the official seal of the Archdiocese on this 16th day of July, 1935.

Rudolph A. Gerken
Archbishop of Santa Fe.

Archdiocese of Santa Fe Archives. Printed by permission.

12. Augustine Aguilar and Other Santo Domingo Officials to Archbishop Gerken, August 6, 1935

The Santo Domingo officials expressed their loyalty to the Church and to the archbishop; they reminded Gerken that the Pueblo had long-established relations with Catholicism, dating back to the reconquest of the 1690s. For over two centuries they had proclaimed their Catholic identity without ceasing their tribal customs, including their right to privacy. In a letter to Archbishop Gerken three men of Santo Domingo said sadly that they could not change their faithful (but resolutely remote) relationship with the Church.

Dear Archbishop Gerken:

The pueblo of Santo Domingo has given long thought to your resolution of July 16, 1935. For hundreds of years at Santo Domingo we have taken care of the Catholic Church. Never before until this time has any church father said to us the things you have said.

We have been Catholic Christians according to our own consciences for these hundreds of years. We have been accepted and ministered to by the church all this time. We have not changed in any way.

When you meet [*sic*] with our officers on July 15th we explained that we could not permit a convent to be established within the pueblo or a resident priest to be placed here. But we were willing and anxious for the priest to come as [it] has always [been] done, and for the sisters to come on Sunday to give instruction to our children.

Then you [wrote] to us that if we would not consent, you would refuse in the future to allow our children to be baptized or to allow priests to perform marriages or to allow priests to come to our church on holy days.

We feel our father that you have been unkind. We do not beli[e]ve it is right to take our religion away from us merely because we will not grant permission to a convent to become established within our pueblo. We do not believe that we are violating any canon of the Catholic Church in the position which we have taken. We do not believe that a community of white Catholic[s] would be punished in such a manner.

Before we rec[e]ived your resolution, our officers went to see you at Santa Fe. But you told them that the priest would not come to our holy day August 4th unless our pueblo should sign an agreement giving the sisters and priest permission to come at all times without exception into our pueblo[.] All who know our life and customs know that such an agreement is impossible and that we have days and occasions when no white man or woman can come among us. [The] demand to permit a convent to be established was omitted from this proposed agreement but another and a more impossible demand was put in.

We can not grant it. We are sad, but we can not change. We are Catholics still in [spite] of what you have done. We remain faithfully your children.

> The pueblo of Santo Domingo
> by Governor and fellows
>
> > Augustine Aguilar
> > Reyes Quintana
> > John Bird

Archdiocese of Santa Fe Archives.

13. Archbishop Gerken to Aguilar, August 8, 1935

Archbishop Gerken responded to the Santo Domingo Puebloans with an authoritative statement regarding sovereignty and Native rites. The archbishop said that the Church is sovereign over the spiritual lives of all its people, and no civil government can interfere with that authority granted by God. He also said that the time had come for the Church to insist that the Pueblo people cease practicing rituals of two religions, one Catholic and one Native. He did not wish to allow them the secrecy necessary to maintain the pattern of dual religious participation.

My dear Friends:

I am directing this letter to you because I find your name the first of three signatures to the letter, which was sent to me under date of August 6th; the others who have signed their names are Reyes, Quintana and John Bird. All three signatures are under the heading by which the letter closes, namely: "The Pueblo of Santo Domingo by Governor and Fellows."

In reply to this letter, I must say first of all that you are not meeting the issue squarely nor fairly. You accuse me of having been unkind to you, which is very unfair to say. I have dealt with you in the greatest of patience and have given you much of my time. That which I have requested of you is my duty, as the Archbishop of this Diocese. You say, that you do not think it is right that I should take your Religion away from you. I certainly do not want to take your Religion away from you, but I want you to accept the entire Religion as it was given to us by Jesus Christ, as it was taught by the Apostles and as it is brought down to us by the Church established by Jesus Christ nearly 2000 years ago and as it is taught by this Church from the beginning until now, and as it is practiced by all the faithful children of the Catholic Church.

You say, that you do not believe that you are violating any Canons of the Catholic Church in the position, which you have taken, and that you do not believe that a community of white Catholics would be punished in such a manner. Now, my dear friends, it is my duty to advise you that you have violated the Canons of the Catholic Church all the time by refusing the Church the liberty to instruct the children and by refusing to permit the people to receive the Sacrament of Penance in Confession and Holy Communion, by failing to send for a Priest when someone is sick and in danger of death, by not having your dead buried by the Priest, and finally by not being anxious to have Mass every Sunday and Feast Day because it is the grave duty of Catholics to hear Mass on every Sunday and Feast Days, when possible. Many white Catholics have been punished much more severely than you are being punished for offenses that are not nearly as grave as I am enumerating above. Before God and before the authorities of the Catholic Church all nations and all races regardless of color and language are the same. As it says in the Sacred Scripture, "there is one Faith and one Baptism and one God, who is the Father of us all." Therefore, we are God's Children and for this reason, we are all brothers and sisters here upon earth. The Catholic Church never makes a distinction and she must insist by her divine institution that her children will accept the entire Religion and that they will recognize and respect the authority established in the Church of God Himself.

I told you repeatedly when I met with you in Santo Domingo, that I did not want to interfere in any of the civil affairs of your Pueblo nor with any of your customs and if I am to do my duty, then I must request that the Church be recognized in its authority to teach and to administer as she has been commanded to do by God. You, as faithful children, of the Church as you call yourself should first of all realize that the worship of God by the Religion to which you subscribe by Baptism and Confirmation, namely the Catholic Christian Religion, must take precedence over other forms of recreation or customs. I, however, have been considerate of you and told you that I did not want to interfere with your customs, which do not pertain to your Religion. If there are days, when you feel that God's representatives, the Priest and the Sisters, are not wanted in your Pueblo, such exceptions could be made. Never, however should this interfere with that which is a Catholic[']s greatest duty, namely: to hear Mass on Sundays and Feast Days. In other words you should allow this to come first and then adjust your own celebrations to comply with these regulations, which are not ours but which are laid down by God Himself. If the Indians of Santo Domingo only would permit their people to be fully instructed in the Catholic Religion, then there would not be all this difficulty. I am, therefore, not unkind to you, as your spiritual father, but I would not be your father in fact if I did not do that which is necessary for the Indians to save their immortal souls.

In your long letter, you do not once refer to the right of the people to receive the Sacraments of Confession and Holy Communion. As long as you deny this privilege to your people, it would simply be forbidden that I would reinstate services at Santo Domingo. According to the teachings of the Catholic Church, no sin is forgiven to Catholics unless they receive forgiveness from the Priest, as God's agent when he hears Confession, because Our Lord said to the first Priests of the Church, "whose sins you shall forgive they are forgiven them." You must also know, that no one with sin on his soul can go to Heaven. If, therefore, you deny your people the right to do that which is necessary to have their sins forgiven and to prepare for Heaven, then what good is there in being Baptized and being Confirmed[?] In other words to continue the old arrangement that a Priest come only once a month and that the children cannot be instructed and that the people shall not be permitted to receive the Sacraments of Confession and Communion, and not be permitted to have a Priest before they die is simply an impossible arrangement. Every Priest, who has ever served you has always told you this. Bishops in the past have been lenient with you because they had hoped and prayed that the people of Santo Domingo would finally be Catholics not only in part but in full. Now, however, it is very evident that the officers and council make it impossible for the Church to hold out hope that the people of Santo Domingo could ever become good practical Catholics, such as all other nations and races are, because the Church is not given the liberty to perform its duty to the people, and because the people are not permitted to do that which is necessary in order to save their immortal souls, namely: learn their Religion well and receive the Sacraments of Penance and Holy Communion.

Instead of considering me unkind, therefore, and make such an unfair and unjust accusation, please understand that I am very unhappy over the entire situation as it now exists in Santo Domingo. I am praying daily very fervently that God will enable you to see and understand your mistake. I have also requested the prayers of hundreds of good pious people for the Indians of Santo Domingo so that they may finally understand that we cannot expect God to compromise, but that we must be subject to God's Holy Will to His law and to His Church. The Indians on the other hand have been very unfair to me, because I came as your friend and father, but you refused every one of my propositions. You would make no concession whatsoever, which is very unreasonable. I, however, understand and repeat that this is due to the fact that the Indians do not know their Religion, otherwise they would not take such a stubborn stand. I, therefore, pray God daily that he will enlighten you and enable you to see and understand that the Church of God is only trying to do that which is good, wholesome and salutary for you, and in this spirit I again ask God to bless you one and all and with every kind wish, I remain,

Most sincerely yours in Xto.,
Archbishop of Santa Fe

Archdiocese of Santa Fe Archives. Printed by permission.

14. John Bird of Santo Domingo to the Editor, 1940

For five years the archbishop's interdict held firm. Negotiations between the pueblo and the chancery finally ended the stalemate, with both sides expressing their satisfaction with the resolution. John Bird of Santo Domingo wrote in 1940 that his people had sustained their refusal to permit outsiders to live among them, and therefore they were continuing to preserve their ancient religious practices. Archbishop Gerken, on the other hand, issued a press release, saying that the pueblo had met all the demands of the Church.

Dear Editor:

In the summer of 1935 Archbishop Gerken asked the Santo Domingo Council for ground within the pueblo on which to establish a home for Priests and Sisters. It was the understanding of the Council that the Sisters were to visit our sick and instruct us on religious matters. The priests were to instruct, hear confession, give communion, marry us and bury our dead according to the Catholic religion.

The Council agreed that it would be alright for the sisters to teach the children. They also gave permission for the Priests to instruct and to marry us. It was furthermore agreed by a majority of the Council that the Priests would continue to hold their church service as before. The whole Council came to clear understanding and firm decision about these matters.

The Council however refused to grant Bishop Gerken's request for the ground for the following reasons:

1. The grounds of the Santo Domingo Pueblo were given for the use of the Indians of the Pueblo. For years the Council has struggled to free our lands from those occupants who were not Indian members. Therefore it was not consistent for the Council to grant Bishop Gerken's request.

2. The whole Council firmly objected to having the services of the Priest at our burial time.

3. The majority of the Council was opposed to the Indians going to Confession.

4. Certain days in the year when there are Indian ceremonies the Council could not permit the presence of any white people within the Pueblo boundaries.

5. It was also agreed any further concessions to any white religious organizations would tend to break down the ancient Indian religious practices which are a normal part of our lives. We could see no reason to give up

our religion custom in which we are happy and to take in their place that which is foreign to our natures.

Bishop Gerken was told of the decision of the Council regarding his request. In reply Bishop Gerken said we were not good Catholics and would have to be excommunicated from the Catholic Church. There was nothing for the Council to do but to accept the order of the Bishop. The Indian people of the Santo Domingo Pueblo continue as always with their old religious customs and with their direct relationship with God.

As far as we know the Indians have never asked any white people to become members of the Indian religion but to the Green Corn Dance on this August 4th only at the Santo Domingo Pueblo a friendly invitation is given to all white people. The Indians have respect for the religion of the white people and we ask that they give us theirs. The Council strictly enforces the rule that no cameras be brought to or used during the Green Corn Dance.

> John Bird, Authorized Spoke[s]man
> for the
> Santo Domingo Pueblo
> Domingo, New Mexico
> August 2nd 1940

On this August 4th only the Archbishop has been granted permission to hold Church Services and to perform marriages at Santo Domingo Pueblo.

Archdiocese of Santa Fe Archives.

15. Archbishop Edwin V. Byrne to the Governor, Santo Domingo Pueblo, December 30, 1943

Edwin V. Byrne succeeded Gerken as archbishop of Santa Fe. In 1943 he sent a form letter to the new governor of Santo Domingo Pueblo, reminding him that his ritual canes of authority come ultimately from God, as temporal rulers are always subject to divine rule. Notwithstanding, Puebloan and Church officials continued to vie with one another regarding their prerogatives.

My dear Governor:

I have just learned of your election as Governor of your people. Today on this feast of the Three Kings you receive the canes of authority as a sign that your people place in you their authority to govern them. I wish to congratulate you on this great honor that is yours, because the conferring of the canes of authority is a proof of the great confidence and affection that your own people have in you.

I am sure that on this day, so memorable in your life, you shall not forget that all authority comes from God. The authority then that is being delegated to you by your people comes primarily from God, the Ruler of all peoples and all individuals. Temporal rulers on this earth are subject in everything to the Divine Supreme Ruler. They should exercise their authority then in accordance and in harmony with the divine laws and regulations.

Allow me, dear Governor, in the name of the Catholic Church, to express my cordial wishes for your success and happiness. May the Light of Our Lord enlighten your way; may His Wisdom direct you and may His Strength fortify you to rule your people with kindness, justice and charity.

Sending you and your people a special blessing as a pledge of my interest in you and affection for you all, I beg to remain, dear Governor,

Very sincerely yours,

Edwin V. Byrne
Archbishop of Santa Fe

Archdiocese of Santa Fe Archives. Printed by permission.

16. Fred Tenorio et al., San Felipe Pueblo, to Archbishop Byrne, March 2, 1949

In 1949 the officials of San Felipe Pueblo wrote to Archbishop Byrne, question-ing a ruling by the priest Julian Hargit, O.F.M., to the effect that the Indians should quit their traditional worship or else risk a prohibition against bap-tism. They said that they had always been taught to respect both Indian and Catholic ways.

Dear Most Rev. Archbishop;

Writing this letter to you gives me a greatest pleasure and honor. Please forgive me if I should say anything that might be offending.

A question has arisen among my people here in my pueblo that prompt me to write you this letter.

It is the question of worship.

Rev. Father Julian who comes to the pueblo to perform masses here, has told us, that we no longer be given a privilege of holy baptism to our new born ba-bies, unless the parents of the new born child vows against the Indian religious worship.

Father Julian claims you gave him that order to carry out.

This question has never been brought up as long as I could or any of my fellow officials could remember. After all we have lived here in this pueblo for many generations and since the time of the first baptism was administrated among our people, not one priest ever did attempt to forbid us to practice our Indian religious worship.

By tradition, we were taught to worship both, Indian ways and the Catho-lic ways. We were taught to respect the Catholic religion as well as our Indian religion.

And this order you have issued could well be the end of our union among us. All through these years, my people has stuck together as one in any event.

There was a time a certain politician drafted a bill to stop our Indian reli-gion. Many friends came forward to help us to defeat that bill which tends to destroy us.

So my dear, great father, if you have given that order, please be advised that we have no any other choice, but to adhere to our ways of worship.

Be also advised that we have no intentions to disrespect the good Catholic faith, we respect it and shall continue to go along respecting it regardless the denial of the Holy Baptism.

I will, thank you, good father, in advance, for your good advice and opinion on this issue.

We remain your humble people, of San Felipe Pueblo

Signed   Fred Tenorio,
Governor of Pueblo
Martin Caudelario,
Lt. Governor
Andres Valesquez
Fiscal Mayor
Joe L. Padilla

Archdiocese of Santa Fe Archives.

17. Archbishop Byrne to Tenorio, March 15, 1949

Archbishop Byrne replied that there is only one true religion, one true Church; all other forms of worship are false and are to be eschewed. He emphasized that nowhere in the world does the Catholic Church permit its members to participate in two religious systems.

Dear Governor Tenorio:

I have read with pleasure your kindly letter concerning Baptism and I am pleased to send you the following answer. As you know, by the Sacrament of Baptism Original Sin, which we all inherited from the first man and woman, Adam and Eve, is washed away, and the baptized babe becomes a child of god and a member of the Catholic Church. You also know that the Catholic Church teaches that, as there is only One, True God, there is only one, true Church, which is the Catholic Church. Since the Catholic Church teaches that all other forms of religion are false, she wants to have the guarantee that the baptized child will be instructed in the Catholic doctrine and not take part in any false worship. Therefore, throughout the whole world the Catholic Church allows a child to be baptized in the Catholic Faith on the condition that the parent of the child or the padrino (madrina) of the child promises that the child will be so educated and will be protected from taking part in false worship.

The Catholic Church teaches the same doctrine to all nations in all parts of the world and has done so from the beginning of her institution. The Reverend Father, baptizing in San Felipe Pueblo, will only ask for the same promises that is made everywhere else. From this, you will see, dear Governor, that the promise of Catholic education and of non-participation in false worship is nothing new, but has always been and always will be the custom and teaching of the Catholic Faith.

If you wish, dear Governor, to talk to me about this matter or anything else concerning the Catholic Faith, I will be very pleased to receive you and any of the Pueblo officials. It is my ardent wish and prayer that our dear Indians of San Felipe Pueblo, who want to be true Catholics, be given all the opportunity and freedom necessary to practice their Holy Faith.

I consider myself, dear Governor, a real friend of the Indians, whom I love dearly. Every day I pray for them, so that they may share in the riches of God's blessings as I myself do. Trusting that this answer will be well received by you and the officials and sending my blessing to all at San Felipe Pueblo, I remain, dear Governor Tenorio,

Faithfully yours,

Most Rev. Edwin V. Byrne, D.D.
Archbishop of Santa Fe

Archdiocese of Santa Fe Archives. Printed by permission.

At Isleta Pueblo the archdiocesan priest, Monsignor Fred Stadtmueller, attempted to prevent the Indians from dancing during Christmas celebrations. He preached in public against Native ritualism and obstructed tribal performances, calling his parishioners "pagan savages." Isleta officials asked the new archbishop, James P. Davis, to remove the monsignor. Failing in that, Andy Abeita, the governor of Isleta in 1965 ordered Stadtmueller to leave the territory, or risk expulsion. In his letter Abeita wrote, "We have traditions, we have ceremonials, some were taught to us by the Spaniards when they first entered this country and we are still practicing these traditions."

Andy Abeita and Archbishop Davis met in order to prevent a crisis; however, Davis would not replace the monsignor and the governor would not rescind his eviction notice. The nub of the issue was whether Isletans could continue to practice their religion – a combination of Native and Hispanicized Catholic forms. In their discussion Abeita stated: "Monsignor says that you can't practice two different religions. Then we are not practicing Catholics, because we take part in our own ceremonies." The archbishop replied, "That is a good statement." In addition, the governor and the archbishop were locked in an investiture controversy: Could a governor evict a Catholic priest appointed by Church authority? Abeita made a public statement of his jurisdiction on June 26; the next day he handcuffed Stadtmueller and led him from the pueblo.

18. An Isleta Committee for Religious Freedom Writes to Archbishop James P. Davis, June 28, 1965

Governor Abeita's actions did not please all of the Isletans. A group called the Committee for Religious Freedom decried the eviction, saying that the pueblo authorities were, in effect, denying Catholic Isletans their right to worship – especially since Archbishop Davis padlocked the pueblo church and refused the sacraments to the territory. Backed by the archbishop, the committee brought a civil case in the U.S. District Court of New Mexico, which ruled in 1969 that the archbishop was responsible for withholding Catholic services to Isleta; all he needed to do was replace Stadtmueller with another priest, which Davis refused to do. Only when Robert F. Sanchez succeeded Davis as archbishop in 1974 did rapprochement take place between the Church and Isleta Pueblo, and a new pastor was appointed.

Your Excellency:

This letter is written in order to clarify the extent of the Isleta Pueblo's Twelve-Man Council participation in the recent eviction of Monsignor Stadtmueller by the Pueblo officials.

We at no time approved or sanctioned such action. We were unaware as to the date and time of this regrettable incident until it had been executed. Unfortunately, the Council was not consulted as to the final course of action taken, therefore, we were unable to deter or temper the end result.

It is our sincere hope and desire that spiritual brotherhood will prevail, and this unpleasant stigma forgotten, so that once again our people will be united. We are convinced that nothing but good will result from a concerted effort on the part of all concerned to resolve our differences, and ask Almighty God for help from this day forward, all misunderstandings will be eliminated by intelligent resolution prior to their development into a catastrophe.

It is a foregone conclusion that we must, as Catholics, have a spiritual leader in the House of God to perform the sacred rites of our religion. We are joined by the Catholics in this community in our request that a Pastor be assigned to our Pueblo at the earliest possible date. Innocent people through no fault of their own may be deprived of those Sacraments so necessary for eternal life if the need should arise. Additionally, there are numerous other services such as marriages, house calls for the sick and aged etc., required and desired.

In conclusion we hopefully pray that our plea for the assignment of a Parish Priest will receive favorable consideration, and that God in His infinite mercy will forgive those who contributed to our dilemma.

> Respectfully yours,
> [signed]
>
> Bart Montoya   Tom Abeita, Jr.
> Juan R. Abeita   Carlos Jojola
> John C. Lucero   Diego Abeita
> Juan B. Abeita   Joe E. Zuni
> Phillip Lente   Robert L. Lucero
>
> Members, Isleta Pueblo Council

Archdiocese of Santa Fe Archives. Printed by permission.

19. Archbishop Robert F. Sanchez to Gilbert Valdez, Santa Fe Fiesta Council, September 23, 1977

Archbishop Robert F. Sanchez tried to create more amicable relations between the Pueblo Indians and the Hispanic community of Santa Fe. In a 1977 letter to Gilbert Valdez, president of the Santa Fe Fiesta Council, the archbishop tried to change the tone of the annual Santa Fe Fiesta, from a triumphant reenactment of the 1690s reconquest (with Hispanics triumphant over Puebloans) to an expression of shared Catholic tradition and faith.

Dear Mr. Valdez,

May God's Peace and Love be with you!

I am writing this letter for two purposes: 1) To express to you, and to the Fiesta Council, my sincere appreciation for all of your efforts on behalf of the Santa Fe Fiestas for 1977. Aside from the unfortunate mistake with our Indian brothers and sisters, I feel certain that all would agree that the Fiesta has been returned to the people of Santa Fe, and the accent once again where it should be, on the spiritual events. No doubt the efforts and examples of many are responsible for this success. 2) I would like to share with you a few thoughts which may assist the Council in their deliberation with the Indian Pueblos toward achieving a mutual and respected understanding.

At the breakfast following the Mass at the Rosario Chapel, I had occasion to share with all present many of my feelings concerning the Fiestas of Santa Fe. You will recall that I strongly emphasized that the Fiestas were not begun to celebrate a conquest of people, but rather, it was begun to celebrate the re-entry of the Colonists into Santa Fe, and the second beginning of harmonious and peaceful living with the Indian people. If Fiesta is to mean anything to us today, it should be an expression of gratitude on the part of all people of the City of Holy Faith for the special blessings that have guided us, peoples of many cultures and traditions, not only to respect one another, not only to accept each other, but even to inter-marry so that our union might be sealed with the mixture of our bloods. Obviously, such a celebration as Fiesta could not be complete without the presence and active participation of our Indian people. I feel certain that if we approach the Pueblo Governors, and the All Pueblo Council, with these attitudes and with these convictions, they will not only welcome our invitation to participate in the Fiesta next year, but they will feel proud that such efforts are being made to correct any past abuses or mistakes, as well as to set a firm foundation, formed from mutual respect and concern for our future relations.

Furthermore, I would wish to add that if I can assist in the mediation and in reaching a mutual understanding, please know that I will be anxious to assist. It would seem to me that a meeting with the Indian Council in the not too distant future would be in order.

Thanking you for your kind understanding, and for your dedication to the Fiestas, while wishing you all God's blessings, I am,

Sincerely,

Robert F. Sanchez
ARCHBISHOP OF SANTA FE

cc: Mr. [Delfin J.] Lovato

20. Delfin J. Lovato, All Indian Pueblo Council, to Archbishop Sanchez, September 26, 1977

Delfin J. Lovato, the chairman of the All Indian Pueblo Council, thanked Archbishop Sanchez for his efforts.

Dear Archbishop Sanchez:

I want to take this opportunity to thank you for your interest and effort in attempting to bring about a more amiable atmosphere during the [recent] Santa Fe Fiesta controversy. Rest assured that the All Indian Pueblo Council will make a concerted effort to establish a meaningful dialogue between the Indian community and the non-Indian neighbors, in the spirit of brotherhood and cooperation.

I look forward to meeting with you to discuss this and other matters in the near future.

Sincerely yours,

ALL INDIAN PUEBLO COUNCIL, INC.

Delfin J. Lovato
Chairman

Archdiocese of Santa Fe Archives.

21. A Yaqui Maestro's Story, 1940

In 1617 the Yaqui Indians of what is now northwestern Mexico first permitted Jesuits to live among them. For a century and a half the Jesuits inculcated Catholic theology, liturgy, and ecclesiology until the Spanish Crown expelled the Society of Jesus from all of New Spain. The Yaquis continued to embrace Catholicism in the absence of priestly authority, creating in effect a semiautonomous Yaqui Catholic religion. In the late nineteenth century Mexican military action against the Yaquis caused a diaspora to the United States, where the Yaquis now live in several Arizona settlements. They continue to practice their own form of traditional Catholicism, with Native officials, rituals, and texts. In 1940 an unnamed Yaqui maestro — a local church leader — told an anthropologist, Edward H. Spicer, the following story about Mary, Jesus, and Joseph.

Mary always had flowers about her. Jesus was born because Mary smelled a flower; this is the way that she remained a virgin. In the time when the Jews were going to crucify Jesus, they wanted a carpenter to make a cross on which to crucify him. They found Joseph and told him to make the cross. Joseph was a good carpenter, but when he went to look at the wood which he had for making the cross, it was all too short, and there was no way in which he could cut it to make a cross big enough. While he was standing there puzzling over it, his son Jesus came and talked to him. Jesus told him that he was God and that, if Joseph went out into the hills, he would find a tree which he could cut down and make a cross out of it. Jesus then went away. Joseph stood for a long time in doubt. He didn't know whether or not to believe that Jesus was God or not. Finally he went out into the hills and found a tree and cut it down. The tree which he cut down was really Mary, because Mary had turned herself into a tree. Jesus and God had planned this out long before and had told Mary to turn herself into a tree. So, when Jesus was crucified, he was crucified on a cross made of his mother, Mary. She holds him embraced in her outstretched arms.

Edward H. Spicer, *Pascua: A Yaqui Village in Arizona*. Chicago: University of Chicago Press, 1940, 254. Printed by permission.

22. A Yaqui Easter Sermon by Ignacio Alvarez, 1941

During the Lenten-Easter season the Yaquis engage in elaborate ceremonialism focused upon Mary and Jesus. Organized by officials called the kohtumbre, *Yaquis reenact the salvific passion, death, and resurrection of Jesus at the hands of the* fariseos, *and particularly the preeminent enemies of Jesus, the masked* chapayekas. *On Easter morning a* maestro *delivers a lengthy sermon to the gathered community of worshipers, praising the officiants and actors, including those who contribute to salvation by portraying God's foils. The* maestro *encourages the Yaquis to conduct themselves morally and to give thanks for God's plan, symbolized most powerfully in Mary's flowers and the blood of Jesus. What follows is an excerpt from a sermon given in 1941 by Ignacio Alvarez, recorded, edited, and translated by Muriel Thayer Painter, Refugio Savala, and Alvarez himself.*

Well, yes, gentlemen, my fathers, mothers, people of the pueblo, equally everybody, my pueblo fathers, mothers, everyone who is now here present, those who came together, assembled for this now in this hour.

I am truly standing before you in your presence in this present hour.

I desire to speak to you about those two or three truths that we are working on here, made by God's example, and made by the example of Our Mother Most Holy Mary.

But first, pueblo fathers, pueblo mothers, equally everyone, with the good permission of the pueblo fathers and mothers, my fathers, with your permission my fathers, I desire to say to you two or three truths about the sermon made by God.

Even though you know it.

And even though you learned it.

But truly thus, in the very beginning (on Ash Wednesday), the men of the church and he, the savior maestro, who own the work with the Lord, made the first benediction.

And equally likewise the women of the church, having that good holy benediction with Our Mother Most Holy Mary, will own the work with her; will own that work with her.

And also equally even the sacristan father who likewise owns the work with her like this.

Yaqui Palm Sunday pageant with Native dance and pantomime, Tucson, Arizona. Credit: *The Indian Sentinel* 2, no. 2 (1921): 325. Photographer unknown. Marquette University, Bureau of Catholic Indian Missions Records. Reproduced by permission.

And equally likewise the singer mother, the altar woman, the flag bearer, the *pasion* bearer, equally all the Kohtumbre…, all who, having owned the Lord's work, now stand here at this present moment, joined together in your presence.

They stood up to the work like this, making the good holy benediction yonder in the very beginning, when ashes were received, receiving them just like this on their foreheads, beginning the holy benediction.

The work of Our Leader, God Jesus Christ, was done because He commanded it like this; He truly created it like this here on earth; truly it seems not bearable, but truly it seems not within reach….

From the very beginning, from Ash Wednesday to the present time, the Pilate father, and the flag bearer father, and just likewise the captain and the sergeants and the soldiers, as well as everyone, embracing the image of Our Leader God Jesus Christ upon their breasts, carried out its holy benediction.

Truly He, owning the work, went about blessing that earth, to each of its four corners.

For seven weeks we worked like this on that holy benediction.

At dawn, and equally at this hour (noon) as well as at the "Ave Maria," at the three hours, the Kohtumbre…prayed like this looking to the Lord; they prayed for just everybody, not only for themselves alone.

Also like the prayers of the maestro father — but truly the prayers of the Kohtumbre are not so many — only the one "Our Father," one "Holy Mary," the "I Believe" ("Credo"), the "Hail Queen," the "Beat Breast" ("Confiteor") and the "Benediction"; truly with these they prayed for everyone on up to the last.

But He, the Lord, here on earth, made it priceless for them; therefore everybody, speaking like that, prayed, looking to heaven.

Therefore now moreover we worked on it like this, on up to this hour, owned the work like this on it, beginning then at the time of receiving ashes.

Doing the work they own on it, as well as the maestro father doing the work he owns in connection with it, they have truly come out with it this way.

Truly they placed it with Holy Mary in her hand, saying they worked on it like this, saying they truly worked hard on it like this; truly not feeling lazy about it, truly with hearts as clear as the one water drop.

Working hard on it, on the commandment that He made, saying that He made it, the Kohtumbre placed it in the Lord's hand like this.

Now then every baptized person and just all the Kohtumbre...worked on it from the very beginning, they who owned the work on it from the very beginning.

Truly the work made at the very beginning, the work made on starting, truly the Lord made it without price, and just likewise He made it the good truth, because here on earth He truly created it without price, truly ordered us to love it, truly ordered us to pray for ourselves with it, valuing it.

Therefore those who have duty like this truly own the suffering because in the seven weeks they will work on it like this.

Therefore the pueblo father, pueblo mother, love it, regard it, because the Kohtumbre does all the suffering for all baptized people, desiring to pray for them.

And the Kohtumbre, just inviting the maestro to do it, owns the work, accompanying the maestro with it, but it is not for the maestro alone.

Truly all baptized persons, desiring to keep those commandments, own the work like this.

Those whom you call Kohtumbre..., and whom you call chapayeka, and equally those whom you call corporal, and whom you call Caballero, truly, they work on nothing else.

In seven weeks, desiring just only to pray for those blessed souls departed, those deceased, somewhere on land, at sea, on wasteland, on rock, they bother you about the ceremonies like this.

But they, being heard or not being heard, or regarded as silly, or even if regarded as being burdensome, just by all the pueblo, even so they invite you to join in the ceremonies, even with feet tiring, or even if not willing to go there, running about, trotting about among you.

Inviting you with the pretty flowers that were strewn there yesterday, on Saturday's sun, and just inviting for it even also the pueblo fathers, pueblo mothers.

But desiring to beseech for you that way about it the thousand holy graces, inviting you with the heavenly glory that the Lord made.

Invite you with it; but already, what truly shall be done; the pueblo, some of them, do not hear them, and just do not respect His word, and act just as if they did not respect His word, even that of Our Leader, God Jesus Christ.

Because many times it is mortifying to do it; even so, it being their duty, they will tire themselves out doing it; but they are poor like this; either sick or doing penance, either sick or doing penance.

But the Kohtumbre worked on it all night through like this, desiring to pray by means of it for all that pueblo, all the baptized people, and all those departed souls.

Thus for this reason, the Lord truly loves him, truly regards him, who has that work like this, that duty like this.

But if he goes out on it perfectly, and then if he comes out on it perfectly, truly that good signature is made for him, that good grace is made for him.

And just for everyone: for the maestro father, and for the singer mother, and just the same for the altar woman, for the flag bearer, and just the same way for the sacristan and the bearers of the *pasion;* just for everyone throughout.

The truth is one; truly God Our Father's truth is not two, truly not three.

God is One, He who made this earth, the world, heaven, all the world over.

He truly is One, being One, truly makes Himself respected.

Being in heavenly light, all over the world; sitting with light all over the world.

Our Mother Most Holy Mary truly is one; truly she is powerful.

Truly, having that good truth up yonder in heaven, she sends it down here to you, nursing you under that holy benediction through day and night.

The Lord created daily bread, sending it down to you like this.

Therefore he who knows his Father will know his Mother.

Truly, on reaching Lent like this, and where the work (of the Lord) exists like this, a person there, although being busy, will request an excuse; or even more, will just even leave his job, and do his duty.

Because these seven weeks truly are not many, are not much, and just don't even exist in all, in continuous time; nor the request asked for, the request asked for like that.

Therefore now, the baptized people who were invited to it like this, who are now here present, you saw it, what that maestro father made, what he spoke toward heaven, that which he begged for.

In the seven weeks, embracing his holy book, he prayed for it, looking toward heaven; he begged for that flower (grace) like this.

Until during these many days, that holy fulfillment was made, right there where your holy temple stands.

In the presence of Our Leader God Jesus Christ, in His house, where the heavenly light comes down, truly came down on the maestro, he asked for the holy flower in the prayers said toward heaven.

Now then, it was shown to you like that, that Our Father's flower, that Our Father's blood.

He, Our Father, hung on the cross with open arms; the blood, touching the earth and splashing down, spread all over the world.

Up yonder, where sits the Lord, the Most Holy Trinity, on the holy throne, up yonder, were truly made the pretty flowers which have been created down upon you.

The good holy heavenly light came down to each of you, to every baptized person.

But with that holy prayer that the maestro prayed toward heaven, right there while he was praying, the holy light was sent down to him.

Now then truly, right there, that man whom you call chapayeka, that man whom you call Pilate, that man whom you call enemy, that man whom you call Jew, that man whom you call cruel, he is said to work against the Lord.

Truly, having made for himself his insignia like this, he works on it like this, works hard on it like this, because even He, being the Lord, at that time gave Himself like this.

But He, pretending, gave Himself as their enemy, but is not their enemy.

Now then, you saw it, moving about with Him there, embracing His image.

The Lord says we should all move about with Him like that, upon reaching every year.

The Lord says thus we should confess; thus we should own that commandment; He says we should own the work with Him, embracing His image.

In the very beginning He made Himself like that, created Himself like that.

Truly gave Himself the journey all over the world — on land, at sea, on wasteland, on rock, in brush, somewhere in impenetrable places, going about among thorns — has shed His blood there, has fallen, was bruised, knees scratched.

And just has had even the worst punishment, has shed blood....

Muriel Thayer Painter, Refugio Savala, and Ignacio Alvarez, eds., *A Yaqui Easter Sermon.* Tucson: University of Arizona Press, 1955, 61–62, 65–68. Printed by permission.

23. Reverend Remy Rudin, O.F.M., Describes O'odham [Papago] Pilgrims to Magdelena de Kino, 1953

In the seventeenth century the Jesuits initiated missions among the Indians of the Sonoran Desert, including the desert O'odham (Papagos) and the river O'odham (Pimas). Father Eusebio Francisco Kino, S.J., arrived in O'odham country in 1687, and before his death in 1711 in the town of Magdelena he had baptized several thousand Indians. With the Jesuit expulsion, Franciscans took over the Sonoran mission in 1768; over the centuries the O'odham developed the tradition of making a pilgrimage to Magdelena de Kino, sixty miles south of the U.S. border in Mexico. There they have paid homage to Francisco: a combination of St. Francis Xavier, St. Francis of Assisi, and Francisco Kino, who is buried there. Reverend Remy Rudin, O.F.M., describes one such pilgrimage in 1953.

Up to a few years ago, one caravan of wagons, filled with Indians, followed another, going southward through Papago-land during the latter part of each September. The wagons would converge on the rough road beyond the Mexican border that leads to the valley of the Rio Magdalena and on to the town of the same name. Hundreds of Papago families were making their yearly two hundred mile trek to honor St. Francis Xavier.

The Papagos still go to Magdalena. But nowadays, with automobiles available and with the bus lines running special excursions, the wagon caravans we used to see have all but disappeared from the desert trails.

To understand the meaning of this yearly pilgrimage and its hold upon the Papagos, it is necessary to take a glimpse into the past. Back in the year 1700 Father Kino, the great pioneer Jesuit missionary of upper Sonora, founded the Mission San Xavier del Bac among the far-off Papagos at a place some miles south of the present Arizona city of Tucson. As the story goes, he acquired a magnificent statue of St. Francis Xavier for his distant new mission, but various difficulties prevented its transfer to its destination, so he finally decided to place it in the church at Magdalena. In the very midst of the ceremonies of installation, Indian tradition says, Father Kino became ill and died. At any rate, a fine old statue of the Saint is enshrined in the church there and the missionary's grave is there.

Mindful of the immeasurable blessings that Father Kino had brought them and knowing his devotion to St. Francis, the Indians in their dark hour of bereavement placed themselves under the protection of the great Apostle of the Orient. Thereafter they spared no effort to make a pilgrimage to his shrine on his feastday, December 3rd. As the years went on, the number of pilgrims increased far beyond the accommodations that the town could offer. Moreover, the weather is usually inclement at the time of the year, so the celebration was advanced to an earlier and more seasonable date. Thus we have the curious anomaly of St. Francis Xavier being solemnly feted on the feast of St. Francis of Assisi, October 4th. But fortunately, in heaven there is no room for jealousy.

Down through the years the Papagos in Arizona often heard about this shrine and its traditions from their Christian Indian relatives to the south. When in the present century missionaries finally came to them with the glad tidings of the Gospel, they were convinced that St. Francis had had a hand in their good fortune. Their newly acquired faith led them also to have recourse to him in every necessity. Today scarcely a home on the Papago Reservation but has a statue or picture of St. Francis, brought from Magdalena and venerated by the household.

Their most special devotion to the Saint is the annual pilgrimage to his shrine. Though every family cannot go every year, yet hundreds of Papagos add to the vast throng of Indians and Mexicans who journey to Magdalena for the feast from all over northwestern Mexico.

This year I had the opportunity to make the trip and to observe this huge and magnificent manifestation of devotion at first hand. I must admit I was almost overwhelmed.

Most impressive is the attitude and actions of the individual pilgrims. Each of them, it seems, wants to personally venerate the statue two or three times. From early to late, Mexicans and Indians crowd about and into the church. Every foot of it is constantly packed. To get from the front door to the altar where the statue is located usually takes three or four hours. For two whole days except at the times of Mass and services, this procession of suppli[c]ants, slowly, patiently, wedges its way to the shrine.

Wherever I went, Papagos from my missionary district would come to greet me; the light in their eyes showed they felt a special joy at finding their pastor joining them in far-off Magdalena. Did they feel, as I did, that here was an example of the unity that is in Christ — a Franciscan missionary from Arizona journeying to Mexico to pay honor to the incomparable Jesuit missionary, St. Francis?

As I observed these people for two days, I was impressed at their devotion. Most of them must have to make sacrifices and put up with many inconveniences in making this pilgrimage. But this they feel is a small price to pay for the opportunity of showing their love for St. Francis.

And there is no doubt the Saint rewards their devotion. In life he often felt a consuming frustration at his physical inability to help all who needed him. Now that he has intimate access to the treasures of Omnipotence, he delights to share them, particularly with the poor of God's children.

Reverend Remy Rudin, O.F.M., "Papago Pilgrims," *The Indian Sentinel* 33, no. 9 (November 1953): 131–32. Printed by permission.

24. Joseph W. Thomas Speaks of O'odham [Pima] Religion and Catholicism, July 22, 1995

Well into the twentieth century the O'odham have participated in three variants of religious life: O'odham himdaq — the ancient religion with its emphasis on nature; Santo himdaq — the Hispanicized devotion to wonder-working saints; and Kaho:liga himdaq — the sacramental system of the modern Catholic Church. Missionaries used to refer to the combination of these three traditions as "Montezuma Catholicism." Although most contemporary O'odham identify themselves with the Catholic way, they often look back longingly upon the aboriginal O'odham way — which they sometimes interpret through the filter of their present-day Catholicism. In 1995 Mark G. Thiel interviewed a Pima Catholic, Joseph W. Thomas, who spoke about his people's traditional religion.

THIEL: Were there any Indian religious objects in your home...?

THOMAS: No, there was no...as far as Indian religion. Indian religion under Pima is not really religion in itself.... Pima's, according to the old way, has to do with nature. And, you kept religion in the Indian way by getting up in the morning and saying your morning prayer in regards to all the different aspects of life that you go through. In other words, O.K., the thing is like your four = [earth,] water, fire, wind,...those were the things you done, those were the only religion you had. Everything you prayed during the day for everything you done. If you mean to hurt anything, to nature, you prayed for that sort of thing to forgive you or if you plant you prayed for it to grow and everything. But Indian religion is more to nature.... Like my wife is a Pueblo. They have dances,...a go-between between the people and the Gods. The Pimas never had that. It was more of a self-contained religion that you grew up with that had to do with nature. My great great uncle was the last...medicine man-type and so I used to remember my uncle would come on his journey..., he used to go all over and come over there to stay. He would sit under this big cottonwood tree and he would teach [my father] songs and teach him the ways of the medicine man, but because of the Catholic religion and when the priest from Tempe, the one who used to come to us far out, he told my father that it cannot be, that is, according to that time, that it's not permissible in the Catholic Church, so either take that or if you don't, then if you take that then you cannot teach the catechism because then they will excommunicate you. So my father chose to be more in the Christian, what he had known as far as his religion, he chose that and he dropped it. And to this day I'm still I guess in my thing I'm still mad at the church for that because now they say bring your culture in, by way of tradition, I would have been, because I would have taken, being the seventh, seventh child, and that's the way it goes. And so I would have been, I would have taken it up because it takes six years to train for whatever the thing is and that's where it goes so I would have been there but because of that I could never get there and it hurts me because I don't know that and yet the Church says now bring in your culture, and I say it's kind of late. You should have said this a long time ago. So,... I still give little talks in regards to Indian religion versus my Catholic religion, how it affected me and all kinds of stuff like that.

THIEL: [What is the relationship] between Catholic spirituality and your Pima spirituality and beliefs?

THOMAS: There's not very much difference. The only difference..., I feel, is that the way it was taught in the pre-Vatican until now. With Vatican II it has come, the Church has come out of its...cocoon, I think I'll say because — I say cocoon because in the past the Church seemed to be, everything was just inside. You weren't allowed to even participate or even mingle with other re-ligions. You were cocooned into a big, say, you're a Catholic, this is what you do, it was strict. And once you left, if you did something from outside of that you were...excommunicated. That was the big scare, and I think to me being a Catholic in the past has been the main instrument that the Church used to keep its family together, keep the Catholics together, was scaring people. And then when they said O.K. excommunication if you don't do this. And so the religion what we have, like I said. Our religion, we have a religion which has to do with nature and has to do with God. We knew about God. We knew what God wanted, our creator of life, which is God to us, and like I said, we had all the things the same as the Church in regards to commandments, which is really what the Church is about. You have the commandments, the other com-mandments in regards to the Church commandments, the six of those. And we had all those, so there was really nothing different. It was just the idea that the Church told us that our religion was heathen, we were heathens because we didn't believe in what they wanted us to believe in, yet if they would have only looked and asked questions they would have found out that all our religion was the same, except for one item, which is Jesus Christ. And so when Jesus Christ was brought into the picture, we were baptized. O.K., so, all they did was made us Christians. But before that we weren't called Christians but we had a reli-gion. And so the strong thing about being a Catholic in my religion was that it was always said, that your religion and I think not only to the Pimas — It has to do with all the Native Americans, it was always said, that your religion, you're heathens if you believe in this.... The thing...is that [they] didn't try to look into it and try to learn if that really is something that was, like, to be a heathen, but I don't think it was. And so I believe that we had religion way before white man came here. And our spirituality was always there because we lived to the way we felt about our religion, how we felt about one another and how we felt about our creator, that we were one with our neighbors. In order to do that we had to be one with ourselves and one with our neighbors, before we can be one with our creator. And that's our thing. If you don't feel that you're one with yourself, and not one with your neighbor, and to say I'm one with my creator, then you're a hypocrite because you're not, you cannot be one. If you disregard your neighbor and not love your neighbor and try to say I love God, you can't do it, because it's through God that love comes. But that's the way were we,...we all treated each other as equals. Our community lived together happily because of that religion. That's how it worked out....

Marquette University, Kateri Tekakwitha Oral History Collection. Printed by permission.

25. Sister Gloria Ann Davis, S.B.S., Tells of Navajo Religion, the Native American Church, and Catholicism, 1975

The Navajos — the most populous American Indian nation in the United States — have received Catholic missions only in the last century; only a small portion have embraced the Catholic faith. Sister Gloria Ann Davis, S.B.S. (her father Navajo, her mother Choctaw), wrote in 1975 that her Catholic training harmonized with her Navajo spirituality, especially the medicinal sacramentalism of the Beauty Way and the peyote rituals of the Native American Church. For her, Catholicism in the American Southwest has provided a means of maintaining and fulfilling the religious culture of her people.

I was born in Fort Defiance, Arizona. We lived there for three years and then moved onto the Navajo Reservation to a place called Lukachukai for nine years. Dad is Navajo from Lukachukai. Mom is Choctaw from Pearl River, Mississippi.

I remember many superstitions we would pick up while out herding sheep with our cousins. If we killed a lizard, say, or horny toad, we had learned that our heart would dry up, so we would lick our hands to prevent this. If it lightninged and thundered while we were out playing, we had to sit down on the ground when the lightning flashed and would get up again only when we heard the thunder.

We often went to visit our grandparents, and when we stayed overnight in their hogan, we slept on sheepskin. I remember many times Grandfather would wake us up at sunrise and give us pollen from a skin pouch. We'd just put our hand in, take the pollen and put it on our tongue. Then whatever was left, we'd offer it up to the east to our Creator. Grandfather would pray spontaneously and tell us to pray in our own way, silently or out loud.

We used to go walking with Grandfather. He made us aware of creation. He taught us reverence and appreciation for nature. He had us stand and listen. He pointed out the sunset, the sunrise, the trees, the wind blowing, the earth. After a rain he'd say, "Come and look; it's beautiful. Smell it." He'd take sagebrush, rub it and make us smell it. It was like Vicks and it really cleared your nose out. He'd have us smell the different herbs.

He always conveyed a reverence toward nature, toward everything, even toward food. He was always gentle. I remember my sister one time taking a knife and stabbing a watermelon, and we really got a lesson out of that. I never forgot it. He said, "Never, never, never do that! We must respect the food that the Great One has given us." And many times when we were growing up, Dad would say the same thing: "Never stab any food; we cut it with reverence."

In those days, too, we took anything that was left over, like the bones and things, and we'd burn them. Even our hair when it was cut — we'd burn it out of reverence, because it was part of life and something sacred. As I look back, I think that this is where I got a real appreciation of God, our Creator — of how he created the sunset, moon and stars.

When I was about nine or 10, Dad was in a terrible accident, and for a time he wasn't himself anymore. Relatives were returning from World War II. Things in society were changing really fast and some Navajos, experiencing this, were turning to the Native American Church. Now the Native American Church is a religion that uses the peyote herb, which they call their sacrament. Their worship is basically an all-night prayer meeting. My dad changed from his traditional Navajo religion (medicine man, squaw dances, and all) and began going to the prayer meetings of the Native American Church.

According to the legend that I heard, this peyote cult started in Mexico with the Mexican Indians. A woman had a vision out in a field and was told to pick up a peyote herb and take it to the men and tell them how to run the prayer meetings.

I went with Dad to the meetings because Mom said he needed support from the family. By the time I was in the seventh grade, Dad had become a "road runner" — the person who runs the prayer meetings. He would get calls from different places on the reservation, and I would volunteer to help him drive. So I drove him quite often to the prayer meetings and I took part in them. On Sundays I would go to Mass.

Looking back on the prayer meetings, I realize that they were very ecumenical. Indians from several tribes and from several traditional tribal religions, Indians from all kinds of Protestant Churches, as well as from Catholic backgrounds, joined in all-night prayer. They would sing and pray in their own languages. Those from a Catholic tradition might say the Hail Mary and Our Father and make the Sign of the Cross. This is where I learned spontaneous prayer — it came easy to me. When I later began going to Catholic charismatic prayer meetings, I was stuck by many similarities.

The Catholic charismatic way of praying is the closest thing I have experienced to the Native American Church prayer meeting, especially in terms of the spontaneous prayer and the ecumenical spirit. This is where we might have an inroad with our people who belong to the N.A.C., which is a kind of steppingstone between the Navajos' traditional religion and Christianity. When people move into the N.A.C., they hear Jesus Christ's name so often from the Christians attending that they can begin relating to Jesus Christ.

One of my great wishes is to some day find N.A.C. members who are willing to put the peyote aside as a sacrament and get them to have a prayer meeting with a sunrise Mass. Many of my people do not find it impossible to belong to both the N.A.C. and the Christian Church. Many N.A.C. members identify themselves with the Christian Churches and consider the peyote as a medicine or drug rather than as a sacrament.

Another vision of mine is to get back to the "Beauty Way" which our ancestors have given us. Beauty Way is our whole way of life — one that teaches us to stay in harmony with nature by not deviating into extremes. When a person goes to extremes — whether eating, sensual pleasure, material goods — he or she becomes ill. In order to get well, people who are ill have certain ceremonial prayers said for them by the medicine man so that they may again walk in harmony with nature (with God, man and oneself). When we walk in harmony with our nature, we walk in beauty, as suggested by a small part of our ceremonial prayers:

> *Beauty before me*
> *Beauty behind me*
> *Beauty above me*
> *Beauty below me*
> *Beauty all around me*
> *In Beauty I walk.*

As a Christian, I see the beauty as God's presence before me, behind me, and so on, and because of his presence I walk in beauty.

I would like to see the Church regard the Navajo customs and myths with respect, and I do know missionaries who have. The Church would be placing before us a terrible block if it denied us the right to continue to treasure what was taught us by our ancestors. It is denied by only those people who are ignorant of our culture.

Jack Wintz, O.F.M., "Respect Our Indian Values," *St. Anthony Messenger* (July 1975): 34–40. Printed by permission.

26. Tony Machukay (Apache) Writes of "The Status of St. John's Mission School," April 22, 1981

One of the most important means of inculcating Catholic culture to American Indians was the mission school, and especially boarding institutions where Indian children left their home communities to be immersed in American Catholic ways. These boarding schools came under criticism as early as the 1920s, and in the last several decades many of them have been transformed into local schools under tribal control. This transformation has not always pleased Indian Catholics who grew up in the boarding school system. In 1981 a San Carlos Apache, Tony

Machukay (now executive director of the Arizona Commission on Indian Affairs), wrote to the Diocese of Phoenix, criticizing its plan to change Machukay's alma mater, St. John's Mission School, into a tribal institution controlled by the Gila River (O'odham) Indian Tribe. Machukay was thorough in his praise of the Franciscans who conducted St. John's for many years.

I. THE RELATIONSHIP BETWEEN FRANCISCAN FATHERS AND KOMATKE VILLAGERS

The relationship between the Franciscan Fathers and local parishioners with respect to St. John's Mission School is unclear at this time and of late, appears to be deteriorating. For instance: (a) It is well known among those interested in St. John's that the Franciscan Fathers have apparently disbanded their original responsibility of overseeing a Catholic mission school. There is every indication that the Education Department of the Diocese of Phoenix also supports the disavowal of the school by the Franciscans and has gone so far as to recommend that the administration of St. John's School be turned over to the Gila River Indian Tribe to be used as an Indian Community School; (b) although the primary reason for the Franciscans' existence in Komatke Village was for the benefit of Catholic Indian people, very little consideration has been given to village parishioners when Mission assets such as used building material or other stored items were either sold or given outright to non-Indian profiteers and beneficiaries. Such actions are unheard of in parishes throughout the Diocese of Phoenix where parish councils have a voice in such matters.

II. LEGAL IMPLICATIONS

Conceivably, the Franciscans could relinquish to the Tribe, all land and property outside the immediate premises of the Church and monastery at a nominal rate of compensation for holdings affixed to the Church lands. Or, the Fathers could simply move out of the Village altogether and negotiate with the tribe on the value of the remaining assets.

III. RATIONALE FOR SEEKING ADVICE FROM LOCAL PARISHIONERS

In any case, the Franciscans are not legally bound to listen to or accept any advice from Komatke parishioners on what direction the Fathers should take, nor are the Franciscan Fathers obligated to transfer the school to the tribe. However, if the priests do see the need and rationale for taking some advice from members of the parish, they should do so with the understanding that their original commitment to establish a church and school in Komatke Village was in response to a request by a particular segment of the tribe; that is, to those tribal members who wanted to also become members of the Catholic faith.

In other words, the original agreement whether formal or not, was effectuated between the Franciscan Fathers and a distinct entity consisting of those Komatke Villagers who intended to become Christians of the Catholic Church.

The final direction for the future of St. John's Mission School should therefore be taken only in close accord with those members of the Village who consider [themselves] Catholic, on whose behalf the Mission and school was established.

While the changeover would involve complicated legal procedures, the ultimate decision is a moral and ethical one which both the Franciscan Fathers and the Diocese of Phoenix cannot ignore....

IX. FRAGMENTED BELIEFS

In contemplating projections for the school, planners should avoid abruptly categorizing the Catholic educational process from religious instruction as much as possible. In most parish schools, such distinct separation is not usually drawn. Furthermore, to tribal people whose traditional way of thinking is infused morally and comprehensively with such forms of life as education, politics, technology, economics, etc., the planned fragmentation is no less than an affront to local villagers who are deeply rooted to and have had a strong faith in Catholic education, religion and tribal tradition as elements of their total belief system.

X. SUCCESS DESPITE DEPRIVATION

To be sure, the calibre of education at St. John's Indian School has not failed Indian students nor have students failed St. John's despite extreme difficulties. In the 1920's, 30's, and 40's Indian boys and girls managed somehow to overcome heat, cold, skimpy meals, meager living accommodations, frugal clothing and insufficient educational aids and supplies, yet still received a sound education and thorough religious instruction. In the 1950's, 60's and 70's, students fared a little better, but compared to BIA or public school systems, St. John's School facilities were somewhat less modern. Defiantly, students remained to complete their education and religious training and complaints were the exception rather than the rule. Summarily, pride and loyalty to St. John's has always been a hallmark of its hundreds of Indian students despite economic hardship.

To its everlasting credit, St. John's staff and teachers have been the mainstay throughout the life of the mission school; facing considerable odds, they have displayed remarkable *perseverance* and *hardwork* when other school systems demanded much less; *loyalty* that is not often found in other schools; excellent *professional skills* not unlike those exhibited in more modern classroom settings; *unselfishness* in confronting low salaries and wages; *generosity* with time in providing spiritual guidance, psychological counseling and career orientation; *humor, discipline, open-mindedness* and good rapport with Indian students; and *endurance* under work stress in a school relatively isolated on an Indian reservation. Without these exceptional qualities exhibited by a dedicated staff, St. John's Mission School would not have survived or existed for so long.

XI. CONCLUSION

In all, St. John's has been a symbol of success spiritually, mentally and physically to hundreds of reservation students who attended St. John's Indian School despite many adversities.

Based on this track record, it is inconceivable that St. John's Mission School should be allowed to die. On the contrary, one would suppose that just the opposition should be taking place; namely, that St. John's School should be allowed to live and be nourished with sustenance and material resources so that the School can continue its religious and educational gains. Toward that goal, plans should be formulated, and that is the message that is being presented in this paper.

Statement by Tony Machukay
former student of St. John's
and resident of Komatke Village.

Marquette University, Bureau of Catholic Indian Missions Records. Printed by permission.

27. Fray Juan Crespi's Journal of Alta California, 1769

While Father Junipero Serra, O.F.M., was founding the first Spanish mission in Alta California at San Diego, Don Gaspar de Portolá (governor of Lower California and military commander of the 1769 expedition), Fray Francisco Gómez, O.F.M., and Fray Juan Crespi, O.F.M., traveled up the coast to a place they called Los Christianos, not far from the future site of Mission San Luis Rey, where Gómez baptized two little girls in danger of dying — the first baptisms in what is now the State of California. The Spaniards also planted a cross, which drew the friendly attention of the Indian people soon to be called Luiseños.

...On the 24th of May, Ascension Day, we arrived at this harbor with perfect ease, without the least mishap or sickness, thank God, having spent in the journey thirty-eight days.

As soon as we arrived, the very same day, before we dismounted about half a league before reaching the Point of the Pines and the beach where we had halted on the first journey, we wished to see a cross which they said they had set up when we started back last December. We were consumed with curiosity to see this cross and the beach, which we had not seen or been on, except those who had explored that place. And so Commander Don Gaspar de Portolá, Lieutenant Pedro Fages, and I, with a soldier, went to see it, guided by the soldier to the place where he knew the cross had been erected. We reached it, looked at it, and examined it again to see if we could find any signs that the bark had arrived, according to the signals formerly agreed upon by the chiefs, but we saw no sign of the bark whatever. We found the cross all surrounded by arrows and darts with plumes stuck in the ground; a dart with a string of sardines, still nearly fresh; another dart with a piece of meat hanging to it; and at the foot of the cross a little pile of mussels, all put there by the heathen in token of peace. All along the road where the camp had halted we found many darts with plumes stuck in the earth. And now, as soon as they saw us, they all came out unarmed, just as though they had dealt with us all their lives....

Saturday, July 22. — This day dawned cloudy for us. About seven o'clock we set out west and climbed a grassy hill. In a little while we entered a valley which turned to the north-northwest, and which communicates with that of Los Rosales. We traveled in the mountains, for they are not rough but open, with hills and extensive mesas, covered with a great deal of grass and grown with live oaks and alders, especially in the little valleys and arroyos, with an abundance of Castilian roses. Three mesas covered with large live oaks were encountered. About eleven o'clock we came to a pool of water, after having traveled some four leagues from the preceding place. This pool of fresh water is in a dry arroyo, which is grown with many alders. We made camp near the pool, and immediately about fourteen heathen, and as many women, with boys and girls, came and showed themselves to be very friendly; we entertained them and made them gifts.

The explorers informed us that on the preceding day they saw in the village two sick little girls. After asking the commander for some soldiers to go with us to visit them we went, and we found one which the mother had at her breast apparently dying. We asked for it, saying that we wished to see it, but it was impossible to get it from its mother. So we said to her by signs that we would not do it any harm, but wished to sprinkle its head, so that if it died it might go to heaven. She consented to this, and my companion, Fray Francisco Gómez, baptized it, giving it the name of María Magdalena. We went then to the other, also small, who had been burned and was apparently about to die. In the same way I baptized it, giving it the name of Margarita. We did not doubt that both would die and go to heaven. With this, the only success that we have obtained, we fathers consider well worth while the long journey and the hardships that are being suffered in it and that are still awaiting us. May it all be for the greater glory of God and the salvation of souls. For this reason this place is known to the soldiers as Los Christianos....

Herbert Eugene Bolton, *Fray Juan Crespi: Missionary Explorer on the Pacific Coast 1769-1774.* Berkeley: University of California Press, 1927, 50-51, 134-35. Printed by permission.

28. Testimony of Runaway Christian Indians, August 12, 1797

The Spanish established missions along the California coast, where Indians were baptized and lived under the rule of the Franciscans and their supporting soldiers. Once christened, the Native neophytes were expected to remain in the missions; however, many tried to escape to their familial villages. The authorities attempted to regain these fugitives, sometimes with military expeditions. In 1797 Governor Don Diego de Borica asked his troops to question the captured runaways of Mission San Francisco — mostly Huchiun Indians — concerning their motives for escaping. Prominent among the reasons were hunger and physical cruelty in the mission, as well as a desire to see relatives at home.

In fulfillment of the decree of Governor and Inspector General Don Diego de Borica, calling for testimony from the runaway Christian Indians of Mission San Francisco captured by Sergeant Pedro Amador during the recent campaign, on this day, July 21, 1797, I brought them before me. Once I figured out who was capable of testifying, I separated them out. By means of the interpreters and in the presence of the witnesses Sergeant Joaquín Pico, Corporal Claudio Galindo, Corporal José Miranda and soldier José Gonzalez, four members of the Catalonian Volunteers, I questioned each one regarding the causes and motives they had for running away from their mission without wanting to return. To these interrogations they responded in the following way:

Tiburcio — He testified that after his wife and daughter died, on five separate occasions Father Dantí ordered him whipped because he was crying. For these reasons he fled....

Magin — He testified that he left due to his hunger and because they had put him in the stocks when he was sick, on orders from the *alcalde*....

Roman — He testified that he left because his wife and a son had gone back to their land, because of the many whippings, and because he did not have anyone to feed him....

Claudio — He declares that he fled because he was continually fighting with his brother-in-law Casimiro and because the *alcalde* Valeriano was clubbing him every time he turned around, and when he was sick this same Valeriano made him go to work....

José Manuel — He testifies that when they went to bring wood from the mountains Raymundo ordered them to bring him water. When the declarant wouldn't do it, this same Raymundo hit him with a heavy cane, rendering one hand useless. He showed his hand. It was a little puffed up, but had movement. That was his reason for having left the mission....

Malquiedes — He declares that he had no more reason for fleeing than that he went to visit his mother who was on the other shore....

Liborato — He testifies that he left because his mother, two brothers, and three nephews died, all of hunger. So that he would not also die of hunger, he fled....

Timoteo — He declares that the *alcalde* Luís came to get him while he was feeling poorly, and whipped him. After that Father Antonio hit him with a heavy cane. For those reasons he fled....

Otolon — He reports that he fled because his wife did not care for him or bring him food. The vaquero Salvador had sinned with her. Then Father Antonio ordered him whipped because he was not looking out for said woman, his wife....

Milan — He declared that he was working all day in the tannery without any food for either himself, his wife, or his child. One afternoon after he left work he went to look for clams to feed his family. Father Dantí whipped him. The next day he fled to the other shore, where his wife and child died....

Orencio — He declared that his father had gone several times with a little niece of his to get a ration of meat. Father Dantí never gave it to him and always hit him with a cudgel. Because his niece died of hunger, he ran away....

Toribio — He stated that the motive for his having fled was that he was always very hungry, and that he went away together with his uncle....

Lopez — He explained that his reason for having run away was the following: He went one day over to the presidio to look for something to eat. Upon returning to the mission he went to get his ration. But Father Dantí did not want to give it to him, saying that he should go to the countryside to eat herbs....

Magno — He declared that he had run away because, his son being sick, he took care of him and was therefore unable to go out to work. As a result he was given no ration and his son died of hunger....

Prospero — He declared that he had gone one night to the lagoon to hunt ducks for food. For this Father Antonio Dantí ordered him stretched out and beaten. Then, the following week he was whipped again for having gone out on *paseo*. For these reasons he fled....

Having concluded the preceding declarations that were legally gathered and which follow the testimony of the interpreters, and in the belief that they represent the truth, I and my assistants sign it at the San Francisco Presidio on August 12, 1797

José Argüello
José Miranda
Joaquín Pico
José Gonzalez
Claudio Galindo

Randall Milliken, *A Time of Little Choice: The Disintegration of Tribal Culture in the San Francisco Bay Area 1769–1810.* Menlo Park, Calif.: Ballena Press, 1995, 299–303. Printed by permission.

29. Pablo Tac (Luiseño), A Record of California Mission Life, 1835

Pablo Tac was born in San Luis Rey Mission in 1822, a Luiseño Indian in Father Antonio Peyri's domain. When the California missions were secularized, Peyri left for Mexico City, then Spain, and took Tac and another boy with him. Two years later the boys entered the Urban College in Rome, where they planned for Christian missionary work. The other youth died in 1837, and Tac died of smallpox in 1841. Under the supervision of a clerical linguist in Rome, Tac produced a document, "Conversión de los San Luiseños de Alta California," probably the earliest literary work by a California Indian. Tac's writing, excerpted here, depicted the founding of San Luis Rey Mission in 1798, its organization under Peyri's rule, and the daily lives of the neophytes.

ARRIVAL OF THE SPANIARDS

When the missionary arrived in our country with a small troop, our captain and also the others were astonished, seeing them from afar, but they did not run away or seize arms to kill them, but having sat down, they watched them. But when they drew near, then the captain got up (for he was seated with the others) and met them. They halted, and the missionary then began to speak, the captain saying perhaps in his language "hichsom iva haluon, pulluchajam cham quinai." "What is it that you seek here? Get out of our country!" But they did not understand him, and they answered him in Spanish, and the captain began with signs, and the Fernandino, understanding him, gave him gifts and in this manner made him his friend. The captain, turning to his people (as I suppose) found the whites all right, and so they let them sleep here. There was not then a stone house, but all were camps (as they say). This was that happy day in which we saw white people, by us called Sosabitom. O merciful God, why didst Thou leave us for many centuries, years, months and days in utter darkness after Thou camest to the world? Blessed be Thou from this day through future centuries.

BUILDING OF THE MISSION

The Fernandino Father remains in our country with the little troop that he brought. A camp was made, and here he lived for many days. In the morning he said Mass, and then he planned how he would baptize them, where he would put his house, the church, and as there were five thousand souls (who were all the Indians there were), how he would sustain them, and seeing how it could be done. Having the captain for his friend, he was afraid of nothing. It was a great mercy that the Indians did not kill the Spanish when they arrived, and very admirable, because they have never wanted another people to live with them, and until those days they were always fighting. But thus willed He who alone can will. I do not know if he baptized them before making the church or after having made it, but I think he baptized them before making it. He was already a good friend of the captain, and also dear to the neophytes. They could understand him somewhat when he, as their father, ordered them to carry stone from the sea (which is not far) for the foundations, to make bricks, roof tiles, to cut beams, reeds and what was necessary. They did it with the masters who were helping them, and within a few years they finished working. They made a church with three altars for all the neophytes (the great altar is nearly all gilded), two chapels, two sacristies, two choirs, a flower garden for the church, a high tower with five bells, two small and three large, the cemetery with a crucifix in the middle for all those who die here....

THE FERNANDINO FATHER

In the Mission of San Luis Rey de Francia the Fernandino Father is like a king. He has his pages, alcaldes, majordomos, musicians, soldiers, gardens, ranchos, livestock, horses by the thousand, cows, bulls by the thousand, oxen, mules, asses, 12,000 lambs, 200 goats, etc. The pages are for him and for the Spanish and Mexican, English and Anglo-American travelers. The alcaldes to help him govern all the people of the Mission of San Luis Rey de Francia. The major-domos are in the distant districts, almost all Spaniards. The musicians of the

Mission for the holy days and all the Sundays and holidays of the year, with them the singers, all Indian neophytes. Soldiers so that nobody does injury to Spaniard or to Indian; there are ten of them and they go on horseback. There are five gardens that are for all, very large. The Fernandino Father drinks little, and as almost all the gardens produce wine, he who knows the customs of the neophytes well does not wish to give any wine to any of them, but sells it to the English or Anglo-Americans, not for money, but for clothing for the neophytes, linen for the church, hats, muskets, plates, coffee, tea, sugar and other things. The products of the Mission are butter, tallow, hides, chamois leather, bear skins, wine, white wine, brandy, oil, maize, wheat, beans and also bull horns which the English take by the thousand to Boston.

WHAT IS DONE EACH DAY

When the sun rises and the stars and the moon go down, then the old man of the house wakens everyone and begins with breakfast which is to eat *juiuis* heated and meat and tortillas, for we do not have bread. This done, he takes his bow and arrows and leaves the house with vigorous and quick step. (This is if he is going to hunt.) He goes off to the distant woods which are full of bears and hares, deer and thousands of birds. He is here all day, killing as many as he can, following them, hiding himself behind trees, climbing them, and then loaded with hares he returns home happy. But when he needs wood, then he leaves the house in the morning with his tumpline on his shoulders and his ax, with companions who can help him when the load is very heavy, and in the afternoon he returns home. His old woman staying at home makes the meal. The son, if he is a man, works with the men. His daughter stays with the women making shirts, and if these also have sons and daughters, they stay in the mission, the sons at school to learn the alphabet, and if they already know it, to learn the catechism, and if this also, to the choir of singers, and if he was a singer, to work, because all the musical singers work the day of work and Sunday to the choir to sing, but without a book, because the teacher teaches them by memory, holding the book. The daughter joins with the single girls who all spin for blankets for the San Luiseños and for the robe of the Fernandino Father. At twelve o'clock they eat together and leave the old man his share, their cups of clay, their vessels of well-woven fiber which water cannot leak out of, except when it is held before the face of the sun, their frying pans of clay, their grills of wood made for that day, and their pitchers for water also of clay. Seated around the fire they are talking and eating. Too bad for them if at that time they close the door. Then the smoke rising, being much, and the opening which serves as a window being small, it turns below, trying to go out by the door, remains in the middle of the house, and they eat, then speaking, laughing and weeping without wishing to. The meal finished they return to their work. The father leaves his son, the son leaves his sister, the sister the brother, the brother the mother, the mother her husband with cheer, until the afternoon. Before going to bed again they eat what the old woman and old man have made in that time, and then they sleep.

OF THE DANCE OF THE INDIANS

Each Indian people has its dances, different from other dances. In Europe they dance for joy, for a feast, for any fortunate news. But the Indians of California dance not only for a feast, but also before starting a war, for grief, because they have lost the victory, and in memory of grandparents, aunts and uncles, parents already dead. Now that we are Christians we dance for ceremony.

> Minna and Gordon Hewes, eds. and trans., *Indian Life and Customs at Mission San Luis Rey*. San Luis Rey, Calif.: Old Mission, 1958, 12–13, 20–22. Printed by permission.

30. Fathers Fernando Martin, O.F.M., and Vicente Oliva, O.F.M., to Comandante General José Maria Echeandia, regarding Citizen Gil, 1826

When Mexico declared its independence from Spain in 1821, the California government of José Maria Echeandia proceeded to "secularize" the Franciscan missions, that is, to separate the neophytes from their status as mission residents in order to become free Mexican citizens. In the case of Citizen Gil (Diegueño) of Mission San Diego in 1826, the process appeared simple enough; however, the subsequent history of secularization demonstrated the government's desire to confiscate mission properties for the benefit of California officials, colonists, and soldiers and to exploit the labor of the emancipated Mission Indians.

Citizen Gil, native of Mission San Diego and carpenter by trade, desires to separate himself from said Mission where he is now, in order to go where he can exercise his trade with adequate profit. In complying with the petition presented by Gil Riela on April 4, 1826, we have to say that he is a Christian from his infancy, having been born at the Mission of parents who are Christians of long standing, that he is of regular conduct, married to Pia who was baptized at Mission San Luis Rey. He is 29 years of age and has three children. His trade is that of carpenter by means of which he maintains himself in some comfort. Therefore he has our leave to separate himself from the Mission.

> Engelhardt Zephyrin, O.F.M., *San Diego Mission*. San Francisco: James H. Barry Company, 1920, 213.

31. Certificate of the Marriage of Malvina Sawebel (Cupeño) and Suanee Mooat (Cupeño), Presided by Catechist Ambrosio Ortega (Cupeño), 1891

In the late nineteenth century descendants of the Mission Indians in southern California remained in touch with their Catholic heritage, mostly in the absence of priestly contact. Catechists such as the Cupeño Ambrosio Ortega took the place of priests at marriages and other rites of passage. This wedding took place at Agua Caliente.

This is to certify that Malvina Sawebel and Suanne Mooat were married according to the Indian ceremony, by Ambrosio Ortega, and witnessed by the

Alcaldes and the people, on this the 20th day of December 1891. Such contract being considered lawful, and binding. Written at the request of Ambrosio Ortega, and signed by me as a witness. J. H. Babbitt. We the contracting parties consider this marriage lawful and binding. Jose Antonio C B, Malvina Sawebel, Ambrosio Ortega.

Marquette University, Juliana Pena Calac Papers. Printed by permission.

32. Memoir of Pala by Father Julian Girardot, O.F.M., ca. 1935

A century after the writing of Pablo Tac and secularization, Father Julian Girardot, O.F.M., described the Luiseño and Cupeño descendants of the San Luis Rey Mission and its outpost at Pala. In 1935 he witnessed Pala funeral devotions, when the people's spirituality especially expressed itself: the ringing of bells, the lighting of candles, the reciting of the rosary, the all-night communing by the side of the corpse, the singing of a requiem high Mass, the offering of gifts at the grave, and the community feasting.

The day's work was finished at 9 p.m. I had gone to the recreation room at the San Luis Rey Mission to spend a little time with the other Fathers. Hardly had I sat down when the telephone rang. It was a sick call for me at the Pala reservation twenty miles away. I took the call, and when I reached Pala I had to turn off the highway, and some distance away, cross a stream of water. It was a dark night but I had no difficulty in getting through the water. Farther on at the foot of a mountain I reached the humble dwelling of the sick man. He was one of the old time Indians of Pala. He was unmarried and lived all alone. He was quite ill and I administered the last Sacraments.

About a week later, while staying at the Pala Mission, I was awakened during the night by the tolling of the Church bells. Someone had passed away and I knew it must be Ramon, the old man I had attended. As soon as a death notice is received, my Sacristan at Pala tolls the church bell regardless of the hour of the day or night. Then everyone knows that a death has occurred.

Now there are many things to be done. The body is taken to the Undertaker. Formerly this was never done. But now most bodies are embalmed. The relatives are informed of the death. This is done by telephone and by word of mouth. The message is relayed to nearby reservations so that within a day the notice of the death has traveled far and wide.

At the home of the deceased, other activities are proceeding. Some of the Indian homes consist of only one room. When this is the case, everything in the room is taken outside. Then benches are placed along the four walls. When the body arrives, it will be placed in the center of the room; two candles will burn at the head and two at the foot of the coffin. If the home should have more than one room, the largest room is cleared and prepared in this manner.

Other men go out to slaughter a beef, for many people will be fed; and others go out to gather a large amount of firewood. The members of the family and close relatives will go to the store and procure a large amount of food. They will also buy six or eight yards or more of varied color Calico or Gingham cloth which will be placed on the grave after the body has been buried. The kitchen is now prepared to serve a large crowd. Kitchen utensils, plates, etc. that may be needed are borrowed from others. If the home of the deceased has a kitchen and room to serve meals, that is used. In the case of the old Indian, Ramon, whose home had but one room, the home of a relative close by is used.

Toward evening the body is brought to the home. Relatives and friends begin to arrive. Indians from other reservations and from distant towns will come. The people come into the house, view the body, place their flowers around the coffin, and sit on the benches along the walls. They remain there for a long time, then they will go outside and others will come in to take their place. In winter-time, a log fire is built outside and benches placed around it that people outside may keep warm. This will keep up all night until the funeral Mass next morning. At the kitchen all the people who come from outside places are fed, and during the night hot coffee is served at various times.

In the room where the people are gathered around the coffin, there is usually a prayer leader. He leads in reciting the rosary and other prayers. He leads in singing some religious songs. He also sings some old traditional Indian songs. And while singing these Indian chants, he beats time with a little instrument composed of a gourd partly filled with little stones and run through on a stick which serves as a handle. This is shaken and gives a rattle effect. Some have a turtle shell instead of the gourd. The rattle sound is about the same. I have seen a rattle used, composed of the outer shell or nail of the hoofs of deer feet, each fastened on a short piece of cow-hide cord in the manner of a bell. These in turn were fastened together on a leather handle. And when the handle was shaken, the little cluster of hoofs would produce the sound of a rattle. This is shaken to beat time for the chant. The praying, singing, and chanting goes on all night. No one retires for the night.

Early the next morning at day-break, the men will go to dig the grave. They will work in the rain when that is necessary. But never will the grave be dug the day before. According to their tradition, someone must always watch the grave after it is dug, or evil spirits might enter it. No one will stay at the graveyard all night to watch it. So the grave is simply dug the morning of the burial. The grave is usually finished by the time Mass begins.

The Mass is always a Requiem High Mass. Three or four Indian women sing the Mass which they do [quite] well. They go from Mission to Mission wherever a Mass is to be sung. The coffin is always opened during Mass. And after the Mass, all the people walk to the front of the church, view the body once more, and drop an offering in the basket that is placed at the foot of the coffin. After the prayers at the coffin the body is carried to the cemetery. After the customary prayers, the coffin is lowered into the grave, and is always placed into an outer wooden box which is then securely nailed shut. Sometimes the clothes in which the person died or other personal belongings are wrapped in a sheet and placed on top of the box. Now one of the men holds a shovel of dirt. And the priest first takes a handful of dirt and throws it in the grave. He is followed by all the other people present. When this little ceremony is finished, a number of men immediately fill the grave. While this is being done, all the people remain and the choir sings hymns. After the mound is completed, several relatives spread yards of cloth over the grave and around the cross that is always planted at the head of the grave. No relative of the deceased may take the cloth. But others not related take the cloth from the grave and will use the cloth for dresses or other such purpose. After this ceremony the spokesman or a relative thanks all for their prayers and help in this affliction and invites all to gather again at the home. So once more a large meal is served, the priest and choir occupying the first table. Then after an exchange of farewells, all depart for their homes.

Reverend Francis J. Weber, ed., *El Caminito Real: A Documentary History of California's Asistencias.* Hong Kong: Yee Tin Tong Printing Press Ltd., 1988, 139–42. Archdiocese of Los Angeles Archives. Printed by permission.

33. Santa Rosa Mission Indians to Bishop Charles F. Buddy, October 16, 1939

When Bishop Charles F. Buddy visited Santa Rosa Indian Reservation as part of Los Angeles–Monterey diocesan outreach to the California Mission Indians in 1939, tribal representatives thanked him for his stay, which inspired the people to "remain Catholic." A Santa Rosa tribal meeting approved a letter to the bishop, which he found "very beautiful" and had it published in the diocesan newspaper, The Southern Cross.

We Mission Indians of the Santa Rosa Band have been taught to conduct ourselves in a Catholic manner and that ideal has been instilled in us from our fathers and grandfathers. They told us that when you first came to California with the Catholic religion it was not forced upon us. And the early Mission Fathers did not try to make us forsake our own beliefs or the manner of expressing our devotion to the deities whom we to this day still hold in reverence and awe. Our people have embraced the Holy Roman Catholic Church as their one Church which we hold in high and holy esteem. But deep in our hearts we have a reverence for the things our fathers taught us. And we still carry on with certain ceremonial[s] for our dead, which do not conflict with our Catholic hearts. Your religion dear Bishop has never denied us this worship or tried to take it away from us.

Archdiocese of San Diego Archives. Printed by permission.

34. Mrs. Mariano Saubel et al., Morongo Mission Indians, to Pope Pius XII, May 23, 1952

Franciscan priests returned to California mission work in the 1920s, but Bishop Buddy of the Diocese of San Diego determined to oust them in the early 1950s over the issue of ecclesiastical authority within the diocese. Some Indians were distressed to see their beloved friars depart. Mrs. Mariano Saubel of

*the Morongo Reservation and several of her Morongo tribal associates protested
directly to Pope Pius XII in 1952.*

I am appealing to you in behalf of the Catholic, Indian people concerning the
withdrawal of the Franciscan Order from St. Boniface Indian School and our
own little chapel on the Morongo Indian Reservation, near Banning California
Diocese of San Diego. Why the Franciscan priest[s] are being ordered out of this
part of the country I don't know. History shows and every one knows that the
Franciscans belong in California. They were the first my people knew. They
are humble and so are my people. They understand us and help us, not only
spiritually but every way possible for our welfare. So again I plead please leave
our own Franciscans with their children.

*When the Vatican forwarded the letter to the diocesan headquarters, someone
in Bishop Buddy's office inquired about the signatories:*

Please inform me 1) How many of these signers have made their Easter Duty?
2) How many assist at Mass & support the Church?

Diocese of San Bernardino Archives.

Part 2

THE FRENCH HERITAGE

35. Reverend William M. Hughes, "The Happiest People in the World," 1913

In the first decades of the seventeenth century, French Jesuits and Francis-cans made contact with the Algonkian peoples of Acadia — Micmac, Abenaki, Maliseet, and the Passamaquoddy and Penobscot Indians of present-day Maine. English opposition hindered the Acadian missions; however, Catholic identity ran strong among many of the Indians through the centuries. In 1913 Father William M. Hughes celebrated three hundred years of Catholic missions in Maine, calling the Catholic Indians "the happiest people in the world" in the pages of The Indian Sentinel. *His essay makes for a sanguine survey of the French missionary efforts and their effects.*

The Three Hundredth Anniversary of Catholic Missions in Maine

The happiest people in the world are the Indians of Maine. Seldom — indeed, nowhere else in the whole country — can there be found Indians without se-rious complaints to make and just grounds to show for their complaints. But these Indians who celebrate this year the three hundredth anniversary of the establishment of Catholic missions among them, are without a single grudge.

They have the happiest dispositions; are the most industrious; the most pleasantly-situated for the following of their natural bent, woodcraft, hunting and fishing; the most favored in their treatment at the hands of the Govern-ment; among the best cared for in the matter of religion; the most Catholic in their history; by nature the most intelligent if judged from their legendary lore; in a word, they are the most favored Indians in the country.

PEACEFUL FACES

The faces of the Penobscots and Passamaquoddies are the most peaceful and the most expressive of peace of soul of any Indians in the land. Their voices, espe-cially those of the young women, are the gentlest, the most musical. It is no dispraise of womankind to add that they are the most talkative, because their talk is charitable and their voices are as resonant as the woods they inhabit and as sweet as the babble of the waters under the paddle of the canoes they ride in. The manners of the people are the politest. Their sense of humor is the keenest, although not the noisiest. Their lives are among the most religious....

CHILDREN OF LIGHT

The Abnakis, or, as they call themselves, the Wapanakis, the men of the aurora borealis, have been, indeed, in their religious history, the children of light. Naturally polite, gentle and virtuous, they responded readily to the appeal, quickly and thoroughly applied the lessons, first of the priests and later of the Sisters, and irrevocably pledged allegiance to the Cross and the faith for which it stands.

In the beginning of the 18th century the governor of Massachusetts, anxious to win the alliance of the Abnakis in war and to accomplish their defection from the Catholic faith, offered to rebuild at his own expense the church at Norridgewock which the English had destroyed. The governor laid down one condition, namely, that the Indians should dismiss their missionary and accept one of his choice. The Indian envoy indignantly replied:

"When you first came here, you saw me long before the French governors, but neither your predecessors nor your ministers ever spoke to me of prayer or the Great Spirit. They saw my furs, my beaver and moose skins, and of this alone they thought; these alone they sought, and so eagerly that I have not been able to supply them enough. When I had much they were my friends, and only then. One day my canoe missed the route; I lost my path, and wandered a long way at random, until I landed near Quebec, in a great village of the Algonquins, where the Black-gowns were teaching. Scarcely had I arrived, when one of them came to see me. I was loaded with furs, but the Black-gown of France disdained to look at them; he spoke to me of the Great Spirit, of heaven, of hell, of the prayer, which is the only way to reach heaven. I heard with pleasure and was so delighted with his words that I remained in the village near him. At last the prayer pleased me, and I was instructed; I solicited baptism and received it. Then I returned to the lodges of my tribe and related all that had happened. All envied my happiness and wished to partake it; they, too, went to the Black-gown to be baptized. Thus have the French acted. Had you spoken to me of the prayer as soon as we met, I should be now so unhappy as to pray like you, for I could not have told whether your prayer was good or bad. Now I hold to the prayer of the French; I agree to it; I shall be faithful to it, even until the earth is burnt and destroyed. Keep your men, your gold, and your minister; I will go to my French father."

THE REAL APOSTLE, AN INDIAN

Charles Meiskwat, an Indian, is the real apostle, the pioneer of faith, among the Abnakis. From Sillery, the Jesuit mission on the St. Lawrence, where he had led a truly saintly life, Charles set out for the Maine wilderness on an embassy of mercy. He had heard that a party of pagan Abnakis were being tortured by pagan Algonquins in spite of the fact that they belonged to the same Algic family, as their language would show. Charles lost his companion, Nicolet, who was drowned in a rapid, but, undaunted, he hurried on in quest of his countrymen. He found them, rescued the victims who were just then being tortured, and brought them back in triumph to Sillery. Here they were first cared for physically. Then they were instructed in the "Prayer" by the Sisters and priests. When they had recovered and been instructed, they sent Charles with one of their number to carry the good tidings of their rescue and new-found faith to their fellow-tribesmen on the Kennebec. One chief returned with Charles to the mission, was instructed and baptized. Others followed and soon every Abnaki village counted its Catholics. Such was the real beginning of Abnaki missions, which dates from 1642.

The catechist, or deacon, as he is called among the Abnakis, has been a great factor in the spread and preservation of the faith. At Oldtown the memory of the saintly, prayerful Sak Bason Swasson (a corruption of the French Jacques Vincent Joachim) is held in benediction. He was the governor, a man of majestic men. He is said to have been a direct descendent of Baron de Castine, who married Madocawando, daughter of the first sagamore. He daily made the stations of the cross. He spent over an hour in this exercise every day. It was for his people, he explained.

Among the Passamaquoddies, Toma Dana (Thomas Daniel) was the rival of Bishop Healy in apostolic work. The Indian could sing all the Mass. Once when he joined with the bishop in intoning vespers, it was a great success. Toma declared "Me and the bishop sing good today. We can't beat nobody." He meant that no one could excel these two.

THE BEGINNINGS

Previous to Charles Meiskwat, scattering efforts had been made by both Jesuits and Franciscans to teach the people the "Prayer." The Jesuits who had begun at Port Royal, Nova Scotia, among the Micmacs, who, in the person of Father Biard, had ascended the Kennebec in exploration but who, in their efforts on the peninsula, had been thwarted by the arrogant young military ruler, Biencourt, finally effected an establishment on Mount Desert Island near the mouth of the Kennebec. This was the mission of the Holy Redeemer, or St. Saviour. It is this mission and the reconnoitering expedition of Father Biard which furnishes the ground for the three hundredth anniversary celebration of the beginning of Indian missions in Maine.

The mission did not live long. It was very soon destroyed by Argall, the notorious buccaneer of Virginia. The baptism of a sick child, which lived, and the death of Brother du Thet, who fell defending himself and companions from the attack of the English pirates, were the only visible fruits of the mission.

About 1620 the Recollects (Franciscans) had missionary stations among the Abnakis, on the St. John's River in New Brunswick. They may have visited the related tribes on the St. Croix. The place is not distant and may be reached by easy water routes. Other Franciscans (Capuchins) were afterwards stationed as chaplains at French posts on the coast. They also had a convent on the Penobscot and an hospice on the Kennebec near tidewater. While the historian Shea found at this period no evidence of work by them among the Indians, the well-known missionary purpose and history of the order and their marked opposition twenty years later to the return of the Jesuits to the Kennebec Indian missions, argue the existence of such missionary work on the part of the Franciscans in Maine.

FATHER DRUILLETTES

It is certain that for a number of years the Abnakis were without a missionary devoted exclusively to them. They sent delegation after delegation to get a priest to come to them. In 1646, Father Druillettes, the Jesuit, was sent and remained on the Kennebec eight months. In two or three months he could speak their dialect better than Indians who belonged to other tribes but to the same Algonquin family. In 1650 the persistence of the Indians compelled his superior, in the face of the dearth of priests, to send Father Druillettes once more to the Kennebec. He remained with the delighted Indians for a year and a half. During this time he made two official visits to Boston as ambassador of the French in the matter of protection for the Abnakis who were by treaty considered British subjects. Father Druillettes offered in return for such protection the valuable privilege of free trade with Canada, which then revelled in wealth of hides and furs. Father Druillettes may, therefore, be considered not only the apostle of the Abnakis, but also the first envoy of trade reciprocity between Canada and New England. He made two journeys from Quebec to Boston for this purpose. His ulterior motive was the protection of the Abnakis, who were Catholics and allies of the French, from the Mohawks, who were pagans, enemies of the French and, at least nominally and when it served the crafty purpose of the Iroquois, allies of the English.

Six years later Bishop Laval of Quebec and Father Jerome Lalemant attempted to restore the fainting if not dying Jesuit Indian missions, whose utter annihilation was foreshadowed in the destruction of the New York Iroquois of the Canadian Huron mission. Some Jesuits were sent to the Abnakis who still kept the fire of faith burning in the wigwam of prayer.

For thirty years, 1658–1688, no word of the Jesuits reaches us from the Abnaki missions. The Jesuits attempted to draw the christians of Maine to St. Joseph at Sillery or to St. Francis at the Falls of the Chaudiere on the St. Lawrence. Some were drawn. So many, in fact, that mingling with the other Algonquins there who had survived the ravages of war and sickness, the Maine Indians by their numbers and zeal made of these missions Abnaki settlements.

In 1684 Father Thury, member of the Seminary of the Foreign Missions, was sent by the Bishop of Quebec to the St. John River Abnakis in New Brunswick; thence one year later to the St. Croix tribe, and finally, after two years more, to the lower Penobscot, where among his beloved redskins he died in June, 1699, regretted by all.

In 1688 the two brothers Bigot, Jesuit founders of the Chaudiere mission, succeeded in thwarting the fisheries company and got the consent of Governor Denonville, of Canada, to resume the work of the Society of Jesus on the Kennebec.

At this time the Franciscans were represented by Father Simon in a mission on the St. John near where the cathedral city of the same name in New Brunswick now stands.

FATHER RALE

The wars between the English and French for possession of the territory of Maine long threatened the destruction of the missions, the annihilation of the Indians and the death of the priests. One of the priests, Father Rale, S.J., stands out most strikingly among them. He lived at Norridgewock, the principal Abnaki village on the Kennebec. He remained here from 1695 until his death, which was accomplished in the second attempt by the English under Colonel Westbrook, in 1722. Though crippled, both legs having been broken, he had eluded his white pursuers, because of the loyalty of the Indians. His life reads like a romance. Living with the Indians in their village during the short planting and harvesting seasons, hunting with them in winter and fishing with them in summer, he became an Indian. But he did not lose the Frenchman's hearty political dislike of the English, especially since the encroachments of the latter were made upon his beloved Indians, as well as upon territory and allies whom he considered by right to be French. It would be but natural that he should feel hostile to the English, who were the enemies of his native land and the plunderers of his adopted children. If there was need of plunder, the French, in spite of Father Rale, could do that to the king's taste. But never could the Abnaki be accused of cruelty while under the guidance of Father Rale. Judged from any standard whatsoever, he is one of the most magnificent types of men who, from any motive in the world, ever labored for his brother man.

The death of Rale brought on an Indian war which lasted three years and which was directed against the Puritans of Massachusetts.

Strangely enough, the other Abnaki missions of the Penobscot and St. John were not disturbed by the English.

Six years after the death of Rale, the church which had been burned by the Puritans was rebuilt and Norridgewock itself, which had been deserted, assumed something like its previous prosperous appearance. The Penobscot mission was left without a pastor by the retirement of Lauvergat, who had been broken down by the opposition of half breed Castines. He found his way to St. John's mission in the northeast.

SOLDIERS OF THE REVOLUTION

Three wars among the white nations deprived the Abnakis of missionaries. First, the war of the Austrian succession, which had no meaning to the provinces, but which deported the missionaries or compelled them to take refuge in the wilderness. The priests of Nova Scotia and New Brunswick suffered terribly and those of Maine were threatened. Only the efforts of the priests who succeeded in quieting the Indians prevented reprisal on the part of the English. Next came the French and Indian war, so-called. This war saw the last of the grand old Jesuits go. He was Father Germaine, who retired to St. Ann's Island on the St. John near Fredericton and thence to St. Francis on the St. Lawrence, where he died. Finally came the war of American Independence, in which the Abnakis bore a glorious part both by reason of the pledges given by them to Washington in 1775 at Watertown, the record of which is a tribute to their Catholic faith and independent spirit, and by reason of the services which they rendered in the war. Forty-one warriors lie buried in the old cemetery at Indian Island. Flag-draped crosses mark their graves. A granite cross was placed by the Daughters of the American Revolution in the churchyard to their memory. In the church nearby these Catholic soldiers, of whom the chief, Orono, who bore a commission in the Revolutionary army, was the greatest, pledged allegiance to their God before fulfilling their pledge of allegiance to the cause now expressed in the Stars and Stripes.

When the war of the revolution was ended, and the first bishop had been named for America, the Indians sought him. They bore the crucifix of the martyred Rale to Bishop Carroll at Baltimore, saying: "If I give to thee today, Bishop, it is a pledge and promise that thou wilt send us a priest." The bishop promised and kept his promise by sending Father Ciquard, the Sulpician priest. He went to Oldtown, where he soon learned the Indian language. Here he remained ten years working throughout all Maine until the time of his departure for the St. John Mission, now in Canadian territory....

RECENT HISTORY...

The Sisters of Mercy who have been the real resident missionaries for thirty-five years deserve a special chapter. Nowhere in the country is the value of the Sisters' service seen to better advantage.

His Eminence, William Cardinal O'Connell, when bishop of Portland, and Rt. Rev. Bishop Walsh have followed in the footsteps of Bishop Healy, who was so devoted to the Indians.

The Indians themselves deserve great praise. They are not perfect. The removal of the curse of intoxicant would make them well nigh perfect. The zeal of the Indian can be seen from the following quaint remark. When one of the young men at Oldtown had committed some minor infraction of the law, an old Indian went to the convent to tell the Sisters about the affair. He was greatly perturbed and exclaimed: "Sister, he has gone and spoiled the whole Catholic religion."

The fine intelligence revealed in their legends cannot be brought out in the limits of this article. The reader is recommended to apply at his library for the Algonquin Legends of New England by Charles G. Leland.

The testimony of Father Maloney, who knew the Indians of Maine at their best and at their worst, may well conclude this account of these people whose ancestors were the first fruits of the harvest of souls among the Indian tribes of the north, the wampum belt, the pledge given that many tribes would surrender to the cross of Christ. Father Maloney writes:

"As for the Indians themselves, I found them a warm-hearted, simple, grateful people, towards those whom they found sincere with them, but suspicious, crafty, and entirely untrustworthy in regard to those who were in any way tricky in their dealings with them. In one word, they are staunch friends, and can be inveterate enemies. They never forget a kindness, nor do they forget, although they may forgive, an injury. My memories of them are of the happiest. Never did I have warmer friends than the Indian friends of the Passamaquoddy tribe."

> William M. Hughes, "The Happiest People in the World," *The Indian Sentinel,*
> 1913, 5–20. Printed by permission.

36. Bishop Amedee W. Proulx's Memo, "Peter Dana Point," October 20, 1982

The twentieth century has tested the faith and happiness of the Passamaquoddies and strained their association with the Catholic Church. Social deterioration accompanied the influx of non-Indians and a large, successful land claim against the State of Maine soured Indian-white relations. In 1982 the bishop of Portland, Maine – Amedee W. Proulx – addressed the difficulty of providing priests and sisters to a community where vandalism, violence, and substance abuse were endemic. Proulx's intervention helped to stabilize Passamaquoddy Catholicism.

Events leading up to Bishop Proulx's intervention

For some years now I have been meeting occasionally with representatives of the Sisters of Mercy, and those who minister at Peter Dana Point to discuss the mission of the Church to the residents of the Mission.

A matter of concern has been the increasing number of incidents of vandalism against church property and particularly the incidents of breaking and entering at the convent. These incidents have generated growing fear in the Sisters residing at Peter Dana Point [because] they are often carried out under the influence of drugs and/or liquor.

On March 22, 1981 the Sisters of Mercy convened a public meeting to address their concerns.

Eighty-six (86) Indians signed a statement stating the need of the Sisters and in religious education.

A committee was to be formed to insure that the enthusiasm and support for the Sisters['] ministry be continued.

Despite this commitment the vandalism has continued.

The departure of Father Laughlin has had mixed effect. Supporters are unhappy, others are relieved. There are mixed signals from the community as to the need for another resident priest.

Father Carpentier did not feel accepted at first. He was seen as a temporary substitute and not truly considered as the Indians['] "own priest."

In discussions with the ministers at Peter Dana Point it was thought that we should wait for clearer signs from the community before a new resident priest be sought for them. This was never discussed with the community.

One of the difficulties arised from the lack of recognized spokesmen for the community. The Tribal Council does not really seem to be representative of the faith community. Yet it cannot be ignored since it has traditional and legal authority in many areas.

There is no "parish council" to speak for the faith community. We discussed the possibility of establishing one and decided against it because the community is thought to be too divided to achieve any peaceful and effective representation of the entire community.

Yet, it was felt that the community needed to be challenged in its faith response and in coming to grips with the violence that is growing in the community.

Here is the outline of the message I tried to convey:

We need to talk about the relationship of the Church with the community of believers at Peter Dana Point.

The church is present at P.D.P. for the sake of Jesus Christ to bring to them the Good News of God's love and saving grace.

Who decides how the Church will be represented?

The Bishop:	in response to their needs
	in consultation with the Religious
	Societies which can/wish to supply personnel.

Fr. J. Laughlin:	His goodness/generosity were abused
	it affected his health
	he had difficulties with administration.
	The Bishop and his superiors decided to remove him.
	He will not return even if he might wish to do so.

Fr. Carpentier:	is your priest.

The Sisters who serve here do so on a volunteer basis. If they have to leave they might not be replaced.

Vandalism:	I am puzzled by it
	It goes against your tradition
	We expect it to stop

I closed with an exhortation on reconciliation and the need to communicate/work together. We then had a reconciliation service.

Our weakness: We really have not been talking with the leadership. They have not been involved in the decisions affecting the ministry in their community.

Some issues which need to be explored:

1. What do they expect of the Church?

2. Why do they want Sisters living on the reservation?
      "   "   "   "   Priests   "   "   "   "   ?
Doing what?

3. Should the Sisters be involved in the school?

4. What about violence?

5. Residence and buildings.

6. Financial support.

7. Who speaks for the faith community?

8. Relationship of the Church to the Tribal Council?

9. The need for the faith community to assume responsibility.

Fundamental problems:

1. The stress caused by the legitimate desire to preserve their heritage and the need to prepare for a healthy relationship with the rest of American Society.

2. Possible lack of adequate ethics to cope with life as they know it today. My theory is that the restriction of this people to life on a reservation has made many of their traditional ethical principles ineffective or inoperable. e.g. lack of discipline in bringing up children. When children needed to learn early in life the art of survival in the wilderness it was important for them to grow up with a sense of independence. Living in close quarters more discipline is required to learn respect for the rights of others. Common vs private ownership.

The principles of anglo-saxon Christian ethics have not been assimilated sufficiently to fill this void. The recent advent of a cash economy on the reservation raises a whole gamut of new problems.

    This, I think, needs to be addressed — cautiously — among the members of the community.

    There are more questions/issues than answers at this time.

AWP
10/20/82

Diocese of Portland Archives. Printed by permission.

37. Reverend Andrew White, S.J., in Maryland, 1639

The Society of Jesus functioned not only in French and Spanish colonies, but also among the English of nascent Maryland. In 1639 Father Andrew White gained the loyalty of the Piscataway tayac (chief), Kittamaquund, by curing him of a disease. The tayac received public baptism with his wife and infant daughter in 1640; however, he died the following year. When Protestants took over the Maryland colony in 1645 the Catholic missionaries were banned and Father White died in an English prison in 1656. The Piscataway allegiance to Catholicism disappeared from the view of outsiders; nonetheless, today there is still a Catholic community of Piscataways in Maryland.

Not long after the coming of Father White to his court, the Tayac was in danger from a severe disease; and when forty conjurers had in vain tried every remedy, the Father, by permission of the sick man, administered medicine, to wit: a certain powder of known efficacy mixed with holy water, and took care the day after, by the assistance of the boy, whom he had with him, to open one of his veins for bloodletting. After this, the sick man began daily to grow better, and not long after became altogether well. Restored from the disease entirely, of himself he resolved as soon as possible to be initiated in the Christian rites; nor himself only, but his wife also and two daughters — for as yet he has no male offspring. Father White is now diligently engaged in their instruction; nor do they slothfully receive the heavenly doctrine, for by the light of heaven poured upon them, they have long since found out the errors of their former life. The Emperor has exchanged the skins, with which he was heretofore clothed, for a garment made in our fashion; he makes also a little endeavor to learn our language.

Having put away his concubines from him, he lives content with one wife, that he may the more freely (as he says) have leisure to pray to God. He abstains from meat on the days in which it is forbidden by the Christian laws; and men that are heretics who do otherwise, he for that very reason thinks ought to be called bad Christians. He is greatly delighted with spiritual conversation, and indeed seems to esteem earthly wealth as nothing, in comparison with heavenly, as he once told the Governor, when explaining to him what great advantages from the English could be enjoyed by a mutual exchange of wares — "Verily, I consider these trifling when compared with this one advantage — that through their testimony I have arrived at the true knowledge of the one God, than which there is nothing greater, or which ought to be greater, in my wishes."

Not long since, when he held a convention of the empire, in a crowded assembly of the chiefs and a circle of the common people, Father White and some of the English being present, he publicly attested it was his determination, together with that of his wife and children, abjuring the superstition of the country, to take the part of Christ; for that no other true deity is anywhere else had than among the Christians, nor otherwise can the immortal soul of man be saved from death — but that stones and herbs, to which, through blindness of mind, he and they had hitherto given divine honors, are the humblest things created by the Almighty God for the use and relief of human life. Which being spoken, he spurned far away from him with his foot a stone which happened to be near. A murmur of applause from the people sufficiently indicated that they did not hear these things with unfavorable ears. But the greatest hope is, that when the family of the Emperor is purified by baptism, the conversion of the whole empire will speedily take place. In the meantime, we heartily thank God for so joyful a commencement of affairs, and are especially encouraged when we daily behold those idols to be the contempt of the natives, which were lately reckoned in the number of deities.

"The Annual Letters of the Jesuits," in Clayton Colman Hall, ed., *Narratives of Early Maryland 1633–1684*. New York: Barnes and Noble, 1967, 126–28. Printed by permission.

38. Reverend Jerome Lalemant, S.J., Describes Joseph Chihouatenhoua, a Huron Convert, 1640

In the early 1630s the Jesuits focused their attention upon the Huron Indians, Iroquoian-speaking farmers of Georgian Bay, whose settled village life seemed conducive to resident missionary efforts. The priests brought with them a message of an all-powerful God and an eternal life after death. They also brought diseases — influenza, measles, smallpox, and so on — that ravaged the Hurons and brought the missionaries under the suspicion of sorcery. In the midst of an epidemic in 1637 some Hurons accused the Jesuits of causing illness; other Hurons turned to baptism in hope of its medicinal powers and in fear of the consuming fires of hell. The most prominent of these converts was Joseph Chihouatenhoua, who persisted in Christian devotions and sought greater theological and spiritual discipline. In 1640 Father Jerome Lalemant, S.J., described Chihouatenhoua's attraction to the spiritual exercises of Ignatius Loyola and his expectation of a heavenly life. In that year, "the Christian," as the Jesuits called him, was martyred for his faith.

It had indeed been one of our thoughts while building a house apart, remote from the vicinity of the villages, that it would serve, among other things, for the retreat and meditation of our evangelistic laborers, who after their combats would find this solitude full of delights: but never would we have believed that the first for whom this house would serve for this purpose was to be a poor barbarian, whose spirit is so far removed from the ideas answering to such occupations. This was Joseph Chihouatenhoua, surnamed here par excellence "the Christian."

On account of the storms which we were anticipating, we judged it proper to inform him with some more particular instruction, so as to strengthen his courage, as the one who was to serve as example to all the others. We then broached the matter to him, and gave him some idea of the spiritual exercises.

"Alas!" he said, "why have you been so long without imparting to me so great a good? I had a thousand times had the thought of inquiring why you did not teach me what I so often saw the two Fathers do who are in my cabin, who pray to God so long without moving their lips: I restrained myself, believing that if you had judged me capable, you would have taught me, and consequently that I must wait to be found worthy thereof." After that, the time was taken for this purpose; but extraordinary occupations coming upon him, one after the other, the matter dragged along. This good man perceived as much, and plainly suspecting, of his own accord, that there might be some ruse of the devil therein, he left in God's hands the care of his family, and in fact came to find us when we were least expecting him. Perhaps one will be glad to know some portion of the sentiments that our Lord gave him during this holy occupation; it will be seen that the Holy Ghost is everywhere the master of hearts.

1. "All my life I have always been occupied; if I died at this hour, what profit would there be left to me for eternity, unless from the little that I have done for the salvation of my soul since I have had the faith? The occupation which I am about to undertake will be forever profitable to me; I must then attend to it more mightily than ever I have undertaken any business in the world.

2. "My God, I come here to know your holy will, and resolve, whatever cost there be, to fulfill it, though it were to cost my life. Unless you give me to know it, — forgive me, my God: a subject to whom his Captain does not declare his desires, is excusable if he do not accomplish them.

3. "Alas, how insignificant is the support of men! Those who loved me the most in the world, and from whom I derive most, — my father and my mother, — are dead; God alone, in his goodness, has served me as father and mother; when I was nowise thinking of him, he thought incessantly of me. I was like a child at the breast, which bites and annoys its mother when she is doing it most good. This great God has called from the end of the world, and from beyond the seas, men who have come for me, and for me almost alone. Alas, my God, how great is your love! Shall I lean on another than you?"

4. On a certain day, he found himself at evening in a great aridity and distraction of mind; when it was a question of giving an account of his meditation to the Father who was directing him, "My brother," he said to him, "I acknowledge, indeed, that I have no sense; I have not said my prayer well, — I straightway found myself at the end of my thoughts. Alas, what is our intelligence!" The Father having asked him how he had behaved on that occasion, he answered: "I said to God, 'Alas, my God, I am nothing; is it for me to bring you any word? I come here to hear you; speak then, in the depth of my heart, and tell me, "Do that;" I will do it, my God, though I should die for it.' Then I said to the Virgin: 'Holy Mary, mother of my Savior Jesus, here I am in your house and in your Chapel; who will do me good if not you? Have pity on me: I have come here to know the will of God; but I have no intelligence, and, if he speaks, I do not understand him. I am nothing; you are all-powerful: entreat your well-beloved son Jesus for me.' Then I addressed myself to the Saints whose relics are here, and the chief part of which gave me much trouble to bring up here from Kebec. I said to them: 'Great Saints, I do not know your names; nevertheless you cannot be ignorant of the fact that I have brought your relics to this country. Have pity on me; pray your master and mine, Jesus, for me.' Afterward, I remembered the pictures which are in this Chapel; and I prayed to the Saints who are depicted there, — especially saint Joseph, whose name I bear."

5. During the meditation on Paradise, he would not stop to consider everything beautiful that one can imagine to one's self in heaven. "My God," he said, "I do not desire to imagine the good things which you reserve after this life for those who serve you, for I have no sense. It is enough that you have said that we should be forever satisfied there; you know the means thereto better than all men can understand. If I fancied Paradise as a place where there are fine cabins,

handsome beaver skins, deer and bears to eat, I would not make you richer than men; there is nothing of all that, but there is much more than all that, since men and all their riches are nothing like yours. They tell me a thousand rare things and beauties of France, which I cannot understand, yet I believe it: why should I not be assured of the ineffable satisfactions that there are in heaven, although they surpass my thoughts? It is enough that you have said that we shall be forever contented there."

6. One day, they bring him a false piece of news, about the sickness of one of his nieces. "What though," he said, "my wife and my children were sick, I will not leave here till the eight days have expired. I console myself in the belief that God sees everything which takes place in my family; I am not the head of it, God is: if he will that all die, who can resist him? My presence would be useless to them now: I shall do more for them here, near God. The devil has done all he could to hinder me from beginning these exercises; he now tries to stop me from continuing them. Those who direct me will judge, better than I, whether I must go to assist those who are reported to me to be sick."

7. One night, among others, having awakened, he proceeded to pray and to consider the providence of God over the guidance of the life of men, — that we were at the disposal of God, just as the dogs which men feed are in their power: that — just as they, when they have a young dog that is turning out bad, kill him in order to obviate the harm that he might do, becoming larger — likewise God, foreseeing that a child will be bad if he become a man, anticipates him with death, by an effect of his goodness which men do not see. Just the same, although we give our dogs what suffices them for their food, they nevertheless eat what they find, and take it where they can. Thus, although God gives us sufficient for life, we are never satisfied; we beat our dogs on these occasions, although we love them: likewise, when we abuse God's favors, he chastises us, and yet he does not fail to love us; but those who serve him faithfully, God loves with more tenderness than a father loves his children.

8. He often said: "I do not longer fear death at all, and I would thank God if I saw myself at the end of my life, in the firm hope that I have, that I should go to heaven: in like manner, I no longer apprehend the death of any of my relatives, provided that they die in the grace of God. When a young woman who lives in her father-in-law's house is invited by her own father to come and spend some months in his house; if he is a rich and liberal man, the father-in-law rejoices in the thought that his daughter-in-law will be much at her ease. Likewise, if some one of our family died, I should have the thought that God, her father, had drawn her to his house: I should rejoice in the same, since she would be better off there than with me."

9. Often, when leaving prayer, he found no words to explain the feelings of his heart, and several times repeated, "taouskeheati iatacan," — "it is a strange thing, my brother." "Oh, how true it is," he added, "that men have no sense; I now begin to know God. Oh, why is he not known! what are men thinking of! and I who speak, — where was my sense? how can it be that one remains infidel: can one sin after that?" He frequently offered his blood and his life for the conversion of his fellow countrymen, and made a firm resolve not to lose

the opportunity to speak of God, and never to blush for professing what he was, — a Christian, even to death.

The days were too short for him, and he often asked whether he might not make a retreat several times a year. In a word, there is no barbarian heart, even in the greatest depth of barbarism, when God wills to take possession thereof. Jesus Christ has no less merited the thanks of the Savages of America than those of the most civilized peoples of Europe.

Since that time we have seen him grow perceptibly in that truly Christian spirit which was found in the primitive Church.

Reuben Gold Thwaites, ed., *The Jesuit Relations and Allied Documents,* 73 vols. Cleveland: Burrows Brothers Company, 1893–1901, 19: 137–49. Printed by permission.

39. Reverend Simon le Moyne, S.J., Describes the "Captive Church" of Hurons among the Iroquois, 1654

Between 1648 and 1653 the Iroquois Confederacy attacked the Hurons and demolished their homeland, including the Jesuit mission among them. When Father Simon le Moyne, S.J., visited the Iroquois capital of Onondaga in 1654 at the Confederacy's request, he found many Huron adoptees, captives, and slaves, including what the Jesuits called a "Captive Church" of a thousand or more baptized Catholics. These Hurons were eager to renew contact with the priests, and through their interest in Catholicism a missionary effort began among the Iroquois in what is now New York State.

On the 7th, a good Christian woman, Terese by name, a Huron captive, wishing to pour out her heart to me away from all noise and in quiet, invited me to go and see her in an outlying cabin where she dwelt. Oh, what sweet consolation to see so great faith in savage hearts, in Captivity, and with no help except that of heaven! God makes for himself Apostles everywhere. This good Christian had with her a young captive of the Neutral Nation, between fifteen and sixteen years old, whom she loved as her own daughter. She had instructed her so well in the mysteries of the faith and in sentiments of Piety, in the prayers that they repeated together in that holy solitude, that I was utterly surprised. "Well, my sister," I said to her, "why hast thou not baptized her, since she has as strong a faith as thou thyself, since she is a Christian in her morals, and since she wishes to die a Christian?" "Alas! my brother," that blessed captive made answer, "I did not think it was permitted me to baptize except in danger of death. Baptize her now thyself since thou dost deem her worthy, and give her my name." That was the first baptism of a grown person performed at Onnontagé, for which we are indebted to the Piety of a Huron woman. The joy which I experienced at this was sufficient to make me forget all my past fatigues. When God prepares a soul, the consummation of its salvation is soon accomplished.

Almost at the same time, I was summoned to a sick man who was reduced to a skeleton, — an ulcer, caused by an ill-dressed gunshot wound, eating away his flesh. I spoke to him about God, the hopes of an eternal life, and the truths of the faith. But alas! the words of heaven found no entrance to that heart, all swelled up as it was with pride; he was thinking only of the present life, and, although he showed me some affection, he could not conceive any for God.

The 8th. I baptize three little dying children, and give and receive consolation at seeing myself in the midst of a Church of trained Christians. Some come and confess, while others give me an account of all their sufferings, and, at the same time, of the blessing that remains to them that their Faith is not held captive in their captivity. They also esteem themselves happy in the knowledge that, when they offer their groans and tears to God, he beholds them; that his holy Providence has a mother's love for them; and that they will be free in heaven. I learn that several, who were cruelly put to death over a slow fire, consoled themselves, at the height of their agonies, with the sacred name of Jesus, which was both on their lips and in their hearts up to their last breath. I inquire after all our old acquaintances, in order to learn their fortunes; and I have reason to bless God at seeing that he is everywhere present, among the Iroquois as well as in the country of the Hurons. I had orders to ascertain what had become of a young Huron woman, a Christian, named Caterine Skouatenhré, whom we used to call "the Nun," because of her great piety and a modesty as exquisite as can be desired in a girl given wholly to God. Her sister told me that she had died while praying to God, having never forgotten him in the whole course of her illness, which had been long. Shortly before her death she said to her: "I am going to heaven, my sister, for Jesus is good and will show me mercy. As for thee, if thou desire to follow me, so that we may meet again in heaven, cherish thy faith more than life. Shun sin as thou wouldst death; and if, by mischance, thou fallest into it, remember that Jesus is good, ask his forgiveness, and tell him that thou wishest to love him." These last words have remained so deeply graven on the surviving sister's heart, that she cannot lose the remembrance of them. The good Soul could not see me often enough, in order to hear about God, and comfort herself, in my company, with hopes of Paradise....

The most touching part of all this to me is that all our Huron Christians, especially the Captive women, have kindled this fire which is burning in the hearts of the Iroquois. They have heard so much good about us, and have been told so often of the great blessings of the Faith, that, in spite of their ignorance of it, it commands their esteem; and they love us in the hope that we will become to them what we have been to the Hurons.

Reuben Gold Thwaites, ed., *The Jesuit Relations and Allied Documents*, 73 vols. Cleveland: Burrows Brothers Company, 1893–1901, 41: 103–7, 119. Printed by permission.

40. Reverend Joseph Marie Chaumonot, S.J., Describes a Pilgrimage to Sainte-Anne-de-Beaupré, 1671

Faith in Saint Anne, mother of the Virgin Mary, came to New France with the Norman and Breton émigrés. Because of her reported intercession during violent storms, the Frenchmen established a shrine for her beside the St. Lawrence River in 1658. She soon was reputed to cure diseases miraculously. A Huron named Marie Oendraka organized a pilgrimage to Sainte-Anne-de-Beaupré in

*1671, accompanied by Father Joseph Marie Chaumonot, S.J. Over sixty million
pilgrims have followed them there over the centuries, including thousands of
Indians from the United States and Canada, whose devotional lives have been
enriched by the experience.*

Viewing the external appearance of our poor Savages, no one would deem them
capable of these Christian deeds and practices, which are dictated purely by devotion, and performed under no constraint whatever. Yet what I am about to
relate shows very clearly that the Holy Ghost makes no distinction of persons,
but works indifferently in all hearts which he finds ready to receive his graces.
Last Spring a widow named Marie Oendraka recalled to my remembrance how
her late husband and a daughter of hers, who were very ill at the time, had made
a Pilgrimage together in a Canoe to [Saint] Anne, to obtain by the intercession
of that great Saint (whom it has pleased God to honor in this country by many
Miracles) either their health or a glorious death; and how, in consequence of
their devotion, they had both died a pious death soon afterward. Then she proposed to me her plan of undertaking a like Pilgrimage, if I approved of it, for the
purpose of paying her homage to her Benefactress; of testifying her gratitude to
her by a present of two thousand Porcelain beads (the jewels of this country);
and, most important of all, of asking her for the same favor for herself and all
her family. I gladly granted her what she wished. "But, my Father," she added, "I
pray you to sanction the offering of the present, which I desire to give to Saint
Anne, not under my own Name, but under that of the Huron Nation. Moreover, as we have our great Protectress, the Blessed Virgin, from Saint Anne, I
should be glad also if we could make this little offering in recognition of that
favor, which I esteem above all earthly treasures." "I give my hearty approval,"
I said to her, "and I will even join the party with the chief men of the Village,
to give this action greater solemnity." "Ah, my father," she rejoined, "since you
are so good, I would like to ask one more favor of you, — to put an inscription
under the present, making known, as a perpetual evidence of our gratitude, our
motives in giving this offering." I saw no harm in granting this request of hers
also. We embarked in fine weather in our bark Canoes, well attended, and accomplished our six leagues with the tide's help, praying and singing Hymns in
the native tongue to the honor of the blessed Virgin and her Holy Mother. We
arrived safely, and all performed their devotions, to the great edification of the
settlers of the place.

Reuben Gold Thwaites, ed., *The Jesuit Relations and Allied Documents,* 73 vols.
Cleveland: Burrows Brothers Company, 1893–1901, 54: 299–301. Printed by
permission.

41. Reverend Paul Ragueneau, S.J., Describes Huron Martyrdom, 1658

*The Iroquois wavered in their attitude toward the Huron Christians in their
midst, sometimes permitting them sacraments and other times killing them
when they professed their faith. As French policy toward the Iroquois alter-*

nated between alliance and warfare, the Huron Christians were accordingly either secure or endangered. In 1658 Father Paul Ragueneau, S.J., described the martyrdom of Dorothée and several other Huron Christians.

It is not merely at the present day that God's designs toward his elect are adorable, and that he finds his glory by ways which are wholly opposed to our own, whose motive principles will appear only in eternity. For, besides our Fathers who were all ready to be sacrificed as victims, but whom it was not God's will to consign to the flames, — although the Iroquois had already prepared their funeral pile, — the sentiments of the Converted Huron women were truly Christian at the death of their husbands and fathers, whose blood gushed forth upon them as well as upon us.

"Great God," exclaimed one, "mingle my blood with my husband's, and let them take my life to-day; never will they be able to take away the faith which I have in my heart."

"My God," cried another, "I firmly believe that you are the All-powerful, though I see your servants slaughtered by your enemies. You did not promise that our faith should exempt us from death; our hopes are for another life, and we must die on earth in order to live in Heaven."

As one of these stout-hearted women, named Dorothée, was being butchered with hatchets and knives at the entrance to the village of Onnontagué, seeing the tears of a little girl eight years old who had been at the Ursuline seminary, she said to her: "My daughter, weep not for my death, or for thy own; we shall to-day go to Heaven together, where God will have pity on us for all eternity. The Iroquois cannot rob us of this great blessing." Then she cried out, as she died, "JESUS, take pity on me!" And her daughter met her death by the knife immediately afterward, uttering the same words that her mother had used: "JESUS, take pity on me!"

Two others, on being burned at a slow fire, cried out from amid the flames that they were dying as Christians, and that they deemed themselves happy that God saw them in their torments and knew their hearts. "Yes," said one, "if our bodies were immortal, the Iroquois would render our sufferings immortal. As our souls cannot die, is it an incredible thing that God, who is nothing but goodness, should reward them for all eternity?"

These mothers embraced their children who had been cast into the flames, and the excess of all this barbarous cruelty could never separate them, — so true is it that the faith and the love of God are stronger than fire and death.

Reuben Gold Thwaites, ed., *The Jesuit Relations and Allied Documents,* 73 vols. Cleveland: Burrows Brothers Company, 1893–1901, 44: 167–69. Printed by permission.

42. Reverend Claude Dablon, S.J., Describes Daniel Garakontié, a Christian Onondaga, 1671–72

One of the most strategically important conversions among the Iroquois was that of Garakontié, who allied himself with the French, served as a negotiator between his people and the French, and thereby gained a reputation as a chief. After his baptism in Quebec in 1670 – taking the name of Daniel – he denounced the traditional religion of the Iroquois and helped form a Christian faction within his community. He died in the winter of 1677–78.

The other circumstance that must give much joy to all who desire to see God glorified in the conversion of these Peoples, is the constancy of their Chief, Daniel Garakontié, in his high opinion of the faith, and in his fidelity in everywhere making open profession of Christianity. He did this with all solemnity two years ago when, after being baptized at Quebec, he declared upon his return, in a public meeting, that he intended thenceforward to discharge no function of his Office except so far as it should be in conformity with God's commandments. This declaration he repeated in a more courageous manner in New Holland, before the Europeans who hold command in that country, and the chief men of all the five Iroquois Nations, who had been summoned for the purpose of concluding a peace with the Loup Nations. The Father informs us in his last letter that Garakontié showed a truly Christian courage, the past Winter, in an illness that brought him to death's door. His relatives and all the village, seeing themselves in danger of losing him, urged him with great importunity to permit, for the sake of being cured, the employment of the usual juggler's arts, which pass for remedies in that country. To this he made constant and strenuous resistance. Nevertheless, a superstitious ceremony was executed in his cabin, after the custom of the jugglers when they undertake to cure some ailment. The Father, hearing of it, felt some suspicion that it had received the sick man's consent. He went to visit him toward evening, and found with him all the elders, — who, believing his death to be near at hand, had come in a body to do him honor, and bid him a last Farewell. The sick man spoke first and said to him: "My Father, I was much distressed to-day on account of the ceremony which was performed, without my knowledge and out of my sight, at the other end of my cabin. 'Alas!' said I to myself, 'what will Teharonhiagannra'" — Father Millet's name — "'think and say of me? He will believe me to be a hypocrite and dissembler.' No, my Father, I have not changed my mind since my baptism, nor am I any longer the man to consent to such follies. I merely suffered myself to be scarified, and a little blood to be drawn from my head; but I do not think that I thereby offended God. I have too much spirit, Father, and have too solemnly promised God to keep his holy law all my life, to resume like a coward the old practices that I have renounced, and now once more renounce, with all my heart. No, my Father, I will never break my promise, even though my life should be at stake." The Father strengthened him in these good resolutions, which afforded the company great edification.

Subsequently our Neophyte, having recovered his health, went down to Mon-real as Ambassador from all the Iroquois Nations, to hold council with the Algonquin tribes known as the Outaouaks, — who held their rendezvous there for the arrangement of their affairs with one another, as well as for the sale of their furs. Now in this assembly of a hundred and fifty canoes, — that is, of more than five hundred Savages of various Nations, — in the presence of Monsieur de Courcelles, Governor of the country, for whom all these Tribes have a very marked veneration, Garakontié displayed his intelligence and good sense, and especially his Faith and zeal. For, after they had finished their negotiations, and ratified the treaty of peace by fresh protestations of friendship and an exchange of presents, he raised his voice to tell them that he had formerly been as they were, — ignorant of the true God, given to the worship of his dreams, and observing all their superstitious practices; but that now he was a Christian and was living a happy life, obeying God's commandments and hoping for a life eternal. He concluded his harangue by exhorting them, with his wonted eloquence, to imitate and follow him.

Such a speech, from the mouth of a Savage who thus frankly declares the feelings of his heart, often produces more effect upon these people's minds than the words of the most zealous Missionary, — as is shown by two very recent instances. This same Daniel Garakontié, says Father de Lamberville in his letter of September 23rd, "having, on his homeward journey, encountered a kinswoman of his who was mortally ill, sought me out, and asked me for some remedy for her. 'My brother,' said I to him, 'the sole remedy that can avail her in her present state is Baptism, to save her from hell. But she is utterly averse to receiving this Sacrament, being obstinately bent on dying like her Ancestors, whom she wishes to go and find in the so-called "land of souls." If thou hast a true affection for her, exert all thy efforts to render her more docile; but make haste, for she has only a little longer to live.' No sooner had I made this proposition to him" — these are the Father's words — "than that genuine Christian, who possesses no attribute of the Iroquois Savage but his birth and name, went to visit her; and wrought on her so admirably by his zeal that she was thereupon sufficiently instructed to receive holy Baptism — to the great satisfaction of all the family." The Father was still unable to gain access to another poor dying creature, for the purpose of speaking to her concerning her salvation, because she showed an intense aversion for such themes, as well as an incredible attachment to the native superstitions. In this difficulty, he had recourse to a woman who was a friend of that family; she was not yet a Catechumen, and did not even attend prayers, but she had some knowledge of our mysteries and was well-intentioned. She met with such success from the very first time when she spoke to the sick woman about becoming a Christian, and cleverly contrived to predispose the latter so favorably toward the Father, that he was made most welcome in her cabin, and she never refused him a hearing thereafter. Being then sufficiently instructed, she was baptized; and, soon after her Baptism, she died a very Christian death. "Thus it is" — says the Father in closing his letter — "that, in spite of intemperance, which reigns here to the greatest excess, and the other obstacles that hell is constantly opposing to the advancement of the faith, we are continually finding souls to win, and fruits of the Blood of Jesus Christ to gather."

Reuben Gold Thwaites, ed., *The Jesuit Relations and Allied Documents*, 73 vols. Cleveland: Burrows Brothers Company, 1893–1901, 56: 41–47. Printed by permission.

43. Remembrance of Kateri Tekakwitha, the Saintly Mohawk, by Reverend Pierre Cholenec, S.J., 1696

The most renowned of all Native American Catholics was Kateri Tekakwitha, baptized in 1676 in a Mohawk village. (Her mother was Algonkian, her father Mohawk; both died in a smallpox epidemic when she was a young girl.) She emigrated to the Jesuit reduction at Kahnawake in the St. Lawrence Valley near Montreal, where she joined the company of other Catholic Indians — mostly Iroquoians — under the leadership of Father Pierre Cholenec, S.J., and other Jesuits. Her intense devotionalism, her privations and penances, her renunci-ation of sexuality, her imitation of Christ, all made her legendary, especially after her death during Holy Week in 1680. Father Cholenec and his fellow priests celebrated her asceticism, even as it may have contributed to her death, and her life and death became central icons of the Jesuit missiology in North America.

Katharine sanctified her work by spiritual conferences. So holy a conversation, together with her zeal for the things of God, had the result that she always came away with new desires to give herself entirely to Him and to put into practice what she had just heard. She found God everywhere whether she was in church, in the woods or in the fields. Lest she live a moment that was not spent for Him, she might be observed coming and going with a rosary in her hand, which led her instructress to say that Katharine never lost sight of her God, but that she always walked in His presence. If rain or extreme cold prevented her from working, she passed almost all her time before the Blessed Sacrament, or she made small objects of mat work, but she did not spend her time visiting other girls in order to play or seek amusement, as those of her age are apt to do on similar occasions.

Weeks so well utilized were indeed weeks filled, that is to say, in the sense of the Holy Scriptures, with virtue and merit. Katharine nevertheless ended each week with a severe discussion in which she gave account to herself of all that had happened; then she had her sins taken away in the Sacrament of Penance, for she went to confession every Saturday evening. But she did so in an extraor-dinary manner, one that could have been inspired by the Holy Ghost alone, who Himself guided her, and who first had given her a love of suffering and, as we shall see later, a hatred of her body.

In order to prepare herself for these confessions, she began with the last part, I mean the penance. She would go into the woods and tear her shoulders open with large osiers. From there she went to the church and passed a long time weeping for her sins. She confessed them, interrupting her words with sighs and sobs, believing herself to be the greatest sinner alive, although she was of angelic innocence. Not only the desire to be always united with God, and not to be distracted by the people, made her love solitude so much and flee society, but also her desire to preserve herself in innocence, her horror of sin, and the fear of displeasing God.

First Communion

Thus lived Katharine from the autumn she arrived at the Sault until Christmas, and because she led such a fervent and exemplary life, she merited at this time a grace not granted to those who came from the Iroquois until several years later, and then only after having passed through many trials, so as to give them a high idea of it, and to oblige them to render themselves worthy by an irreproachable life. This rule did not hold for Katharine; she was too well disposed and desired with too great an eagerness to receive Our Lord, to be deprived of this great grace, so she was promised some time before the feast that she might receive Him on Christmas, after she had been instructed in the mystery.

She received the good news with all imaginable joy, and prepared herself for the great event with an increase of devotion suitable to the exalted idea she had of it. It must be admitted, however, that it was at this First Communion that all her fervor was renewed. The ground was so well prepared that only the approach of this divine fire was necessary, to receive all its warmth. She approached or rather surrendered herself to this furnace of sacred love that burns on our altars, and she came out of it so glowing with its divine fire that only Our Lord knew what passed between Himself and His dear spouse during her First Communion. All that we can say is that from that day forward she appeared different to us, because she remained so full of God and of love of Him.

All this will seem very surprising in a young Indian, but it will seem even more so when I add that, having afterwards had the happiness of receiving Holy Communion frequently, she always did so with the same disposition and fervor she had the first time, and undoubtedly she received the same love and manifold graces from Our Lord, who seeks only to visit us in this Sacrament of Love, and who puts no limits to His grace, when He comes in contact with hearts disposed to receive and profit by them, as was the case with Katharine. This fact, moreover, was so well known in the village that at the time of general Communion the most devout women hastened to place themselves near her in church, claiming that the mere sight of her exterior was so devotional and ardent at those times that her example inspired them and served as an excellent preparation for approaching the Holy Table in a proper manner.

A Winter at the Hunt

After Christmas it was time to go on the hunt. Katharine also went with her sister and her brother-in-law. This was a sister by adoption only, who had been in the same lodge with her among the Mohawks. It was neither the wish to divert herself nor the desire for feasting that made Katharine take part in the hunt (which is the reason most of the women go), but only to satisfy this good sister and her husband. God doubtlessly wished that she should sanctify herself in the woods as she had done in the village, to prove to all the savages, by the beautiful example she gave, that virtue may be practised equally in both these places. She continued the exercises of piety she had practised in the village, making up for those she could not do there by others that her devotion suggested to her. Her time was regulated as that of a Religious.

She prayed before dawn and finished her day with the common prayers according to the praiseworthy custom of our Indians, who say them together morning and evening, and although she said the former while the others were still asleep, she prolonged the latter until late into the night, while the others slept. After the morning prayers, while the men ate and made preparations for the all-day hunt, Katharine retired to solitude to pray again, approximately at the time that the Indians heard Mass at the mission. For this purpose she had erected a small shrine on the bank of a stream. It consisted of a cross she made from a tree. There she joined in spirit the people of the village, uniting her intentions to those of the priests and prayed to her Guardian Angel to be present there in her place and to bring her the fruits of the Holy Sacrifice.

When she thought the men had departed for the hunt, she returned to the cabin and occupied herself there all day long in the manner of the other women, gathering wood, fetching the meat of the animals that had been killed, or making necklaces in the cabin. During this latter occupation she always invited the others to sing some devotional hymns, or to recount incidents of the lives of the saints and narrations she had heard at church in sermons on Sundays and feast days. In order to encourage them, she was often the first to begin these discourses.

She had two purposes in this: first, to avoid bad conversation and frivolous talk, which only distract the spirit; secondly, to preserve constantly her fervor and union with God, which was as strong in the forest as if she had been at the foot of the altar in the village. It was for this reason that her principal occupation and the one she took the most pleasure in was to gather wood for the cabin, for being alone she could satisfy her devotion, talking intimately with her Divine Spouse; and her humility, in working for the others, by acting as the servant of the cabin; and her desire for suffering, by tiring her body with continued toil of a painful nature.

She found another means of penance by a more spiritual and secret exercise. She would fast while there was an abundance of good meat, for she would cleverly leave the cabin to gather wood before the sagamite was ready and would not return until evening. Even then she ate very little and afterwards spent part of the night in prayer in spite of her extreme fatigue and her natural weakness. If in the morning they made her take nourishment before going to work, she would secretly mix ashes with the sagamite to take away any pleasure she might have in eating it, and to leave her nothing but gall and bitterness instead. She also practised these mortifications in the village whenever she was able to do so without being observed.

She never became so attached to work, either in the woods or in the cabin, that she forgot her shrine. On the contrary, she took care to return there from time to time so as to satisfy the hunger of her soul while she subjected her body to a fast. She went there morning and evening and several times during the week. She ended her devotions by harsh chastisement which she administered to herself with rods, for she neither possessed suitable instruments nor did she know of their use, for she had undertaken this kind of penance in secret, and under the direction of the Holy Ghost alone.

Although Katharine's life in the woods was most praiseworthy, and even of great merit to herself, nevertheless she was not happy there, and it was easily seen by her bearing that she was not in her own element. The church, the Blessed Sacrament, the Masses, the Benedictions, the sermons, and other similar devotions in which she had taken so much pleasure in the short time she had been at the Sault, held a powerful charm, constantly drawing her towards the village, and claiming her heart and all its affections, so that if her body was in the forest, her spirit was at the Sault. Thus the sojourn in the woods, which generally is so agreeable to those of her sex because they think only of having a pleasant time, and amusing themselves, being far away from all household cares, soon began to be a burden to her, for which she felt a great aversion....

Katharine, having returned to the village, thought only of recovering the graces she had missed while in the woods. She recommended her visits to the church with her ordinary fervor and eagerness and joined her instructress again that she might profit by her pious exhortations during their work. Easter was drawing near; and those who were not far from the village, on the hunt, returned to the mission according to their custom, to celebrate the great day. It was the first time Katharine celebrated it with us for the great good of her soul. She assisted at all the services of Holy Week, and admired all these solemn ceremonies, receiving from them a new esteem for religion. She was so touched by sweetness and consolation that she shed many tears, especially on Good Friday during the sermon on the Passion of Our Lord. Her heart melted at the thought of the suffering of the Divine Savior; she thanked Him a thousand times for it, she adored and kissed His cross with feelings of the most tender gratefulness and the most ardent love. She attached herself to the cross that day with Him, taking the resolution to repeat on her virginal body the mortifications of Jesus Christ for the rest of her days, as if she had done nothing until then. On Easter Sunday she received Holy Communion for the second time, and did so with the same disposition and ardor and spiritual fruits she had on the feast of Christmas....

Reverend Pierre Cholenec, S.J., "The Life of Katharine Tegakoüita, First Iroquois Virgin" (1696), from the original manuscript kept in the Archives of the Hotel Dieu Monastery, Quebec: *The Positio of the Historical Section of the Sacred Congregation of Rites on the Introduction of the Cause for Beatification and Canonization and on the Virtues of the Servant of God Katharine Tekakwitha, the Lily of the Mohawks.* New York: Fordham University Press, 1940, 254–59, 262–63. Printed by permission.

44. Christian Daniel Claus, "Memorandum at Onondaga," 1750

Through the colonial wars for the North American empire the Iroquois stood between the Catholic French and the Protestant English. As late as the mid-1700s there were still Iroquois in New York with Catholic leanings, although in central New York Catholicism was steadily losing its hold. At Onondaga in 1750 a Catholic chief was observed in friendly debate with a Protestant compatriot regarding the relative merits of their respective faiths and their suspicions regarding the French Jesuits. Conrad Weiser, a noted translator, recorded the discussion; Christian Daniel Claus translated it into German, and here it has been rendered back into English.

One evening, two Indians had a dispute about religion; one professed the English [Anglican] the other the Roman Catholic. Mr. Weiser appended this dispute to his journal (and I later translated it into German). To wit:

Ganachquajéson, one of the Indian deputies, who was a protestant convert, had a discussion with one by the name of Jahaswuichdiuuny, with whom we stayed and [who professed] the Roman religion. He is now the most sublime or king. Jahaswuichdiuuny asked Ganachquajéson whether it was true that such and such an Indian (he named him) had quite desperately uttered, that he would have to go to hell after his death and live with the devils. Ganach. replied that the man had [indeed] said so but he had been very sick having had restiveness and great temptations to his soul in firmly insisting on his point of view and it had been lasting a good while but in the end he [the man] had become a bit doubtful.

Jahas. said: When [in spite of] being baptised you will have to go to hell, what good is your baptism? For he who is [baptised] by the two French priests, will never be damned. We ourselves should hold to our covenant of baptism but the Fathers report that they pray for us and after death get us out of hell with their prayers and then we have the choice to go either to the place where the French Fathers and the other good people move or where our forefathers went. The Fathers are able to obtain either for us.

Ganach: What you are telling me about prayer, the power and effect of your French Fathers and your choice to go where you want to after your death, is a misunderstanding. Your Fathers mislead you. It has been made known by the Creator of heaven and earth that after this life none but the good and pious people shall live with Him and the evildoers and godless, those who are without repentance and faith in Jesus Christ, will stay with the devils. There is no salvation for a bad [person]. Let your Fathers say what they want.

Jahas: Perhaps both our and your Fathers are right. As they are different in nation and language, they may have understood the Creator in a different way. Our Fathers tell us that they are able to talk to the blessed who really reside in heaven and learn everything from them; and your Fathers say that they have a book that was written by the Creator Himself. But our Fathers do not want to grant them that but say that they have the original of that book and yours have nothing but the copy, written by someone who did not even understand it correctly.

Ganach: The book about which we are speaking is the very same among all the nations and our Fathers have the same that yours have, which all admitted. There is no difference but that your Fathers say they can talk with the souls that reside in heaven. It is they that cause all the misfortune and error for they teach you lies, which run counter to the things that are written in that book by the Creator Himself; this is also the reason why your French Fathers do not want to let the common people have these books lest their fraud might be discovered.

Jahas: I admit that the French Fathers take us in at times. I once asked my Fathers, whether I would be forced to go to heaven where the Fathers and all the good people went or not? He told me no. I asked another one to search the heavens whether my grandfather was there and he promised to do that for me; he told me the other day that he had seen him there. Thereupon I held it up to him how he [my grandfather] had been able to get in there in spite of having hated the French Fathers and their religion like poison. He once had even caught a Father and taken him to Onondaga so that he [the Father] could be burnt to ashes alive; he [the grandfather] commanded his children and grandchildren to kill the French Fathers whenever they could get them into their power. Thereupon the French Father answered that he had perhaps mistaken the person and said he wanted to look once more; when I visited him a few days later, he reported to me that he had indeed made a mistake as the person whom he had taken to be my grandfather, had really been my father's grandfather; my grandfather was in hell. I told him he was a liar as I was certain that my great-grandfather had entered the blessed land where the Indian forefathers had gone after their death. And this is the place, Brother Ganachquajéson, where I also wish to go and nowhere else. We are being taken in by the white men in this world and if we do not pay attention, they will make us their slaves.

Ganach: Although I am unable to inform you thoroughly about the doctrine of our Father, I am much amused to hear from you that you would rather go to our forefathers than to the place where the French Fathers go.

Helga Doblin and William Starna, eds. and trans., *The Journals of Christian Daniel Claus and Conrad Weiser: A Journey to Onondaga, 1750.* Philadelphia: American Philosophical Society, 1994, 20–23. Printed by permission.

45. Reverend Michael K. Jacobs, S.J., to Bishop James J. Navagh, March 9, 1961

In 1755 Catholic Iroquois — mostly Mohawks — from Kahnawake formed a satellite community called St. Regis at Akwesasne, straddling the St. Lawrence River between what is now the United States and Canada. The difficulty of tending a parish that lay in three bishoprics (Ogdensburg in the United States, Valleyfield and Alexandria-Cornwall in Canada) was compounded when non-Indians settled all around the reservation and, at the same time, a traditionalist religious movement arose among the Indians, which made them critical of white culture, including Catholicism. Father Michael Karhaienton Jacobs, S.J., a Mohawk from Kahnawake, served as resident priest at St. Regis from 1936 almost until his death in 1988. In 1961 he wrote to his bishop in Ogdensburg, bemoaning the travails of pastoring the St. Regis Mohawks.

[Excellency],

I want to thank your Excellency for your kindness and great patience in receiving me last Wednesday, March 8th, to discuss once more on the spiritual interests of the Indians of Saint Regis, Hogansburg, New York.

The problem of the assistance at Mass on Sundays, is a serious matter and we both want that our Saint Regis Indians be more fervent and attend Mass, every Sunday if possible.

I — Let me put down, by writing, the possible reasons, why, I think, they miss Mass so easily. I am not looking for excuses, but we must try to understand, their mentality, their character, their way of thinking, as *Indians,* and relatively recent converts to Christianity.

The sound principles of Christianity, belief in the Article of Faith, [the] seven Sacraments — all these truths, they believe and they accept and practise, I hope, enough to be saved....

Concerning [Sunday] Mass, frequent reception of the Sacraments, supporting the Church, Catholic education, Church societies, working for the Church, they haven't got it.

Reasons?

1. For two centuries, as Government Wards, supported by the Federal Government, they have given nothing and they have received everything: they expect to be supported; they say: "The White Man has taken their lands — the Government must help us — give us money, pay for our bills, — *no taxes.* ... And the Government does pay their bills: Doctors' fees, [medicine], hospital, education of children and with many, federal aid for food, clothing and other necessities.

They are used to get everything free and with many, they intend to remain, as such. If they can get it who can blame them?... After all, the White Man has taken their lands.... That is how they reason....

2. Now transfer that mentality to the Church. The Church had to treat the Indians as minors, unable to give anything to the Church. But in the minds of many of the Indians, they expect everything free from the Church. Insist that they give their share to the support of the Church and they will simply stop going to Church. They want everything free... and even with no work they expect to go to heaven.

All their lives: No sacraments... no Sunday Mass, no Commandments, no support of the Church, but at the end of their lives, they do expect the Church, *its priests,* to give them the last Sacraments and thus, perhaps they can get to heaven some day....

Against such back-ground, we will perhaps understand, somewhat, the thickness of their skull, their stubbornness, their resistance to civilization, their opposition to the White Man and their present attitude of *"Nationalism"* their somewhat *"Neo-paganism".*...

Only the Catholic Church has succeeded in transforming the mentality of our Catholic North American Indians.

Only God and His grace, His Infinite Patience and Mercy, His Predilection for sinners and, I am sure, His Infinite Love for All Races and in particular for the Red Race, the Indians of North America, that we can boast of the Saint Regis Catholic Mission, still existing, since its foundation, over 200 hundred years ago, in [1752] — the oldest Catholic Church, in the Diocese, after that of "La Conception" Father Picquet's Church of Ogdensburg, in the midst of 1750's.

We have come a long way since, — and we still have to work hard, with *much patience* and *humility* before we can say that our Indians of Saint Regis Mission are equal in Faith, religious Convictions and fervor, like the Irish and the French-Canadians, who have embraced the Faith many, many centuries before the Indians of North America did.

II — How can we solve the Problem?

What problem?

1. Assistance at Mass, on Sundays...

2. Support of the Church (la Dime: the Tenth of earnings)

3. Catholic Education: first, parochial school to 6th. Grade, in Hogansburg, N.Y., and then High School, in Massena, N.Y.

1) The older generation: we cannot change their mentality....

2) The young generation: we can educate them, in Catholic Schools — good education — strong religious convictions — training of character forming good habits of receiving the Sacraments, — Mass, on Sundays.... The future of the Catholic Church in the St. Regis Reservation is in the Catholic Parochial School....

1. The Assistance at Mass on Sundays:

The Masses, on Sundays, in the Saint Regis Church, are as follows:

a) 7:00–Low Mass: it is a convenient time for some, even for the Irish, from Hogansburg. (I have some who come regularly to this Mass.) It shows that the White Man is welcome to our Church — like the Indian should be welcome in St. Patrick's Church.

I do not believe in *segregation,* and to break that attitude, we must start, at home — we are Catholics and we *must practise true* Christian Charity, *love of neighbor.* An Indian should be taught to go to Church — In Fort-Covington, Bombay, and Hogansburg, as well. The Indian saying: "*We are not wanted*" *must be destroyed....* If we do not teach them that they can go to Mass, in these churches, then when they live abroad, in Syracuse, Rochester or Buffalo, they will not go to Mass there either; because "They will feel that they are not wanted."

Here, Excellency, I know that I am going against your opinion; but I am sure you will try to understand me, like you try to understand those who have gone to see you, in delegation some time ago.

If we want our Indians to go to Mass, on Sundays, when they are away from the Reservation — then we must teach them, that they can go to Mass in Hogansburg, on Sundays, "if they *prefer* to do so."

Because:

a) It is the nearest church....

b) and because they don't have to report to the Customs (as some complain) — This is just a *pretext.*

c) [because] those who complain of St. Regis Church are all *English-speaking Indians*...they should go to Hogansburg, it's the closest church....

To me, I hope His Excellency will forgive me:

The Indians who complain of the distance and hardship of going to Church in Saint Regis — they are hypocrites, two-faced people, envious and jealous and victims of the illusions of the devil; they are protestants in mentality, they want to run the Church, they want to be Church trustees; it's what they can get out of the Church, is their aim; and not what they *do* and *give* to the *Church.* . . . Excellency, it is the Indian in me . . . I have struggled against that protestant and pagan mentality for the last 23 years. My zeal is sincere: I want the good of the souls, God's Greater Glory — Am I not the minister of the Good Shepherd? My Master did not teach me to sacrifice my life to preserve the lives of His sheep? . . .

Have two National Churches for the Indians, within two miles of each other: it is dividing their forces — it will weaken their strength — *even their Faith* and they will become an easy prey to the ravenous wolves: The Mormons, The Witnesses of Jehovah, The Seventh Day Adventists, the Pagan Indians, Long House, Mad-Bear Anderson and their gang of pagan Indians.

I do not believe in two Churches for the Indians of Saint Regis — If the Irish are good Catholics, as they should, then let them open the doors of the Saint Patrick Church and allow with Christian Charity, and brotherly love, the Indians to attend Mass, in Hogansburg, if that is what some Indians want: let them have it....

But, I assure His Excellency, that it is *only* a small number of Indians who want a Church in Hogansburg. The majority, (if not all), are perfectly *happy* and satisfied to come to Church in Saint Regis, like their forefathers did.

In Saint Regis they can go to Confession in Indian, pray in Indian with the Congregation they can sing or hear the High Mass, sung in Indian — hear the sermon in Indian.

They have all the advantages: no church to build, nor pay its debts — no special [contribution] of 100 or 200 dollars a year that they will never give; only one collection at all the Masses, no envelopes, no tithings to give to the Church yearly.

If ever I mentioned these things to them: the idea of a new Church — debts and dues to pay — they would go on a Warpath — (and, I pity the victims....)

But, above all, there will be *even less people,* going to Mass on Sundays. — They will say for sure — "All what the priest wants is money, money...." — "It's too expensive to be a Catholic[.]" — Besides the other denominations offer money to the Indians to go to their meetings.... And we can guess the results....

I am sorry to annoy Your Excellency, and I must continue where I left off:

Three Masses on Sundays:
1) 7:00 and 8:30 a.m. low Masses
2) 10:30 a.m. High Mass.

If Your Excellency desires a fourth Mass: we can have it, either in Saint Patrick's Church, Hogansburg; or Saint Regis Church–Quebec. Sunday evenings at 8:00 P.M.

Father Albert Burns, S.J., my Assistant, and myself will alternate and both of us binate, every Sunday. I await Your Excellency's wishes and we will comply.

We will do everything possible to increase the assistance at Mass, on Sundays.

It is *not a question of distances* — ... it is a question of *good will... convictions, generosity* and *perseverance* on the part of the Indians.

Your Excellency can help us by his prayers, merits and credit before the throne of God. I pray, do penance, fast and humble myself. I am subjected to humiliations, hardships, opprobriums, and alone, I cannot do much — but with your help, Bishop, with your prayers and God's grace, His Infinite Mercy, I hope to convert my Indians to a more fervent Christian life.

Sunday after Sunday, I say to my people:
a) pray every day;
b) Mass, every Sunday,
c) receive the Sacraments every month.

Bishop, please help me and help our Saint Regis Indians, by your prayers and your merits.

2. Support of the Church — "la dime" or tithings to give to the Parish, yearly.

Excellency it will take very long before we can change [the] mentality of the Indians.
a) When I first came here, Sunday collections amounted: $2.50. Our predecessor got $120. a year; now we receive $3,500. a [year].
b) [T]he Parish visits: they gave in food: potatoes, corn, preserves and one Indian said to me: the priest said: "One cent per person:" we are three in the family and he said I give you more, and he handed me five pennies:
c) Now [they] give $2.00 per family —
d) Moreover, the American Indians are unable, (because they don't want to give) to give 50 percent, their share in the Church fuel expenses: It costs the Church and Rectory $1300. — I worked hard for six weeks before Christmas, with Raffles and Bingos and Church Organization to make $435.; I was $200. short of the goal.
e) This year nobody gave anything towards Church insurance $313.35, because I collected $435. and they think it will take care of everything. Without the support of the Bishops of Ogdensburg and Valleyfield. Valleyfield gives $400. a year; Ogdensburg gives $1200. a year; the two Missionaries of Saint Regis would have a tough time to live, with-

out these grants. Life is already, hard enough, in Saint Regis, why build another Church? It would be financially and humanly too hard, impossible.

3. The answer to our problem?

A parochial School, in Hogansburg from Grade 1 to 6th inclusively, with Sisters to teach our children: It is building for future generations:

    a) Our children from the age of six will receive a Catholic education; Religion will be taught thoroughly; Frequent Confessions and weekly Mass, on Friday at 11:00 A.M. with Communion; —

    b) And more important: Sunday Morning Mass: Children's Mass at 9 o'clock — where the parents can bring their children to Mass in the auditorium of the Parochial School —

To me, *this is the solution*

It is *feasible* and *practical:* —

First: we have the [property] three to four acres of land: We have the Residence or Convent for the Sisters; Ideal location for a school: Six-class rooms-Cafeteria (a must for pupils), an auditorium or recreation-hall, — this auditorium will be used for weekly Mass on Fridays, at eleven o'clock, *Children's Mass,* on *Sundays* at 9 or 10 o'clock — Parish organizations, like parties, dinners, bingos, raffles to raise funds to contribute to pay expenses of the up-keep of the school-teachers' salaries, etc....

I warn, His Excellency, that the Indians will pay perhaps one-third of these expenses; the rest two-thirds will have to come from the Bishop (perhaps from the Negro and Indian Collections[)].

It is an enormous project, very expensive and only His Excellency can assume the grave responsibility. On the other hand, it means salvation of souls — Catholic education for Indians, preservation of faith and Greater Glory of God.

I beg His Excellency to accept the Challenge and I repeat as in my previous letter, you will build a great monument to the survival of the Indians, their Race and their Faith.

                Your humble and obedient servant in Jesus Christ,

                      Michael K. Jacobs, S.J.

46. Reverend François le Mercier, S.J., Describes the Anishinabe Encounter with Catholicism, 1668

By the 1660s the French Jesuits had progressed westward by paddling and portaging to the crucial junction of Lakes Superior and Huron, the rapids they called Sault Ste. Marie. The Indians of that area called themselves Anishinabe — now known as the Ojibwas. They and their close linguistic relatives of the Great

Lakes region, the Menominees, Ottawas, and Potawatomis, received the missionaries, whose efforts at evangelism progressed by stops and starts. For each baptism there was doubt regarding the motive of the Native recipient.

As Pointe du [Saint] Esprit has been hitherto the seat of all those upper Missions, I am going to begin to relate the progress of the Gospel, and the establishment of the Kingdom of God, in that place; but at the same time I must not fail to mention the great obstacles that are encountered there.

Dissimulation, which is natural to those Savages, and a certain spirit of acquiescence, in which the children in that country are brought up, make them assent to all that is told them; and prevent them from ever showing any opposition to the sentiments of others, even though they may know that what is said to them is not true. To this dissimulation must be added stubbornness and obstinacy in following entirely their own thoughts and wishes; this has obliged our Fathers not to admit adults so easily to Baptism, — they being, moreover, brought up in idolatry and licentiousness.

"But finally," says Father [Allouez] in his Journal, and in one of his letters written at the Sault on the 6th of June, 1669, "God caused me to know, after several trials, that it pleased his Divine Majesty to show pity to one nation in particular that desires, every member of it, to embrace the Christian Faith. It is one of the most populous; it is peaceful, and an enemy to warfare, and it is called the Queuës coupées; but it is, besides, so addicted to raillery that it had, up to that time, made child's play of our Faith." This people gained their first acquaintance with the Gospel in their own country, by the great Lake Huron, at the time when our Fathers were there; and they afterward received instruction from the late Father Menard, in the place where they are now. Finally, during the two or three years that Father [Allouez] spent with them, they continued to receive instruction constantly, without embracing the Faith, — until last Summer, when the Elders made speeches in its favor in their Cabins, in their Councils, and at their feasts.

"That was what obliged me," says Father [Allouez], "to pass the Winter with them at Pointe du [Saint] Esprit, for the purpose of instructing them. In the beginning of the season, having been called to one of their Councils, I let them know the news that two Frenchmen had just brought me; and told them that at length I felt myself obliged to leave them, in order to go to the Sault, because, after my three years among them, they were unwilling to embrace our holy Faith, — there being only children, and some women, who prayed to God. I added that I should leave that place immediately, and that I was going to shake the dust from my shoes; indeed, I took my shoes off in their presence, in proof that I was leaving them altogether, and did not wish to take anything from them away with me, not even the dust that clung to my shoes. I informed them that the Savages at the Sault, wishing to become Christians, had called me, and that I would go to them and instruct them; but that if, after some years, they did not become Christians, I would do the same thing to those at the Sault that I was doing to these now.

"During all this address I read, on their faces, the fear that I had inspired in their hearts; leaving them then to deliberate, I immediately withdrew, with the intention of going away to the Sault. But an accident having detained me, by a special providence of God, I was soon a witness to a change on their part that can only be attributed to an extraordinary stroke of grace. By common consent, they abolished Polygamy entirely; they did away with the sacrifices that they had been accustomed to offer to their genii; they refused to be present at any of the superstitious ceremonies observed by the other nations in the vicinity; in a word, they showed a fervor like that of the Christians of the primitive Church, and a very great assiduity in all the duties of true Believers. They all took up their abode near the Chapel, in order to facilitate for their wives and children, during the Winter, the instruction that is given them, and in order not to let slip a single day without coming to pray to God in the Church."

Such, in general, is the state of the Mission at Pointe du [Saint] Esprit. I am going now to describe in detail some of the most remarkable conversions. An old man who died on Christmas day, after preparing himself for death, shall head the list.

The Savages told Father [Allouez] that, after his Baptism, he had had a vision of two roads, one of which led upward, and the other downward; and that, according to his own account of the matter, he had taken the former, but that he had had much trouble in following it, as it was very narrow and difficult. They added that he had seen the downward road as very wide, and well-trodden, like that which leads from one Village to another. I cannot pass in silence the Baptism of the first adult of that nation. As he was their Captain, and a man of excellent understanding, well fitted for Christianity, he was the first to make a speech in favor of the Christian Religion, and to say publicly that the doctrines that were preached to them were true, and that, for his part, he was resolved to obey the Father. His name was Kekakoung. That holy freedom in speaking for the Faith gave the impulse, as it were, to all their minds, and inclined them to submit to the Gospel.

One man sixty years of age did not have very much trouble in becoming a Christian: he assured the Father that all his life long he had acknowledged a great Spirit who included in himself Heaven and Earth; that he had always invoked him in his sacrifices; and that he had received help from him in pressing need. The man was given the name of Joseph at his Baptism.

The example of another old man confirms the same thing. He relates, with deep feelings of gratitude toward this sovereign Spirit who saved his life, that, when they left their own country, they were obliged to take flight on the ice of the great Lake of the Hurons, in order to escape the Iroquois and the famine that pursued them everywhere. They had no provisions, and maintained their families only on the fish that they harpooned each day under the ice. Now it happened that sixty of their men, who had gone out to seek the means of subsistence, were carried away by a great field of ice that was detached by the violence of the wind. More than half died, either from cold or from hunger. This old man was preserved on that floating ice for the space of thirty days, and at length leaped upon another piece of ice, and thence to the land, — being unable to render sufficient thanks to that Spirit, more powerful than hunger, cold, ice, winds, and tempests, to whom he had directed his prayer.

When he heard about God for the first time, he recognized at once that he was that mighty Spirit who had saved him, and he resolved from that moment to obey him in all things.

Finally, Father [Allouez] observes, in his Journal, of another man of the same age, that he could not marvel enough that he had lived so long with no knowledge of the true God; and that he had often said to him during his instruction: "Is it possible that we old men, who have a little sense, have been so long blind; and that we have taken for divinities things that serve every day for our use?" A hundred persons of that nation, partly adults, partly Children, have already received Baptism. As to the Hurons who took refuge in that country, thirty-eight have been baptized. In the other nations are counted over a hundred persons more, to whom Baptism has been given.

An unmarried woman, forty-four years of age, who had shown constancy and a singular affection toward our holy Faith, was at length baptized. The continual temptations to which she was exposed, and the persecutions that she suffered on account of her beauty, made one fear at first to give her Baptism; but her noble spirit gained the day, and she declares openly that she will never marry.

She was confirmed in this resolution by what she had once heard Father [Allouez] say in regard to the Virginity of the blessed Virgin, and the vow of chastity taken by Nuns; and she went back to her own country with this holy purpose, in which she will have the Holy Ghost as her sole director until it shall please God to send some Missionary thither.

Father Marquette writes us from the Sault that the harvest there is very abundant, and that it only rests with the Missionaries to baptize the entire population, to the number of two thousand. Thus far, however, our Fathers have not dared to trust those people, who are too acquiescent, and fearing lest they will, after their Baptism, cling to their customary superstitions. Especial attention is given to instructing them, and to baptizing the dying, who are a surer harvest.

Reuben Gold Thwaites, ed., *The Jesuit Relations and Allied Documents,* 73 vols. Cleveland: Burrows Brothers Company, 1893–1901, 52: 203–13. Printed by permission.

47. Reverend Dablon, "Of the State of Christianity at the Mission of Saint Marie du Sault," 1670

Father Claude Dablon, S.J., found the nomadic ways of the Anishinabe an obstacle to conversion. Even more difficult to overcome was the deeply entrenched Native religion, inculcated through totemic associations and vision quests, which made the spirits a personally felt presence among the Indians from their earliest days.

The nomadic life led by the greater part of the Savages of these Countries lengthens the process of their conversion, and leaves them only a very little time for receiving the instruction that we give them.

To render them more stationary, we have fixed our abode here, where we cause the soil to be tilled, in order to induce them by our example to do the same; and in this several have already begun to imitate us.

Moreover, we have had a Chapel erected, and have taken care to adorn it, going farther in this than one would dare promise himself in a Country so destitute of all things. We there administer Baptism to children as well as Adults, with all the ceremonies of the Church; and admonish the new Christians during the holy Sacrifice of the Mass. The old men attend on certain days to hear the word of God, and the children gather there every day to learn the Prayers and the Catechism.

The assiduity shown by them, joined to their docility, would have already much increased the size of that Church, if the Devil did not hold them, as if enchained, by the most detestable of all the customs existing among the Savages. This has already been touched upon in the preceding Relation, and we shall discover more and more its pernicious effects.

It consists in each one's making for himself, in his early years, a God which he reverences then for the rest of his days, with superstitious and ridiculous veneration. It is this which they believe to be the sole author of their good fortune in all their enterprises of war, fishing, and hunting; and so they wear its ineffaceable hieroglyphic, — marking on their skin, as with the graver, the representations of the Divinities that they have chosen.

Now this is the way in which they create the Divinity. When a child has reached the age of ten or twelve years, his father gives him a lesson, imparting to him the necessary instructions for finding out what will be his God thenceforth.

First, he has him fast for several days, in order that, with his head empty, he may the more easily dream during his sleep; for it is then that this fancied God is bound to reveal himself to him, so that the sole object of all their ingenuity and all their exertions is to see in their sleep something extraordinary, which then takes for them the place of a Divinity.

Accordingly, when morning has come, the father questions his son, very seriously and with great secrecy, on all that has occurred during the night. If nothing has appeared to him, the fast must be begun again, and followed up until finally something is formed in the empty brain that represents to him either the Sun, or Thunder, or something else about which he has often been talked to; and, immediately upon awaking, he tells the good news to his father, who confirms the image in his thoughts. Consequently, after he has been brought up from infancy in this belief and has continued all his life to honor this God of his imagination with divers sacrifices and many feasts which are held in his honor, it is almost impossible to free his mind of this cursed superstition when he has grown old in it, or even passed some years.

At first we believed that it was only the young boys who were brought up in these stupid notions; but we have since learned that the little girls also are made to fast for the same purpose; and we find no persons more attached to these silly customs, or more obstinate in clinging to this error, than the old women, who will not even lend an ear to our instructions.

Despite these obstacles and many others, which the Devil raises up to check the course of the Gospel, in the two years since the beginning of this Mission we have baptized here more than three hundred persons, of all ages, from the earliest infancy up to extreme old age.

One of the first fruits of this year was an Old man of seventy, who died after the Baptism which Father [Allouez] conferred upon him on the road. Last Summer, during his journey up hither, the Devil, who regarded the old man as a victim that had been assured him for a long time, forgot no expedient to prevent this move, so managing matters that, two days before his death, — the very day appointed for his Baptism, — the Canoe which bore the Father went astray in the Lake of the Nipissiriniens. But we have reason to believe that this dying man's Guardian Angel assumed the guidance of the Missionary during the night, and conducted him safely through the darkness to the rendezvous of the others, where this good Catechumen was baptized. The Father — who was passionately determined not to give up hope for his patient, in order that he might help him in the last struggles — was sorely afflicted when he saw, on the morning after losing his way, that his Canoe, by some misfortune or other, was separated from the body of the rest; and he could not join them either during the day or during the following night, and was even almost in utter despair when, by an un-hoped-for piece of good fortune, he notwithstanding reached the entrance to Lake Huron, very late. There he found his sick man, — in the death-agony, but with his reason still unimpaired; and after he had been prepared by all the Observances necessary in his critical condition, he died a Christian death on that night, leaving us very evident signs of an altogether special providence acting for his salvation. We have every reason to believe that God showed him this mercy as a reward for the great services that he rendered these Missions, even when he was still a Pagan, at the time when the same Father [Allouez] came up to these Countries for the first time. All the other Savages forsaking the Father, and being unwilling to take him in their Canoes, this man alone, against the will of all the others, procured his passage; and by this means he has been, in some sort, the cause of all the blessings that have since been enjoyed by these Missions. And it was the will of Providence that, on the very route on which he had rendered this service, he received holy Baptism from the same Father whom he had so courageously assisted.

Among a number of young children whom we baptized, four girls of the same family gave evidence of the strength and courage that the Grace of Baptism imparts. For, after they had received it in our Chapel, when they had returned to their Cabin and were openly glorying in the fact that they were Christians, an old woman who was strongly attached to her superstitions, rudely scolded them, — telling them, among other things, that Baptism was invented only to cause death, and that they must fully expect to die soon. "Very well," they replied, "we will die, but we will die Christians, and will sooner have our souls torn from our bodies than the Faith from our hearts."

Ought not that noble spirit to touch the most hardened and the most barbarous? Perhaps it is God's will to touch them still by an incident which appears extraordinary enough here. A short time after our arrival we had baptized two twin children, one of whom died a few days later; and, because we had not yet any Cemetery, the relatives suspended this little body in the air, after their usual custom, placing it on a scaffold, and then retired into the Forests to pass the winter. A pack of Wolves, pressed with hunger, coming out of the woods, pounced upon this little body; but they, — after they had devoured the skins and even the colored glass beads with which it was covered, — through a protecting influence that was altogether marvelous, did not touch at all the body itself, as being a thing consecrated by holy Baptism.

We shall see what effect this will have on the minds of these poor Infidels. We ought to hope for much, especially from the great number of innocent souls, the souls of so many children who died after Baptism, and who, without doubt, present themselves immediately before God's Throne, to ask for the conversion of their relatives and the people of their country.

Reuben Gold Thwaites, ed., *The Jesuit Relations and Allied Documents,* 73 vols. Cleveland: Burrows Brothers Company, 1893–1901, 54: 139–47. Printed by permission.

48. Reverend Dablon Describes Diseases and Baptisms among the Anishinabe, 1671

Father Dablon found success in baptizing the Anishinabe during times of disease. Some sought miraculous cures thought to be effected by the christening waters; others gave themselves over to the Jesuits' God in order to gain heavenly reward at their deathbed. Whole villages dedicated themselves to Jesus and individuals ceased the practice of polygamy.

... God himself may be said to have stretched forth his hand to draw these peoples to him, — in the same way, relatively speaking, that he made his Apostles labor for the conversion of the Pagans, by the miraculous cures which he wrought through them.

Father Gabriel [Druillettes], one of the oldest Missionaries in Canada, where he has been engaged in converting the Savages for more than twenty years, fortunately came to our succor. No sooner had he landed here than a grievous disease broke out among the greater part of our Savages; yet, instead of checking the course of the Gospel, it, on the contrary, brought it into great repute by many wonderful cures. This made such an impression on these peoples' minds that, by the grace of our Lord, they declared themselves openly for the faith; and all the elders have publicly promised to embrace it when they are sufficiently instructed.

It will be well to relate here some of these cures, in order to thank God for them, since he does not disdain to show his mercy to these poor Barbarians.

One of the chief men — Apican by name — of the Nation known as the people of the Sault, being troubled with a severe inflammation of the throat, accompanied by much vomiting of blood, — which he had been throwing up for two days, without being able to eat or sleep, so tormented was he by this cynanche, — was exhorted by Father Gabriel to have recourse to God. No sooner had he done so than he found himself instantaneously freed from his sufferings, and able to come to Church and thank our Lord. "Prayer alone," said he, "without any medicine, has cured me. The thing is done; I pray now, and I am determined to be a Christian." His wife, two of his children, and some of his grandsons also, on being seized with the prevailing disease, visited the Chapel only twice before they were cured.

A good old woman more than eighty years of age, summoning the Father, said to him as soon as he entered her Cabin: "It is all over with me, I am a dead woman; for, besides my old age, I am being killed by a severe pain in my loins, and a burning heat that is consuming my whole body. To-morrow I shall be no longer living." The Father instructed her, inspired her with trust in God and the Blessed Virgin, and, after causing her to make the sign of the Cross, left her. No sooner had he gone out than she fell asleep, and, on awaking, she had neither fever nor pain in the loins; and in the morning, when she had expected to be borne to her grave, she had strength enough to visit the most distant Cabins, and tell her relatives of her very sudden cure, inviting them to accompany her to the Chapel to thank God therefor[e]. Thither, in fact, she went attended by her nearest kinsfolk, — who, as well as herself, were under obligations to return thanks to our Lord. Among them were her daughter, who, the very first time the Father made her pray, was cured of a grievous fever and a paralysis of both arms; her son-in-law, who had often been cured, at the Church door, of fever and other ailments; and her granddaughter of five or six, who, the first time she was carried to the Chapel, was cured of a bloody flux from which she had long been suffering. Now it was a beautiful sight to see that good old woman, with her relatives, prostrate on the Church floor, lifting hands and eyes to Heaven, and offering this short prayer: "You, O great God, by the power of the Faith alone, have driven death from my home, and I am under a remarkable obligation to you; but as my age, so advanced as it is, does not admit of my long reaping the fruits of that favor, my children are much more indebted to you than I, since you have renewed their life and enabled them, for a long time to come, to enjoy the blessing that you have bestowed upon them."

Another woman was immediately cured of a swollen leg; and soon after, being in danger of dying in childbed, "Jesus," she cried, "you who cured me of the disease in my leg, and who did so love children, take pity on a mother and her offspring. I am dying, and my boy with me." She did not die, nor did her boy; her faith was too great.

A girl was suffering such violent attacks of fever that she had lost hearing and speech in consequence; her mother brought this deaf-mute to the Church, and carried her back to her cabin in perfect health.

Another woman did not need to come to the Chapel to be cured of diseases of several kinds with which she was afflicted at the same time. She prayed in her cabin, and on that very night all her ailments were dispelled.

A child had lost the use of one eye; and, as soon as the Father had made him pray to God, he could see with it as well as with the other.

The most common malady was the bloody flux, which spread through the whole Village, so infecting the atmosphere that even all the dogs were going mad with it, and dying. Meanwhile God preserved all those poor Savages who had recourse to him in prayer; but to enumerate them would be wearisome.

We must not, however, omit to say that these signs of favor were not confined to the people of the country, but were also shown to strangers passing this way.

A young Kilistinon, seized at Montreal with an ailment which, during the past year, swept off many Savages, was in a very feeble condition. Upon arriving here from the other side of the river, he was so low, jaundice having spread over his whole body, that he had been unable to eat a mouthful for three days; and was even left without power to move, as if he were already dead. The Jugglers had striven to cure him, using all their diabolical superstitious practices, but to no purpose. The Father went to see him in the afternoon, instructed him, and made him pray and promise to become a Christian. No sooner had he thus pledged himself than he suddenly felt new life in his whole body, and on the very next day he crossed the river to come and offer his thanksgivings in the chapel. The other Kilistinons, learning how their compatriot, at death's door though he was, had so easily escaped death, and had already embarked to continue his journey, came in crowds to the Church, and pressed the Father for instruction, offering their children for Holy Baptism. "Do not cry," they said to them when the children moaned in their sickness; "do not cry, Baptism is going to cure you."

A young man of twenty-two years, belonging to the Monsounic nation, arrived here at the same time, more dead than alive, and on the point of expiring, owing to the attacks of a fever so violent, and a chill so difficult to overcome, that he did not feel the fire applied to him, even though it burned him. The Jugglers had employed their songs and superstitious ceremonies without stint to cure him, in spite of which he continued to sink constantly, and was in a critical state when the Father visited him. After instructing him, he left him in a much better condition. His relatives, to complete his cure, recalled the same Jugglers; but their superstitious performances produced no effect except to reduce him to a worse state than before. This poor young man, recognizing the offense that he had committed in letting those wretched Jugglers perform over him, was yet unable to have recourse to the Father, because the latter had taken his departure by boat; but turning to God, he begged his forgiveness, and was immediately cured. Thereupon his uncle, one of the most noted Jugglers of the country, having retraced his steps and returned to the spot, declared aloud, in the presence of a large body of Savages, that his nephew publicly asserted that he had been cured by prayer, which the Father had taught him.

Another young man of another Nation, who had suffered for four days from a retention of urine, had no sooner prayed to God than he was freed from it; and he came to the Chapel to offer his thanksgivings.

God made use of these very uncommon cures, and of many more like them, to touch our Savages' hearts; in consequence of which, on the eleventh of October, 1670, all the principal elders of the country repaired to the Chapel in a body, and made a public declaration before all the people that at length the Sault was Christian, and that the God of Prayer was the Master of life. For, said they, when the atmosphere was so tainted that even the dogs did not escape unaffected by it, nevertheless not a person died, not even a child; but, on the contrary, all the sick, young and old, great and small, were most miraculously cured as soon as they began to pray — and many even without the Father's presence.

After this solemn avowal, publicly made in the Chapel, the oldest and most influential man of the whole Village entered, and related the following, in the presence of all the assembly: "Yesterday evening," said he, "I was so ill from a knee that was swollen to the bursting-point, and with grievous pains all over my body, that I thought my last day had come. While I was in this condition, the Father entered my cabin, and had no sooner made me pray than, on the instant, I was so entirely cured that I hastened hither, without the least difficulty, to relate this wonder to all of you — but, much more, to thank you, O great God; for you alone have restored me. I used to profess that I could restore the sick to health by my jugglery, but I was lying and deceiving them when I made such a promise. But I was myself deceived of old by the wicked Manitou, who is nothing but a demon of Hell; and him I renounce, acknowledging henceforth only the great God as the sole master of our lives, whom we are to believe and obey. My wife has experienced the truth of this, as well as I. The pains of which I was cured yesterday evening, seemed to be transferred to her; for she felt them last night all over her body, suffering incredible agonies. I applied the same remedy to her case as the Father had employed to deliver me, and all night long I did nothing but pray for her, saying again and again, 'JESUS, you cured me; I was dying, and you made me live. My wife can endure no more. You are good, and have as much power over her ailment as you had over mine. I love her, and she will love you and become a Christian.' After my prayers, all her pains vanished at daybreak, as had mine on the preceding evening; and she will soon appear here, full of gratitude, together with her daughter-in-law, who, when unable to walk except on her hands and knees — so serious was her case — was cured after a novena of Prayer."

This speech was received with applause and delight by all the other old men, and by all the young people, who filled the Chapel; and they repeated many times, "The Sault prays, the Sault is Christian." It has likewise changed much in appearance. Those who had left their first wives are taking them back, while those who had several are keeping only the first, and discarding the others. The Chapel is filled on Sundays with old men, women, and young children, who there hear and sing God's praises; and who are prepared for Baptism by public and private instruction, which is given day and night in their Cabins and in our House.

Since the Father's arrival here, he has, in less than six months, Baptized more than six-score children, most of them in the Chapel, with all the ceremonies of the Church.

The Devil was by no means pleased that this Mission should be so greatly blessed by God, nor could he endure the rendering of such honor to God in this Chapel, which was built a year ago. The Baptism of more than three hundred persons, and the continual singing and proclaiming of God's praises there, doubtless stirred the wrath of Hell against this infant Church. A fire, the cause of which could not be discovered, broke out in the Chapel last winter, — on the 27th of January, 1671, — and reduced it entirely to ashes, as well as the house of the Missionaries, who were able to save from this conflagration nothing but the blessed Sacrament. But if God allowed the demons this sort of vengeance, their malice did not greatly profit them; for soon another Chapel was erected, much superior to the former one; and in it there were baptized in a single day as many as twenty-six children, as if to consecrate it by such Holy Ceremonies.

Reuben Gold Thwaites, ed., *The Jesuit Relations and Allied Documents,* 73 vols. Cleveland: Burrows Brothers Company, 1893–1901, 55: 117–31. Printed by permission.

49. Leopold Pokagon to Bishop Frederick Rese, 1830

The Potawatomis of the southern shore of Lake Michigan intermarried with Frenchmen in the late seventeenth century and maintained their Catholic identity even as the French missions came to a close in the eighteenth century. In 1830 a delegation of Potawatomis visited Father Gabriel Richard in Detroit, seeking instruction and asking for a permanent priestly presence among them. The bishop of Detroit, Rt. Rev. Frederick Rese, came to the Potawatomi village of St. Joseph and baptized several Indians, including Pokagon (possibly of Ojibwa or Ottawa birth), who took the name of Leopold. Shortly thereafter Pokagon sent a written request for a black-gown.

Father, Father, I come to beg you to give us a Black-gown to teach us the word of God. We are ready to give up whiskey and all our barbarous customs. Thou dost not send us a Black-gown, and thou hast often promised us one. What, must we live and die in our ignorance? If thou hast no pity on us men, take pity on our poor children who will live as we have lived, in ignorance and vice. We are left deaf and blind, steeped in ignorance, although we earnestly desire to be instructed in the faith. Father, draw us from the fire — the fire of the wicked manitou. An American minister wished to draw us to his religion, but neither I nor any of the village would send our children to his school, nor go to his meetings. We have preserved the way of prayer taught our ancestors by the Black-gown who used to be at St. Joseph. Every night and morning my wife and children pray together before a crucifix which thou hast given us, and on Sunday we pray oftener. Two days before Sunday we fast till evening, men, women and children, according to the tradition of our fathers and mothers, as we had never ourselves seen Black-gowns at St. Joseph.

Annales de la Propagation de la Foi, 4: 546. Reprinted in Cecilia Bain Buechner, *The Pokagons.* Indianapolis: Indiana Historical Society, 1933, 299. Printed by permission.

50. Reverend Louis Baroux Records Elizabeth Pokagon's Last Words, 1851

The Pokagon clan remained Catholic stalwarts through the nineteenth century. Leopold's widow, Elizabeth, left the following words to her family on her deathbed in 1851, recorded firsthand by Father Louis Baroux.

Like him, Chief Pokagon, she was baptized and preserved her first fervor to the end. In her last illness she prepared for death with the most edifying resignation. I, myself, was ill at the time. Several times during the day she sent to see if it were possible for me to rise and go to hear her confession and administer the last sacraments. The evening of her death, message after message was sent. I was unable to refuse such ardent entreaties. I was so weak that it was necessary to help me to get into a cart. I lay down upon a little straw and thus proceeded to the presence of the dying woman. After receiving the last sacraments and thanking me she told me she was glad to leave this world and join those who had preceded her.

All the savages love to visit those who have reached the threshold of eternity; they love to hear and meditate on their last words. It is like a sacred charge which they keep in their families. All were eager to visit for the last time the wife of their chief for whom they justly grieved. Simon Pokagon, the youngest of the children, wrote the last recommendations of his mother and these were preserved as a precious will. He gave me a copy.

First word. I am going to see my dead children to whom I will be united.

Second word. It is dangerous to love this world. God has opposed it.

Third word. My children, love God with all your heart, all your mind, and all your strength. This is the first and the greatest commandment.

Fourth word. God wills to see me.

Fifth word. My children, you must all go to confession and baptize your children.

Sixth word. The Great Spirit is in Heaven. He is a Good Father to us.

After having pronounced these last words she rendered her soul to God at eight o'clock in the evening, Oct. 3, 1851.

I have never seen anything more touching than the last moments of a savage. It is always the same spirit of faith which animated them. What has impressed me the most is that perfect calm, admirable resignation, that ardent desire with which they leave the world to go to God. They are animated by all these saintly dispositions because their life has been entirely spiritual and wholly detached from the goods of the world.

Cecilia Bain Buechner, *The Pokagons*. Indianapolis: Indiana Historical Society, 1933, 314–15. Printed by permission.

51. Antonine Denomie (Ojibwa) to Monsignor Joseph A. Stephan, October 4, 1888

Antonine Denomie, a Catholic Ojibwa Indian at Odanah, on the Bad River Reservation in Wisconsin, wrote in 1888 to Monsignor Joseph A. Stephan of the Bureau of Catholic Indian Missions, complaining of pagan and Protestant activity in the area. Denomie also reported on united opposition to the way in which the 1887 Allotment Act was being interpreted by U.S. government bureaucrats.

Rev Dear Father

This is to let you know that since you came here, the pagan, or dancing Indians, and one Catholic, (Blackbird) (who took up 80 acres in the village known as the Indian Farm) have united themselves with those of Protestant Indians, in protesting against all movements of the Catholic Indians and Halfbreeds, threatening to [expel] anyone who might aid the Catholic cause, and I think is instigated by an outsider. I am aware some of them have been liberally supplied with provisions, while the most needy is left out. The protesting Indians will shortly send a petition to Washington, which will not be signed by Little Cloud John Denomie, our head chief and speaker, and myself [their] writer (or clerk.) I think the sooner a stop is put to this dancing the better it is for the children, and the advancement in General. They have been holding a powwow the last two or three nights, but we would unite with our pagan Brothers in opposing Senator Chandler's Bill. [I]t provides no allotments be made unless it is for cultivation. Now, children cannot cultivate. It is the main desire of the Indians that children should have something in the future provided for him by his ancestor. [Therefore] he is in favor of giving children 80 acres instead of 40 acres.

2nd. Many children have already had 80 and reaped the full [Benefit] therefrom.

3rd. Many of the Indians and Halfbreeds have had [their] second allotments, and have reaped the full [benefit] from the pine thereon.

4th. The Injustice that would Incur on those left out would be unimaginable, as there are more than one half of them. The Indian wants to keep what land there will be left, for he even thinks of those yet to be Born, more than those of old men, who will soon fall to [their] grave.

So Good Bye, Rev. Dear Father.

From your affectionate child

A Denomie

Marquette University, Bureau of Catholic Indian Missions Records. Printed by permission.

52. John B. Masskogijigwek (Ojibwa) to Monsignor Stephan, December 10, 1890

John B. Masskogijigwek, a Catholic Ojibwa in Minnesota, wrote in 1890 to the Bureau of Catholic Indian Missions to request a larger church to accommodate the Indian congregation at Red Lake Reservation.

Very Rev. dear Father:

We Catholic Indians of Red Lake are writing you a letter today telling you what is going on here. We are out to tell you the truth and nothing but the truth. We are perfectly satisfied with the Sisters' school here. Our children are taught well; this is indeed a great benefit to them. And they are coming more and more into the school; at present there are from 55–60 children here in the Sisters' school. We tell you this, if you would help, that the school building be enlarged, a little, especially for the boys, so that afterwards also a "brother" could come and teach the boys in the school.

And our church is very small and in a very poor condition. Many Indians have to stand outside of the church during Divine Service on Sundays, as they cannot all go into it. Not even 1/3 of all the Catholic Indians here can go into our small church. This is the reason we tell you this, that you may know how we are. We hope and wish some day that a church be built in a short time. We beg of you that you may assist as herein as much as it is in your power. This is the earnest wish of us all.

This is all, we tell you and we all greet you.

Marquette University, Bureau of Catholic Indian Missions Records. Printed by permission.

53. "Cha-pah-kes-kut — Ghost Dinner," St. Michael's Church, October 21, 1979

In recent decades it has become common among Iroquoian and Algonkian Catholics of the Northeast and Midwest to meld their ancient Feast of the Dead with All Souls Day in the Catholic calendar. At St. Michael's Church on the Menominee Reservation in Wisconsin a "Ghost Dinner" has become a tradition that combines tribal and Catholic identities.

There is an old custom on the Menominee Reservation of celebrating the feast of ALL SOULS DAY with a special dinner to honor the spirits of the dead[.] This has come to be called "The Ghost Dinner." In the past these dinners were sponsored on a family basis and they still are, where that is possible. Circumstances, however, make this increasingly difficult so St. Michaels in Keshena offers an opportunity to keep this old custom alive on a Parish level, conscious that we are a family — brothers and sisters in Jesus Christ.

The old timers tell us that it has been the custom on this occasion to bring food for the dinner that was particularly pleasing to some of their beloved dead and share it in their honor. Food is never lacking, there is plenty for all. Instead of an ordinary pot-luck dinner this becomes a feast of delicate and sometimes exotic dishes with an abundance of wild game and forest foods prepared the way grandpa or mom used to like it.

This is not an affair to raise money or promote the social life of the community; it is an extension of our religious observance of All Souls Day. "It is a holy and wholesome thought to pray for the dead" (II Mac. 12/46) and this is on[e] of the ways of honoring our dead, keeping their memory alive and reminding ourselves that we will one day join them in the spirit world. It is also an excellent opportunity to acquaint our young people with one of the venerable customs of our past.

This year our Ghost Dinner will be November 1st, on the eve of All Souls Day, after a Mass in which the names of all those buried from our Church during this last year will be mentioned.

Marquette University, Sacred Heart Franciscan Indian Mission Records. Printed by permission.

54. The Diaries of Louis Riel, 1884–85

In the nineteenth century the Anishinabe and other Indians of present-day Manitoba intermarried with fur trade company personnel, creating in their offspring a recognized populace known to this day as Métis. In 1869 the Métis of Red River fomented an unsuccessful revolt against the formation of Canada, led by a former seminarian, Louis Riel. In the following years during which Riel lived in Montana, he continued to preach an apocalyptic message of spiritualized politics. Riel composed the following passages in Montana as he was about to embark on the second Métis rebellion in 1885, which ended tragically for the Métis and for Riel, who was hanged by the Canadians.

June 4, 1884

...Leader of the Manitobans! You know that God is with the Métis; be meek and humble of heart. Be grateful to God in complete repentance. Jesus Christ wants to repay you for your labours. That is why He is leading you gradually along His way of the cross. Mortify yourself. Live as a saint, die as one of the elect. Implore the Saviour to spare you at all costs from the pains of the next life. Do not be concerned about your enemies, your false friends who mistreat you. You will see what will happen to them; you will see with your own eyes how some of them will end. Oh, how pitiful it will be! Pray for them. Forgive them.

Take consolation. God wants you to enter immediately the joys of eternal life as soon as you die. Request, seek and find perfect contrition.

Take consolation. God gives you the means to educate your children and to raise them far away from the wicked, in the most pious of sanctuaries, if you wish. There your children will grow up, one day to carry on your interrupted labours, which God will recommence and cause to flourish. Your wife is worthy. She loves you.

Sacred Heart of Jesus! My spiritual director told me at the beginning [of my public career]: "Riel, you will succeed when everyone thinks you are lost." I have believed in his words because of You. I believe that God our Father will fulfill the promise which Your priest made to me. In the name of the Father, in the name of the Son, in the name of the Holy Spirit, I will succeed when everyone thinks I am lost.

Sacred Heart of Jesus! I am lost in an ocean of inextricable complications. For the sake of Saint Joseph and of the Virgin, Your Blessed Mother, make me succeed. You are the inspiration. Your divine Spirit can easily show me the path I must take to conquer and triumph. Man-God! Bless me according to the intentions of Your Providence, which we love when we do not understand them. Deliver me from the [United] States.

My God! Be my support! My God! Be my support! My God! Be my support!

Sacred Heart of Jesus! In Your mercy and overwhelming love, please bestow upon me the successes, victories and triumphs which are the lot appointed for me by divine prescience, but of which I have made myself unworthy through my sins. O Sacred Heart of Jesus! Sanctify me! Give me the blessings which were destined for me. For the sake of Your name, rehabilitate me! Restore me to the heritage of Your blessings.

Sacred Heart of Jesus! Give me perfect contrition as well as the mortification which You love. Be with me so I can do penance as I ought. Detach me from all things. And please grant me all the precious goods of this life, that I may use them as they should be used, solely in the interest of Your greater glory, for the honour of religion, for the salvation of souls, for the good of society, for my most perfect san[c]tification, according to the charity of God's plans!

Oh! Sacred Heart of Jesus, make us really understand that this world is simply the antechamber of eternity. You give us the goods of this life only to put us in the position of more easily being able to win the wealth of eternal life....

April 19, 1885

I hear the voice of the Indian. He comes to join me, he is coming from the north. He is in the mood for war.

I see five horsemen coming down the hill. They are riding at an angle to the river. They are on the south branch on the east side. There are two in front, then comes one by himself; his horse is spotted, light-coloured, almost piebald. The last two are side by side. I think they are hiding. These riders are Métis, judging by their horses.

I see a large number of Indians, they are on the other side of the river. They are single file, they are following our path, most of them are in a hurry. Every day new Indians come to increase their number, they have the same purpose as we do. Courage, my people, courage....

Thomas Flanagan, ed., *The Diaries of Louis Riel.* Edmonton, Canada: Hurtig Publishers, 1976, 26–27, 66–67.

55. Houma Indian Church Records, Diocese of Houma-Thibodaux, 1843–1911

The Houma Indians of southern Louisiana intermarried with French, Spanish, and African Americans during the colonial era; through the nineteenth century

American officials thought of the Houmas as an assimilated or extinct people. They became a "free people of color" — not blacks, not whites, descended from Indians but not legally Indians themselves. Nonetheless, the Houmas maintained their Indian identity and social solidarity, in no small part through the records of births, baptisms, marriages, deaths, and burials kept by the Catholic Church. The Billaux-Billot family tree can be traced as far back as 1765 in Louisiana. In 1835 Jacques Billaux and Rosalie Courteau — who was chief of the Houmas until her death in 1885 — gave birth to Jacques Constant Billaux, who was baptized eight years later. In 1865 Alexandre Billot, another offspring of Jacques Billaux and Rosalie Courteau, married Marguerite Felicite Verdin. In 1867 Rosalie Courteau herself was baptized at the age of eighty. There are hundreds of entries for the Billots and for the other common Houma family names in the Diocese of Houma-Thibodaux.

BILLAUX, Jacques Constant (Jacques & Rosalie COURTEAU) b. 7 April 1835; bt. 6 Jan. 1843. St. Joseph Church, Thibodaux....

BILLOT, Emile Antoine (Jacques & Anne BILLOT) b. 10 Jan. 1860. Sacred Heart Church, Montegut....

BILLOT, Rosalie Pomela (Charles & Honorine DARDARE) b. 5 Feb. 1864. Sacred Heart Church, Montegut....

BILLOT, Alexandre (Jacques & Rosalie COURTEAUD) m. 21 Sept. 1865 Marguerite Felicite VERDIN. Sacred Heart Church, Montegut....

COURTEAUX, Rosalie (Joseph & Marie Anne PIERRE), bt. 27 Jan. 1867 at age 80 yrs. Sacred Heart Church, Montegut....

BILLOT, Barthelmy, at age 78 yrs., d. 19 July 1911, buried 20 July 1911, Sacred Heart Church cemetery, Montegut....

Diocese of Houma-Thibodaux Archives. Reprinted in Reverend Donald J. Hebert, *South Louisiana Records: Church and Civil Records of Lafourche — Terrebonne Parishes,* 12 vols. Cecilia, La.: Reverend Donald J. Hebert, 1978–85. Printed by permission.

56. Choctaw Letters from Union, Mississippi, to Reverend William H. Ketcham, 1917–20

The Choctaws of Mississippi received their first sustained evangelism in the 1880s, but without federal recognition they began to move to Indian Territory after 1900 in order to join their relatives who had removed there in the Jacksonian era. In Oklahoma, Reverend William H. Ketcham translated a Catholic catechism into Choctaw in 1916; as director of the Bureau of Catholic Indian Missions he lobbied successfully for federal recognition of the Mississippi Choctaws. When it was gained in 1918 many Choctaws returned from Oklahoma. The following letters display the respectful affection held by the Choctaws for Reverend Ketcham. The letters were written (and read) in

Choctaw and have been translated into English under the direction of Dr. Clara Sue Kidwell in 1998.

Letter from Buck Shoemake and Buck Williams to Reverend Ketcham, February 26, 1917

Hello, hello. Yes, my dear friend.

I received your kind letter this very day and was very glad, so I am answer so soon. At the present time, I am still doing fine as all the other Choctaws — we are all fine. Day after day, I am reading this Holy Book always, and also at nights, I am studying this book. However, I still do not understand all the laws yet; but however, if God intends for me to know, I will learn all the laws, I guess. Yes, and I believe that was so, that you said it was very, very cold in Washington, but here in Mississippi, the weather has been rather warm in recent days. However, I think there [will] be cold days yet. Yes, and in this Newton County, seven little children were washed.* And there are nineteen adults who are Christians. Yes, and myself — I want to learn all the books very much; however, I do not have money so I can not go to school — I am always, every day, I want to go to school but this is all I can do always.

Easter Sunday will be here soon and I think about it, and so, I am asking you, and again, before the Easter Sunday, could we just play ball or some kind of game? I want to know for certain. So you must tell me plainly. This is all and I am your dear friend[.]

I will be looking for an answer soon, Yours truly

Letter from Shoemake to Reverend Ketcham, March 17, 1917

My dear friend-truly;

A few days ago, I received and read your dear letter. And I was very glad. That is — at this very present, I am doing well still and the other Choctaws are all doing well also — as I sit and answer [your] letter. You said you did not know how to write but as I see [your] letter, I think you write very good. I believe you even write better than I do. Lo, and do you think the Choctaws who are Catholic and elders, who had a wife, but now are separated should still be serving as elders? I believe that they, as I . . . see it, are still sinning. Recently, we are not having church services here. Father Tucker has not come so there are not services. Well, I like to read the letters you write very much. You write the Choctaw language very well. Well, this is the end and I rest.

Your friend always.

Well, I get my mail at Union, Mississippi now RFD #2, Box 32. This is where I get my mail. Good bye[.]

Yours truly

---

*Translation note: the word *kami* means "wash" as in "wash the face." It may refer to conversion as in baptism or to confirmation.

Letter from Shoemake to Reverend Ketcham, December 22, 1917

Hello, hello, my dear friend

Yes, it is true. I received your kind letter and I was glad to hear that you are doing fine, so I sit and give you an answer. Presently, I am still doing alright. And all Choctaws are doing fine. And I am going to ask you something. I have been mistaken about how many days, meat is not to be eaten. I thought it was only on Friday when meat was not to be eaten, but I have learned that there are days in some months when meat was not eaten. So, I am asking you to tell me correctly. Write a paper on the days meat is not to be eaten and send it to me.

I want a medal to wear and I want something* like the Christians usually have. This is all and I rest, and I was glad to hear you say you be good. This is all [your] true friend.

Letter from Jim Davis to Reverend Ketcham, August 19, 1919

Yes, my dear friend. I am very sick as I sit and write to you. Yes, I received one of your book. The white man is causing some problem for us Choctaw Catholics here. He is telling them that the Catholics are not true (not faithful). Then he is baptizing these who have joined the Catholics (forcing them).

Is this all the words to the Choctaw Catechism song book? If there is other words, you must write them down and send it to me. Then we will sing it.

> Holy Spirit
> You must come
> You must bless us
> You must bless us

If those words have more words; you must write them. Send it to me. If there are words to this song about — "Jesus was on the cross" and if you have no problem, write it and send it to me. We will all have a singing. There is singing at my house every Sunday. I rest. I look for an answer soon.

Letter from John Charlie to Reverend Ketcham, February 10, 1920

Dearest W. M. H. Ketcham

You are a dear man, my friend. Well, all is fine with me as I sit and write to you these few words. Before this year, I lived and worked in Tucker, Miss. Mission land, but I moved about 14 miles west from Tucker. I lived on a borrowed white man's field — part of the year. I would still be living at the Tucker church, but I moved out because the white man did not think the Choctaws were always right. But I am not turning loose of the church. The Choctaws were even forbidden to use the hymns by the white man. So, we have quit singing, even though, we liked singing much. Yes, and again — I would be very happy if you would find out and tell me if the news made and coming from Washington that

---

*Translation note: "medal to wear" is the possible translation of *beres pene*. "Something" may refer to a "rosary."

the Choctaws in Philadelphia Miss will be getting na habena* is true. I have not seen your words written for a long time, so I will be happy if you send me an answer in a few days. Well, again — I have no news so I rest. I will be looking for an answer soon.

Because of the Holy Word of God, I rest in peace I say Amen.

I am your dear friend[.]

I am. This is one you learn Christmas song chorus: "I come for all."

Marquette University, Bureau of Catholic Indian Missions Records. Printed by permission.

57. Reverend Louis Taelman, S.J., Obituary of Louis Ignace La Mousse (Flathead), 1927

After the War of 1812 a party of Iroquois fur traders from Kahnawake, Quebec, led by Ignace La Mousse, settled among the Flathead Indians in the Rocky Mountains and piqued their interest in Catholicism. Ignace acted as missionary and then prayer leader among the Flatheads and encouraged them to seek permanent association with Catholic priests. In the 1830s four delegations of Flatheads journeyed eastward to St. Louis in search of a pastor. The last pilgrimage encountered Father Pierre Jean de Smet, S.J., who answered their call the following year, thus beginning formal Catholic missions among the Rocky Mountain Indians. In 1927 Father Louis Taelman, S.J., noted the death of Ignace's last living son, Louis Ignace La Mousse.

On the fifth of last month at St. Ignatius Mission, Louis Ignace died at the ripe old age of 91. His death was edifying and holy, the crown of a truly Christian life. Louis had spent most of his years working for the Fathers here at the mission. Always reliable and honest, he was truly the right-hand man of the Brother in charge of the farm. His devotion to the Church came before all other considerations. The blessing of God was upon him. And no wonder, for he was the son of the famous Grand Ignace whom Father Palladino, in his book, "Indian and White in the Northwest," rightly calls the apostle of the Flathead.

Louis was the last link that united the present day with the first beginnings of Christianity among these Indians. When his father, Grand Ignace, was killed by the Sioux Indians in 1837 in an attempt to fetch the Catholic missionaries from St. Louis to the Flathead tribe, Louis was a little over a year old. His father was an Iroquois Indian. As history tells us, a band of Iroquois, twenty-four in number, some time after 1812, left the mission of Caughnawaga, near Sault St. Louis on the St. Lawrence, and, crossing the Mississippi Valley, directed their course westward. The leader of the band was Ignace La Mousse, better known as Grand or Big or Old Ignace. By a mysterious design of Providence, they reached the land of the Flathead in 1816, were kindly and hospitably received, and here the wandering band concluded to remain. The ties of friendship soon ripened into stronger ones by intermarriage, and from this on, these Iroquois became members of the Selish or Flathead nation.

---

*Translation note: *na habena* refers either to "gift," "per capita," "land," or "aid."

Louie Sam (Coeur d'Alene), prayer leader of the "Soldiers of the Sacred Heart," an early sodality. Sacred Heart Mission, De Smet, Idaho, ca. 1940. Credit: Photographer unknown. Marquette University, Bureau of Catholic Indian Missions Records. Reproduced by permission.

Grand Ignace soon acquired an ascendancy over the tribe. This influence he wielded for the temporal and spiritual welfare of his adopted brethren. He taught them their prayers. He taught them how to baptize their babies, how to bury their dead and how to plant the cross on the graves. He told them the advantage and necessity of having blackrobes or Catholic missionaries among them, by whom they could be instructed and taught the way to heaven. In consequence, a strong desire grew up among the Flathead to get the blackrobes spoken of by Old Ignace, with the result that four expeditions were organized to St. Louis for that purpose. The last of the four was successful. The first expedition having failed in 1831, a second one was resolved upon in 1835. It was Grand Ignace himself this time who offered to go. He took with them two of his sons, Charles and Francis, and reached St. Louis late in the Fall after many privations and sufferings. Ignace pleaded the cause of the Flathead with Bishop Rosatti, and with the latter's assurance that the missionaries would be sent as soon as possible, he left with his two sons and safely returned to the mountains.

Eighteen months having passed after Grand Ignace's return and no tidings of any blackrobe being on the way, a third expedition went forth in the summer of 1837. This third delegation consisted of three Flathead, one Nez Perce and Grand Ignace himself, the leader of the party, five in all. Passing through the country of the hostile Sioux at a place called Ash Hollow on the South Platte, they fell in with a large party of that tribe. Being attacked, our little band bravely defended themselves, killing some fifteen of their assailants. But greatly outnumbered, all five perished in the unequal struggle. Grand Ignace was dressed like a white man and had been ordered to stand apart with the whites who were traveling in the same company. But he spurned the command and preferred to share the lot of his adopted brethren. Thus perished Grand Ignace, apostle of the Flathead. Francis, his son, died eight years ago at over ninety years of age. Of him, Father Palladino says that perhaps in the whole Missoula County there was not a man more respected by white and Indian than Francois Saxa, the name by which he was known. And now the last son, Louis, half Iroquois and half Flathead, has also passed away. Only grandchildren, great grandchildren and great, great grandchildren are left here on the reservation to transmit the name and virtues of the original Grand Ignace upon whose descendants the blessing of God is visibly resting.

May his soul rest in peace.

Reverend Louis Taelman, S.J., "Louis Ignace La Mousse: Son of the Great Ignace La Mousse, Apostle of the Flathead," *Indian Sentinel* 7, no. 1 (winter 1927): 28–29. Printed by permission.

58. Anthony Del Orier, William H. Tinker, and Louis C. Reveard (Osages) to the Editor, *Freeman Journal,* April 16, 1874

In 1869 the United States initiated a national program for the administration of Indian reservations. Called Grant's Peace Policy, it was inspired by reformers from the Society of Friends (the Quakers), and it entrusted the management of Indian reservations to Christian missionaries. The Board of Indian Commissioners assigned various denominations their reservation territories, and by and large the Catholics were excluded, much to the consternation of Catholic Indians such as these Osages of Indian Territory, who wrote a complaint to the Freeman Journal *in 1874.*

Sir, I beg leave to insert an article in your wide spread paper, about the manner in which we Osages are treated. Indeed the grievances are so many that there is a rumor of burning all the improvements made by our Quaker Agent. Perhaps $25,000 is annually wasted for the Government officers and employees; [w]hen it was stated last summer that an attempt had been made to rob us at one stroke of $400,000.00 as mentioned in Kansas papers, we became mistrustful and indignant.

When we made our treaties with Government in 1865 and 1869, we begged of the Commissioners, to let us retain our Catholic schools, and missionaries; this was the expectation of the whole Osage nation without a single exception. In this hope of good times we began to select our officers, and prepared rules to be carried out under the advice of our good missionaries; for they have been like fathers to us for upwards of twenty years even now they visit us occasionally when the cry of joy is heard by every family; these used to live frugally among us; they visited and consoled our sick etc. No wonder therefore our Chiefs consulted them on all important affairs.

When Agent Gibson came among us he was kind and spoke well of our missionaries; we took him for a good Government Officer, to pay us our annuities and to promote our interests, and because he took our part against the white intruders on our lands we began to like him; but after we had sold to Government all our old reservations a tract of land 300 by 50 miles, and were moved on our new homes in the Indian Territory then Agent Gibson began to exercise Despotism. Our Osage Chiefs were no longer consulted, and their complaints at the many and [great] expenses have been and are disregarded; however they and their [counselors] remained peaceful, they only complained bitterly in their private counsels, discontent is on the increase our privation of Catholic schools and missionaries surpasses all our other evils.

Our Chiefs have asked the Agent for them... in each public [Council they] transmitted [petitions] to higher authorities; they have begged President Grant to give to them this just demand, but all in vain. When the Osages saw a costly storehouse built and occupied by quaker teachers; they grew sorry and put their hands to their mouths, it seems to us that the Government officers study plans to profit for themselves for the large amount of money due to the Osages by the late treaties.

The country around the Agency swarms with quakers all employees fed by our money, no wonder if an Osage [counselor], whom the Agent had lately degraded from his office, should tell these new comers that by spring he will drive these intruders from the Osage lands; these I suppose are sample threats but show the bitter feelings of Osages.

When lately our chiefs and head men petitioned and asked for Catholic Schools the Agent told them that no religion should be taught at school that

Indian tourists from the Osage Reservation, Pawhuska, Oklahoma, at the Church of the Holy Sepulcher, Jerusalem, Israel, ca. 1919–32. The group donated this U.S. flag to the church, which was blessed by Archbishop Albert T. Daeger, O.F.M., of Santa Fe, New Mexico (front row center). The Osages have been uniquely prosperous since the discovery of oil on their reservation in the late nineteenth century. Credit: Photograph by G. Felici. Marquette University, Bureau of Catholic Indian Missions Records. Reproduced by permission.

children should be left free to choose their own religion when 21 years of age; this doctrin[e] is new to us and we wonder; however this new doctrin[e] of freedom seems unreasonable to Agent Gibson himself, for he lately made known to his employees, that those who didn't attend to his religious prayers and Sunday schools would be dismissed from employment; so we gradually withdrew from the employ of the Agent. I myself with many of my schoolmates, joined the U.S. army 12 years ago, we served three years we were never forced to attend any religious worship, and were allowed Catholic worship whenever an occasion was offered.

There are 3000 Osages, if all are not Catholic, all have a predilection for Catholic schools for Osage children, at present male and female children are mixed, and taught by female teachers, whose conduct is not always edifying there are likely 30 children at school (when I left school some years ago we were 200 scholars)[.] The Agent having dressed those children in blue large soldiers clothes, had offended their parents; and these fearing that morality was not well guarded at school called home the larger half. The cry for Catholic schools is universal, it is the great end of the present Osage Delegation at Washington.

Peaceful Citizens of large Cities call us Indians cruel, and barbarous: they know not our family affections, and our love for our children, neither do they know that by the Indian treaties with Government Officers, secretary of the Interior is made the exclusive manager of all the funds; he entrusts these funds to the management of inferior officers; and an Agent is finally placed over the Indians (*at present, with absolute authority*). Our chiefs and head men sold to Government within the last eight years upwards of (8) eight millions of acres of Osage lands, say at the rates of an annual income of 75 or 80 thousand dollars; hitherto we have received [through] the Agent or superintendent from 30 to 40 thousand dollars [annually]....

How are the other 40 thousand spent[?] Indians are sometimes forced to retaliate; every wound they inflict bring[s] us nearer to annihilation. Is there no pity for Indians!...

Marquette University, Bureau of Catholic Indian Missions Records. Printed by permission.

59. Lakota Sioux Chiefs to President Rutherford B. Hayes, 1877

In 1877 Lakota Sioux leaders Little Wound, Red Cloud (both of Pine Ridge), and Spotted Tail (Rosebud) requested of President Rutherford B. Hayes that Catholic priests and sisters be assigned to their reservations as teachers.

Little Wound, September 26, 1877
...My Great Father, I have come here to tell you about another thing. I wish to have all the provisions that a white man has — the animals that he has, so that I can learn and bring my children up in the same way the whites do theirs. We want farming implements of all kinds to cultivate the soil. I also want a Catholic Priest; and that is all I have to say.

Red Cloud, September 27, 1877
...We would like to have a school house — a large one, that will hold plenty of people. We would like to have Catholic priests and Catholic nuns, so that they could teach our people how to write and read, and instruct us how to do....

Spotted Tail, September 27, 1877
...I would like to say something about a teacher. My children, all of them, would like to learn how to talk English. They would like to learn how to read and write. We have teachers there, but all they teach us is to talk Sioux, and to write Sioux, and that is not necessary. I would like to get Catholic priests. Those who wear black dresses. These men will teach us how to read and write English....

National Archives, M1282, Letters Sent to the Office of Indian Affairs by the Agents or Superintendents at the Pine Ridge Agency, 1874–1907, Microfilm Reel 1. Printed by permission.

60. Reverend Henry Grotegeers, S.J., "Instruction by Means of the Two Roads," 1931

Reverend Henry Grotegeers, S.J., was superior of Holy Rosary Mission on the Pine Ridge Reservation in South Dakota, 1916–1920, where he used the Two Road Catechism in his evangelism. In this excerpt he focuses upon the salvific life of Jesus and the founding of the Catholic Church. The manuscript is dated December 10, 1931; however, he is said to have left Holy Rosary in 1928.

This picture is called the two roads, the good road, and the bad road. The good road leads to heaven, and the bad road to the home of the devil.

If we desire to go to heaven, three things we must observe: 1 — We must believe all what God has revealed. 2 — We must observe the commandments of God. 3 — We must receive the seven Sacraments. 4 — There is one God, but there are three Persons in God whom we must adore, the Father the Son and the Holy Ghost. These three are one God. They possess all things: all alike. One Wisdom, one Kind....

4000 years after the creation of man God sent the promised Saviour and who was born in [Bethlehem]. The Saviour lived for 33 years on earth; for 30 years He lived in [Nazareth] and rendered common labor thereby teaching us an example.

For three years He taught the people of Juda by counsel including us the road to Heaven and showing to us and proving to us that He is the true God by some wonderful miracles.

On our account He gave Himself to suffer, died and was buried. But after three days He rose from the dead. He lived and remained 40 days on earth. He instituted His Church permanently and then went to Heaven; He dwells in Heaven now.

The Saviour is the son of God, God is His Father and the Holy Virgin Mary His mother. St. Joseph is His foster-father. When Jesus was yet small he watched over Him, and God commanded him to do this.

Jesus lived as Man and lived as God. (i. e.) for instance, He possessed all what [men] possesses and as God what God possessed, thus is the meaning.

Thus as a man He possessed body and soul, understanding and mind and as God He possessed wisdom, intellect and power. Therefore He is the Greatest; and loves us most dearly. Hence we should honor and love Jesus by observing His want and we must fulfill all he wants us to do in all good will. And thereby in the future we will be happy with Him in Heaven for all eternity.

Those who have no love for the Saviour and who are not obedient to His want, and when death takes them they will suffer forever with the devil in his home. Therefore first, remember these things.

We should be obedient as well as dutiful to His Church. Because His name Jesus is taught to us and His road to Heaven is shown to us: "He who listens to you, listens to me," Jesus said. Those people who lived before Jesus came lived in the dark, so we also live year after year. But Jesus came and brought light to earth, and hence we live in His light. We are now living in the light of the Saviour and His Church and His road to Heaven is presented to us which is bright like that of the sun. REFERS TO PICTURE "TWO ROADS" YEARS BEFORE CHRIST IN BLACK, THOSE AFTER IN RED. 12-10-31....

The Two Roads Picture Catechism depicted the two roads of good and evil, to be used in instructing the Indians in the essentials of the Catholic religion. Based upon pictorial catechisms employed by missionaries in the Northwest as early as the 1840s — particularly the Catholic Ladder of Father Francis Norbert Blanchet — Lacombe's Ladder marked Christian history from creation to the late nineteenth century and presented its viewers with a crucial choice, either to walk the path of the Church to communion with God in heaven, or to orient one's life toward the Devil and hell. Because it easily transcended language barriers, Catholic missionaries and Native catechists used the road picture catechism extensively in evangelizing Native peoples across the United States and Canada. Credit: Reverend Albert Lacombe, O.M.I., and published in Montreal, Canada, ca. 1880. Marquette University, Holy Rosary Mission — Red Cloud Indian School Records. Reproduced by permission.

God gave us the ten Commandments. We should observe these very carefully, if we want to enter Heaven. God gave us these Commandments on Mount Sinai the first time through Moses. God created us. Therefore He is our Master, and he could give us Commandments; it is His right. It is His authority.

Marquette University, Holy Rosary Mission — Red Cloud Indian School Records. Printed by permission.

61. Bishop Joseph F. Busch to the Catholic Indians of the Diocese of Lead, ca. 1910–15

Reportedly written by Joseph F. Busch, the bishop of the Diocese of Lead (now Rapid City, South Dakota), this document warned the Catholic Indians of the spiritual dangers – drinking, traditional dancing, and divorce – that might prevent them from entering the kingdom of heaven. His letter, ca. 1910–15, expressed the moralism of the Church and its emphasis on the afterlife in its evangelistic message.

To the Catholic Indians of the Diocese of Lead.

Beloved Brethren:

A good shepherd must not only feed his flock, but must also protect it from danger. I, therefor[e], who have been appointed the shepherd of your souls must not only see that you are instructed in the Faith and strengthened by the Sacraments, but must also warn against all spiritual dangers.

"The devil like a roaring lion goeth about seeking whom he may devour," and among the things he makes use of to destroy your souls, there are especially three, and they are so dangerous, that I must ask you to turn away from them and to have nothing to do with them in any way.

The first is drinking intoxicating liquor.

The Indian must put away the desire for strong drink, for it is the helper of the devil, it makes man sick and poor, takes away reason, brings sorrow to wife and children and therefor[e] "no drunkard can enter the kingdom of Heaven."

The second danger is Dancing and all the Old Customs of the Indians, because they are used by the devil to put what is bad into the mind and the heart of him who takes part in these practices.

I am sorry to see that there are many who think there is no harm in these customs, but I warn you to give them all up or you may be sorry in Hell forever. Work hard against these customs which please the devil and lead many away from Christ and from Heaven.

The third danger is Divorce. "What God has joined together, let no man tear asunder." This is the commandment of Christ and he who breaks this command is an adulterer, and no adulterer can enter the kingdom of Heaven.... Those who wish to marry should go to the priest or the Catechist to be well instructed for this Holy Sacrament, then they will learn that a Catholic can be married only by the priest and can never be divorced and marry another, as long as the other partner lives. I am very sorry to hear that lawyers and even parents often coax people to get a divorce. They are working for the devil, who will reward them in Hell.

I hope all Indians will listen to my warning and turn away from the...dangers I have named. I pray God to bless all who are obedient, and will ask God to punish all who are disobedient and give a bad example by working for the devil, that they may be converted from their wickedness, be saved from the deceits of the devil and become good children of their Father in Heaven.

Joseph F. Busch,
Bishop of Lead

Marquette University, Holy Rosary Mission—Red Cloud Indian School Records. Printed by permission.

62. St. Joseph Society, Organization Rules, January 1917

Catholic missionaries organized the first St. Joseph and St. Mary sodalities among the Lakota Sioux in 1884. They were structured similarly to traditional men's and women's sodalities as mutual aid societies; however, membership was limited to Catholics married within the Church who had received first communion. The members were to observe the Sabbath, catechize their brethren, and avoid polygamy and drunkenness. They were to be adult models of Christian virtue. The earliest known written rules for the St. Joseph Society date to 1917. Father Paul I. Manhart, S.J., transcribed them in 1965.

a) The Catholic Church is *one*, and the Pope is the head; all its members have the Pope as their father. The name of Jesus stands guard over the Catholic Church throughout the world. For Jesus asked St. Peter: "Peter, do you think you love me; then what would you feed my sheep[?]" Jo. 21.15.

b) The Pope lives in Rome because St. Peter died in Rome, he being St. Peter's successor and the father of all, and all must listen to him.

c) The Pope as father appoints and ordains Bishops, his helpers and heads of areas or dioceses.

d) Bishops, like the twelve apostles of Jesus, listen to St. Peter, listen and do as they are asked. Bishops who are heads of dioceses also have helpers. And these are priests. Bishops and Priests all over the world to spread the words of the Gospel: Baptize the people and preach to them so they might be given recognition in Heaven. For Jesus Christ said: "He that heareth you heareth me; and he that despiseth you despiseth him that sent me." Lk. 10.16.

e) So therefore, the Priests who are sent by the Bishop the people are to listen to. Priests are our fathers. For when they baptize, they give a new and everlasting life. "Amen Amen I say to you, unless a man be born again of water and the Holy Spirit, he cannot enter into the kingdom of God." Jo. 3.5[.]

f) The Priest feeds our Spirit or Soul to strengthen us for our new life. They preach to us and give us food, the Holy Banquet and Holy Food. They heal a sick spirit; when we confess our sins and we are given absolution, the sins are taken away and our souls are healed. They are called fathers because they guide us to eternity. Therefore, we should love them and listen to them. For St. Paul said: "If you should have ten thousand instructors in Christ, yet you have not many fathers. For in Christ Jesus, by the Gospel, I have begotten you." 1 Cor. 6.15.

The First Rule

    I. Honor and listen to the priests of the Bishop of the diocese.

    II. All those who want to be a member of the St. Joseph Society must be Catholics; non-Catholics cannot be members.

    III. They will not hold Indian pagan rites, positions, dances, [superstitious] practices.

   IV. To be a member of the St. Joseph Society, a man may have but one wife, be in a Catholic marriage, and not a divorced man.

   V. He will take good care of his family, with food and clothing.

   VI. He will go to Church every Sunday and Holy Day of obligation.

   VII. He will confess his sins and go to Holy Communion at least once a year.

   VIII. [Not included.]

   IX. He will not use intoxicants.

   X. He will attend every meeting, providing he is not sick. He will pay ten cents to the treasurer if not there.

   XI. Fifteen cents a month will be paid to the treasurer.

   XII. The Society will help a member who is sick; food and clothing will be given to his family. They, the chairman and sick committee chairman, will decide what will be given them.

   XIII. A sick member will be visited by at least two members after being notified by the chairman of the sick committee.

   XIV. Money from the funds will be used to pay for the digging of graves. All will wear Society emblems for the funeral; a Society banner will also be carried in front of the casket; they will help and comfort the family.

   XV. A member will have his child baptized and given Catholic instructions and Catholic schooling.

   XVI. Anyone who wishes to become a member will notify the President and will undergo an examination for qualification. If he qualifies, he becomes a member.

   XVII. All members must learn the Our Father, Hail Mary and Apostles' Creed, the six precepts of the Church, and he shall not go to Protestant Churches.

   XVIII. Officers preside for one year. They will be changed in October. They can, however, be re-elected to the position.

   XIX. They shall not have long hair. St. Paul said: "If a man wear his hair long, it is degrading to him." 1 Cor. 11.14.

Rules for Officers

   1. The [*President*] should be a God-fearing, religious man, wanting to work for charity, possessing an education, and knowing, how to give comfort to those who mourn. He should understand and be able in the use of

prayers. This is the man we would want. He is to illustrate by his own good conduct [in] life how others are to live.

2. The *Treasurer* should be one who is dependable and truthful. He is to be able to read and write and keep a record of money. Every three months the priest and the officers review the records. There will be two appointed people [to] go over the record of the treasurer to investigate and also count the money in his possession.

3. The *Vice-President* will be a man also good, and he should understand the ways of St. Joseph. His words, his labors — that is the man we want as vice-president. He should be a man always observant of things, and the people should work along with and respect him, and try to imitate the life of St. Joseph.

4. The *Secretary* to be selected should be able to read and write and be able to perform his own duties. He is to keep a register of names of the members and carry the minutes of the meetings. He should write communications for officers and members when asked.

5. The *Chorus Leader* should sing well, and know all the songs, and be able to lead in them and teach them to others.

6. The *Committee for the Sick* should consist of two members (man and woman). These are their duties: When a member is sick, they should visit him immediately, notify the priest and officers. They should then remain there to look after him.

7. When a meeting is in progress, the *door-keeper* is to keep away, anyone who may interfere, and if there be some who arrive, he is to inquire inside whether they are to be admitted or not. Moreover, he is to see that other members keep the meeting-house in order and clean. He is to look to it that nothing is damaged.

8. The *cemetery committee* should consist of two members. Their duties are: to see that the cemetery be in good order, and broken fence is repaired immediately. He is to remove the weeds and he should place a crucifix at the head of each grave.

Cooperation among all members means that there should be willing help, so that much can be done. The work in preparing a soul for heaven is a work that requires patience. The devil is always working to destroy these aims along the way. Some evil men tempt good members. And they tempt us to sin mainly when one is attacked while alone. In this case, he is quickly tempted to sin. But many men form an organization and working together accomplish many things, and they try to win others to become members. That is why we should wear the clothing of St. Joseph. Working as he did, under him, all members are to follow his example, how he prayed, how he died. That is the teaching we must learn. So those who are members of the St. Joseph Society know that if they follow his example perseveringly, St. Joseph will help them. St. Joseph will bless and help them in sorrow to rise above their sadness and keep the devil out of their lives and watch over them. Every member of St. Joseph who appreciates his membership will remain a member always. He will sympathize with his fellow members, love them, advise them, and so we become brothers to one another.

Marquette University, Holy Rosary Mission — Red Cloud Indian School Records. Printed by permission.

63. Parishioners, St. Paul's Church, Yankton Sioux Reservation, to Reverend Ketcham, May 14, 1920

On occasion the Sioux Catholics rebelled against the authority of their pastor. In 1920 Dakota parishioners of St. Paul's Church on the Yankton Reservation in South Dakota petitioned Reverend Ketcham of the Bureau of Catholic Indian Missions to sack Father Sylvester Eisenman, O.S.B., for removing their Native catechist and dismissing the St. Joseph and St. Mary societies. Eisenman did not lose his post.

Our Dear Father & true Shepherd

We the Members of the St. Paul Catholic Church of Yankton Indian Reservation do hereby Petition you in Regards to the action & conduct of our Pastor Father [Sylvester]. We are sorry to tell you the father is not doing Right he favor few and making trouble for us he has Discharged our Catechist Mr. William Randell with out any cause and we don[']t like it he takes Everything on his own Sho[u]lder and says he can do as he think best and he has ap[p]ointed a new catechist with out the will of the members and also Dismiss the St. Joseph & St. [Mary] Society and We had a meeting and the majority of the members voted to keep Mr. Randell as their catechist and they don[']t want Father as their Pastor if you don't take Father [Sylvester] a way from here we will not come to church and hear Father Preach[.] We don[']t like the way he is [managing] the affairs he don[']t want to forgive any one so we have Determined to have him Dismiss away from here this is the will of Mr. Thunder Horse, Eugene Bull, John Littleowl, Amos Sitoka, and the will of the Majority of the Members of the church.

[22 signatures follow.]

Marquette University, Bureau of Catholic Indian Missions Records. Printed by permission.

64. Obituary of Leah Rooks (Lakota), "A Rose of the Bad Lands," by Reverend Eugene Buechel, S.J., 1921

Sometimes the missionaries found the life (and death) of young Indian women to be filled with sanctity and composed obituaries to honor their virtues. Father Eugene Buechel, S.J., wrote one such piece in 1921 at St. Francis Mis-

*sion, Rosebud Reservation, South Dakota, for Leah Rooks, a recently deceased
Lakota.*

"Bad Lands" — you think of barren fields and rocky places — and have no use
for them. And yet God's own greatness reveals itself right there. While seeing
them from a distance you may not care to visit them at midday in summertime but you cannot easily turn your eyes away from those strange formations
before you, remnants seemingly of another world and built by another race
for a kingly people. With but little imagination you see ancient cities, castles,
cathedrals, amphitheatres, and a lot of other things that are not there.

Nor are they useless, for many a stockman put up his log house right close
to them, as the numerous narrow valleys offer good feed and shelter to his cat-
tle and horses. Yes, their name is "Bad Lands," but they are part of God's own
flower garden all the same.

Let me tell you of a fair June rose that grew there and was claimed by the
heavenly gardener on June 22, 1921. It was my treasured privilege to watch over
that charming rose of the Bad Lands when He came to take her home.

Leah Rooks was a pupil of the St. Francis Mission Indian School, St. Francis,
So. Dak. Ill health, however, compelled her to take more than one undesired
vacation. And it was no small sacrifice on her part to leave her school and the
church where her God dwelled. Born Nov. 10, 1903, Leah was received into the
church Sept. 22, 1914. Going to a Catholic school meant trying to overcome
herself gradually, and she succeeded so well that after a while her good conduct,
fine manners, and gentleness made her a favorite with everybody. But the real
beauty of her God-loving soul shone forth most brightly when she felt that
her prediction, made frequently among her friends, that she would die before
them, was to come true.

There she lay emaciated and suffering, weak in body, but strong in faith,
hope, and love. You saw her crucifix pinned right over her heart. Her scapular,
too, and a medal of the Sacred Heart were in full view. Her beads were placed
back into her right hand at her request ever so many times. These were her
trusted weapons, and truly, I never noticed in her the least sign of fear or worry.

How joyfully she welcomed the priest when towards evening he arrived having travelled 42 miles hurriedly at her bidding. "O, Father, I am so glad you
came. You must stay with me until I die." To be sure, I gladly gave my word, for
it meant seeing a saintly soul off to heaven. She certainly made use of the priest's
presence, but never annoyingly for there was no more thoughtful girl than Leah.
While suffering intensely, she made nothing of herself, but rather thought of the
wants of the healthy people around her, the priest included. She feared being a
burden to her loving parents and relatives. At the same time she had a grateful
look or word for every little favor done. It gave her pleasure to hear from the
good Sisters and her friends and she begged me to remember her to me and all.

But these seemed to be her last words for this world. When after Holy Communion I asked her what else I should do for her, she said sweetly: "Ask Jesus to
let me die soon, for I want to go to heaven." Henceforth the priest seemed to be
the most important person and she would hardly ever permit him to leave her

for any length of time. But this was from no fear. Death was to her nothing but the gate leading to heaven. And as to her past life she remarked: "It pays at the end to have led a good life." So when in due time I said to her: "Leah, I think you will go soon," she showed no surprise but simply replied: "I think so too, Father." And she would hear no weeping in her presence. Even in the very act of dying her face seemed to disapprove of the wailing that no doubt, she heard.

But what she cared for was speaking to God and hearing about Him. No prayer was too long and none too many. She wanted the prayers of the Church and her favorite devotions in honor of the Sacred Heart and the Blessed Virgin Mary until late in the evening when she asked me to rest a while. But at 2 o'clock when her own great day was beginning to dawn, she had her father call me again. I shall never forget those wonderful hours of the early morning spent with her as she was waiting for her God, whose presence we seemed to feel. The sight of her, as she lay there, angel like, with folded hands and eyes closed whether she was speaking or listening, would have brought tears to any man's eyes. O, could I but show that beautiful picture to every boy and girl, to let them see how praying elevates us, and how it is a grand privilege and not a burden to speak to God in prayer.

After hours of patient waiting the end came and everything the way she had laid it out for herself. Once more she said with me the acts of faith, hope, charity, and contrition. Once more the priest raised his hand to impart the last absolution, and she bowed down her head to meet her Savior while the prayers for the dying were recited.

"O how beautiful is the chaste generation with glory: for the memory thereof is immortal, because it is known both with God and with men. When it is present, they imitate it, and they desire it when it hath withdrawn itself, and it triumpheth crowned forever, winning the reward of undefiled conflicts. ...Being made perfect in a short space, she fulfilled a long time, for her soul pleased God." (Wisdom, IV 1, 2, 13)

Rest in peace, Leah, and may God, for whom alone you were longing, be your rich reward. May we all understand as well as you did that heaven is our true home, and may our death be as happy as yours.

Marquette University, Holy Rosary Mission — Red Cloud Indian School Records. Printed by permission.

65. John Goes in Center [John Bull] (Lakota), Affidavit, February 7, 1931

Catholic morality required that Indian converts follow Church rules regarding marriage and divorce. In 1931 the Lakota John Goes in Center of Pine Ridge Reservation requested an annulment of his first marriage so that his second marriage might be declared valid.

I, John Goes in Center (also called John Bull) being sworn in depose and say:

that I was married by Father Bosch, S.J. to Elizabeth (Lizzie) Bird Necklace (now called Poly Holy Rock) on December 30 - 1895 in St. Joseph's church,

Bear Creek, now called Hisle, S.D. The witnesses being Mr. & Mrs. John Lodeau. We both are fullblood Sioux Indians.

We remained together less than one year. A child was born to us, but it died. Then she always wanted to go home to her mother again. She went to see relatives in Kyle and Porcupine and finally got back to her mother. Then she married a man called Holy Rock and has now a large family — all protestants.

I myself also got married again to Kate Lip and we have many children — all baptized Catholic although Kate Lip is no Catholic. She wants to be Catholic when we first make this marriage right and holy.

We could not get our marriage straightened out, because we were told that the first marriage was right.

But I say that the first marriage must have been wrong. Lizzie Bird Necklace did not really want to marry me, as she told [expressly] several times. She did not want to go to the church. When coaxed she went in but came out again before the ceremony. But people followed her and brought her back. Then she did not answer in a loud voice when the priest asked. She was not a bashful girl, but she was contrary and when she gave her hand she [wrapped] it into her shawl. She had no intention to stay married with me. So I think it was a wrong marriage from the beginning.

I beg the Bishop to declare that first marriage null and void and entirely invalid before God and men.

> Marquette University, Holy Rosary Mission — Red Cloud Indian School Records. Printed by permission.

66. Minutes of the Golden Jubilee Catholic Sioux Congress, Holy Rosary Mission, Pine Ridge Reservation, 1938

Beginning in 1891 and every year thereafter, members of the St. Joseph and St. Mary Societies and their families gathered in midsummer for Catholic Sioux Congresses. The annual gatherings served partially as a replacement for the banned Sun Dances, as thousands of Siouians celebrated social and religious solidarity. Criers greeted dignitaries, including bishops and papal representatives. Everyone shook hands solemnly, then proceeded to Eucharistic processions, devotions to the Blessed Sacrament, hymnody in Lakota, Dakota, Latin, and English, and requiem services for those who had died during the year. Delegates gave speeches and passed resolutions (e.g., against peyote use and divorce, or for greater federal funding for Catholic boarding schools), and the various sodalities displayed their regalia. In 1938 at Pine Ridge the delegates celebrated the fiftieth anniversary of Holy Rosary Mission's founding.

JUNE 21

The meeting was called to order at 1 P.M. The following officers presided: Wm. Patton, Pres.; Ray Hernandez, V. Pres.; Wm. Bush, [Assist.] Sec.; Emil Afraid of Hawk, Temp. Sec.; Thos. Yellow Bull, Treas.; Peter Red Elk, Critic.

Following the invocation by Rev. Father [Buechel], S.J. of St. Francis, So. Dak.; a hymn was sung and a welcome speech was given by Peter Red Elk of Manderson, So. Dakota.

A roll call of the thirty Churches and Stations of the Pine Ridge and Rosebud Reservations preceded a very interesting talk by Father Bernard, O.S.B. of the Standing Rock Reservation in both English and Dakota.

The meeting was then turned over to the St. Mary's Society for business.

Evening Session

After a few numbers by the Holy Rosary Mission Band quite a few delegates who had arrived late reported from Yankton, Standing Rock, and Arapaho, Wyoming.

The evening was given over entirely to the alumni. Quite a few of the old-timers who attended the opening of the mission school in 1888 were present and gave interesting and amusing accounts of the difficulties of those early days. It was hard getting acquainted with the strange customs of living a regimented school life; it was hard getting acquainted with the white "Blackrobes" with their strange manners of life; new ways of reckoning time had to be learned, for the Indians had no days of the week, months and years as the white men did; strange were the teachings of the new religion; the sign of the Cross was a subject for laughter and regarded as superstition by the pagan Indians; [i]n time darkness became light to them and today's fifty-year celebration is a wonderful lesson of the progress made in such a short time.

JUNE 22

After the Solemn High Mass celebrated at the bower, Father [Buechel], S.J. gave a very instructive sermon in fluent Dakota language.

Rt. Rev. Bishop J. J. Lawlor of Rapid City arrived unexpectedly and after greeting the Indians gave an excellent talk on "Salvation of Souls" through an interpreter, Emil Afraid of Hawk. Because the Bishop's stay was short, the Confirmation ceremonies were held immediately and at 11 A.M. eighty-three men, women and children were confirmed.

Afternoon Session

Mr. James Grass, Sr., the "Door-master" opened the meeting.

Wm. Fills the Pipe, delegate from St. Bernard's Church, presented a resolution from his local society which read as follows:

> "Resolved that all Catholic Churches in the Indian Field Camps where no Catechist resides be presented to the Reverend Bishop for such Catechist appointments."

This resolution caused much excitement among the delegates and officials because the present session of Congress did not happen to have the necessary

Pearl Brewer (Lakota) and Seth Irving (Lakota) in "Lily of the Mohawks" school play at Holy Rosary Mission, Pine Ridge Reservation, South Dakota, ca. 1938. In 1938 Holy Rosary students reenacted the play at the Golden Jubilee Catholic Sioux Congress. Credit: Reverend Joseph A. Zimmerman, S.J., Marquette University, Bureau of Catholic Indian Missions Records. Reproduced by permission.

papers, such as rules and by-laws, to justify and solve such a resolution at such a time. A thorough search was made through the old records, but to no avail. Finally a messenger was sent to secure copies of the general rules for Congresses from the Superior of Holy Rosary Mission. In the meantime it was moved and seconded to use the Constitution and By-laws of the General Owancaya Meeting temporarily. The result of the votes was 33 in favor and 15 against. This motion did not bind, however, as copies of General Rules for Congress were found. It was too late for any further business so the meeting adjourned at 6 P.M.

Evening Session

Meeting was called to order and the usual hymn was sung. During the fore part of the day the Rosebud Delegation tabled a resolution which read as follows:

"We, the Catholic members and people of the Rosebud Indian Reservation, do hereby respectfully request the authority of the Catholic Congress to take action in beheading or checking various matters which now cause backsliding among our Church members, namely: Peyote, Yuwipi, Wiyon Nonpapi, and Divorces.

In doing this we must do it in a systematic way so as not to slander.

It is better to encourage more of our helpers and to better their wages and to call on our good Catholic friends and peoples of the East."

Action could not be taken until now that such rules were available. Speakers explained the nature of the resolution and as the delegates were still studying the problems, Sister Lucy, a native Nun, entered the meeting. Immediately it was arranged for her to speak to her people. Truly it was a great surprise to the people to hear Sister Lucy speak very fluently in both Dakota and English. She gave a very instructive talk. Following it all lined up and shook hands with her. Great inspiration was experienced at an appropriate time of the Congress. It made everyone feel very happy.

Because it was getting late, the resolutions that were pending were postponed until the following day for further action. Meeting adjourned at 11 P.M.

JUNE 23

At 9:30 A.M. Rev. Father Goll, S.J. opened the meeting with a prayer. Two distinguished pioneers of the St. Mary's Society, Mrs. Jarvis and Mrs. Clara Holy Skin whose ages ranged past the 80's were given an honor. Rev. Fr. [Buechel] told some interesting things about these ladies as far back as he could remember them. They were the originators of the St. Mary's Society at Holy Rosary. In return for the honor given them Mrs. Clara Holy Skin rose and leaning on her cane gave a short talk of thanks.

Mr. Isaac Deon, delegate from Yankton, was the next speaker; he gave an excellent talk on saving our souls through good work of Catholic Action. Mr. Alonso Moss, an [Arapaho] Indian from Wyoming, gave an excellent talk through interpreter Emil Afraid of Hawk about the new organization "Tekakwitha Temperance Society" which the [Arapaho] Indian boys and girls of Stephen's Mission accepted and organized.

Resolution adopted at Rosebud General Meeting on June 11, 1938 at Our Lady of Good Counsel and presented by Harry Iron Wing and Geo. Whirlwind Soldier was put to vote. Result: 62 in favor and 5 against. It was moved and seconded that the resolution now adopted should immediately take [effect]. The motion was withdrawn after some long discussions.

Afternoon Session

Meeting called to order at 1 P.M.

Harry Iron Wing again explained the resolution of the previous day but it appeared that there was still some confusion with its passage so finally he moved the withdrawal of the resolution. The President overruled Mr. Iron Wing's motion; he ordered to proceed with the resolutions adopted by them at the General Meeting for Congress to consider. The Secretary read:

"Resolution of equalizing each Indian Child's school appropriation regardless of what school they attend."

Mr. Edward Stover of Oglala moved that this Congress be authorized by its members to request equal per capita allowances which each Indian child is entitled by treaty rights whether they attend parochial or Government schools. There was no second so it was dropped. The resolution was reworded:

"The Catholic Congress respectfully asks the Secretary of the Interior to instruct the Commissioner of Indian Affairs to consider the wishes of the parents of Indians school children as to the school which these children are to attend. We Indians want that the Catholic Mission schools be allowed to fill to their capacities and that the contract be extended to this full number."

Jas. Henry Red Cloud moved and it was seconded by Chas. Randall to accept this resolution which was read and construed by the Secretary. The vote was 28 in favor and 4 against.

At this time W. O. Roberts, Supt. of Indian Affairs, attended by M. G. Ripke, Chief Clerk, W. O. Nicholson, and Eugene Clement, School Supervisors arrived and Mr. Roberts gave a brief but pointed talk on the good work being done among the Sioux by the Missions.

Tom Stabber presented a resolution to assess fifty cents to each chapel for incidental purposes for Catechists. No action was taken. The President explained that such resolution already had been adopted.

Wm. Fills the Pipe tabled a resolution that St. Bernard's Church have a Catechist. John Eagle Louse seconded and it was passed 29 to 11. He further tabled a resolution to request the Rt. Rev. Bishop to allow and fill in all vacant chapels where there are no Catechists. It was seconded by John Eagle Louse and passed 30 to 7.

Geo. Whirlwind Soldier moved to elect secretaries for the Congress. Vote unanimously in favor.

Henry Leed, nominated by Geo. Whirlwind Soldier was elected but because of difficulties was declared invalid and Henry Iron Wing, nominated by James Grass, was officially elected. Louis P. Mouseau was elected by 23 votes.

Evening Session

Before the meeting was opened for business Catechist James Grass, Jr. made the spiritual report of the Congress. During the three days there was

1 baptism

6 first communions

83 confirmations

600 confessions were heard

1000 received communion

The meeting was opened for discussion.

Ed Stover made a suggestion that for the next Annual Congress all of the various reservations who are members of the Congress should help to collect funds for the expenses.

Joseph Yellow Fat of Standing Rock explained to Congress that his people are preparing to unveil a sculptured monument in memorial of the pioneer Rt. Rev. Bishop Marty, known as Tamaheca, in full regalia sometime next year in June at Kenel, So. Dak. It was here that Bishop Marty rendered his last confirmations to his beloved Standing Rock Sioux Indians. Joseph Yellow Fat further expressed his thanks to the executives of the Congress and the people for the courtesies he received during the deliberations of Congress. He furthered an invitation to the Oglalas to be present at the memorial festival.

The President reread the report of expenditures for the Jubilee Congress, which totaled $510.63. During the Congress:

722 adults received rations.

111 adults were fed three meals a day.

833 total number of adults receiving care during the congress.

Rev. Fr. [Buechel] as usual gave very good advice to the people of the Congress. Everyone was silent to hear the wonderful Teton Sioux language which Father used very fluently in his speech.

Geo. Whirlwind Soldier moved that the next Annual Congress for 1939 be held on the Standing Rock Reservation, seconded by Wm. Fills the Pipe. Vote 59 in favor, none against.

James Red Cloud expressed thanks to the people of the Congress, in particular to Rev. Fr. [Buechel], S.J. for his kind assistance and good counsels during the three days of the Congress.

Mr. Isaac Deon also extended his sincere thanks to the Congress for the good cause that all of the speakers made, the courtesies of the women's Society and that they were well taken care of in the line of food. Mr. Deon made a strong talk against the use of Peyote among his tribe. He emphasized very much against the wretched drug because little children ranging from seven years up are forced to eat peyote. Something should be done immediately to suppress this.

Mr. Yellow Bull expressed his thanks especially to Mr. Peter Red Elk who was kind to furnish 210 pine poles to be used for the bower at the Congress. It made him happy to hear the fine remarks made of the skilled labor done on the bower by some of his people who selected a very [appropriate] place at the shrine of Our Queen of Holy Rosary.

Mr. Wm. Red Hair and President Wm. Patton praised Emil Afraid of Hawk for his skilled work in building the bower. Mr. Patton announced and ordered that the bower remain on the place for the rest of the season as [it] will make a nice recreation place for the youngsters upon their return to school.

Mike One Star of Rosebud also expressed his thanks to the Oglala for the nice treatment he experienced during the Jubilee Congress.

Quite a few speakers gave their views of the Jubilee Congress. Among these were Father Daniel of Marty S.D., Jas. Grass, Mrs. Julia Deon and Catechist Ray Hernandez. All of these remarks were of encouragement to keep up our Catholic religion.

There being no further business Congress adjourned at 11 P.M.

Hymn No. 58 "God Be With You Until We Meet Again" was sung and all took part in shaking hands for a cheerful farewell and departure.

> William Patton, President
> Wm. Bush, Assist. Secretary
> Emil Afraid of Hawk, Temp. Secretary

Marquette University, Holy Rosary Mission — Red Cloud Indian School Records. Printed by permission.

67. Correspondence of Nicholas Black Elk, Lakota Catechist and Medicine Man, 1907–34

Black Elk Speaks *is about Black Elk's early life as a medicine man among the Lakota Sioux Indians of the Northern Plains. Today it is the most popular book about American Indians, but few readers know that the holy man Black Elk became a Christian and spent most of his life as a catechist with Jesuits in South Dakota. Steeped in both Lakota and Catholic traditions, Black Elk was christened "Nicholas" on the feast of St. Nicholas, December 6, 1904.*

As a catechist between 1907 and 1916, Black Elk dictated many spiritual letters addressed to his friends and relatives. They were published in the missionaries' Lakota language newspaper, Sinasapa Wocekiye Taeanpaha, *meaning the "Black Robe Church Newspaper," at St. Michael's Mission, Devil's Lake Reservation, Ft. Totten, North Dakota, and distributed in Indian reservation communities throughout the Northern Plains.*

Translated from Lakota to English under Reverend Michael F. Steltenkamp, S.J.

Letter to the newspaper written at Pine Ridge Reservation, Manderson, South Dakota, November 12, 1906, published March 15, 1907.

Since the last Sioux Congress and at the present time, I have visited the Rosebud Reservation. The people there told me that they want churches built on their own districts. I was pleased to hear these people are interested in God. As I was present there, they took up a collection for me, and these people donated to me.

[Acknowledgments follow, listing names and donations.]

I thank these people for doing a great deed for me. I know all these came from God. I spoke mainly on Jesus — when he was on earth, the teachings and his sufferings. I myself do a lot of these things. I suffer and I try to teach my people the things that I wanted them to learn, but it[']s never done.

In my sufferings, my eyes are failing, and also my health is failing. So I will tell you that all of you (and myself, that it or we) are like sheep among the wolves ready to be eaten up. And you know when one sheep is surrounded by wolves it has no place to go. That's how we are. We are ready to be eaten up.

So my friends and relatives, we should stand together and do what is right and be patient. That way God has something good for us all the time.

These people want to accept God and they ask me to get a catechist in these communities. So I told them that the districts of our reservation have catechists... and that these people pray on Sundays when the priest is not around.

I will encourage you people that you donate at least a penny to these catechists, so that they can continue on their work in the name of God. While we're still living on earth, we should be thankful to God for putting us here on this earth. And God has promised us a place when we die, and I'm pretty sure he'll never forget us.

Letter to the newspaper written at Pine Ridge Reservation, Manderson, South Dakota, October 20, 1907, published December 15, 1907

...Last May, Edward White Crow lost his wife. And at that wake I said these words: My friends and relatives and St. Joseph and St. Mary Society present. What I want to tell the mourners is this. Every one of us has to die some day and we are not going to live for a long time because God has sent us on this earth for a short time. But what I want to tell you is: have faith in God and remember to go to church every Sunday because this is where you can gain wisdom. And when you pray to God, all your sorrows and whatever that comes your way will disappear, because God is there to help you.

This woman was very active in the St. Mary's Society. So now she has gained the gates of heaven because she has worked very hard for God. Now what I'm going to say again is this: that Julia White Crow was a very kind woman. I saw her work many times, and she tried her best to do what she was supposed to be doing — sewing, and helping out in the meetings, cooking — and we are going to miss this woman because God has called her.

God the Father, and Jesus Christ — I pray to them often that St. Joseph's and St. Mary's Society will never fade away. Some day this is going to happen: because the present generation is beginning to turn. But let us train our younger ones to continue on the work that we've been doing. I'm very old now, and my days are numbered. So, my friends and relatives, what I'd like to say is, at least, God have pity on you during your mourning.

And last July I went to Indianapolis, Indiana. There I met with the White people in a meeting and I was really glad that I have heard and seen with my own eyes the things that they are doing. And we should do the same thing here, but it is very hard for us to do the things that the white people are doing because we have very few things to work with. But again, we must depend on God to help us. My friends and relatives I speak to you from the bottom of my heart. Please try and do the things that we're supposed to do. Let us not forget the main person — that is Wakan Tanka [God]. And the priest or the bishop has told us that we are never to be afraid because God is always with us.

Now last September 20th, I went on a trip again. This time to Montana where they called me and invited me to go there. And it was difficult for me

Black Elk, second from right, front row, St. Elizabeth's Church, Manderson, Pine Ridge Reservation, South Dakota, 1936. Credit: Photographer unknown. Marquette University, Bureau of Catholic Indian Missions Records. Reproduced by permission.

[because they spoke a different language]. But they have organized a St. Joseph and a St. Mary Society, and I was really glad that these people, too, were interested in the organization. And I spoke at that meeting and congratulated them because they, too, have interest in the great family, the Holy Family.

So I will now close that you should all pray, and always remember to pray for each other.

Letter to the newspaper written at Pine Ridge Reservation, Manderson, South Dakota, no date, published July 15, 1908.

I will be going on a journey to Wyoming, the land of the Arapahoes. We are bringing Good News [about Jesus Christ] to these people — I and Joe Red Willow. They have selected us to go to the Arapahoes. We are invited by the majority of the people, and we had a really big meeting with the Arapahoes and what they want to know about is the St. Joseph and St. Mary's Societies. So we did the best we can. We told the Arapaho people that we, too, are very poor, and that there is no difference between them and us because we are both Indians. And they asked me to say a few words to the members there, so I told them about the St. Joseph and the St. Mary's organization. First how to conduct a meeting. And then I told them about the order of the meeting: that you've got to have a president, a vice-president, a secretary, treasurer, a critic, and a door-keeper. And then they were so enthused that they are going to start their own St. Joseph and St. Mary Society there. And then they asked me how they should pray, so this is what I said to them. When you say the Our Father, remember that there is one Father and one Son. This is what you've got to believe. And after my talk, they were so interested so they want us to go back to the land of the Arapahoes again, in the near future.

What they want to know is how to pray. So I asked Fr. Westropp to send our prayer-books so they can translate in their own language [Arapaho]. Then they will have a prayer-book. While I was talking, I was talking in my own native [Lakota Sioux] language and Mr. Red Willow was translating my talk [into English for retranslation into Arapaho] because I do not talk English well. I know a few words and that is it.

The next thing that I will be talking about is how to elect officers. And we told them that you select a person who is worthy — that has knowledge of being a leader, and that's the person that you select. And the vice president is the same way, in case the president is not there, then the vice will be there to take over. And the next position is the secretary. The secretary is to keep the minutes. And I told them that whatever they say are the main points that's what the secretary should write down and make it a good minutes. And a treasurer is responsible for all of the money that's been collected so as to keep an account and report this at each meeting. A critic is a person that if a person gets out of line, he should correct them and still accept it. And a doorkeeper is to shake his hand, then he will close the door and charge a fee for opening the door again. This is the organization of the St. Joseph and St. Mary society. They had a big election of officers while we were there. Andrew Jackson, president; Alfonso Goes In Lodge, vice president; Mr. Big Head is treasurer; Black Coal is secretary; Alfonso Moss, catechist.

The next Catholic Congress is in Rosebud. These officials are planning to come there, and to get more ideas while the meeting is going on. And there's many people who are suffering. The superior [of St. Francis Mission] told me to help these people and I went to every lodge, to help them. Fr. Westropp came by and talked to me about going back to the Arapaho. And he said he had received a new donation to build a church and a meeting house and I was really glad that they are beginning to take hold of their own and I hope in the near future that they start organizing and do the things that we are doing over here. So Fr. Westropp has told me that we are going to install some more catechists in our area, the Pine Ridge Reservation. The place where they are going to install these new catechists is at St. Paul's in Porcupine District. So now I will close my talk and wish you the best, and I will shake my hand from the bottom of my heart and I will remain as your friend,

Letter to Msgr. Ketcham, Director, Bureau of Catholic Indian Missions, written at Pine Ridge Reservation, Manderson, South Dakota, January 9, 1912.

Would like to notify you that I have live up to nineteen twelve and would like to notify you about my condition. Last nineteen hundred & four I became a [catechist] and during that time & at the present date. I have had a number join our flock and I expect I have quite a number more in the future but I am in a critical condition at present. Therefore I gave you thanks in Christ and wish for you to remember me in your prayers. I am now going to make my head way to Hot Springs for a treatment. I will be in Hot Springs 18th of this month. Therefore I beg you to find me a little help and would like to hear of you too and if our Saviour gives me help on my sickness and restore my health I will again look into our business among my Catholic Sioux's. I sincerely wish to hear from you soon. In the name of our Saviour we praise you.

Yours in Christ
Nicholas Black Elk

Marquette University, Bureau of Catholic Indian Missions Records. Printed by permission.

In 1930–31 the poet John G. Neihardt interviewed Black Elk and in 1932 published his life story as Black Elk Speaks. *In this book Black Elk described his Lakota spirituality, including his visions and ritual performances as a young man, and he expressed nostalgia for traditional Lakotas ways. No mention was made of his Catholicism. The Jesuits at Holy Rosary Mission were distressed at the portrayal of the catechist they knew so well as an unreformed traditionalist, and they sought a corrective. In 1933 Black Elk was seriously injured and requested last rites. He was granted them, and when he recovered in 1934 he signed two documents in which he disavowed the contents of* Black Elk Speaks. *The first was typed in English and Lakota and signed by Black Elk, his daughter Lucy C. Looks Twice, and Reverend Joseph A. Zimmerman, S.J.*

BLACK ELK SPEAKS AGAIN — A LAST WORD:

I shake hands with my white friends. Listen, I speak some true words. A white man made a book and told what I had spoken of olden times, but the new times he left out. So I speak again, a last word.

I am now an old man. I called my [priest] to pray for me and to give me holy oil and the Holy Food, the "(Yutapi Wakan)." Now I will tell you the truth. Listen my friends.

In the last thirty years I am different from what the white man wrote about me. I am a Christian. I was baptized thirty years ago by the Black-gown priest called Little Father (Ate-ptecela). After that time all call me Nick Black Elk. Most of the Sioux Indians know me. I am now converted to the true Faith in God the Father, the Son and the Holy Ghost. I say in my own Sioux Lakota language; Ateunyanpi; — Our Father who art in heaven, Hallowed be thy name — as Christ taught us to say. I say the Apostle's Creed and I believe every word of it.

I believe in seven holy Sacraments of the Catholic Church. I myself received now six of them; Baptism, Confirmation, Penance, Holy Communion, Holy Marriage, and Extreme Unction.

I was for many years a regular companion of several missionaries going out campaigning for Christ among my people. I was nearly twenty years the helper of the priests and acted as Catechist in several camps. So I knew my Catholic Religion better than many white people.

For eight years I made regular Retreat given by the priest for Catechists and I learned much of the faith in those days. I can give reasons for my faith. I know whom I have believed and my faith is not vain.

My family is all baptized. All my children and grand-children belong to the Black-gown church and I am glad of that and I wish that all should stay in that holy way.

I know what St. Peter said about those who fall away from the holy Commandments. You white friends should read 2 Peter 2–20, 22. I tell my people to stay in the right way which Christ and His church have taught us. I will never fall back from the true faith in Christ.

Thirty years ago I was a real Indian and knew a little about the Great Spirit — the Wakantanka. I was a good dancer and I danced before Queen Victoria in England. I made medicine for sick people. I was proud, perhaps I was brave, perhaps I was a good Indian; but now I am better.

St. Paul also turned better when he was converted. I now know that the prayer of the Catholic Church is better than the Sun-dance or the Ghost-dance. Old Indians danced that kind for their own glory. They cut themselves so that the blood flowed. But Christ was nailed to the Cross for sin and he took away our sins. The old Indian prayers did not make people better. The medicine men looked for their own glory and for presents. Christ taught us to be humble and to stop sin. Indian medicine men did not stop sin. Now I hate sin. I want to be straight as the black-gown church teaches us to be straight to save my soul for heaven. This I want to do. I cheerfully shake hands with you all.

Nick Black Elk
Lucy C. Looks Twice
Joseph A. Zimmerman, S.J.

In the second document of 1934 Black Elk claimed to have spoken to Neihardt of his Catholic faith, but that Neihardt left such material out of his book. In effect, the letter blamed Neihardt for dwelling on the past and accused the poet of inventing a paganized Black Elk.

"DEAR FRIENDS," September 20, 1934.

Dear Friends: —

Three years ago in 1932* a white man named John G. Neihardt came up to my place whom I have never met before and asked me to make a story book with him[.] I don['.]t know whether he took out a permit from the agent or not[.] He promised me that if he completed and publish [*sic*] this book he was to pay half of the price of each book[.]

I trusted him and finished the story of my life for him[.] [A]fter he published the book I wrote to him and ask [*sic*] him about the price which he promise [*sic*] me on the books he sold[.] He answered my letter and told me that there was

---

*Historical note: Neihardt's interview took place in 1931.

another white man who has asked him to make this book so he himself hasn't seen a cent from the Book which we made[.]

By this I know he was now deceiving me about the whole business[.] I also asked to put at the end of this story that I was not a pagan but have been converted into the Catholic Church in which I work [*sic*] as a Catechist for more than 25 years[.] I've quit all these pagan works[.] But he didn't mention [these] last talks[.]

So if they can['t] put this Religion life in the last part of that Book also if he can['t] pay what he promised I ask you my dear friends that this Book of my life will be null & void[.] Because I value my soul more than my Body[.] I['t]m awful sorry for the mistake I['t]ve made[.]

I also have this witnesses [*sic*] to stand by me[.]

I['t]m yours truly
Nick Black Elk

*My name is not Amerdian [*sic*] but he is lying about my name[.]

Marquette University, Holy Rosary Mission — Red Cloud Indian School Records. Printed by permission.

68. Pine Ridge Petition to Mrs. Franklin D. Roosevelt, March 5, 1934

In an attempt to stop the loss of Indian lands and cultures, the U.S. Commissioner of Indian Affairs, John Collier, initiated an Indian New Deal for the Franklin D. Roosevelt administration in 1934. Collier issued federal directives to respect traditional Indian religious practices; he established tribal governments on the model of the U.S. Constitution; he questioned the wisdom of boarding schools, which removed Indian children from their parents in order to wean them of their Native ways. At Holy Rosary Mission and many other Catholic institutions, Collier's reforms were anathema. The Church authorities arranged for Pine Ridge Catholics to sign a petition to Eleanor Roosevelt, the president's wife, protesting the threat to mission boarding schools.

Dear Mrs. Roosevelt:

We, the undersigned Indians of the Pine Ridge Reservation, write to you as one parent to another. We know you [are] a good mother who has raise[d] your children as good christian men and women and we want to do the same with our children.

Mr. Collier, the Commissioner of Indian Affairs has started a program that he calls the FIVE POINT educational plan, which means the end of our mission boarding schools. The missionaries have been our friends for years and have helped us in every way and now Mr. Collier who doesn't know the good the Mission schools have done like we do, is going to stop them from taking our children. It is our money that has helped to pay for these Mission Schools and they have not [cost] the Government a cent.

The United States Supreme Court in the Quick Bear case said that we had a right to use our money to have our children receive religious education at our own cost, and that to prevent us from doing so would prohibit the free exercise of religion, which is one of the most precious rights of the American citizen.

We know that you would not want some man who does not know your family affairs like you do to stop you from sending your children to a religious school at your own expense if you wanted to do so.

We Indians have read and heard about you and we hope our cry to you will be heard. We know how busy your husband is and how little time he can give to us poor Indians but won't you please see him and help us. As a mother you know that our children are more precious to us than anything else. Please help us, Mrs. Roosevelt.

[Attached to the letter were hundreds of Indian names.]

Marquette University, Holy Rosary Mission — Red Cloud Indian School Records. Printed by permission.

69. Freeman A. Mesteth (Lakota) from South Dakota State Penitentiary to Reverend Ted F. Zuern, S.J., March 7, 1993

On the night of May 29, 1981, in Rapid City, South Dakota, Freeman A. Mesteth (age twenty) and Walter Dale Means (age nineteen), son of American Indian Movement activist Russell Means, burglarized the St. Isaac Jogues parish rectory while reportedly under the influence of alcohol and drugs. The pastor, Reverend Richard G. Pates, S.J. (1919–89), was shot and wounded and the associate pastor, Reverend James V. "O.C." O'Connor, S.J. (1920–81), died of a heart attack. Catholic Lakotas viewed both priests as longtime benefactors and advocates of Indian people. Mesteth served seventeen years in prison and was incarcerated again following a parole violation. Father Ted F. Zuern knew Mesteth and his family well as a pastor. Father Zuern had baptized Mesteth and his younger brother Arlen in their infancy. (Arlen died from abuse in state foster care.) When Mesteth wrote this letter his alcohol-dependent mother was suffering from a diabetic coma.

Dear Fr. Zuern,

I'm sorry it has taken me awhile to write and thank you for visiting my Mother and praying with her. I am also thankful for the address of the Rev. Richard Pates. I still have not written to him as I am still attempting to muster the courage with which to do so. I will get to it sometime soon though. I know what I would like to say to him as well as Fr. Pates['] other family members. It's just taken me some time to do it.

One never really thinks about how much is thrown away when one commits a crime and loses his/her freedom. I never really thought about the spiritual imbalance in my life and the great void that is there as a result of not praying. All the anger and frustration that has been with me ever since I was a little boy sometimes gets the best of me. I have been working on it though.

I don't mean to sound like I'm trying to place the blame on anyone or my imprisonment is not just. It's just so hard at times dealing with the racism that exists in here. If I ever make it out of here I don't ever want to come back to such a place as this. I truly am sorry for what I did to Fr. Pates. I am also sorry about Fr. O'Connor. I never intended for anyone to die that night. I also never seen anyone have a heart attack before.

My life seems so meaningless at times I often wonder what my Dad and younger brother are doing in the spirit world. There was times in my life during my confinement that I often called out to my Dad, Grandfather, little Brother, or Grandma to come after me. With my Mother being where she is at now and the condition she is in it just makes it that much more difficult at times.

Fr. Zuern, I thank you for forgiving me and extending my apologies to the congregation of the St. Isaac Jogues Parish. I don't know how my one time co-defendant, Walter D. Means, feels. I can't speak for him, but I feel I owe you people. Before I leave this world I will give something back to the Rapid City community which Fr. Pates and Fr. O'Connor served.

You're a [good] man Fr. Zuern and I'll pray for you as I pray for Fr. Pates and Fr. O'Connor. I remember one time when we lived out at Sioux Addition. My Mother and Father went to Pine Ridge to check on their lease checks and why they never received them. We didn't have much to eat at that time and my Sister Dotty was the oldest there and she watched over us younger ones. I believe she sent Joy and Ardenna down to the Mother Butler Center on West Blvd. to ask you for help. You brought the girls back along with a few sacks of groceries. My little Brother Arlen was about 3 years old at that time and my Mom and Dad took Gibby as he was only 1 years old at that time.

We used a kerosene lamp in those days but I remember Dotty praying before we ate our meal and she thanked God for you and the food you had brought us. Although we didn't have much in those days I still believe they are the happiest days in my life. Dotty is married and living in North Carolina. She has a son who is named after my younger Brother Arlen. I spoke to him a couple of times although he is still very young and it was a bit difficult to understand.

Well Fr. Zuern, I'll end this letter here. I'll be transferred to a different prison on Monday. It is somewhat rougher and I must admit I am a bit afraid, but that[']s prison life. If anything should happen to me I feel a lot better knowing that you have forgiven me. I also thank you for all the help you have given to my family. Peace to you Sir.

Sincerely,
Freeman A. Mesteth
21165

Marquette University, St. Isaac Jogues Records. Printed by permission.

70. Reverend Joseph P. Logan, S.J., Report on Catholic Missions among the Indians, Diocese of Seattle, August 16, 1948

The Catholic Suquamish Indians of Puget Sound found themselves overwhelmed by non-Indian vacationers and weekenders who attended Mass at St. Peter's Church, where the Suquamish had buried their dead for several generations. Father Joseph P. Logan, S.J., noted that the Indians' resentment of the intrusion kept them away from church. He also remarked that some Catholic Suquamish participated in the Indian Shaker Movement, begun in the Northwest in 1882 and still a spiritual presence in the region.

St. Peter's
Suquamish, Wash.

It is very difficult to get any response from the Indians. They are not well-organized, they are scattered over the whole of the parish, since they do not live on a reservation for the past several years, and there are very few family units. Most of the remaining Indians are single, or have married into white families who have no religious affiliations.

The few who do come faithfully to Mass are exemplary Catholics. There is, in an outlying section of the parish, a little community called Little Boston, where a sort of Shaker Movement has some little influence among the Indians. Many of them were nominally Catholics at one time.

Only a full-time priest could have much influence on these Indians, and then I don't know how much it would be. I feel that a good deal of their apathy to the church is the result of resentment that the whites have moved into their church in such numbers that they have practically taken it over. That is what a couple of the old-timers have told me.

Joseph P. Logan, S.J.

Archdiocese of Seattle Archives. Printed by permission.

71. Swinomish Tribal Community to Bishop Thomas A. Connolly, March 18, 1971

With a large non-Indian population surrounding the Indian reservations in the Archdiocese of Seattle, and with a shortage of priests following the Second Vatican Council, Archbishop Thomas A. Connolly selected to close St. Paul's Church on the Swinomish Reservation in 1971. The local priest said that his ministry was not reaching a sufficient number of Indians there, and with another Catholic church nearby, it seemed imprudent to duplicate his efforts. When the priest announced the closing, members of the Swinomish community, non-Catholics as well as congregants, petitioned the archbishop to keep the church open. Notwithstanding, Archbishop Connolly decided to discontinue regular services at St. Paul's.

Your Excellency:
It has been called to our attention that an announcement was made through the bulletin of the St. Charles Church of Burlington that Masses at St. Paul Church of Swinomish were to be discontinued with next Sunday, March 21st, being the last Mass.

We, the families and Catholic members of the Swinomish Indian Reservation, prayerfully wish to be heard with compassion on the matter of the discontinuance of Masses at the St. Paul Church, Swinomish Indian Reservation. We plead to you, Your Excellency, with every fiber of love in Christ's name, to hear our plea.

Should the Masses be discontinued at St. Paul, the members of Swinomish will again experience the ravaging power of a system to which the Indians have been exposed for the last 150 years. We have in the past been saddened by actions of the United States government in the handling of Indian affairs, and have become somewhat calloused to this. In this particular instance, however, the spiritual hurt will be long lasting and, with our cultural spiritual beliefs virtually extinct, we find this action of closing the church extremely difficult to accept as an act of God.

We, the undersigned members of the Swinomish Indian Reservation, express our thoughts and prayerful desire to have the decision of closing St. Paul's Church reversed and to have Sunday Masses continued. And we pledge earnestly to attend Masses as often as it is possible for us to do so in the future.

The following are samples of typical verbatim comments uttered by members of the Swinomish:

We just got this church going and now we have to close it. If we let it go now, our younger children that just started to know how to go to church will forget their religion. This is going to be a big loss for our reservation. We just as well not have a church standing up. Our children will not know how to pray. It's our children I am worrying about. It is bad enough now. Our Catholic will really go down to nothing. That church was built before my time. The young generation are the ones we have to think of.

John R. Paul

This church has always been open since 1925. That is the year I moved here. There always has been this church even though there was no priest to come here. They say there are not enough priests to go around. Father Hartnet had a hard time too when he had to say three Masses every Sunday, even though his heart started bothering him. We had priests that cared for the Indians in the earlier days — especially Father McGrath and the late Father Hartnet.

In 1925 when I first moved here, I did not know about this church. I lived in a tent then just about below the church and I used to hear a bell ringing every Sunday morning, so one day I walked up there knowing there was no priest around. When I went into the church, I found one old lady there all by herself praying. Since then I have been going to this church and it is the only church I have been going to.   Lucinda Joe

I think the St. Paul Church is the only spiritual connection that our people, the members of the Catholic religion, have. If it is closed now, we lose all our spiritual help.   Helen Ross

I am retired from the navy after twenty years of service plus seven years with Federal Civil Service. It seems to me that after all these years of what we call democracy, things haven't changed but a very little amount for the Indian people. And yet we ask so little.

I had also made arrangements for new church pews from the Naval Air Station at Whidbey Island. These are considered surplus and we were to install them at our own time in the very near future.

I, my wife and children beg to keep the church continued.

Andrew McDonald

The first priest taught the people how to pray and sing hymns and used to visit the people. Prayers and hymns were in Indian. When I was a little boy I used to remember that priest that used to visit the homes once in awhile, but he used to travel in horse and buggy to Burlington and to LaConner, and when he didn't come the people even still used to go to church. When the priest stopped coming then the people began not to go to church.

Richard Peters

We would miss having Mass every Sunday and keeping our children in touch with God — right here on our own reservation so close to home within walking distance — to be with Christ once a week. For the sake of our children and ourselves we need to keep our faith and to keep our church open. I would not know what to do without having to visit God every Sunday.

Beverly Peters

For myself, I have been attending Mass at this church since I have been on Swinomish back in 1948. And it was hard when St. Paul's was closed for several years. I have tried to attend as often as I possibly could. My son, Rodney, has known what Catholic religion is, as St. Paul's opened just when he was old enough to start understanding what it is to be a Christian boy. I would like Mass to [be] said at St. Paul's even if it could be said during the week, just so long as we can continue to hear Mass.

Bernadette A. Billy

We, the undersigned, prayerfully request Your Excellency to use your position in Christ's name to keep our church, the St. Paul Catholic Church of Swinomish, open with Masses to continue as in the past. We further feel that a pastor should be assigned to our reservation to do the work that has long been needed to rejuvenate church work among the Indians. What we have now is tantamount to no pastor at all. We would be happy to discuss this with you at a later date.

Your careful consideration on behalf of the Indians of Swinomish will be appreciated.

Yours in Christ's Name,
Members of Swinomish Indian Reservation
Tandy Wilbur *et al.* [51 names]

We, the signers of this paper, are concerned, non-Catholic members of the Swinomish Indian Reservation. [14 names]

72. Martin J. Sampson (Skagit) Lectures on Catholicism's Spiritual Power, May 16, 1977

Northwest Indians who have reflected on the conversions of their ancestors to Catholicism have suggested that they were attracted to the faith because it seemed so much like their traditional spirituality. In a speech given to students at the University of Washington, Martin J. Sampson, a Skagit elder, tells how Father Eugene Chirouse, O.M.I., told the Indians in the nineteenth century about the spiritual power of Catholicism and how the Indians compared that power to their own. Sampson emphasizes the similarity of powers expressed in the songs of traditional shamans, Indian Shaker curers, Christian hymns, and operatic arias. Translated and transcribed by Vi Hilbert, a Skagit linguist.

You folks, my people (standard salutation i.e. Dear Friends,)

We are gathered here today to reminisce about the way our ancestors were when the strangers arrived long ago.

They arrived and the Indians asked them[,]

"Who are you?

Where are you from?"

The strangers said,

"We are from Boston!"

"Oh! Boston."

That's how they come to know this.

At the present time as we are gathered here, we know that the Bostons are Americans.

Then these strangers came, there were many of them (they became many).

Then the religion came.

This "press yourself religion!" (sign of the cross religion).

It arrived.

([T]hose preaching this religion) took the Indians and told them this.

"We are all (brothers & sisters) one people, everyone on this land."

So they accepted this (religion).

The leader of this religion said,

"In the beginning we were all one people."

Now today, this 'press yourself (sign of the cross)' religion was given by *Jesus Christ* son of the supreme one.

The priest, Father Chirouse said to them, he said this, "it is the will of the heavenly father, though your body dies, your soul will live.

It just returns from whence it came."

This was what the priest tells the people of Christ's message.

Then he said,

"Your breath that gives you life stays here on earth.

But yet this returns from whence it came."

Then the people said[,]

"We believe the same thing.

Our breath leaves us.

Our bodies return to the earth, yet our souls live."

The people just said to him.

The beliefs were the same, they thought the same thing.

The "press yourself" religion and their own.

Yet where the Indians went was close.

Where their souls are.

There is a land where the Indians go.

There is nothing but summer there.

The Indians are always singing there.

They are always happy.

Someone with spirit power will go there.

If someone is ill and the Indian doctor can't cure him.

He is unable to help him.

So those who know how, go to the first land of those who die.

They call it, "beltedaq."

These people go, now they sing this spirit power song....

It was after the people saw that the 'press yourself' religion was the same as their beliefs that they accepted it.

That was why the Indians accepted religion.

The priest said to them[,]

"You will go way up high where you will be forever!"

Then the Indians asked the priest, "do you folks go to the first land of the people who die?"

He said, "no, we don't go there, that is called purgatory."

The priest doesn't go there.

Yet the beliefs are the same.

The Protestant religion was brought now.

It was introduced to the Indians.

Then, after that, those from Boston came, the Americans now.

We would like to buy land to live on....

We went to the reservation when I was just three months old.

To Tulalip.

We moved to Swinomish.

There was now a school at Swinomish.

I will (say it in English), 1894 was when the school was built.

Just four grades, one, two, three, four. That's all there was.

Father Chirouse's school though went to the sixth grade.

That was where he taught religion.

Then I went (to school).

I kept going through the fourth grade.

I didn't quit going to school because I couldn't quit until I was past 16 years of age.

I continued, a child going to school....

So it is that the white people have always kindly wanted to help us.

They want for us to learn things.

This desire is present to this day.

Christianity gives us strength to this day.

The education that is given by white people, what is written.

It is present to this day....

If it were not for Christianity there would be no Indians today.

You can see they are still fighting on their lands.

We, here on what we call America, Oh, our country is good.

I wouldn't have known about school.

My son, my daughter wouldn't have gone, we just have two children.

They wouldn't have known Christianity.

They wouldn't have known about writing.

We wouldn't have been here where we are, if it were not for Christianity.

This religion, it doesn't matter what it is, Catholic....

Well, this doctoring power there are many songs for it.

They fast, for how long, ten days they would go far away.

It is said by those who write.

The white people write about it.

That which they call Mt. Rainier, it is as though they pray to Mt. Rainier.

No, only if it is good ground, sacred ground would there be spirit powers present.

That is no longer possible today, because if you were to go to camp at Mt. Rainier, or Mt. Baker.

In the morning there you would find,

There a beer bottle, and over there, and there, no more is there a good place.

There are no spirit powers there any more, because the white people who come here have caused them to be no more by what they bring there....

It has become polluted, the earth is contaminated now.

This warrior power, this song.

You would go and sing over there.

Your sins would go away and you would be given a song.

That was the way it used to be.

During the present time, one of my cousins...did this.

He used to sing a spirit power song of our ancestors during the river drive.

He went then, became a Shaker,...then his spirit power from our ancestors changed over to become a Shaker.

It is the same spirit power only it too becomes a Shaker.

Here is the spirit power song of our ancestors.

> *SONG* ʔayewe, hu?...
>
> To the one who travels
>
> Listen to, the one who travels
>
> Listen to, the one who travels

Then after he became a Shaker. (sung as a Shaker song.)

Then there are those of us who come along later, we go to church.

> *SINGS* (in Latin, *adeste fideles*)

When I was confirmed in church,...the priest, a doctor in the French army, been a professor, a grand opera singer, he taught me how to sing.

He was a beautiful singer, and by the way, I was a WMCA secretary when I was

confirmed in the Catholic Church.

So I was on both sides of it, but anyhow.

The old priest said, "When you sing, have confidence, walk.

Have respect, don't be like a little child...."

> *SINGS* an aria from an opera.

Lushootseed Research Archives. Printed by permission.

73. Faye LaPointe (Swinomish) to Monsignor Paul A. Lenz, September 26, 1979

Faye LaPointe, a Swinomish Catholic, wrote to Monsignor Paul A. Lenz of the Bureau of Catholic Indian Missions in 1979, encouraging a Catholic Indian ministry of celebration rather than hellfire and damnation, a ministry more in keeping (she said) with Native American spirituality.

Dear Monsignor Lenz,

My name is Faye LaPointe. I am an enrolled member of the Swinomish Tribe in the state of Washington. My husband, Bob, and I are living in Tacoma where we are raising our 11 children. We are members of St. Leo's parish.

I'm writing to you because I just received the September issue of the Bureau of Catholic Indian Missions newsletter and was fascinated by the news of the August convention. I would like to have been in attendance but, like most of my people, lacked whatever it takes to initiate such participation.

I have worked for the Puyallup Tribe, the Muckleshoot Tribe, the Tacoma Indian Center and the State of Washington since 1973 in the areas of human services. I have been privileged to serve the weakest of God's people and blessed to learn from them.

Since I was educated in "white man[']s country" I had learned to think with my head. Which, by the way, is all but useless in Indian country. I had to be re-educated and begin again to think with my heart. By listening to my heart and the heart beats of my people I was allowed to see Jesus in their eyes. It is a most painful experience to say the least. But then, so was the life of Christ.

From my experiences I have come to [believe] that Indian people have suffered enough. We have had enough of John the Baptist's Hell fire and damnation. We want and need leaders like Jesus Christ. Ordained men and women that will help us come together in celebration. Celebration because as we read the scriptures we find that Jesus loved the people that were socially and economically oppressed. They were always persecuted and always helpless. They suffered the same kinds of social and spiritual illnesses that we do today. He ate with them, drank with them, sang, danced and prayed with them. He celebrated the final coming of our Father for it will be truly a joyous occasion for all of His people.

If one stops to think about it, Indian people today are very much like those that Jesus loved to be with. We asked for the same miracles, i.e. kill our oppressors, give us power and riches. And, as always, he very tenderly, [patiently] says to us "EAT MY BODY AND DRINK MY [BLOOD] AND YOU WILL HAVE ETERNAL LIFE." Now that[']s powerful and something we can relate to. It[']s something like Mother Earth and everything She supports.

It always blows my mind to see highly educated people trying to pound spirituality in the heads of my people[when all they really have to do is let it come out of our hearts. He is in fact in the hearts of all of my people. Unfortunately, we sometimes have to build high walls around Him to [survive]. Some of us even manage to kill Him again because we are afraid and can find no help.

I could go on and on but I'm sure you have heard all of this before. In closing I'd like to thank you for your work with my people and offer one word as a possible way of unchaining the hearts of Indian people. You guessed it, the word is *CELEBRATION.*

Be assured that I will pray for you and all people that are about our Father's work.

> With a wish for the peace of Christ
> I remain respectfully yours,
> Faye LaPointe

Marquette University, Bureau of Catholic Indian Missions Records.

74. A Public Declaration to the Tribal Councils and Traditional Spiritual Leaders of the Indian and Eskimo Peoples of the Pacific Northwest: In care of Jewell Praying Wolf James (Lummi), November 21, 1987

In 1987 Archbishop Raymond G. Hunthausen of Seattle and nine other Christian denominational leaders signed an ecumenical public declaration to the

*Indian and Eskimo peoples of the Northwest, apologizing for their churches'
participation in the destruction of traditional Indian practices. The signatories
affirmed the rights of Indians to engage in traditional ceremonies and praised
the ancient wisdom of their aboriginal religions. They placed the declaration
in the care of Jewell Praying Wolf James, a Lummi who was leading efforts to
protect American Indian religious freedom.*

Dear Brothers and Sisters,

This is a formal apology on behalf of our churches for their long-standing
participation in the destruction of traditional Native American spiritual practices. We call upon our people for recognition of and respect for your traditional ways of life and for protection of your sacred places and ceremonial
objects. We have frequently been unconscious and insensitive and have not
come to your aid when you have been victimized by unjust Federal policies
and practices. In many other circumstances we reflected the rampant racism and
prejudice of the dominant culture with which we too willingly identified. During the 200th Anniversary year of the United States Constitution we, as leaders
of our churches in the Pacific Northwest, extend our apology. We ask for your
forgiveness and blessing.

As the Creator continues to renew the earth, the plants, the animals and all
living things, we call upon the people of our denominations and fellowships
to a commitment of mutual support in your efforts to reclaim and protect the
legacy of your own traditional spiritual teachings. To that end we pledge our
support and assistance in upholding the American Religious Freedom Act (P.L.
95–134, 1978) and within that legal precedent affirm the following:

1) The rights of the Native Peoples to practice and participate in traditional
   ceremonies and rituals with the same protection offered all religions
   under the Constitution.

2) Access to and protection of sacred sites and public lands for ceremonial
   purposes.

3) The use of religious symbols (feathers, tobacco, sweet grass, bones, etc.)
   for use in traditional ceremonies and rituals.

The spiritual power of the land and the ancient wisdom of your indigenous religions can be, we believe, great gifts to the Christian churches. We offer
our commitment to support you in the righting of previous wrongs: To protect your peoples' efforts to enhance Native spiritual teachings: to encourage
the members of our churches to stand in solidarity with you on these important religious issues; to provide advocacy and mediation, when appropriate, for
ongoing negotiations with State agencies and Federal officials regarding these
matters.

May the promises of this day go on public record with all the congregations
of our communions and be communicated to the Native American Peoples of

the Pacific Northwest. May the God of Abraham and Sarah, and the Spirit who lives in both the cedar and Salmon People be honored and celebrated.

Sincerely,

The Rev. Thomas L. Blevins, Bishop
Pacific Northwest Synod—
Lutheran Church in America

The Most Rev. Raymond G. Hunthausen
Archbishop of Seattle
Roman Catholic Archdiocese of Seattle

The Rev. Dr. Robert Bradford,
Executive Minister
American Baptist Churches of the Northwest

The Rev. Elizabeth Knott, Synod Executive
Presbyterian Church
Synod Alaska-Northwest

The Rev. Robert Brock
N.W. Regional Christian Church

The Rev. Lowell Knutson, Bishop
North Pacific District
American Lutheran Church

The Right Rev. Robert H. Cochrane
Bishop, Episcopal Diocese of Olympia

The Most Rev. Thomas Murphy
Coadjutor Archbishop
Roman Catholic Archdiocese of Seattle

The Rev. W. James Halfaker
Conference Minister
Washington North Idaho Conference
United Church of Christ

The Rev. Melvin G. Talbert, Bishop
United Methodist Church—
Pacific Northwest Conference

Marquette University, Bureau of Catholic Indian Missions Records. Printed by permission.

75. Joan Staples-Baum (Ojibwa) to Archbishops Raymond Hunthausen and Thomas Murphy, April 20, 1988

In 1988 various Indians of the Archdiocese of Seattle wrote to the two archbishops, Raymond Hunthausen and Thomas Murphy, asking that the Church renew its efforts to provide a ministry directly to Catholic Indians. Joan Staples-Baum, a part-Ojibwa living in Tacoma, expressed the loneliness of Indian Catholics who felt ill at ease in mainstream parishes. Hunthausen created the Pastoral Ministry to Native Americans and appointed Staples-Baum a coordinator of the effort.

Dear Archbishop [Hunthausen] and Archbishop Murphy:

It is with a heavy heart that I write this letter asking for your support in establishing a Native American Indian Apostolate within the Archdiocese of Seattle.

Mr. Burton Pretty-on-Top, a member of the Crow Nation from Montana, expressed my sentiments precisely at the National Tekakwitha Conference in Phoenix last summer. My soul jolts now as it did then as I repeat his words. "When the Holy Father invited the Native American People to participate in the World Day of Prayer for Peace in Assisi he acknowledged us as being part of the human race"! He repeated this statement three times and each time it pierced my heart. Judging from the complete silence and stillness among the thousands, Native and Anglo alike, he had laid open a deep wound.

I have lived in the Archdiocese of Seattle area for two years now and am appalled at the lack of Church involvement with the Native People. I admit to a slow anger arousing within me when I see the commitment the Church has made to other minorities within the diocese.

We, as a People, did have a strong spiritual identity in the past. Our culture was thriving. Tradition was such that all people were taken care of within their tribe from birth to death. Each was responsible in some way for the survival of the group as a whole. We had a purpose.

Slowly that changed. A new people converged upon us bringing their own beliefs and traditions. We were forced, threatened and even killed to abandon our way of life. We became a [beleaguered] minority. And Yes, you as a community had some responsibility in this [desiccation]. I will not belabor this point, as we have all heard it before and it is best to put it behind us and to move forward.

In Pope John Paul II['s] speech to Native People in September, 1987, in Phoenix he appeals to the local churches to acknowledge Native Culture and Traditions, as have many before him. Pope Paul III proclaimed "the dignity and rights of the native people of the Americas by insisting that they not be deprived of their freedom or the possession of their property." I feel it is time for action from the church.

The May, 1977 American Bishops' Statement on Native Americans states that our Catholic faith is thriving "within each culture, within each nation, within each race, while remaining the prisoner of none." I speak as an Urban Indian when I say that it is very lonely to be a Catholic Native American in the Archdiocese of Seattle. I have to go North to Tulalip, Bellingham (Lummi) or LaConner (Swinomish) if I want to pray with my Native People. We have churches that serve the Blacks, Hispanics, Asians, etc., why not the Native American Indian?

I am experiencing great turmoil within as I write this letter and want both of you to know that any animosity depicted is evidence only of my personal struggle to be true to the Catholic [Church] which I love. But I must also be true to my Native Spirituality which I also love and is an intrinsic part of my being. I speak from my own woundedness for other Native People who have expressed [similar] struggles.

Please be with us to share in our sorrow, our celebrations and traditions; as we have been with you in yours; that we may learn together the true meaning of Christ's Peace on Earth.

Peace,
Joan Staples-Baum

Archdiocese of Seattle Archives. Printed by permission.

76. Robert Joe's Story, "The Deer Named Fish," 1992

The Swinomish Eucharistic minister Robert Joe often tells a story to his Catholic audiences — sometimes Jesuits, sometimes gatherings of the National Tekak-witha Conference, and so on — which expresses the ambiguities involved in Indian conversions to Christianity.

A priest came to an Indian village. He performed religious instruction and baptized the whole village, except for one elder, who resisted conversion. So, the priest visited him and finally baptized him, giving him a new, Christian name.

The priest told the elder that there were three rules he was compelled to follow: go to mass on Sunday, confess your sins on Saturday, and abstain from eating meat on Friday.

Pretty soon, however, the priest found the elder on a Friday, cooking venison in a pot. He asked him, "Why are you eating deer meat rather than fish?"

"I am eating fish," the elder replied.

"Don't lie to me," said the priest.

"I'm not lying," said the elder. "This *is* a fish. When I killed a deer, I took it down to the river and baptized it, and I changed its name to 'fish'."

Christopher Vecsey, *The Paths of Kateri's Kin*. Notre Dame, Ind.: University of Notre Dame Press, 1997, 352. Printed by permission.

Part 3

LEADERSHIP, URBAN MINISTRY, AND INCULTURATION

77. Reverend James Chrysostom Bouchard, S.J. [Watomika], ca. 1850–57

James Chrysostom Bouchard, S.J. (Watomika, "Swift Foot"), a Delaware Indian, a convert to Catholicism in 1847, ordained a Jesuit in 1855, and a missionary in California from 1861 to his death in 1889, was the first American Indian ordained to the Roman Catholic priesthood in the United States. Born in 1823, in Indian Territory (now Kansas), Watomika was French on his maternal side — his mother having been captured by Comanches as a child, and having lived her adult life as a thoroughgoing Comanche, married to a Delaware. Watomika grew up culturally as a Delaware-Comanche: hunting buffalo, participating in war parties, paying close attention to his dreams and visions. After the death of his father, he attended Marietta College in Ohio, became a Presbyterian, and then a Catholic. Bouchard's early Christian spirituality reflected the Delaware pattern of fasting and dreaming. In ca. 1850 he had a dream in which members of the Society of Jesus served as his guardian spirits.

I dreamed a celestial guide conducted me into Heaven, and there showed me, far in the upper Heaven, five circles of glowing stars, in the center of which there was one star more significant than the rest. Asking my guide the meaning of this, he responded: "The outer circle represents those members of the Society of Jesus who die out of office; the fourth represents all who die as rectors; the third represents the missionaries of the Society; the second represents those who have died as provincials; the first represents the Generals — and the central luminary represents St. Ignatius, the holy founder of the Society of Jesus...."

If one looks at the lives of the first American Indian priests, one can see the tension created by their desire to assert their Indian identity in the face of Church policy to mute it. It was Watomika's desire, as a Jesuit and as an Indian, to serve as missionary to his own people — if not the Delawares, then at least the Indians of the West, and he hoped to accompany Father Pierre Jean de Smet, S.J., on his missionary journeys. Nevertheless, his superiors forbade such a vocation. Because of the conflict between his wishes and the order's commands, he came close to quitting the Jesuits. Father de Smet encouraged his patience.

157

Letter from Bouchard to Father de Smet, July 1, 1857

VERY REV. AND DEAR FATHER IN CHRISTO [*sic*]:

My health has been very poor for the last few days — pain in the breast and debility — owing probably to the extreme heat which we have now to endure. — His Lordship has promised to let me go and spend some weeks at St. Mary's Mission in order to recuperate. I expect to leave this place some two weeks hence, and I shall not return before the 1st of September. Would you have the kindness to answer this in time for me to receive it before my departure.

I presume Revd. Fr. Provincial [John B. Druyts, 1811–64] has already hinted to you that I am not too well pleased with my present situation, that is to say, I would prefer to live in community with our own brethren, to that of living with secular clergymen; — I have stated to him my reasons for this preference, and I do hope the day is not far distant when I shall have the unspeakable pleasure of either residing at one of our missions, as I have long desired, or of being employed in some humble capacity in some one of our other residences. I write not thus to elicit your favour or influence in my regard, for I have all confidence that Rev. Fr. Provincial has my best interest at heart, but simply because I know that I have a place in your paternal sympathy and love.

I have paid two visits to my Delaware friends since my arrival in this city. — The second visit only a short time ago. This time, I spent some days with them, which I passed very agreeably in visiting my relations. My old uncle, Capt. Ketchum, received me with open arms. He was quite sick when I arrived at his house, but he was so overjoyed at seeing me as to quite forget his illness. He had a world of news to tell me. — Some good, some bad. — And a world of business to be attended to for the tribe, which he was anxious to entrust to me as if he expected me to succeed him in the chieftainship. — But, owing to my Rule, I declined undertaking any secular business, even for my dearest friends, — though, I must say, that I did it with regret; for I would gladly be the first to call U.S. [*sic*] to an account for his connivance at the violation of the late treaty with the Delawares, for the unpaid for reservation ceded to the government some 50 years ago (in Ohio), and for the unjust appropriation of Delaware funds by wicked and selfish agents, and a host of other things.

My friends are all anxious to have me reside permanently among them. They have even expressed a desire to have me preach to them — but, in this, I should, no doubt, be much opposed by the heretical missionaries, of whom there are no less than four different sects, viz. — Moravians, Baptists, Methodist — South and North, and their particular adherents. When I think of their conversion to our holy religion, of which they are entirely ignorant — a dark cloud rises before my eyes, not the faintest gleam of hope penetrates my heart; I can but weep and mourn over the ruin of a beloved people, a people who deserved a better fate; but what better fate could be expected from an [infidel] government, an avaricious nation, whose only God is the almighty dollar, whose only shrine of devotion the territories of the weak and [defenseless].

— Oh! my heart saddens, sickens, when I look at the future of my people, wronged, perverted and crushed by the bloody hand of a so-called *Liberal*

Government. — Adieu, dear Father. Pray for me. Your unworthy Brother in corde Jesu. Respects to all.

WA-TOM-I-KA, S.J.

...Pray for me. Write soon. I would that I could always be with you!

Letter from de Smet to Bouchard, July 8, 1857

P.C. REVD. AND DEAR WATOMIKA:

I received your kind favor of July 1st, and thank you greatly for it. I hope you will frequently write to me, and should you have any amount of leisure, favour me now and then with an Indian legend or anything appertaining to them — all being most interesting and most acceptable to me. Have courage, good Father; your health, I hope, will improve, for you have a large field open before you. I have no doubt that you will be able to do a great deal as yet for the chief of the Leni-Lenapi and the whole tribe. Should I ever be sent back to the Indians, I would assuredly ask for you as a companion, should you be willing to consent. It breaks my heart when I hear of the misfortunes of the Indian nations.... Though old and fit for nothing here, I might perhaps, with the grace and assistance from above, be fit as yet to do a little where there is nobody to do it, in saving children and other well-disposed Indians.... Tell me something of the good and worthy Monotawan, your dear mother. Your uncle must have put you au courant of all what [*sic*] concerns her. I pray daily for her:

Rae Vae servus et vere amicus in Xto [The servant and true friend of Your Reverence in Christ],

P. J. DESMET, S.J.

John Bernard McGloin, *Eloquent Indian: The Life of James Bouchard, California Jesuit.* Stanford, Calif.: Stanford University Press, 1950, 64, 75–76. Printed by permission.

78. Two Letters of Lansing M. Jack (Tuscarora) to Monsignor Stephan, November 9, 1889

On occasions men of Indian descent felt the calling to the priesthood and sought help from the Bureau of Catholic Indian Missions. In 1889 a Tuscarora, Lansing M. Jack, wrote from Boston, Massachusetts, to Monsignor Stephan of the Bureau of Catholic Indian Missions, asking for aid in entering a seminary. There is no known record of his attendance at Niagara University.

Respected Father: I am going to state here all the necessary information of which you might require to learn more as to what I have written you last night for. Now you will understand that I have communicated with Rev. Fr. Kavanagh, President of "Our Lady of the [Angels] Seminary" on Niagara University, Suspension Bridge, N.Y. in regard to any scholarships there. Father Kavanagh requested me to write to Bishop Ryan of Buffalo, N.Y. for all the particulars pertaining to my obtaining a permanent scholarship in that University. Sometime ago I wrote to Bishop Ryan of Buffalo, N.Y., to that effect. He asked me for references and previous history so I am now in want to have you to give the reference concerning me, to Bishop Ryan of Buffalo, N.Y. as you will [meet] him personally at Baltimore or at Washington during the celebration.

Since my [oculist] Dr. Derby has advised me to continue my studies I have made my mind to study for priesthood if you will make some arrangement for me to Bishop Ryan of Buffalo, to attend Niagara University and will I [perfect] these I will enter the Seminary and complete my vocation in life.

I have great consolation when my [oculist] Dr. Derby of this city said I will be able to continue my studies, as I had no hope of recovering of my diseased eyes and was very sure that I was going to lose one of my sight. You can if you will to ask my [oculist] in regard to my eyes through Rev. Fr. Corcoran of the Cathedral in Boston, "Asst. Priest."

Hoping you will see Bishop Ryan of Buffalo N.Y. while he is in your vicinity. In so doing I am sure He will give you warm reception in the affairs as he knows great deal about my tribe namely "Tuscarora Indian." We are in his diocese.

You know what I have promised you as to my plans in future which I had better to state again in few words. (1.) I believe that Catholic Church alone loves the Holy Scriptures and her faith agrees wondrous harmony of every letter in the word of God. (2.) I am desirous to be perfected for Catholic missionary to go and labor among the Catholic Indian Missions, under the care of the Church. (3.) I want to be educated in the University of Niagara under J.S. (4.) I am willing to continue my studies until I will complete my course and remain thus in case of sickness. (5.) I will try to perfect myself for our Master no matter how long it will take me to become Priest. This is my vocation in life.

Yours in Christian love,
Lansing M. Jack
Tuscarora Indian

Rev. Fr. Stephan

I am desirous to be perfected for priest to go among the Catholic Indian Missions in *Far West* when I am thus qualified.

I have applied for scholarship in Niagara University "Our Lady of the [Angels]" Suspension Bridge, N.Y. so now what I want from you is to inform Bishop Ryan of Buffalo, N.Y. all the particulars about me in regard to my plans and vocation in life. I am inclined to think that he will be in Baltimore Md. during the convention.

I am going to be a faithful Catholic as I promised you but my sore eyes permits me little. My [oculist] says I will be able to continue my studies so I have made my mind to study for priest if you will make some arrangement for me to Bishop Ryan of Buffalo.

Hoping to hear from you soon after you have seen personally Rt. Rev. Ryan.

Yours Truly
L. M. Jack
Tus. Indian

Marquette University, Bureau of Catholic Indian Missions Records. Printed by permission.

79. Albert Negahnquet (Potawatomi), Letters from Urban College, Rome, to His Family and to the Bureau of Catholic Indian Missions, 1901–3

Albert Negahnquet is often called the first full-blood American Indian priest in the United States. Born in Topeka, Kansas, in 1874, the Potawatomi studied at the Urban College, Propaganda Fide, in Rome from 1900 to 1903, when he was ordained. In his letters to his relatives — written in English although he was more comfortable in his native Potawatomi language and occasionally he wrote postcards in his native tongue — he described his experiences in the seminary. He told of his intent to become a clergyman for the good of the "ignorant Indian." He wrote of his encounters with Pope Leo XIII. He revealed the rough and tumble racism of the seminarians, including his own. And he acknowledged his heavy drinking, a failing which persisted through his troubled career as a priest.

January 27, 1901

Dear Sister,

I will now answer your letter I received at Xtmas. I was very pleased to hear something from S.H. Although I don't think that I can interest you much about Rome, but to say that you received a letter from Rome, I will write one to please you but very short. I can only tell that Bro. Gregory came to see me twice. He is no more in Rome. He is at Sacro Speco where St. Benedict built his first Monastery. I received a letter from him not long ago. He likes Sacro Speco but I think it is very cold there and they have no fire in most places. I know where the place is for I was near there last vacation. It is on the mountains. I may go and see him next vacation.

The cold has been very keen in Rome. We have no fire in the Colleges. My ears were frozen a little. Many have their hands swollen from cold. It is now getting milder. We had snow on the 3rd... which is an unusual thing in Rome. We had good snowballing. There is a "nigger" or African in my department. We snowballed him. He thought he was going to die. He nearly turned white. He has never seen snow. He thought as soon as it touched him he would die. He called for our prefect at the top of his voice. We washed another's face perhaps it was the first washing he ever had for [he] took sick the next day.

You naturally want to know how I like the Propaganda. I answer that I am very contented. All the students are nice and very lively. We have fun nearly the whole time. We almost frightened one Oriental to death. We were five in a room making each other's tonsure (for I have the tonsure now). This fellow came in to look on, they caught him and sat him on a chair. I took a razor and put soap on his head. He must have thought I was preparing to scalp him. Some saw that he was really scared they let him go. Then I had my head shaved. I thought they were flaying me.

I had to have an examination before I took the tonsure. I was afraid I would be stuck on some things. But luckily I had good old Irish Dominican in to examine me. I had no trouble in passing. He only made [me] translate some Latin and recite my prayers in Indian which I did very easily. Then he said, "Bravo! Bravo! Good."

The following Sunday I had to go [to] the Archbishop of Rome to get the Tonsure. There were about forty of us to get the Tonsure. The Scissors happened to be dull. The Bishop took a lock of my hair but he could not cut them. He had to leave some go. You must know that I have very coarse hair. All the minor orders were given besides some were ordained subdeacon, deacon and priest.

On the tenth of Jan we had the Propaganda Academy. It consists in this. All give a speech in their own language. That is each language known is spoken. I spoke the Indian. There were persons of distinction present about seven Ambassadors and seven Cardinals. The English Cardinal Vaughan was there. Also the Irish Cardinal Logue. The English Cardinal lessened the Estimation people had of him for when he saw a student called out (who is a Boer) to give his speech in Dutch, he went out and didn't return. It was very odd because the subject was absolutely religious and free from politics. The papers say that he is an English fanatic. There were forty one languages spoken. It took three hours to finish the whole thing.

You undoubtedly want to know if I have seen the Holy Father. I saw him about five times. I had the good luck to obtain a place near his throne when he closed the holy door. He was able to walk about without assistance. He started the foundation of the Holy door. That is, he laid bricks across the threshold. After that he intoned "Te Deum" and then gave his Blessing.

I understand that Mary was obliged to go home. I hope she will soon be able to return to school, and that Mother is well by this time.

If you see Bro Tim, tell him to say a "Sunday prayer" for me or *"to shove in a few for me."* When you write again ask about things that would interest you so that I will be able to write with an end. You might ask simply about Rome but I'll answer that now. It is the dirtiest city in existence, with half-starved soldiers and beggars. Rome is nothing without the Churches and the Colleges. Next time I will write more! I remain your affectionate brother, Albert.

April 20, 1901

Dearest father: —

I just received your letter.... I am writing this while the others are asleep. We are obliged to go to bed after dinner for an hour. This is owing to the climate in Italy. You might want to know what I was doing when you wrote that is on the same day. Well here it is, though it is interesting only to one knowing Rome.

(*From my diary*) — *April 7.* — *Monday in Holy Week.* "This morning I did not get up for the Angelus. And only got up after debating whether I should stay in bed or not during mass. I decided to get up. The bell rang for mass while I [was] washing. Consequently I was late. The Rector saw me going to mass after the others at the *Madona.* (Mary's statue) The Vice celebrated mass for the community — Baho, McCormac and Maloney were absent at breakfast table — (stayed in bed) After breakfast I went to see McCormac and then Maloney. (in their rooms) We started for a walk (at 10.a m) for some catacombs out to *Aqua Acetosa*

Reverend Albert Negahnquet, Chaplain, with Potawatomi Indians (most likely relatives) at St. Louis School, Osage Reservation, Pawhuska, Oklahoma, 1924. Credit: Photographer unknown. Marquette University, Bureau of Catholic Indian Missions Records. Reproduced by permission.

(mineral water). We took shelter from the Rain near a Villa of a Pope Julius II. Rain...having ceased we tried to continue our walk but were obliged to go back to shelter again. Then we made up our mind to pull for the city (Rome). It was not long before we had our dinner. We had not *"tempo libero"* (no reading during dinner). After dinner we had our game (like "black man") then our *sleep.* I did not get up for the spiritual reading. This afternoon we went to St. Praxede near St. Mary Major. After that we took a stroll by the station and Praetorio. The man who sells the La Voce (a paper) gave Bonville a stanza of his own make. That evening after supper McKenna syringed Manshouga's (an African [nigger]). Then I went to bed. After saying my prayers, [nigger] was singing. I was about to squirt water in his mouth. He opens his mouth big enough to put watermelon in his throat. McKenna took my syringe and poured half pint of water down his throat."

I have written something from my *diary.* Though I am not faithful in writing every evening. I am very tired sometimes and I put it off to another time. I intend to take down every thing I do while in the Holy City, so that I might be able to say something when I go back and let anyone read who wants to.

I have been expecting a letter from Joe for about five months. I was on the point of writing to Haskell to ask whether he was dead or not. It has been a long time since I wrote. I am afraid I will repeat some things I already told you. I want to say this much. That I have taken the "propaganda oath," namely never to join Religious Order of any kind and to go back straight way to my country, or home, and never to leave it without the permission of the Propaganda or the Pope. This will give me the right to stay in Oklahoma no matter who would want to remove me unless I wanted. Some bishops hate this because the Propaganda Students are immediately protected by the Pope or by the congregation of the Propaganda. There are other obligations besides these. One is to keep the congregation informed of one's self so that they could remove one from one climate to a better, if necessary.

I am glad to know that you are all well. This is the heaviest burden I have not to know how you all are faring. Even I am afraid you might have some thing heavy in store for me when I don't hear from you at a notable time. I am satisfied always to know only that you are well — At present I am well as can be — This morning I was somewhat *stiff* from jumping yesterday. Otherwise I am very well, and felt good after reading your letter. I would like to see Sacred Heart in its ashes. You say on Palm Sunday was cold with you. We had a hot day here; my diary says. "*No sun, no rain, but pleasant.* I saw *deer* in the park."

I am very glad that all our acquaintances are well. Tell them that I am always glad to think that I will have the pleasure to see all of them when I return. It is for their sake that I have left home and parents, that is the Indians. It was not because I wanted to have the name of crossing the Ocean that I almost broke my heart to leave my mother. I would have preferred to stay at home near my mother and father had I sought to please myself and took no interest in the Indians. I thought I could do some thing for them. Even when I left Sacred Heart, I intended to study law that I might do some useful service to the ignorant Indian. But knowing that I could do more for the Indian as a clergyman I took my studies, which I hope to finish not long hence. Time is flying like the mischief. I cannot realize it. It doesn't seem to me more than two months I am in Rome but it is over one year. I have to prepare for examination to have the minor orders. I had [an] easy one for the Tonsure. I had an old Dominican friar to examine me. I heard that some are really devils to *stick* the students, especially us Propagandists, the Jesuits and the Capuchins are the most dreaded. This reminds me of the examination I passed in my studies. I was in despair, but to my surprise I passed a good one. I had the best reports in the hardest study in Dogmatic Theology. I knew Moral Theology well enough since this year I have learned Moral Theology so that I could be able to hear confessions. So well it is explained, [professor] is best in Rome.

July 2, 1901

My Dear Sister,

I received your very welcomed letter on the 30th. It took fourteen days to reach me. It is about the fastest I have had yet. I am delighted to know that you have improved so much. I noticed with pleasure that your penmanship is very nice now. Before long I will be ashamed to write because yours is superior to mine. I am sorry I did not receive both of your letters. I got one you wrote aft Sacred Heart was burnt down.

I got one from *Chaksek* and one from John in which he prophesied that I would not write to him. I am writing now. I will send him one before we go out to the villa or country house. [We] will go in two weeks. I want to write a good one. We have not much to study, only we have to write some tracts on theology to see who gets the praeminum. I am not going for it. Though I will have to write something.

I just finished my examination. It was terrible before, I was nearly out of my bean. I have a headache. I was sick last night after I was examined. I could hardly walk to my room after supper and at supper I could not eat anything for about five days I lived on nothing. The reason was that I did not prepare very well during the year. I commenced only about ten days before the examinations. I almost made myself sick. Besides my Bishop was here that made me distracted. I could not study well. He came to see me twice and I went to see him twice. I had dinner with him last week, namely on the 27th of June. I got him to say mass for us on the 29th of June in the College. I just came from where he was stopping to bid him goodbye when I got your letter. And I got a letter also from Fr. Gregory (Bro Gregory) at Subiaco on the same day.

The Bishop was very good. He was very pleased with my report. I told him I would be ordained two years from now. He was delighted to hear it. He said, "I was afraid you would stay here three years! But that's good! Two years are nothing." He told me as he was leaving to take good care of myself, and that he was very pleased at what the Rector told him about me. Of course this gives me encouragement. I am happy he is satisfied with my progress I can say from [here] I am doing very well, and very contented. I will have [a] good time with the boys as soon as my spell of fatigue is over. I have unbearable headache after all the fuss.

Besides it is very hot. The heat is strange. It is not like here at home. The heat at home is no doubt very hot but I could stand it. But the Roman heat has something about it which puts a person out altogether and causes one to be very weak. I used to laugh at those who were afraid of the heat. They would not go out for a walk. But now I have changed my mind. When we get to the country it will be alright, for we will be on the Mountains. Sometimes they are covered with clouds. There is a hill near us. It is above the clouds. They strike it about half way. There is also a fine lake against the house. It is about six miles around it. We used to catch crabs on the [...].

There is a Palace of the Pope, it is a grand place. The [one] in which Pius IX died is there. And the things he used to write with, they are of gold. There are very fine pictures also. But he cannot go there, the Italian government would not allow him. You must know he is a prisoner in the Vatican he cannot go out. He is very old I saw him good many times. He was very pleased with the Bishop's report.

You did not tell me why you had to go home. Was the reason obliging you? You must be quite an actress to act the Drama "Light throw Darkness." I saw it played some place. Something like it or I must have read it. I saw good many plays since I am in Rome. Before Ash Wednesday we can go and see the theaters for two weeks.

I hope you will enjoy your vacation. If you are well, you want nothing more. Health is the main thing for good times. It would be well now. I would not give any one a rest. Yes, I heard of Tim and the others being ordained priests. Also Bro Laurence. The little fool invited me to be present at the ordination and at his first mass. His invitation consisted nearly in a book with ribbons tied to it. It costed like the mischief to have come by mail, but happily he paid for it. I am going to write and give him [a] piece of my mind. I am very glad to know that he is a priest now. I heard of poor Sylvester dying. He was my special spiritual friend. Many a holy talk he gave me and many a good laugh I had on him. But he is now no more. *Requiescat in Pace.*

I am surprised at Joe, he never wrote since the beginning of December. I wrote about four times but no answer. I am going to register a letter to see where he is. I wish you had told me his address! No one told me from home, in fact, I never asked for it. Do you know where Father MacSolley is? That priest who used to drive in people in church. John knows him well and I want to know where the old Captain is and also Doctor Wycough. I suppose Joe will complain to Father that I don't write. I have the same injury to fall back on. It is true I know he is in Topeka but I don't know his address. He advised [me] to write to Haskell and it would be alright and so I did. But he should [have] taken a proper care. It has happened his letters were intercepted at Haskell once before when I wrote from Sacred Heart. And also when he was in Kansas, there was another Joe Negonkot. I am sorry for I took special pains to write two of them well and make them interesting and I sent two of my photos another time. But neither of these do I know if he got them or not. Perhaps his letter did not reach me which could easily be, as the mail is not very safe here.

You don't know the reason why Father has gone to Kansas I suppose. But I guess it [is] over land matter. He is travelling. He was there last year Joe told me in his last letter. He said he was surprised to see him in H.I. [Haskell Institute] as he was to see me. You can read John's letter for it's our interview for I intend to tell him all about my trip. I did not understand your writing where you say you had to go down in the cellar so many times. I forgot all about cyclones. I was scandalized to think the sisters and girls [were] going down there so often. I thought you went down to drink beer and wine as I used to do in the good old Sacred Heart. I thought you girls were almost as bad as I used to be. I drink [a] good deal of wine yet. I drink about half a gallon a day. Well you [have] cyclones to fear, as I think from you going down in the cellar but we have something more serious to fear here in Rome and also in the country. Destructive earthquakes take place now and then. We had one in Rome not long ago. I was studying for the evening, about 3 P.M. All at once I heard something as if some[one] was running through the hall. I looked about and saw my wash towel and pictures moving on the wall of my room. Then my chair began to move as if some[one] was trying to throw me off. I look to see who it was. I could have thought it was the devil. It reminded me of being thrown about while coming on the ocean. I heard my companions in the hall somewhat excited. I went to see what was up. They were very much frightened especially one he is a Turk. He was yellow from fright. Then I knew what it was. I began to laugh at them. They said, "Are you not frightened?" I said "No, I wish it would come on again, it's just like being on the ocean." They are afraid because they were nearly destroyed out in the country before I came. They were sleeping when it came on. Some ran out in their shirt tails, and others slept on till it was over. The day we felt the shock it came on again at night but it was not much. And during school we thought it was come on. Some professors and students were about to run out. Our professor kept on talking as if nothing was going on. The bells were ringing in some parts of Rome and injured some buildings. Some said I was very cool blood not to mind it as I did. But I think after a good scare I will be changed.

I hope Father Clement will come and see me when he is in Rome. He is not in Rome yet I am quite certain of it. I heard from Fr. Gregory the same time as I got your letter as I said before. I like to see my old companions once again. I understand Fr. Joachim is in England. What is the matter, all are scattered, my old companions.

I must close wishing you good health and good vacation. If you write tell me the address of Joe because I may not hear from [him] when you write. Address, *Villa di Propaganda* Castel Gandulfo, Italia

I remain as ever your Affectionate Brother,
Albert.

St. Gregory's Abbey. Printed by permission.

Letter from Negahnquet to Reverend Ketcham, Bureau of Indian Catholic Missions, March 18, 1903

On the verge of his ordination, Negahnquet wrote to Reverend Ketcham of the Bureau of Catholic Indian Missions, from whom he received a commission to serve as a priest to Indians and whites in Indian Territory. He served there and then with Reverend Ketcham in Washington, D.C. He worked for an Indian mission in Minnesota and returned to Oklahoma, but his alcoholism followed him from post to post. He left the priesthood in 1929, married, divorced, and in 1941 was reconciled to the Church. He spent his last three years in residence at Sacred Heart Priory in Oklahoma.

I received your kind letter yesterday. It was against my will that I could not answer it at once. Even now I will not be able to answer it properly. Indeed you have waited a long time, but you would have had a letter from me before my ordination, for I intended to visit you the first after I arrived in New York. Though I have not written but you must not think that I could forget all the kindness and interest you have always bourne towards me. I have always kept you also in my daily prayers and heart since that night I bade you good bye at Antlers. It is ever with grateful remembrance that I look back on those days at Antlers and to the days of "long ago" when that "Black eyed pupil" used to run about with Bow and arrow at Sacred Heart and whom you congratulate as one of the high aims, but I don't think he can take off his hat simply and say: "Grazia tanto" as if those compliments were his by right of merit.

As I mentioned already that I look back on the past very often. After examining my course of time and circumstances, I cannot congratulate myself as one who aspired to high aims simply for the nobleness of purpose, but I can only claim the praise that I have had a well meant intention and a calling which I could do nothing else but obey. With such convictions I have never wavered.

I got a letter from the [?] some time ago. He seems to want me home soon. He wanted to know when I could be home, I could not be home before July, unless we are ordained early. There could be possibility three of my class must go home they are either mad or exhausted in health. We are losing a fourth at present. [H]e locked himself and prayed the whole time, eats nothing now. I am sorry for him, he was always kind to me and did all he could to make time pleasant for me, even we are great friends if I must own it, he and I were to be as Deacon and Sub-deacon respectively on the feast of St. Joseph. Now I have to go on as Deacon. I was present rather I had the good luck to see the Pope on his 25th anniversary[.] It is wonderful how he has life, his entrance into the Basilica is like the sudden apparition of a heavenly messenger sent to console a depressed people. He was not well, he coughed when passed near where I was. You heard about h[is] tiara that was given on the day of his jubilee. It is precious and well made no doubt. I don't like it, it looks too Medieval. From the crown it sends to a point so that it has a shape of the lead of a sharp pointed cartridge, that the first of the crowns is the largest the middle smaller[,] the last not two inches in diameter (judging the appearance). Whereas the others he has worn until now are just the contrary. The top crown the largest on the tiara.

I saw Bishop Dunne at the polyglotta of Propaganda. He seemed to be glad to see me. At least he said so. The American students were effusive in their congratulations and thanks because I represented America. I must close hoping to see you soon and thanking your kindness once more. I remain yours most sincerely in Christ.

Marquette University, Bureau of Catholic Indian Missions Records. Printed by permission.

80. Letters of Reverend Philip B. Gordon [Ti-bish-ko-gi-jik] (Ojibwa), 1913–24

Philip B. Gordon was born in Wisconsin in 1885 of mixed French and Ojibwa ancestry; his Indian name was Ti-bish-ko-gi-jik ("Looking into the Sky," or "Gift of Heaven"). He attended seminary in Rome and received his ordination in 1913, yearning for an assignment among his own people. In a letter to Reverend Ketcham of the Bureau of Catholic Indian Missions, he observed several hundred Ojibwa "pagans" in need of conversion, and he felt a duty to "these neglected people."

September 21, 1913

Rev. and dear Father;

I fear, Rev. Father, that my biographer will not have very much difficulty in proving that I am an Indian as far as the "roving disposition" goes. Here I am at St. John's Abbey. And thereby hangs a tale.

During my summer travels, I visited among other interesting places, the different Chippewa Indian Missions in the diocese of Crookston. Up to the time of this visit, I had always thought that the Indians of Wisconsin were in pretty bad shape. I used to think that if any people needed my poor services in the days to come, it would be my "home" Indians, those around Odanah or Reserve, for instance. But just imagine the Red Lake Mission with only one priest and several hundred Pagans, less than 20 miles away. Again at White Earth, not five miles from the priest's house are several hundred Pagans and the priest never visits them!! (I don't mean Father Aloysius.)

Truly, if I have a duty, it is to these neglected people. Most of them, I understand, don't speak English and all, of course, are very ignorant (which goes without saying.) On the other hand, the Indians living in Northern Wisconsin are fairly well attended to. Real old time Pagans are no more.

Hence it is that I am now studying for "your friend" the Rt. Rev. Ordinary of Crookston. The first thing he did was to have me proceed to St. John to prepare for ordination sometime before Christmas. In the meantime, I have to secure my "Exeat" from Superior which I have applied for. Until I get this document, of course, I will hardly presume to make any regular preparation for my first Holy Mass....

> With every best wish to the whole force,... I am Rev. dear Father,
> Your most humble child in Christ,
> Philip B. Gordon [Ti-bish-ko-gi-jik.]

Marquette University, Bureau of Catholic Indian Missions Records. Printed by permission.

Father Gordon had little time to settle in among the Ojibwas. In 1915 the Bureau of Catholic Indian Missions sent Gordon to Lawrence, Kansas, where he served for a year as chaplain to the Catholic Indian students at Haskell Institute, the federally funded school for Native Americans. At Haskell, Father Gordon combined his Indian and Catholic loyalties in a personal crusade against religious discrimination at the institute. In Gordon's view — and evidence shows him to have been correct — the authorities at Haskell functioned as Protestants, discouraging Catholic Indian organization and spirituality among the student body. The following letters from Lawrence, Kansas, give a sense of Gordon's strident tone, which embarrassed high-ranking members of the Catholic hierarchy.

Letter from Gordon to Cato Sells, Commissioner of Indian Affairs, October 11, 1915

Dear and Honorable Sir:

Your letter of Oct. 4 with reference to my request for an accurate list of Catholic pupils has been received.

Since I sent my telegram (September 28) and since your letter has come, I have received a third list of Catholics. This third list is fully as inaccurate and as unsatisfactory as the previous ones. In a brief roll-call yesterday, I discovered

Reverend Gordon, center, at a Catholic Sioux congress in South Dakota with Lakota catechists and missionary Reverend Henry I. Westropp, S.J. (back row, left), and Reverend William M. Hughes, then lecturer of the Bureau of Catholic Indian Missions (back row, right), Yankton Sioux Reservation, Ravinia, South Dakota, 1915. Father Gordon addressed the Sioux on the banks of the Missouri River at what was believed to be the exact spot where Reverend de Smet first met the Sioux in 1839. Credit: Photograph by Joseph Fastbender. Marquette University, Bureau of Catholic Indian Missions Records. Reproduced by permission.

six Catholic girls present at my service whose names do not appear on the "list of Catholic pupils." The names of several boys are omitted from the "accurate list."

Incidentally, I might mention that eleven boys and eight girls were absent from the service. (The service is compulsory.)

With out waiting for your answers to the one or two other matters, I wish at this moment to call your attention to the following facts existent here. These facts were called to the attention of your Mr. Wise several weeks ago but as yet nothing appears to have been done to our satisfaction. The facts are these:

1. The Y.M.C.A. of Haskell keep their Secretary (who is well-paid) on the grounds. He uses a Government room (a room in the Large Boy's Building) lighted and heated it would seem by the Government. I have been told that the occupancy of this room encroaches on the dormitory space. Last year this Secretary had his father likewise quartered at the School.

2. The Y.M.C.A. and the Y.W.C.A. have special rooms set apart for them and pains are taken to have these rooms properly labeled and advertized as the Y.M.C.A. and the Y.W.C.A. rooms. The new gymnasium nearing completion have rooms particularly fitted out for the Y.M.C.A., perhaps furnished for them. The piano standing in this [Government] room is rented to the pupils.

The proceeds without much doubt go to the Y.M.C.A. The Y.W.C.A. room seems to be used exclusively for the Y.W.C.A.

3. Catholics are not allowed (as at Carlisle and other places) to have union meetings of a Sunday evening. Various reasons are advanced for this peculiar regulation, the strongest of which appears to be that such union meetings do not have the approval of the Y.M.C.A. Catholics are therefore denied their distinctive religious service Sunday evenings. They must follow the Y.M.C.A. method.

4. The authorities do not think it feasible to allow the Catholics downtown Church services except once a month on trial. I asked for at least two Sundays. The chief opposition seems to come from Miss Stilwell who complains of the extra work required to fit out the children for such a service. The children are almost unanimous for at least two Sundays.

5. Several Catholic pupils have lately requested a change in their religious affiliation, from Catholic to something else. Two gave as their reasons "religious persecution and the hard time Catholics have."

6. Pupils are listed either as Catholic or Protestant. Although there appears to be several Pagan children here not baptized in any church, still there seems to be no third list. During the year, these "Protestants" are baptized into some Protestant church, chiefly the Baptist sect. Miss Stilwell, you will recollect, was formerly a Baptist missionary. The Catholic church rarely has a convert from Paganism. In fact, I know of none at all at Haskell.

I trust that you will take up these points at your earliest convenience and have them cleared up to our satisfaction. I should not like very much indeed to call upon our congressional friends in a matter like the present one but I will state that I mean to get satisfaction. I do not want you to take this as a threat but you will understand that I mean business.

In the meantime, my dear Sir, believe me, Yours very respectfully,

(Signed) Philip Gordon, Catholic Chaplain of Haskell Institute

Inserted as number 7. Reports are in circulation that I am bringing a religious war on at Haskell, that I am personally quarrelsome, that I lie, etc. I, myself, have been the subject of much deceit. The truth seems to be that up until now, the Catholics have been content with very little. Now that I have asked for more and for a proper balance, I am the subject of considerable malignancy or supposed malignancy. Of course, this will be denied by the parties concerned. How could it be otherwise?

Marquette University, Bureau of Catholic Indian Missions Records. Printed by permission.

Letter from Gordon, "Dear Catholic Parent," November 1915

Dear Catholic Parent:

Attention is called to the fact that our Catholic children are suffering inconveniences in the practice of their religion at the Haskell Institute located here.

You are kindly requested to communicate with Mr. John R. Wise, Superintendent Haskell Institute, Lawrence, Kansas, and to Hon. Cato Sells, U.S. Commissioner of Indian Affairs, Washington, D.C., as soon as possible to the effect that unless Catholics are allowed to worship in their own way and unless they receive at least as much encouragement as Protestants and Protestant organizations have received and are receiving, you shall have to consider the advisability of removing your child (or children) from that school.

The Y.M.C.A. and the Y.W.C.A., distinctively Protestant organizations are fostered by the Haskell school authorities and several Catholics have lapsed into Protestantism from the effects, it would seem, of constant association with these organizations.

Your children, dear Catholic parent, are in danger of losing their Catholic Faith as conditions are at present and it behooves you to have a care.

Help us to keep your children Catholic.

Father Philip Gordon (Ti-bish-ko-gi-jik)
Indian Priest

> Marquette University, Bureau of Catholic Indian Missions Records. Printed by permission.

Gordon was removed from Haskell in 1916. In 1918 he achieved his wish and took over an Ojibwa parish at Reserve, Wisconsin, where he served with vigor. He also devoted great energy to political matters, agitating against the Bureau of Indian Affairs and in favor of Ojibwa land claims. He began to associate with national organizers of American Indians, such as Dr. Carlos Montezuma (Yavapai) and Dr. Charles Alexander Eastman (Dakota), and locally he placed himself at odds with the Franciscan priests and St. Joseph sisters, especially through his criticism of their boarding school for Indian children.

Letter from Gordon, Lac Court Oreilles Reservation, Reserve, Wisconsin, to Reverend Oderic Derenthal, O.F.M., May 19, 1919.

...I have written to the Rev[e]rend Sisters with reference to board for Dr. Montezuma of Chicago, an Apache* Indian and Dr. Eastman of Boston, a Sioux Indian. These gentlemen are visiting our Chippewa country in a lecture tour and I am guiding them through our different reservations.

The purpose of the Meetings is to set our Indians in the path of a little independent thinking. Now they appear to be like babies, badly over-nursed. What the Indians need is a few thoughts along the line of progressive living. For instance, in Odanah, you are doing perfectly right in having the Indians support their own Church, including the salary of the pastor. Here in Reserve, where would we be without our outside aid? I believe if the Indians were made to support themselves they might do better....

> Marquette University, Sacred Heart Franciscan Indian Mission Records. Printed by permission.

---

*Historical note: Dr. Montezuma was a member of the Yavapai tribe, sometimes mistaken for their neighbors, the western Apaches.

By the early 1920s Gordon was the subject of governmental and ecclesiasti-cal investigations, and he was being called a troublemaker and worse. Accused (inconclusively) of sexual improprieties (with a report written by Dr. Eastman), he was forced by Church superiors to resign his Indian post in 1924. While resigning, Gordon protested his innocence.

Letter from Gordon to Reverend Hughes, January 28, 1924

Reverend dear Father Hughes:

Yours of the 19th instant at hand. I appreciate your continued interest and I trust that eventually we may come to understand each other and be quite will-ing to give and take and bear with one another our respective "faults" if I may use that term. I do not know whether you will ever admit that *you* ever made a mistake.

To begin with, I do not believe you and I will ever agree fundamentally on Indian affairs. You believe in supporting at all odds and at any cost the Indian Office. This is and maybe *must* be your policy as a matter of expediency. I am of the opinion that while the Indian Office is not through and through rotten, it is sufficiently decayed to warrant a discussion as to a change. It is basically wrong and has been characterized by three things: Ignorance, stupidity and at times dishonesty. But even Satan himself is the cause of much good in that he keeps a lot of people out of hell because of his reputation. The Bureau of Indian Affairs has been the instrument of some good, no one will deny but that it has been responsible for some terrible conditions is also something none but the partisan-blinded can refuse to gainsay. Witness the White Earth destitution this winter which I have seen with my own eyes.

Now as to the "serious charges which have been preferred against you," per-mit me to say that quite serious charges have been from time to time preferred against quite innocent people including some of our friends, the good German people, whose innocence some of us are now rather late in admitting.

As a matter of fact, my resignation is now in the hands of Bishop Pinten who, I imagine, is quite competent to judge me, he never having been here and never having met my accusers one of whom was lately in County jail and an-other of whom recently returned from State Prison. The Bishop, no doubt, will refer to Inspector Eastman's sagacious report for the facts in the case. I do not mean to object in the least to any procedure indicated by His Lordship and you will understand that I do not want any action on your part in any capacity. We will permit the Bishop to consummate his plans and I am sure I for one am going to be satisfied.

The closing line of your letter in view of the present procedure makes me feel like this: You write "I do so want to help you. Is it possible that you will not let me?" Well, I felt as if I was drowning a while back and wrote to you at that time that I needed help. You wrote back that the Indian Office should be allowed to proceed, etc. Well, now that I am metaphorically "drowned" and about to be buried, you ask "Is it possible that you will not let me save you from drowning?"

Bishop Pinten is proceeding in the regular canonical way. Vide Canon 1431-2.

I feel that the time is most inopportune for a change inasmuch as I am in the midst of building. As a part concession, my resignation is effective May 1st to give me just a little time to gather up stray threads of little debts and pledges not yet paid. In this connection, I am making another very local appeal or rather some good friends of mine are making it for me. I am anxious to quit this place even with the board and with just a few dollars in the treasury, say $10.

Right here, if it is possible for the Bureau to join in this last thing I plan for Reserve, I would appreciate $100 or $200 dollars. If the Kekek Will is approved in your favor, of course, there will be quite a healthy balance in your favor even supposing I leave the few outstanding small obligations unpaid by May 1st.

I am leaving an unfinished church which has cost to date something like $22,000. There is a Rectory attached which will cost about $500. to complete. You will be furnished with my written Report before I leave.

My resignation is not yet public pending formal acceptance by the Bishop. It is understood that I am voluntarily resigning and I suppose anything pertaining thereto will emanate from the Bishop's House.

Please remember that I will have nothing to do with any petitions or letters or requests from the Indians to withdraw my resignation. I will be like old P. Pilate: Quod scripsi, scripsi [That which I wrote, I wrote].

> Very sincerely yours,
> Philip Gordon

PS. I did not heckle Supt. Allen. I happened to ride back in the same Pullman on our way from Washington. He actually invited me to propound questions as he said he wanted to have an accurate idea of the subject abroad. I had him mail you a copy of his answer because you wrote that I had made a misstatement on Indian citizenship to the Dearborn Independent reporter which statement as concerns the Menominees was accurate. At least the statement is accurate as far as Allen goes. However, you may know better than he.

N.B. I am withholding announcement of my resignation until Easter as there would be an agitation here that might result in actual bloodshed, for instance the impact of one Indian's fist upon the nose of another would be bloody to some extent.

Marquette University, Bureau of Catholic Indian Missions Records. Printed by permission.

Father Gordon was assigned to a non-Indian parish — which he took as punishment for having identified too strongly with his Native American kinsmen, and for having crossed the all-powerful Indian Bureau. For two more decades until his death in 1948 Father Gordon maintained his public Indian identity: encouraging the passage of Indian New Deal legislation in the 1930s and blessing the president and members of Congress in an invocation in the House of Repre-sentatives in 1943. Nevertheless, Church officials denied him a return to Indian ministry.

Letter from Gordon to Reverend Hughes, May 16, 1924

Reverend dear Father Hughes:

The attached letter is herewith returned. I think you had better write direct to the Right Reverend Bishop in regard to this matter. I do not think my successor has as yet been appointed, or at least he has not yet taken charge.

I am now located in a typical farming district, a rural parish in our richest county. My parish is mostly Irish, a few scattered Germans and one or two [French] families. There are however, some few Indian families near here but fallen away. I am told there are at least six such families.

Isn't it strange that all my activity in behalf of the Indians has not as yet drawn a single word of either thanks or appreciation from my superiors, that is, the Bishop and your Bureau except the mild words contained in the letter you wrote May 8th and this was only because of my interest in the dead and evidently did not include the living. Or is Indian work ever the most ungrateful task?

> Sincerely yours,
> Philip Gordon.

Marquette University, Bureau of Catholic Indian Missions Records. Printed by permission.

81. Letters from Lakota Candidates, Novices, and Sisters of the Congregation of American Sisters, 1891–93

Reverend Francis M. Craft, descended from the Mohawks and sent as a missionary to the Sioux in the 1880s, put into motion an idea set forward by Bishop Martin Marty, O.S.B., to establish orders for Indian women as St. Benedict had done among the Goths and St. Boniface among the Germans in the Middle Ages. In the late 1880s Craft encouraged several Lakota women to join the Benedictine sisterhood; however, when they experienced difficulties in the novitiate, Craft blamed their troubles on racism and determined in 1891 to found the Congregation of American Sisters, designed specially for the Lakotas.

In 1891 several of the novices wrote to Father Craft, expressing their concern at his having been shot at Wounded Knee the previous December, when U.S. troops fired on Lakota Ghost Dancers.

Letter from Susie Bordeaux, Claudia Crowfeather, Mary Blackeyes, Jane Moccasin, Nellie Dubray, and Alice Whitedeer, from St. Francis Xavier School, Avoca, Minnesota, to Reverend Craft, January 25, 1891

Dear Rev. Father Craft,

We will write to you again and tell you that we are all well and happy. We heard from the newspaper that you were shot. Oh! Father, you cannot imagine how sorry we were but afterwards we heard you were getting better. Since we heard that you were wounded we say five "Our Fathers, Hail Marys, and Glorias" at the end of our morning and night prayers every day so I am sure Father, it is our prayers that our dear Lord hears and has spared your life. We hope with all our hearts that you will get perfectly well very soon — for we are indeed anxious to see our good Father Craft who has done so much for us poor Indians. We hope you will come soon for we are waiting patiently to see you. Did you get the letter that some of us wrote to you Father? We addressed it to Fort Yates it was written two days before you were wounded. We got a newspaper from New York and your picture was in it so one of us cut it out and put it in a frame and we will not be satisfied until we hear that you are perfectly well and see you with our own eyes. Thank you Father, over and over again, for all you have done for the poor Indians. We hope and trust that you will get a reward for all you have done after you have passed out of this world to that happy house in heaven. Father all of the children are very anxious to see you and send their love and best wishes to you beloved Father.

Asking for your blessing and a remembrance in your prayer. We remain Dear Father your Affectionate children in J.C.

> Susie Bordeaux
> Claudia Crowfeather
> Mary Blackeyes
> Jane Moccasin
> Nellie Dubray
> Alice Whitedeer

Catholic authorities had misgivings about Craft's order of Lakota novices and wished them to remain in closer contact with Church and government officials. Craft kept the women at the Fort Berthold Reservation.

Letter from Jane Moccasin, Claudia Crowfeather, Mary Blackeyes, and Alice Whitedeer to Reverend Craft, June 27, 1891

Dear Rev. Father Craft, —

You remember Bishop Marty wanted us to write to him and say why we would not go back to Standing Rock. We wrote to him and told him we would not go there and why we would not. We hear now that he told them about it at Standing Rock and they say we must go back. We will *not* go back to Standing Rock because if we do we know the people there will keep us and will not let us be Sisters. Please dear Father — help us and take us to the Convent at Yankton. You are our relative and our guardian, and you are the only one we can trust. You want us to stay here at school three years more before we go to the Convent, but we want to go now because we are afraid something may happen to keep us from going. If you die or go away somewheres who will help us? Three years is a long time and a great deal may happen. Mary Blackeyes is willing to do as you say and stay at school three years more but she says you must take care of her all the time and not let any one take her to Standing Rock and then

Congregation of American Sisters from Standing Rock Reservation, North and South Dakota, with their chaplain, Reverend Craft, at their hospital in Havana, Cuba, ca. 1898. These sisters, Josephine Two Bears, Ella Clarke, Bridget Pleets, and Anthony Bordeaux, were nurses and the first American Indian women to serve in the U.S. Armed Forces. Sister Anthony Bordeaux died and was buried in Cuba with military honors, and Sister Bridget Pleets treasured her apron on which dying soldiers wrote their names and addresses so she could notify their families. Credit: Harmon & Shaw of Atlanta, Georgia. Marquette University, Bureau of Catholic Indian Missions Records. Reproduced by permission.

you must take her to the Convent at Yankton. Dear Father, it makes us feel so sad when we see that everyone wants to ruin our vocations. God made us like the whites and gave us vocations like theirs, and why can't we have them? No one has any right to tell us where to go. We have learned that we are in a free country and you always taught us to want to be free Americans like the white people. If you mean what you say please help us now. Don't ask us to wait any more but take us to the convent now. We would go now ourselves, but we have no money and we hear so much against our vocations that we are afraid we will not be allowed to go. Please help us dear Father. We ask you this in the holy name of Jesus. If they won't take us at Yankton take us to any Convent you like so we can save our vocations. If you can take us to a Benedictine Convent we would like that best. Working for your blessing dear Father your obedient children in J.C.

> Jane Moccasin
> Claudia Crowfeather
> Mary Blackeyes
> Alice [Whitedeer]

Craft's special project was the vocation of Josephine Crowfeather, who from her youth was known as an incarnation of the legendary Lakota ideal, White Buffalo Calf Woman. She was regarded by her people as a sacred virgin; hence her vows were consistent with her tribal image. Catherine became the first superior and mother prioress-general of the new order, but within a year of her vows she died of tuberculosis.

Vows of Mother Mary Catharine (Josephine Crowfeather, Sacred White Buffalo, Ptesanwanyakapiwin), O.S.B., November 1, 1892

In the name of our Lord Jesus Christ. Amen.

I Mother Mary Catharine of the Order of Saint Benedict (Josephine Ptesanwanyakapiwin), O.S.B., Superioress and Mother Prioress General of the Indian Congregation of the Order of Saint Benedict, of the Dakota nation of the Diocese of Jamestown, North Dakota to the honor of Almighty God, of the ever blessed Virgin Mary, and of our holy Father Saint Benedict, and of all the Saints, by the simple vows, vow, profess, and promise Stability, and the conversion of my morals, Poverty, Chastity, and Obedience according to the Rule of the same holy Father Saint Benedict, and our Constitutions, in the presence of God, and of his Saints, whose relics are exposed in this Church, and of the Reverend Father Francis Mary Joseph Craft, Director of this Congregation, and of the Sisters of this Congregation and Community[.] In the name of the Father, and of the Son, and of the Holy Ghost. Amen.

In witness thereof I have signed this with my own hand, at this venerable place, Sacred Heart Chapel and Mission, Fort Berthold, North Dakota, in the year after the Incarnation of our Lord, eighteen hundred and ninety two, on the first day of November, the feast of All Saints.

Mary Liguori became the second Prioress General of the Congregation of American Sisters. In the 1890s as many as twenty Lakota women joined the order, at least as novices; however, they received little support from the Church, despite Liguori's letter to Monsignor F. Satolli, the papal representative in Washington, D.C. Indeed, the sisters and Craft were accused of immorality, and by 1898 Craft was prohibited by the Commissioner of Indian Affairs from entering any Lakota reservation. Most of the women drifted from the order; however, Craft and four remaining followers volunteered for nursing service in the Spanish-American War in Cuba. The last one left the Indian sisterhood in 1903.

Letter from Mother Mary Liguori, O.S.B., to Monsignor F. Satolli, February 13, 1893

Most Rev. Father in Christ,

The great interest you take in the progress of the Church in America, assure us that you will be pleased to hear that there is now established, for the first time in the history of the Indian missions, a Congregation of Indian Sisters.

The object of our Congregation is to labor among the people of our own race, to make them good Catholics and prosperous and progressive Citizens of the United States.

Our Sisters are all Indians, and their director, Rev. Father Craft, is also of Indian descent. This is the first organized effort of Indians to labor for the conversion and civilization of their race.

We have heard with the greatest pleasure of the establishment of a permanent apostolic delegation in the United States, and we feel that the Indians, the real aboriginal Americans, should be among the first to welcome to their country the honored representative of our Holy Father, to offer him their allegiances, and to ask his blessing.

In the name of our Indian race we welcome you; we thank the Holy Father for sending you to represent him among us; we thank you for the hope of progress and prosperity your coming has given us; we offer you our homage and allegiance as the representative of our Holy Father, and we beg your blessing and the blessing of the Holy Father on us and our work.

With best wishes for your happiness and the success of your apostolic labors, and again asking your blessing and a remembrance in your holy sacrifices and prayers, we remain, Most Reverend Father in Christ. Yours sincerely in the Sacred Heart of Jesus.

> Prioress General of the Congregation of Indian Sisters
> of the Order of St. Benedict
> Mother Mary Liguori, O.S.B.
> Subprioress.

Francis M. Craft Papers of Thomas W. Foley, Dunwoody, Georgia. Printed by permission.

82. Lizzie Obern's Biographical Sketch of Sister Edwardine Denomie, F.S.P.A., 1909

Born into a strong Catholic home to an Ojibwa mother and a mixed-blood Ojibwa-French Canadian father (John Baptiste "Little Cloud" Denomie), Sister Edwardine "Lizzie" Denomie (1872–96) entered the Franciscan Sisters of Perpetual Adoration at age twenty after aspiring to religious life since childhood. Both she and Lizzie Obern came from the Bad River Reservation, Odanah, Wisconsin, and attended the local St. Mary's Boarding School. Lizzie Obern was also of mixed Ojibwa and non-Indian ancestry and was about thirteen years old when she wrote this story.

Sister Edwardine Denomie was born in Bayfield, July 9th, 1872.

She was really a remarkable child, and rarely played with other children. She seemed to love prayer, and at the age of four she gathered the other children together, and knelt and said the Stations before the pictures in the room. When six years old, she would say the Our Father and Hail Mary by her mother's tub when she was washing. When questioned why she did this, she replied that she did not want her mother to forget God while she was working, and at the same time wanted to help her, being too small to work she prayed that God would help her, so she would not be so tired. It was the same way when ironing was to be done.

When seven years of age she asked her papa to build an altar, which was done willingly. This being finished, she asked her mamma for a statue and the good mother not having a statue, gave her a sacred picture. The altar being completed, she wanted it blessed, so Father Servatins, an old Franciscan Father, came and blessed it for her. Every morning regularly she would gather her sisters together, and, kneeling before her altar pray devoutly.

When seventeen she received a proposal of marriage from a young man. She at first consented, but one day said she knew, through her conscience, that God did not wish her to marry, for she did not belong to herself but to God. She told this young man that her affection for him would never be any different from that of a sister for a brother. At the same time, her mother bought her a hat trimmed with flowers, and she told a girl friend to tell her mother to take the flowers off her hat. She was afraid her mother would be displeased with her, if she should ask herself.

Every morning she would pray so much that her mother had to interfere, as she was afraid it would affect her little girl's health. One day she said, "Mother, I am going to pray now, until my prayer is answered, for I wish to know my vocation, or whether I should go to the convent or not.["] Some days later she came to her mother and said, "God has answered my prayer. He said I should not marry that man, but should go to the convent." Her mother inquired, "How did God tell you that?" She replied, "Mamma, my conscience tells me, I feel it."

Shortly after, she entered St. Rose Convent, La Crosse, Wis. Her conduct there was ever edifying and she made rapid progress in the science of the saints, as well as in her studies. She was a very talented musician, and her progress in this branch was particularly noticeable.

At an early age she was ripe for heaven, and began to show signs of serious pulmonary trouble. Her superiors, thinking she would be benefited by her native air, sent her to St. Mary's, Odanah, where she was to fulfil the duties of organist.

Arrived there, she failed rapidly, and her parents wished to take her home. At first this seemed quite right to her, but when she realized that she had made the sacrifice of her home forever, by her consecration to God in the religious state, she no longer wished even to hear of it. God seems to have rewarded her in a special manner, for this sacrifice of natural affection, for she seemed particularly happy whenever her parents left her sick-room, and exclaimed: "When they go, Jesus comes!"

Just before her death, she desired to have the Miserere recited; her constant ejaculation in her suffering, was, "Here below O Lord, burn, scathe, spare me not, if thou dost but spare me in eternity." She died reciting the responses to St. Joseph's Litany.

Father Chrysostom, the director of her youth, held the funeral services in the old chapel of St. Mary's, and paid a glowing tribute to her saintly life and holy death. Her remains were taken to Ashland for burial.

The sisters of St. Rose Convent love to think of her as a beautiful wild flower, whose perfume long remained, but which faded all too soon.

Lizzie Obern, "Sister Edwardine Denomie," *Noble Lives of a Noble Race.* Minneapolis: Brooks Press, 1909, 210–11.

83. Small and Big Happenings among the Inuit Sisters of the Snows, 1933–39

With five Inuit (Eskimo) postulants, Father John P. Fox, S.J., founded the Sisters of the Snows in Hooper Bay, Alaska, in 1932. Annie Sipary, who had been a catechist for many years, was the first superior. She was "a crack shot, as good as any man," and led the sisters in hunting and fishing for their sustenance. Anna Marie Yupanik was one of the Inuit postulants. Despite its success Bishop Walter J. Fitzgerald, S.J., disbanded the community in 1944. Dr. Steve Jacobson provided critical details for the translation note.

April 16, 1933 by Sr. Anna Marie Yupanik.

Easter Sunday. No Mass as Rev. Fr. is not here. Meditation as usual for Novices. At 9.00 a.m. Called people to Church, many people in church. Few protestants came also, said prayers in common. Annie gave a good [explanation] on the Sufferings and [Resurrection] of our Divine Lord as the protestants say that the Catholic Priests put our divine Lord to death. Paul an ex catholic caught two seals yesterday so he thought that it would be a good idea to [spend] Easter by giving a share to these poor hungry people as they are short of food. Everybody old and young even little children each with a wooden plate or pail went up to get their share, late in the evening. Nathalia his wife came and brought us seal meat as we had not gone up to get our share. Martina gave the children a little candy that was in a box all melted, after a while an old couple came and told Annie that they had come down because they had heard that Martina was giving out candy. Before supper the daughter of Jacob the [Lutheran] preacher came down to pay a visit to the Novices. Evening prayers at the usual time....

July 24, 1935 by Fr. John Lucchesi, S.J.

Nothing unusual today, except that 5 children got into our garden during night and pulled out a lot of potato plants, cabbages and radishes. The 2 boys got a spanking from Fr.; the 3 girls were made to kneel in the classroom for a spell and all received a good scolding from their folks. The *spanking*, the first one given by Fr. to any one of the village since the opening of the mission created quite a sensation. The general effect seemed very good. The spanking was nicely

Sisters of the Snows, Convent of the Little Flower, Hooper Bay, Alaska, ca. 1932–44. Credit: Reverend John P. Fox, S.J. Marquette University, Bureau of Catholic Indian Missions Records. Reproduced by permission.

taken, and the mothers of the 5 little thieves came each with 1/2 doz. fish to pay damages. Of course, the fish were refused, but we were glad to notice that the parents did not think of backing their children. . . .

November 1–2, 1936 by Fr. John Lucchesi, S.J.

All [Saints'] Mass at 6 o'clock for Sisters at which Sr. Agnes takes 1st vows. Second Mass 7:30. Over one inch rain fell during last 12 hrs. Roof leaking badly above communion railing and in class room. Also both stove pipes. Lunch at 12 and Dinner at 5 o'clock. Benediction 7:30 with sermon. 8:45 little program for Sr. Agnes in dining room. It consisted of little recitations, songs and poetry both original and gleaned here and there, and a little original 2 act skit by Srs. Elizabeth, Marie and Mary Fanning.*

The latter composed the skit entitled "Saints." Everybody had a good laugh. Little lunch of cake and orange juice after program. . . .

All Souls. Three consecutive masses beginning 6:15. People not all dried out yet; many of them spent all night of All Sts. Standing up insteading [*sic*] of sleeping

---

*Historical note: Sisters Elizabeth and Marie were Inuit Sisters of the Snows whereas Mary Fanning was a non-Native Jesuit lay volunteer from Chicago.

as dripping was as bad in igloos and kazga* that it was impossible to find a dry spot to sleep, or even keep from getting soaked except by standing. Dripping in igloos such that it put out candles when Fr. was administering Holy Communion to a sick woman in her igloo. Very high tides and refugee mice everywhere; village practically an island. Quite a bit of wood blown in from the bay, and from the bars across the bay to the beach south of village. New tin roof put on lean to running along north and east side of original mission building. Srs. Martina and Superior go out to see & gather any logs the wind drifted in and that may not yet have been picked up by the natives....

April 7, 1939 by Fr. Fox.
Good Friday.

Due to storm we had very poor crowd at mass yesterday; for same reason no exposition during day, but weather calmed down by evening and we had the usual Holy Hour at 7:30 P.M. offered up [especially] for our fallen-away Catholics and negligent Christians of Hooper Bay. All in all the people spent about the poorest Lent since Fr. Fox came here. The general attendance at morning mass, stations of the cross and evening devotions was never so poor at this season of the year. Cause? Don't know any special one beyond ordinary laziness. Even attendance at Sunday Mass beginning to fall off [especially] among the children, so that Fr. has begun calling absentees of children at the end of services....Both in spiritual as well as in material things the people are, as a rule, hard to manage, being very intractable and selfish, and none of the older ones know any English so that it is hard to talk to them except through an interpreter. For Father knows only enough [Inuit] for ordinary conversational purposes, but can not yet preach or instruct in [Inuit] unless he writes what is to be said....

Gonzaga University. Published by permission.

84. Geraldine Clifford (Lakota) to Reverend John F. Bryde, S.J., October 28, 1949

In 1949 a young Lakota woman from the Pine Ridge Reservation, Geraldine Clifford, wrote from St. Mary College, Xavier, Kansas, to Father John F. Bryde, S.J., of Holy Rosary Mission, Pine Ridge Reservation, informing him of her vocation to the sisterhood. Both of her parents were teachers at Holy Rosary and Clifford grew up in the boarding school there. She has served her order, the Franciscan Sisters of Charity, for more than forty years and today conducts the St. Francis Home for Children, which she founded at Manderson, Pine Ridge, as a shelter for abused Lakota children.

---

*Translation note: a men's communal dwelling, or *kashim*. *Kazga* is perhaps an old-fashioned spelling with faulty hearing, which is now spelled *qasgiq* or *qaygiq* in the Hooper Bay area.

Dear Mr. Bryde,

It was swell getting a reply from you right away because I was anxious to hear what you would think about it. I had plenty time to think this thing out before answering you, and I'll try to answer all the questions you asked me.

First of all the idea is stronger than ever. I realize fully what I would be giving up as a religious — namely giving up men for God; that is being a virgin.

I got the idea when the Nuns from Marty came to Rosary last year to talk to us about vocations. I didn't give it real serious thought because I was afraid to. I thought I couldn't give up all the things that the world had to offer. That is because I didn't want to be one then. The thing that made me change my mind was — when I came here I thought I couldn't stand it. Being so lonesome I couldn't even eat. Then I found consolation in the Chapel. I went there often. Then there was Sister Vincentine in "Life of Christ." She said, "You have only one life to live. Are you living it to the fullness? This is your once. Are you doing God's will?["] That is what turned my life upside down and changed my outlook on life.

About finishing College, the thing that worries me is the fact that my good parents are paying alot of money in sending me here. Besides that I got a loan to pay for part of it. If I were to go to college for four years, I would have to work a long time to pay back the money after finishing college. I couldn't expect the folks to do it for me. If I were planning on joining the convent here, I wouldn't have to worry because I could just finish my college education in the convent.

But I don't want to join here. I want to go to Marty. I feel that I can do more for my people there. This is another reason why I feel I should be a nun. I have been thinking about how many Indian people are going wrong and how few vocations there are among the Indians. If someone would only start the ball rolling at Rosary maybe some one would follow the example.

The thought of being a nun fills one with an unearthly happiness and peace. I feel that I want to follow Christ always and do his Holy will no matter how much it costs.

Don't worry about me not mixing with the kids here. I find it very hard to hold myself back from them. They don't seem to realize that time is valuable. They always want to have a good time.

I am so glad that you told me in your letter about Daddy praying for a vocation for one of his children.

[Sister Geraldine Clifford]

Marquette University, Holy Rosary Mission — Red Cloud Indian School Records. Printed by permission.

Sister Geraldine comments from St. Francis Home, Manderson, South Dakota, October 3, 2001:

"At the time that I decided to become a Sister, the Franciscan Sisters of Penance of Christian Charity, my congregation, could not accept Native American women. I have come to realize that this policy was imposed on my congregation because we are an international congregation directly subject to Rome. The ban was lifted in 1949.

"When I returned home from St. Mary's College in the summer of 1950, I had still planned to enter the convent [of the Oblate Sisters of the Blessed Sacrament] in Marty [South Dakota]. However, when I confided this intention to Reverend Lawrence Edwards, S.J., he said, 'Why don't you join our sisters? You will be able to continue your education and also return to serve your own people on this reservation some day.' Both aspects have become facts.

"Upon hearing Father Edwards state the above, I knew immediately that entering the Franciscans was God's will for me. Needless to say, my Sisters rejoiced that I asked to enter with them. I am most grateful to Lawrence Edwards, S.J., for his discerning advice to me!

"Finally, in Mr. Christopher Vecsey's book, Where the Two Roads Meet, Mr. Vecsey states that my brother, Gerald Clifford, and I attended an international meeting where Gerald used the pipe in praying with the participants. That is true. However, I would like to state that it was my Congregation under the leadership of Sister Christine Pecararo, the Minister General of our congregation in Rome, who invited Gerald and myself to give a retreat to Sister representatives from every province throughout the world — ten provinces in all. When my congregation became conscious of the fact that Native people's spirituality had been repressed by all Christian churches, the leadership made every effort to open themselves to the spiritual gifts of the Native people."

85. Sister Anthony Davis, O.S.B.S., on the Origins of an Indian Sisterhood in South Dakota, June 1994

In an interview in June 1994, Sister Anthony Davis, O.S.B.S. (Ojibwa), narrates the events leading up to establishment of the Oblate Sisters of the Blessed Sacrament in 1935 at St. Paul's Mission, Yankton Reservation, Marty, South Dakota. She was raised on the Turtle Mountain Reservation, at Turtle Mountain, North Dakota, and includes references to the global influenza pandemic of 1918, which hit Native Americans with exceptional severity.

Interviewed and edited by Mark Thiel.

Well, when I was three my mother and father died...in the influenza [pandemic] in 1918 [Turtle Mountain Reservation, Turtle Mountain, North Dakota]. They died the same day...and then...[that] day my grandfather took over...and made my adoption papers....I lived with my grandparents till I went to [boarding] school [and]...I used to come back at summertime for vacation....[D]uring that time my grandmother died, but my grandfather was still living....[W]hen I became a teenager, I went to St. Michael's [Mission School, Devil's Lake Reservation, St. Michaels, North Dakota] and then every summer I came home.

...[T]hen when I went to Marty [St. Paul's Mission School, Yankton Reservation, Marty, South Dakota], I came home the first three summers and then I asked my grandfather if I could become an Oblate Sister....[T]hat was a new order, we never heard of...[it] anywhere...[but]...there's about thirty-five of us who used to get together and have meetings on becoming sisters....[T]hen finally, Sister Clarent, one of the Blessed Sacrament sisters that used to teach at the kitchen...used to listen to every one of us talk and then...talk to us, too.

[She told]...us about religious orders [and] how they lived.... So one day, she said, "Now that we have meetings and meetings, let's go and ask Mother 'La-Guardia' if we could do something about it. I've been telling you all these things about religious orders, maybe we could do something." See, Father Sylvester [Eisenman, O.S.B.] says she was our founder, [our] superior for Marty....

So one day, one Sunday when we met, three girls offered to go ask Father Sylvester to start our order....[W]hen he saw the girls going over there he thought they were coming to listen to the radio, because it was electric. [But] they said, "No, we came to see you. We want to ask you something." "Oh," ... "What could it be?"... "We want to be sisters." "What?" [said Father. So they repeated,] "We want to be sisters." "Well,"... "How many of you?" [They] said, "35 of us." "Are you sure?" We said, "Yes! We've been having meetings all year with Sister LaGuardia and Sister Clement...." " "Well, [he said,] I'll ask a bishop." So he called a bishop that same day, and... said, "I'm going to give you my answer tomorrow." So the girls came over, so he brought that message to us. So we were all anxious to hear what the bishop said.

The next day, Father Sylvester came over and he said, "I want to see those 35 girls." So we all gathered in that recreation hall. He come over and he says, "Girls,...I've had a nice talk with the bishop. He was surprised and pleased. But,...he's giving you all a test. Go home for the summer and if you all come back, you can start. But if only seven come back, you can still start. So, we all went home [and] seven of us came back. It was 1935...[and] there was seven of us girls...all from different tribes [and]...all Indians....[I]t's what Father Sylvester wanted, just all Indian girls. Mother Mary of Lewis came to be our Superior, [from]...a house in Philadelphia—[the] Blessed Sacrament Sisters.

So on October 6th, we were received as [postulants]. We had a silver-gray habit. We wore black stockings,...nun veils and a cape, a black cape for our elbows,...a white collar, and the length of our dress was about eight inches from the floor. Father Sylvester said he could not see us dragging all the trash with our skirts being so long and...he didn't want us to have a scapular, because they always get caught on a wire fence. He said his got caught on the wire fence all the time....So that's how our [original] habit was made....

Marquette University, Kateri Tekakwitha Oral History Collection. Printed by permission.

86. Reverends René Astruc, S.J., and Louis L. Renner, S.J., Describe William Tyson, the Late Eskimo Deacon, 1994

The Second Vatican Council called for greater lay leadership in the Catholic Church. In the mid-1970s the American Church was ordaining Indian men as permanent deacons, especially in the Great Lakes and Plains regions. In Alaska the Jesuits began an extensive program of training Eskimos for the diaconate, and one of the most prominent was William Tyson, ordained in 1977 and an effective apostle among his people. When he died in 1993, two Jesuits wrote his obituary.

He was a man of the tundra, and a man of Alaska's largest city. He was a man equally at home in the world of the Eskimo and in the world of the white man. Throughout his long life he was "a man for others." He entered this world near the mouth of the Yukon River, and he left it as an ordained deacon with two bishops, 12 priests and five deacons present at his funeral, which was held in Anchorage's Catholic cathedral.

According to Church records, William Nugwaralrea Tyson was born to Ignatius Preuchuk and Josephina Tyson on 23 February 1916 at Akulurak. He was baptized five days later. He was to spend most of his life in the Yukon-Kuskokwim delta, the native land of the Central Yup'ik Eskimo people of which he was a member. In those days there were no large communities, just small scattered camps to which the people moved according to the season. From his father William learned the skills needed to survive in this environment: hunting, trapping, fishing.

In 1927, at the age of 11, he was sent to St. Mary's Mission at Akulurak to get some schooling and training from the Ursuline Sisters and Jesuit priests and Brothers staffing the mission. He made his first Holy Communion there on 2 February 1928 and was confirmed there that same year. Before receiving these two sacraments, he admired the medicine men, the shamans, because of their spiritual powers. But after receiving his first Communion, according to his own words, "something went out of me and a great light came in me." He also stated that at the time of his confirmation a great desire to serve his people came into him and that this desire never left him.

His first wife, Pauline, left him with four children, when she died of tuberculosis. The youngest, a little girl, died a month later. (William was to experience more family sorrows before the end of his life. Five sons died under tragic circumstances.)

While Pauline was still alive, William traveled all over the area surrounding the Akulurak mission helping the priests visiting the various camps and translating for them. Father Segundo Llorente, one of the priests for whom William interpreted, said of him: "Without any doubt, William became the best interpreter in the land. He was so good that while he spoke the eyes of the people were fixed on him as though he were an apparition from heaven." While helping the missionaries, William supported his family by hunting and fishing.

On 31 August 1948 William married Maria Arsanyak Julius, a student at the mission school. Soon after, they left for Nunaqaq to assist Father Norman Donohue there. William served not only as interpreter, but also as carpenter, teacher, postmaster, store-keeper, radio operator. He spent much time with the people. They needed his help; he responded selflessly.

Tuberculosis — so widespread in Alaska at the time — necessitated William's leaving his family and going to the sanatorium in Sitka in 1950. He found the separation from his family painful. With weekly letters he kept in touch with them. After his return, he made a special point of being always real close to his family. According to his family, he was the first to admit that he by himself made up only half a person and that his wife Maria made him whole. Maria said, "He taught me never to be alone."

The Tyson children were very well taught and trained by their parents, both in the Native traditions and in the Catholic Faith. Daughter Rose — interviewed by EXTENSION Magazine — said, "Being with my Dad, holding on to his hand — like when we were going to the store — is my favorite childhood memory." She said, "He passed on his faith just by being who he was." "God is my best friend," she said, "I try to love Him like I love my family."

Eventually William with his family moved to St. Marys on the Andreafsky. There he took part in local government and community development. He was active in Eskimo dancing as a choreographer, drummer, singer, dancer. He explained Native customs and the meaning of dances to the uninitiated.

William and his family were faithful members of the St. Marys parish community. When the Eskimo Deacon Program was started in 1970, William was recommended and advanced for it by his people as a candidate, one of the seven in the original group. It is William and his wife Maria who deserve credit for the design of the diaconal vestment worn by the Eskimo deacons during liturgical functions to this day. It closely resembles the traditional Eskimo parka. On the outside of the parka, over his chest, the deacon wears a simple cross hung loosely from the neck.

William was one of the first translators for the deacon workshops and liturgies. In 1971 he, along with three other Eskimos and two priests, met in Tununak on Nelson Island for the purpose of producing an acceptable translation into Eskimo of the common prayers of the Mass and of the Communion liturgies presided over by the deacons-to-be. What they produced was judged "a major achievement." It was left to William to attend to the fine points concerning orthography and to type the Eskimo translations.

While in training for the diaconate, William was involved also with the Alaska Land Claims issues. He was an original member of his regional corporation. With other members he chose "Calista" (the worker) as a name for the new corporation, indicating thereby again his sense of service to his people. Here again he, the recognized expert as a [translator], played a major role. While on the Calista board, he was sent to Washington, DC, to sign official documents. Because of his knowledge of the people in his region, he was put in charge of enrollment and of the distribution of shares and of maintenance of official records. He had to move to Anchorage, because corporation headquarters were located there. His family followed him.

The 26th of January 1977 was an especially memorable day in the life of William Tyson, for on that day, in Anchorage, he was ordained to the permanent diaconate by the Apostolic Delegate to the United States, Archbishop Jean Jadot, assisted by Archbishop Francis Hurley of Anchorage, retired Bishop Francis Gleeson, and Bishop Robert Whelan, Ordinary of the Diocese of Fairbanks, for which William was ordained. For the occasion Maria had made William a beautiful new parka-vestment.

After his ordination, Deacon Tyson continued to attend the Eskimo Deacon Workshops and the annual retreats held for the Eskimo deacons of the Diocese of Fairbanks. When visiting the villages for his work, he was asked to celebrate liturgies for his people. They appreciated his homilies. During his Anchorage days he longed to be with his own people in their home region. He even talked of going back to the delta of his origins to live in a tent as he did at times during his younger days.

When Pope John Paul II visited Anchorage on 26 February 1981, Deacon Tyson, as the representative of all the Eskimo deacons, assisted at the altar. In 1983 he was officially appointed to the Office of Native Ministry of the Archdiocese of Anchorage. As such he was a real inspiration to the Native community, urging them to be true to their roots as Eskimos and as Catholics. He fostered traditional Eskimo drumming and dancing. With his wife, Maria, he visited the Native Hospital, often acting as an interpreter there. And every Sunday, priest or no priest, he gathered the people for prayer and Holy Communion. As long as his health allowed, he and Maria went to the Highland Mountain Correctional Institution to be available to the inmates for counseling and to share with them traditional stories, to sing and dance Eskimo dances for them.

Father René Astruc, S.J., long-time director of the Eskimo Deacon Program and close acquaintance of Deacon Tyson's, recalled the following:

"William's sense of humor was well known. If I can indulge in a personal story. I remember the time my mother traveled from France and was visiting St. Marys in the spring of 1971. The day we arrived William asked when we were to leave. We were to stay ten days. He then said that we should come and eat at his place the day before our departure. When we arrived at his house, the table was full of the most wonderful food from the region. Before we went on, William went to the next room and came back with a pail full of snow and planted in the middle of it a bottle of Cold Duck. (In those days St. Marys was not yet a dry village.) No need to say we had a good laugh about that."

During his life William and Maria Tyson served in many different capacities, generally as bridges between cultures and between the young and Elders. For many years they were parent volunteers for the Johnson[-]O'Malley Program and board members of the Indian Education parent committee. They worked with students from pre-school through college in preserving Native arts, crafts, clothing and dancing. They inspired the Greatland Traditional Dancers, which performed throughout Alaska and in the Lower 48.

William Tyson received many awards and was honored both locally and statewide, both for his efforts within the Church and within the Native Community. He was named Elder of the Year by the Alaska Federation of Natives, Parent of the Year by the Alaska Native Education Council, and Community Member of the Year by the Cook Inlet Tribal Council/Johnson-O'Malley Program.

"*Culingailama wii atuayuitua...* " sang the singers to the beat of the Eskimo drum as the body of Deacon William Tyson was brought into Holy Family Cathedral in Anchorage on 30 December 1993. (He had died of cancer the day after Christmas.) When it was halfway down the aisle, Archbishop Hurley sprinkled the casket with holy water, recalling William's baptism. Then the singing and drumming began again:

"I would like to give you my spirit, but I have no drum. I can not dance.
The word of the Creator comes to us over the water.
The word of the Creator comes to us by the heat waves over the ground.
The word of the Creator comes to us through thunder and lightning.
I would like to give you my spirit, but I have no drum. I can not dance."

At the end of the song William's drum was placed on the casket as a reminder of his call — to reach his people through the teaching of his songs.

On the day of his ordination to the diaconate Holy Family Cathedral was filled by his many friends. It was no less so on the day of his funeral. Concelebrating with Archbishop Hurley were Bishop Michael J. Kaniecki, S.J., Ordinary of the Diocese of Fairbanks, twelve priests and five deacons.

Eskimo Deacon William Tyson, as a man of the drum and of the cross, as a man for others, touched the lives of many. He will long be remembered as a major figure in the state of Alaska and in the Catholic Church in Alaska.

Reverends René Astruc, S.J., and Louis L. Renner, S.J., "Deacon William Tyson: 'A Man for Others,' 1916–1993," *Alaskan Shepherd* 32, no. 4 (July–August 1994): n.p. Printed by permission.

87. Reverend Zuern, "A Study of the Catholic Potawatomi Indians in Topeka and Their Practice of Religion," March 21, 1958

Father Zuern analyzed the conditions of Potawatomi Indians who left their Kansas reservation for Topeka and experienced there a sense of alienation that Zuern hoped his Church could overcome. He saw, however, that the Indians were alienated from the Church and its non-Indian populace and needed a special urban ministry to make them feel at home, a ministry that understood the Potawatomi desire to engage in Native rituals as well as Catholicism.

During the past fifteen years considerable numbers of Catholic Potawatomi Indians have moved from their reservation in Jackson County, Kansas, to neighboring towns and cities, especially to Topeka. The Jesuit Fathers who have ministered at Our Lady of the Snows Church on the Potawatomi Reservation during these years have become steadily aware that the practice of their religion by the Catholic Indians who left the reservation has been poor. The situation in Topeka was more noticeable because of the large number of Indians living there as compared with the number in Manhattan and the smaller towns, but no exact information has ever been available....

In this area there are two active "Indian religions." One is the Society of the Sacred Drum which has gathered and organized ritualistic...dances and sacrificial and other rites of traditional Potawatomi religious practices. There also seems to be a blending of Christian ideas into this "religion."...The other "Indian religion" is called the Native American Church, or colloquially the peyote cult....

Points of jurisdiction and canon law cannot be easily discussed with Indians in general. They do not have a legalistic mentality. Those who have adjusted most satisfactorily into non-Indian society will recognize the existence of Church laws but will expect the priest to obtain any exceptions needed for him because he wants to practice his religion as his Catholic parents used to do when there was no need for permission from city priests. Those who are most pathetically caught between the collapsed Indian culture and the worst elements of contemporary American civilization hardly grasp the complications of any law, canon as well as civil, and suspect that they are being rejected when reasons of law are offered as the excuse for denying them a request. Undoubtedly, this is an area in which education is necessary for the wandering Indian, but experience shows that education by rigid applications of law drives the Indian of this condition from practicing at least the externals of his religion in the case of canon law; and in the cases where state laws are concerned the uncomprehending Indian goes as he will and takes arrest as just another evil in life.

No record... exists of a pastor in the area denying his permission for an Indian child to be baptized at Our Lady of the Snows, yet in one instance a pastor in a small town near the reservation expressed displeasure at [an] Indian couple, living within the boundaries of his parish, regularly attending Mass at Our Lady of the Snows and asking to have their children baptized there. According to canon law he has a just complaint; he has a right to be displeased.

From the Indian's viewpoint he fails completely to understand the couple's standard of values, for without experience of it, a non-Indian can scarcely imagine the affection which Indians have for Our Lady of the Snows church, the Indians' church. Catholic Indians who have not practiced their religion for years will still look upon Our Lady of the Snows as a place especially belonging to the [Potawatomis] and will make contributions to its maintenance. For Indians who do practice their Catholic religion it is the best, almost the only, place to attend Mass and receive the sacraments....

A consideration of the Indian's sense of "the holy" seems necessary for a good view of the whole problem connected with religion. Actually, the discovery of this sense of "the holy" so widespread through a people is a wonderful experience for any Christian non-Indian. It seems related to the sense of mystery which primitive people have before the wonder of natural phenomena and which is lacking in modern non-Indian Americans oriented by scientific explanations of phenomena....

Sometimes an Indian will stop coming to Mass regularly for no apparent reason. When questioned, he will say something like, "Oh, I don't feel like going now." That seems to be just what he means. Apparently (and this statement is based on information offered in all seriousness by an Indian who has broader and more successful associations, than the average Indian, in modern non-Indian society and who probably appreciates more fully the differences between Indian and non-Indian attitudes and tendencies), something is lacking in many Catholic... Indians' sense of obligation to attend Sunday Mass, many priests who have had long experience with Indians agree that many of them do not understand the meaning of the obligation to attend Sunday Mass as does the average non-Indian American Catholic....

During the questioning required to make this survey occasional mention would be made of some individual who was a baptized Catholic but who attended the ceremonies and dances of the Drummers, as members of the Society of the Sacred Drum are called. Further questioning revealed that usually these Indians had no idea of abandoning their Catholicism but merely wanted to dance some Indian dances. One old Indian woman pointed out that as there is a sacrifice of Christ in the Mass so the Drummers have a sacrifice by burning food at their ceremonies, but the religious significance of the Drummer ceremonies does not seem to attract Catholic Indians. The attraction lies in the Indian character of the ceremonies. While there are Indian dances that are purely social and without religious significance, in the local area there is hardly any opportunity now for such dancing, nor is there any other social [activity] that is thoroughly "Indian."

It seems that even the Indian who has adjusted without any noticeable conflict into modern non-Indian society feels the need for some occasional cultural identification with the traditional ways of his people. Opportunities for such identification in this area are rare. That fact combined with the fact, noted earlier, of the Indian's readiness to drop everything and go off to an Indian pow-wow some hundreds of miles away should indicate how the Indian values on a different scale than do other Americans. He craves identification with his people. For many of the older Indians merely to have an opportunity to gather with other Indians seems to [be] enough. For those who want something more active the dances of the Drummers seem...to be the only "Indian" thing left.

Though this phase of the Topeka Indian situation does have a religious aspect, the fundamental problem here is not on religious but cultural grounds. In confirmation of this local Indian attitude toward the Drummers is a recent popular account of the peyote cult which takes the place of the Drummers in other areas. A Catholic Indian who participates in the peyote religion is quoted, "This religion is the one thing left that's really Indian, and not borrowed from our white brothers. No matter how poor or rich an Indian is, or how long he's lived among white men, he yearns for Indian ways." The tragedy is that the Indian just quoted apparently fails to appreciate the blending of Indian and Christian ideas in the peyote cult, which was unknown before 1890. The Drummers also are reported to have some Christian ideas mixed with their Indian ceremonies, so that they are not offering something traditionally; "Indian," in the truest sense. Even here there is modification by social evolution, yet the damaging effect on the Indians' Catholicism remains....

Marquette University, Bureau of Catholic Indian Missions Records. Printed by permission.

88. Milwaukee Indians to Archbishop Rembert G. Weakland, O.S.B., November 1977

In Gallup, Tucson, Albuquerque, and Los Angeles, in Chicago and Minneapolis, in Rapid City, Sioux Falls, Salt Lake City, and Denver, in Spokane, Tacoma, and Seattle, in Sault Ste. Marie and Grand Rapids, in Syracuse and elsewhere across the United States, the Church has initiated urban Indian ministries. One of the successes of urban Indian Catholicism has been in Milwaukee, where the Indian parish, the Congregation of the Great Spirit, was established offi-cially in 1989, after more than a decade of planning. In 1977 a delegation of Milwaukee Indians led by the Menominee/Ojibwa John Boatman sent a letter to Archbishop Rembert G. Weakland, requesting a Catholic ministry to Native Americans. Although the Indians attended several parish churches throughout the city, the letter said, they felt the need to worship together, in order to express the pan-Indian culture that they were developing together.

I'm sorry to bother you so early in your position, but this is a matter I'm sure you would want to be informed of; that is the need of the Native Amer-icans for the service of the Church in the Milwaukee Archdiocese. There is no spokesman, no program, no agency, in the Archdiocese for this group of people; many of whom are Catholic; so possibly this matter may not be presented to you by another.

In Wisconsin there are six tribes as such ([Menominee], Chippewa, Win-nebago, Oneida, Stockbridge, Pot[a]watomi) on eleven [reservations] or areas, none of which are in Milwaukee Archdiocese. [Menominee] are 85 percent Catholic. The Franciscan Fathers of the Sacred Heart Province, whose provin-cial headquarters is in St. Louis, administer the Church's service to the missions in the Native Americans areas (with the exception of Neopit, Wisconsin, where a Green Bay Diocese priest is serving where no Franciscan was available). How-ever many Native Americans have migrated to or were placed in cities in hopes of finding better conditions and chances of employment; but have been met with the frustration of adjusting to a new culture of a rushing, impersonal city quite opposed to their culture. Professor John Boatman of the University of Wisconsin–Milwaukee estimated in 1975 a Native American population of eight to ten thousand in Milwaukee. His estimate is allowing for an invisible minority population avoiding census, hence creditors or other such problems.

In Milwaukee there is a parish, St. Michael's with which Native Americans identify; a man, Bob McGlinn, who is highly respected in the Native American community and who is also active in the Spanish permanent deacon program; and other parishes which happen to serve individual Native Americans who ask for help there. But there really is no continuation of the services specifically for this group of people begun in the reservations.

The Native Americans are basically a very spiritually-oriented people; they are a communal people; their culture accepts very beautiful values of coop-eration, humility, and respect for all living things. A life-long interest in this culture and one year of service among these people has left me with a deep re-spect for the culture, a love for these people, a compassion for their [sufferings], and with friendships like I've never had. In the past both the Church and the government looked upon this culture negatively. Their spirituality was called pagan; the boarding schools served to weaken the social system which might have served to sustain many individuals. The Church looks upon the Indian way more positively now. One priest working among these people called their old religion the purest form of religion. After my experience on the reservation I personally think that there is a place for white persons in the Church serving the Indian people to "find out from them who Christ is, that is, discover the Gospel and the Christ of their culture" and to stand with these suffering people — to encourage them and give them confidence to dare to follow their own initiative in returning to, retaining, or searching out the depth of a way of life in God of which remnants of the original may have been handed down.

Rather than just point out a need, I would like to make a suggestion in hopes that it may be translated into practical administrative terms. I propose the appointment of a person who can minister beyond the boundaries of a parish, yet work within a parish; who can act as [liaison] to and work with various Native American organizations in Milwaukee; who can refer needy Native Americans to appropriate resources and interested people to appropriate Native Americans; and who can help organize desired or needed programs in justice and education. In this way the Native American community knows the Church cares about them but will not do everything for them, rather help them achieve their own goals. On basis of my own experience and a few priests involved in ministry to the poor, I recommend that someone in the Church be able to visit their homes when they trust enough, as this means so much to a person who thinks so little of himself. Finally, I suggest some means of gaining feedback from the Native Americans themselves, be it in the form of a census, or meeting with existing organizations of Native Americans so that these people themselves can let their needs be known or what service may be relevant.

To provide such a service to the Native Americans today may not be easy as some are not well disposed to the Church at the present time; but, as I'm sure you know only too well, Jesus sends us with the Gospel to the alienated and hostile as well as to those well-disposed to us. And the only way a personal, communal people such as the Indian people can meaningfully accept the Gospel is in a personal commitment requiring a ministry which elicits this. Efforts to establish such a ministry can only result in a spiritually alive part of the Archdiocese.

Marquette University, Siggenauk Center Records. Printed by permission.

89. Archbishop Weakland to Sister Mary Margaret Troy, S.S.M., December 8, 1977

Archbishop Weakland responded by hiring Sister Margaret Troy, S.S.M., for a half-time Native American ministry in a parish where many Catholic Indians lived. In his letter to Troy the bishop revealed his own Indian heritage.

Dear Sister,

Your letter of November 23rd was indeed of importance and of interest. It was the first letter I had concerning the problem of Native Americans in the Archdiocese of Milwaukee. I was most grateful for all of the detail and for the positive suggestions. Right now there are so many things to be faced, but I can see the importance of the Native Americans and especially those who come to the big city. I will be in touch with St. Michael's on the matter and see what can be worked out so that someone will be in touch with them, as you suggest in your own letter.

The other day we had a meeting of the Wisconsin Catholic Conference, and I see that this would be a good subject for the entire state to discuss and will talk with the people in charge so that it can come up at one of our meetings in the near future.

I have a special interest in this problem because of the Indian blood that I have in me. The family story is that my ancestors came to the Baltimore colony in 1637 and then in 1692 went northward into Pennsylvania where they married among the Indians. When I was a boy we were hardly permitted to talk about this, as my great-aunts and -uncles thought it a disgrace. Now we are extremely proud of that heritage.

Thanks again for sharing this concern with me. Have a Blessed and Happy Christmas.

Sincerely yours in the Lord,
Most Reverend Rembert G. Weakland, O.S.B.
Archbishop of Milwaukee

Marquette University, Siggenauk Center Records. Printed by permission.

90. Anita Hamley to Board Members of the Siggenauk Center, September 25, 1979

The Milwaukee Catholics called their ministry the Siggenauk Center, named for a pan-tribal Indian leader from around the time of the American Revolution. In creating liturgical forms that would suit the pan-Indian Milwaukee community, the Siggenauk Center aroused some opposition from conservative Catholic Indians who felt that Catholic allegiance should mean forgoing native ritualism. In 1979 the Ojibwa Anita Hamley addressed these and other concerns (excerpted here) to members of the Siggenauk Center board.

Dear Board Member:

...I would like to present some concerns that I have as a board member....

I have a concern about the undue amount of Native American religion that John Boatman wants to put into this Christian program. Are we losing sight of our purpose for forming and allowing Sr. Troy to submit a proposal in the first place? I don't remember us wanting to hire drum chiefs before. I really have to take a stand on this point. I am a Christian! That means that I have one god — Yahweh — and my brother is Jesus Christ who sends the Holy Spirit to comfort and guide me. (Like right now.) I can't and won't compromise that position. This is a Catholic group right now — I'd like to see the Christianity flowing throughout it with no distortions.

You know, at the Tekakwitha Conference on the last day we had a general meeting and covered several points. One of the questions that was brought up was who wanted to see a Liturgy Committee (I guess on a national scale that would incorporate parts of the Native American culture with the Roman rite

Mass). I raised my hand as those who were around me did but there was another group, and yes, a much larger one that did *not* want a Liturgy Committee. In trying to puzzle that out, I came up with one idea—that people were too afraid to have a return to the witchcraft that is in the Native American Religion that they didn't dare even incorporate things like symbols, etc....

What are we responsible for? When do we meet? Who are we responsible to and for whom to supervise? These are really valid questions as is the money question if we want to be a viable group. It could also have its legal ramifications, not to mention it will facilitate working together much easier.

I think we have to get our own preamble together a lot better if we want to be credible. What is our main philosophy? Are we just another social work agency that helps people with some of their problems? Are we a special and unique community that is trying to live gospel (which is very similar to the Brotherhood ideals of the American Indian)? Are we formed so that people can learn more about the Catholic Church? About Christianity? As gospel living are we putting into effect "Bear one another's burdens" by providing some social services and counseling? Is this going to be a fun place to have potlucks, home Masses, and fellowship with other Indian people like ourselves? What do we want? Remember, we *are* the Siggenauk Project!...

Sincerely,
Anita Hamley
Board Member
The Siggenauk Project

Marquette University, Siggenauk Center Records. Printed by permission.

91. Proposed Mission Statement for the Siggenauk Interfaith Spiritual Center, January 15, 1989

Through the 1980s the Siggenauk Center held numerous gatherings for Milwaukee Indian Catholics — and for non-Indians and for non-Catholics, too. The directors tried to balance Indian and Catholic elements: powwows and Masses, task forces on social justice issues, celebrations of feast days. They acquired a sympathetic non-Indian pastor; they published a newsletter. As the Siggenauk Interfaith Spiritual Center took shape, just as it was about to become the Congregation of the Great Spirit in 1989, its board issued a statement of purpose, indicating four primary areas of ministry: religious enhancement, human service, social justice, and culture.

Statement of Purpose, Goals and Objectives

I. PURPOSE:

The purpose of the Siggenauk Interfaith Spiritual Center is to promote interfaith spirituality based on the Gospel and on the cultures, traditions and beliefs of the American Indian community. The Center shall include in its ministries four collaborative integrated service functions; namely,

1) the religious or spiritual ministry,

2) the human service ministry[,]

3) the social justice ministry, and,

4) the language and culture ministry.

II. GOALS AND OBJECTIVES:

In order to fulfill the purpose of the Siggenauk Interfaith Spiritual Center, the ministries shall strive to achieve the following goals and objectives:

A. GOAL #1: to establish a unified, interfaith ministry on the individual, familial, organizational and community levels which will nourish the spiritual needs of the American Indian population.

    1. OBJECTIVE #1: to arrange for a weekly interfaith support and prayer time which will be especially responsive to the contemporary spiritual needs of American Indian people.

    2. OBJECTIVE #2: to serve as a support group and as advocates for American Indians interested in entering a ministry and to search for funds for ministerial training programs.

    3. OBJECTIVE #3: to function as a contact group for the Interfaith Conference of Greater Milwaukee and for various religions.

    4. OBJECTIVE #4: to facilitate the sharing of resources in order to effect mutually beneficial support for every religion which seeks to tend to the spiritual needs of its American Indian constituents.

    5. OBJECTIVE #5: to secure a centralized location wherein American Indians may gather to worship together in accordance with their beliefs, wherein American Indian religions may conduct [ceremonies] to spiritually support their memberships.

    6. OBJECTIVE #6: to serve as a vehicle for networking and collaboration with organizations with comparable project goals.

B. GOAL #2: to offer programs addressing human services needs in the American Indian community.

    1. OBJECTIVE #1: to network with all existing programs which encourage spiritual support in the Indian community, such as prison support, AODA, youth groups, and elderly programs.

    2. OBJECTIVE #2: to address the concerns most affecting the American Indian people seeking assistance at the Center's facility.

    3. OBJECTIVE #3: to address crises in the American Indian community, such as basic food, clothing, housing and household needs; to address needs not presently being attended to, such as funeral support, emergency travel expenses, and infant care.

   4. OBJECTIVE #4: to organize volunteers to welcome persons com-
      ing to the Center facility for assistance.

   5. OBJECTIVE #5: to seek volunteer participation in the functions
      and programs of the Center and its associates.

C. GOAL #3: to be active advocates in the broad area of American Indian
   issues relative to social justice.

   1. OBJECTIVE #1: to organize workshops and a speakers' bureau
      which will offer presentations to promote greater understanding
      among congregations and the general populace.

   2. OBJECTIVE #2: to collaborate with existing organizational efforts
      in advocating for American Indian issues.

D. GOAL #4: to develop language and culture programs which will ensure the preservation and maintenance of American Indian cultures and
   traditions.

   1. OBJECTIVE #1: to maintain an atmosphere of mutual respect and
      free communication consistent with American Indian cultures and
      traditions.

   2. OBJECTIVE #2: to present workshops which feature American
      Indian elders and other persons knowledgeable about traditional
      customs and ceremonies.

   3. OBJECTIVE #3: to disseminate to American Indian people and
      the general populace knowledge of language, culture and heritage
      through the production of multi-media publications.

   Marquette University, Siggenauk Center Records. Printed by permission.

92. The Story of the LaBelle Family "Spirit" Picture, 2001

*In 2001 Susanna LaBelle-Boyd (Ojibwa) of Milwaukee wrote the following essay
describing a photograph of her family members, taken on October 8, 2000. Her
words express the pervading spirituality at the core of American Indian Catholic
religious life.*

Last year on October 8th, 2000, we celebrated 24 years of my mom's death.
I called up all 11 of my brothers and sisters and invited them to Holy Cross
[Cemetery] for a ceremony on my mother's anniversary. Well, eight of them
showed up, along with my son Matt, two nieces and a grandson of my sister
Pat. We gathered at my mom's gravesite and cried, laughed, prayed and shared
mama stories. We still miss her very much! We had a Native American Catholic
ceremony with Tobacco, Cedar, Sweetgrass and Sage. My brother Bob is a Viet-
nam Veteran and had his Eagle feather on his hat and he used it to "smudge" us
as we prayed. It was a beautiful gathering. We headed over to the mausoleum
to pay our respects to our cousin, Jerry Starr. He was one of the 3 men killed

The LaBelle family spirit picture, Holy Cross Cemetery, Milwaukee, Wisconsin, October 8, 2000. At the San Diego, California, Tekakwitha Conference in August 2001 Susanna LaBelle-Boyd gave away individual copies to thousands of Native Catholics who consistently voiced their concurrence with the above interpretation of spiritual reunification. In the original color photo, there is a clear image of a willowy nature visible. This black and white reproduction makes it visible, but just barely. Credit: Courtesy Susanna LaBelle-Boyd. Marquette University. Reproduced by permission.

at the Miller Park "Big Blue" crane accident July 14th, 1999. The mausoleum was closed and my family was heading back to the reservation and had a long drive before them and got ready to leave. Well, I told them that Jerry wasn't in that closed building, his spirit was out here, as I waved my hand towards the open sky. Little did I know how much he was there, among us. So again we cried, prayed and shared Jerry stories. We really miss him, too. We prayed for the widows because the trial against the "Big Blue" crane owners was starting the next day. We believe that our prayers were answered because the widows were awarded 99 million dollars and we continue to keep them in our hearts and prayers. As we were getting ready to leave, we gathered together and took this photo. This is how the picture turned out. I took the photo to our Native American Catholic parish, Congregation of the Great Spirit, and shared it with our Priest, Father Ed Cook. He said, "It's what we as Native Catholics call 'Spirits, Angels or Ghosts, take your pick!' " Well, I chose to call them "Spirits"! I took the photo to the UWM [University of Wisconsin — Milwaukee] Pow-wow that same month and showed a Cherokee Medicine Man. He waved his hand over the spirit on the left side of the photo and said, "This Spirit is female" and I knew it was my mom because she is *hugging* my son Matt. He then waved his hand over the rest of the picture and said, "These spirits are mostly males." Our family believes that the spirit on the far right is our cousin, Jerry Starr. There are many spirits all around us and we feel very "Blessed" by this event. MiiGwetch (Thank you in our language) for letting us share our "Spirit" Picture.

Marquette University. Printed by permission.

93. Transcript of the First Medicine Men and Pastors Meeting, Rosebud Lakota Reservation, February 13, 1973

The most sustained (and the most thoroughly documented) example of theological dialogue between Christians and American Indians, the Medicine Men and Clergy Meetings, took place on the Rosebud Reservation between 1973 and 1979, orchestrated by Father William F. Stolzman, S.J., of St. Francis Mission. The participants at these bi-weekly conferences included Jesuits, Lakota medicine men, Episcopalian priests, and other interested and knowledgeable parties. The subject matter, recorded and transcribed by Stolzman, included everything relevant to religious life. The following excerpt is from the first meeting, February 13, 1973, in which the Lakotas Moses Big Crow, Arthur Running Horse, Charles Kills Enemy, Ben Black Bear, Sr. and Jr., George Eagle Elk, Iva Black Bear, and others engaged Fathers Stolzman, Harry Elgsaer, and John McCurack in a cross-cultural comparison of religious claims. What is the nature of revelation? What are the purposes of ritual? How does one discern spiritual presence? To what degree are Catholicism and traditional Lakota religion comparable systems?

STOLZMAN: We are gathered here tonight to talk about the things of God. This is a holy assembly, and we want to speak about the holy things, which God has revealed to his people. God has spoken to all peoples throughout the history of the world. He has spoken to them in different ways.

Tonight we would like to learn and share the ways that God has spoken and revealed himself to the Lakota people. How he has revealed Himself through the Pipe, through the Four Directions, through the Inipi, and through Yuwipi. And we have much to share and much to learn. And one of [the] things that we should realize is that every man is given different gifts by God. And so two men can come to understand different things about certain realities. A man — one man when he looks at this light, can see the color white — see how wonderful that color is. Another person can look at this and see glass. And so talking about the same thing, different people can say different understanding of things. And so because we have differences of opinion, or different understanding of things, we should not be ashamed or we should not worry. Because they are both right, if they are speaking the truth. For that is both white and glass. Now I may be wrong, perhaps that is plastic. But then by further talk and discussion, we will learn more about the truth and things that God has given to us. It is only by talking and sharing, that we really can come to understand the revelations that God has given to us. For we all do not understand everything. Only One understands everything. That is God Himself. And so I would encourage the men tonight to be able to give us what they understand by the Holy Things of God. Which God has given to his Indian People.

Let us Begin with a prayer.

O Lord God, We are so pitiful and so much in need. We desire to know You more and more. We want to strengthen our people. And we want to grow strong through the things that you have given to us. Give us the courage, to speak of your wonderful things, give us the courage to be able to truly share our faith with one another, so we may really...be a holy people. We ask this prayer through Christ, Our Lord. Amen.

Now without any further comments — many more words are possible — But I think perhaps to break the ice, maybe we could go around the table or maybe some of the Indian men could volunteer, — to tell us first who were some of their main teachers about Lakota religion, about the things of God given to the Lakota people. Each one of us has had special teachers. Where did we learn the most about God? Was it from a person? or perhaps in a vision that we received? Art, could you say anything about that?

RUNNING HORSE: I want somebody to interpret.... [Lakota speech]

BLACK BEAR, SR.: (English text)
Perhaps...let me go through it first. First of all Art mentioned the Pejuta Wicasa which we call the medicine man and there is no one who could be called one today. Because the medicines were given to them by the supernatural not in the same way that the doctors use medicine.

That was the first idea, then the Yuwipi. I imagine that everyone might understand what Yuwipi is. It's almost comparable to the Mass. Here is the way I understand it: Of course the process — the man who is performing it will be wrapped and laid in the middle and prays with the peace pipe. And someone will unwrap him during the prayer. This will be a spirit, I believe. And the power would come through the spirit. Now this — we may elaborate on these later on. — As far as the Canumpa, the peace pipe — before — 2000 years ago — there was no such thing as — peace pipe — or as a religion so that a man was put on a high hill by himself and just raised his arms and prayed. And one incident when this one particular man did this. He had his arms upraised and was praying. He prayed, "Wakantanka, have pity on me. I don't want anything bad to act on me." (Yes, that's a prayer.) While he was praying, the peace pipe appeared on his hands, so after that they used the peace pipe to pray with. OK. Like the Mass,...it is said for people whose spirits would live long, forever. And this is the same idea that they have praying with the peace pipe, and the Yuwipi. So that the people may have a long life or an eternal life. And following that he expressed the idea that we should teach our children about the religions, I guess. So that they may work for this. These are just some points that I picked up....

There is something I forget to say about Art's talk. He expressed the same thing, the fact that you take the Canumpa or peace pipe on faith. In other words, we don't understand very much or very well, but we use it. He is saying are we meeting here...to go back to the same thing, in a way. Because...the spiritual life of the Indian has been destroyed. So he expresses the fact that he is happy about this meeting. That from this meeting we can start to understand each other and that we could return with something concrete and significant, something that he can get out of the meeting. That's about the extent of it....

STOLZMAN: Moses, do you have anything you would like to say about Indian religion?

BIG CROW: Why, yes.

I came here at the request of Mr. Kills Enemy and Frank Pickett Pin. I gathered...that the fathers here want to understand the Indian religion. Is this right?...We all pray to the same God as in the non-Indian religion. They are sitting right here so they can correct me. We pray to the same God but this is the Indian religion and our ways. 2000 years ago they didn't have no pipe to pray with so they go out on the hill and with outstretched hands they say "Wakantanka." As I understand it my grandfather always said "Tunkasila Wakantanka," meaning God. For in the old days it was God. There is only one God and somewheres down the line the pipe was brought down on earth and it is still laying up in the Green Grass somewhere near Eagle Butte up there. I have touched it twice. But as Arthur puts it, I think he means this: that through the peace pipe, — he didn't say *peace* pipe, I think — you get to be an old man, you reach a ripe old age. I think he doubts whether this can save the soul. But in the non-Indian religion we say Mass and this to save our souls. He made the statement that that is to save our souls. To be with God, but since if the non-Indians did not come across we would have this peace pipe, I think this would work the same way, I think this would save souls, so we can see our creator....

Now I believe the opening remarks were, "How did you get to be a medicine man?" or "the vision quest"? It was the opening remarks was it not? May I say that to them in Indian? (Lakota text)....

Now there is Yuwipi and Lowanpi. And these three [men] here are not Yuwipi. These here they sit in the center. They are not Yuwipi. A Yuwipi, as one of them explained, has his hands like this backwards. (Moses puts his hands behind his back.) In between the fingers they are tied with small thongs, leather thongs, like this. (Moses indicates how thongs go around fingers.) Then they put a blanket or quilt over him and they tie him up. As he lays there, they sing. There are certain songs, too,...to give medicine. All of these are certain songs. And every [one] of these medicine men here have different (ones)[,] they are not alike. They perform — maybe each of these has their own ways. So there is a Lowanpi and Yuwipi. So these three here are Lowanpi-men. This here is a spider (indicates Charlie Kills Enemy). And he is fasting. When he said Hanbleciya he said fasting. For the Eagles — to be an Eagle-Medicine-Man. That's just like you priests that you study years and years — that is the same way with these medicine men. They fast and they go through a lot of hardship. Sometimes they get it right away, and sometimes they go years and years of fasting. But to my understanding, they fast every year....

I grew up in this Catholic school here. And I go to the sweat lodges and I fast. I'm going out to be a medicine man. If they — if the Creator feels I am to be qualified, yes — if not I just keep trying. Thanks, it's sort of a thanksgiving for all the benefits He has bestowed upon me since I've been blind....

And now in these times, the chaos, the wars, everything all over the world, people are wondering. Like somebody said we should turn to our religion. And this is when the Indian would turn to the peace pipe, our pipe. This is our religion before the non-Indians came over. So we turned to this. To be a non-Indian we was taught in schools, so too the religion. I am a Catholic. I've been a Catholic all my life. So when I feel like a non-Indian I go to Church. (Laughter) And when I feel like an Indian I go to the sweat bath and go to the ceremonies....

KILLS ENEMY: I wanted to straighten out something here regarding Mr. Big Crow['s]...remark that the pipe will save a soul. Both of my grandfathers, Grandpa Chasing Crane and Kills Enemy told me that this pipe will save no soul. Well before the white man come and brought the churches over, see there's nobody baptized in those days. There's no baptism. So they are dead! Where them souls go to?...

I have a pipe, myself, so I pray with it. With the man that takes care of this pipe and I had a council with him there. I had council with him and inside the sacred pipe, and he said that the same thing my grandfather told me that the pipe would never save a soul. But it would be for health just like the way I said, for peace and happiness, but not to save a soul....

But that's the way my grandfather told me and my grandmother that pipe never would save a soul....

EAGLE ELK: (Lakota text)

BIG CROW: Regardless of which religion, the Indian or the non-Indian, he has to think for the best of it and try to do what is right.

EAGLE ELK: (Lakota text)

BIG CROW: So if they do right and they do it right, he thinks that this *will save* a soul....

Mr. Black Bear says that he would like to comment too. He says the pipe and the Catholic faith are both alike.

BLACK BEAR, SR.: (Lakota text)...

BIG CROW: His belief is: that regardless of which religion, the Catholic faith or the peace pipe, way of religion, if he does it right and lives accordingly, when he dies, he believes his soul will be saved. This is his belief, he says....

STOLZMAN: Do people use the pipe to pray for the welfare of those that are dead?

KILLS ENEMY: The only way I know is — they use this pipe when death comes in the relationship.... They take this pipe and give him smoke, they fill a pipe, pray for him, and give him smoke.

STOLZMAN: By praying for the living?

KILLS ENEMY: Yea, by praying for the living, and the dead too.

STOLZMAN: And the dead, too.

KILLS ENEMY: Yes.

STOLZMAN: It quiets the soul?

KILLS ENEMY: Yes. That's the way I understand, but you can ask the other medicine men too....
  (Lakota to other medicine men)

BLACK BEAR, JR.: The beliefs they had, that the spirits did not leave earth and that the soul, as far as the soul goes, there was no clear understanding what — as to afterlife. So that he wouldn't be praying for — the welfare of the soul. As you say just for the quieting of the spirit. That's the way I understand it....

STOLZMAN: It has been mentioned how the sweat bath strengthens and heals the body. In the sweat bath can there be strengthening and healing of the soul as well? Not to save a soul but — to help it, to help the soul....

ELGSAER: ...When a person in good health goes to a sweat bath, what is he trying to get? — God's help?...

KILLS ENEMY: Well he's already well but he goes in there for problems, to pray for (spiritual — prompt by Elgsaer) yes spiritual problems, to pray for problems he or she has. That's why he she goes in there.

ELGSAER: In doing this is he asking help of God?

KILLS ENEMY: Yes.

ELGSAER: In his problems? OK.

KILLS ENEMY: Yes. There's two ways: for health and for problems....

STOLZMAN: In a sweat bath, a man prays to spirits, the grandfathers and to God....But has any man ever seen a vision of God, Wakantanka and received power directly from Him?...

EAGLE ELK: (Lakota text)

BIG CROW: A long time ago a man was in a war party....

RUNNING HORSE: (Lakota text)

BIG CROW: He is going on this war party to battle with his enemies or to steal horses. — There we go again stealing horses — (Laughter)....Before he left, he prayed to God that if he came back alive, that he was going to do one of these sacred ceremonies....
  Nowadays this pipe is sacred to us. So if we pray to God seriously, we receive from Him what we pray for....

RUNNING HORSE: (Lakota text)

BIG CROW: His answer is, they do not see God, but He gives them power. Meaning He answers their prayers I guess.

EAGLE ELK: (Lakota text) — (Laughter by medicine men.)

BIG CROW: I'd better get out of here. (Laughter by medicine men.) He is asking this same question to these fathers. (Laughter by all.) I'm neutral. He says these fathers put in a lot of years learning to be priests. Do they see God? (Is this good!)....

STOLZMAN: I would ask the second part of the question, also. Can a man — does a man always receive help from God through a spirit, through the spirits... and from the powers He has put into the world? Or does he or can he receive help directly from Wakantanka?...

KILLS ENEMY: The only way I understand it, the way I pray my ceremonies is, the spirits the eagles or the spider are called as the spirits. We don't pray to them. We ask for help from them to pray for us to the Almighty. That's the way I operate mine, I don't know how they operate theirs. But that's the way I operate mine. So these spirits can help us pray or help me pray. That's the way I operate mine....

MACURAK: I think when George asked this question before, he was not just being rhetorical[,] I think that out of fairness because he has shared things with us so sincerely, I think we ought to at least try to give him an answer. Now the only thing that I could give at the moment would be the words of Christ Himself. And he said, I believe it was to Phillip, who was asking him since He was going away and they didn't know where. And he was going to the Father. Christ told him, "No man has ever seen the Father." "But he who sees Me," he said to Phillip, "sees the Father." So we ask ourselves the question that Christ asked the Apostles another time. "Whom do men say that I am." If when we see Christ, whoever saw Christ, also sees the Father. And Christ seems to be saying that He is something more than just man. And today when the Indian people become Christians, who do they say Christ is? Just a great man? a Prophet? Or do they believe in faith that He is also God? Thank you.

BIG CROW: ...I think it works both ways now. You do not see Him but you use His words. You pray to Him. This I think answers both questions on either side.... Boy, I got out of that one. (Laughter)....

STOLZMAN: In the Inipis, and some of the Inipis I have attended, when the flap is closed, and the holy man has prayed for the coming of the spirits, his guardian spirit or the spirits, there appear sparks around the holy man. (Lakota text)....

Some people say that the sparks are made by the spirit. Other people say that the sparks are made by the holy men. (Lakota text)....

I wonder if the answer to these two questions is not something similar to the Mass. In the Mass it cannot be said that the priest, as a man, changes the wine and the bread into the Body and Blood of Christ. (Lakota text)....

Would it be correct to say that in the Inipi and in Yuwipi that the sparks are made through the power of God, through the power of the spirits by the holy man — that is the holy man, by the power of the spirits, makes the sparks....

KILLS ENEMY: The only way I know is that I have medicine that the spirits approach. The medicine that I use. The small medicine bag that I use, that the spirits approach. And when they come in the small blue sparks come in which indicates that the spirits appear. Yes, that's God's power, yes, that's from God[,] it couldn't be from anywhere else. They are made from God. And that's my belief, you know. That is what I believe. That's why I try to control them, I don't like no evil spirits to fight their way up there....

MACURAK: ...Now it could be through good spirits or through a bad medicine man doing this thing themselves or it could be bad spirits....Now they have already said it could be dangerous, one of them has said that. So he's obviously thinking of bad spirits too, of performing these things. Just for the sake of honesty, I think it should be said. And there is a danger and that is why the fathers hesitate of approving anything that is so unusual that it is hard to explain. It's by the results that you can eventually judge....

BLACK BEAR, JR.: (Lakota text)

BIG CROW: (Lakota text)

BLACK BEAR, JR.: (Lakota text)

IVA BLACK BEAR: (Lakota text) (Laughter): I even say my Lord's prayer in there. (Laughter)

KILLS ENEMY: Maybe what you are thinking of is demons. Ha, ha.

EAGLE ELK: (Lakota text) Iva laughs. (Laughter)

BIG CROW: He says (Moses laughs) I don't like to say white men, I'll say non-Indians. (Laughter) He says if these non-Indians didn't come across with the devil, then we'd be alright. (Laughter) (Moses is broken up.)...

RUNNING HORSE: (Closing prayer) Ateyapi na Cinca na Woniya Wakan caje kin on. Amen. (Prayer from Sursum Corda)

Marquette University, St. Francis Mission Records. Printed by permission.

94. Reverend P. Michael Galvan, "Native Catechesis and the Ministry of the Word," 1987

The Tekakwitha Conference publishes the Tekakwitha Conference Newsletter *in which Native American Catholic leaders and members of the Catholic hierarchy address questions of concern to the conference membership. In 1987 Father Michael Galvan, an Ohlone Indian from California, tried to provide a guide to catechesis, balanced between official Church teachings and the wisdom of American Indian traditions. His hope was that American Indian Catholics might draw upon the heritage of both religious cultures in order to become inculturated followers of Christ.*

INTRODUCTION

My grandmother never wasted any words. Often she spoke in cryptic sentences whose meaning took years to discern. I remember that when my cousins and I would irritate her that she would send us outside to play. We always were to play in certain areas: near the chicken coop, next to the rosebushes, by the doghouse. Every now and again, she would come outside and tell us to play in another part of the yard. I never understood why she did this. But no one ever questioned my grandmother's commands. Years later, I asked her what she was doing. She told me in a very few words, "You were bad because you had forgotten where you were." Other people might express such a statement with words such as alienation, lost or confused identity, sin. For my grandmother, and for Native Peoples, such realities take concrete, physical shape....

The experience of God manifests itself both in individuals and in communities. For Roman Catholics, we experience God as individuals shaped by a common Tradition and Scripture. However, each of us relates to Tradition and Scripture in our own unique ways. Our faith, as a result, springs forth from a dialogue between the individual, the community, and God. In recent years, a greater sensitivity has appeared in regards to various cultures and languages. We have discovered that one's culture and language affect how one believes. In this article, I will explore how the culture of Native Americans affects and contextualizes our faith.

In a person's faith life, we can discern various movements: initial conversion, times of rest, ever-deepening life-long conversion, and times of doubt and struggle. In every moment, however, we notice that humans respond to God's call. For Christians, the fullness of God's revelation is expressed in Jesus Christ. Therefore, when we look at the New Testament, discipleship is characterized not by the memorization of certain principles or texts but by a life-long following and living with the Messiah. A Christian disciple is not bound primarily to a doctrine but to the person of Jesus. The call which Jesus issues to the disciples is a simple but profound one — "Follow me." The question which faces Christians is how do we follow Christ.

Jesus' directive was to continue the proclamation of God's revelation. To share in the mission of Jesus is to participate in proclaiming the Word, in celebrating the sacred mysteries, and in serving one another. *Sharing the Light of Faith* points out three ministries which support these aspects of the Church's mission: the ministry of the word, the ministry of worship, and the ministry of service. While we distinguish these three ministries for the purpose of study and reflection, we need to remember that they are inseparably linked. We cannot proclaim the Word without putting the Word into concrete and particular actions. Furthermore, we cannot do either of these ministries without being nourished and challenged by a life of worship and prayer.

As we can distinguish different movements in an individual's faith-life, we can distinguish various movements in the ministry of the word: pre-evangelization, evangelization, catechesis, re-evangelization, and reconciliation. Catechesis presumes that individuals have already been converted to a faith in the Lord Jesus. What we encounter in catechesis is a deepening of an already existent faith. Catechesis speaks to the faith life of people and must, therefore, address the whole person: social, intellectual, emotional, spiritual, physical and cultural. As Richard J. Hater writes, catechesis calls a Christian

> ...to hear, understand, interiorize, and respond to God's word in acts of service and celebration. Catechesis simultaneously firms up individual faith and initiates into the community. If either of these is deficient, catechesis will not accomplish its full purpose.

As a result, we need to address ourselves to the question of faith before we can determine the nature of catechesis. Especially since the Second Vatican Council, we have begun to move away from an understanding of faith as a belief in certain doctrinal statements to faith as a dynamic, living relationship with God. In the former understanding of faith, catechetics concerned itself with the transmission and memorization of data. Such an approach can be seen in such classic question-and-answer texts as *The Baltimore Catechism*. The catechetical language is definitional and has only one meaning. When faith is seen as relational, the element of mystery heightens; language becomes evocative and symbolic. *Sharing the Light of Faith: National Catechetical Directory for Catholics of the United States* represents such an approach. When one takes into consideration Native Traditions, the catechetical text, *Builders of the New Earth*, becomes not only possible but necessary. In this latter approach, catechetics calls forth transforming experiences.

This shift in catechetical approaches is discussed by John Paul II in *Apostolic Exhortation on Catechetics*. While upholding the importance of the content of catechetical materials, John Paul maintains that adaptions may be necessary for the communication of the Gospel. Such adaptations may be necessitated by age, culture, language or by ecumenical concerns. In regards to cultural adaptions, he states: "...catechesis will seek to know these cultures and their essential components; it will learn their most significant expressions; it will respect their particular values and riches. In this manner it will be able to offer these cultures the knowledge of the hidden mystery and help them to bring forth from their own living tradition original expressions of Christian life, celebration and thought." If we follow the Holy Father's lead, it would not be an adequate proclamation of the Word if we were simply to utilize Western catechetical materials and not adapt them to the Native American experience. If our goal is one of transformation and not simply one of transmission, inculturation becomes a necessity.

This need to produce catechetical materials which would be developed primarily for Native peoples served as the motivating force behind a consultation with Native Catechists which was held in November, 1982. The Tekakwitha Conference served as the co-sponsor of the event along with the USCC's

Department of Education. Sr. Mariella Frye, the USCC representative for Catechetical Ministry, reminded the native catechists that their work fit within the framework of the catechetical ministry of Jesus. As she stated,

> Like Jesus, the catechist begins with people's experience, sheds the light of the Gospel message on that experience, and explains what Jesus is asking them to do when they follow him.

The tension that has existed for Native Catholics has been well documented. One can read such classic works as *Black Elk Speaks, The Sacred Pipe,* and *The Sixth Grandfather* to see the Lakota holy man's struggle. Patrick Twohy's *Finding a Way Home* illustrates this in a more contemporary setting. The experience of Native Peoples with the Tekakwitha Conference further substantiates this [phenomenon]. For many Native Catholics, the tension between practicing the Native ways and the Catholic ways has been paramount. To deny either our Native or Catholic roots causes some identity confusion. How does one be Native and Catholic at the same time? How does one become transformed into Christ?

We need to remember that transformation, conversion, does not occur in relation to certain abstract principles but in response to one's experiences and stories. In other words, if Native Americans are to be transformed, converted, to the Lord, this conversion must take place within the context of their own experiences and stories. What types of experiences and stories do we need to address in a Native Catechesis?

First, we must realize that when we deal with Native Americans, we are not encountering one culture. Each nation, tribe, and clan have their own particular and unique culture and tradition. The culture of the shepherding Navajo differs from the fishing culture of the Tlingit and both differ from the hunting culture of the Lakota. It is important to attend to these tribal differences in [catechetics]. In addition, the degree of contact with the dominant Western culture varies. Some Natives, especially those living in urban areas, may have lost, to some degree, contact with their roots. Yet, they experience some dissonance between their familial up-bringing and the dominant culture.

Second, lest we lose all hope of successfully undertaking a Native catechetical ministry, there are common threads and elements which Native cultures share. We can distinguish the following common threads: the relationship with words (story), the relationship with time (expressed often in ritual), the relationship with the land, the relationship with all creatures. Let us discuss each of these elements in further detail.

As I mentioned in the introduction, my grandmother spoke in very few and short sentences. The multiplication of words destroyed the beauty and the sacredness of words. This reverence for the spoken word resulted from a deep reverence for breath. A person's breath expresses one's very life. So, words express one's very self not merely one's thoughts and ideas. When these words create familial and tribal stories, they express the very life of a people. As a result, Native peoples tend to express themselves more in stories, in symbolic language. Such an approach is not counter to the Gospels but is rather similar to the manner of the New Testament. If we read the Gospels, we find Jesus constantly responding to people's questions with stories. The challenge of such an approach is that there can be many different interpretations of a story. As we mentioned above, though, such a symbolic approach characterize[s] present catechetical methods.

We can not leave the relationship with stories at this theoretical level, however. For Native peoples, not to tell our stories, not to live our lives out of our tribal stories, means that we experience a death to our full identity. We are both Native and Roman Catholic. Catechesis, however, does not advocate the death of a culture.... Instead, as John Paul II has advocated, we need to utilize these stories to express the Gospel. I recall one woman religious asking me how this might be accomplished. A method I have found useful is to parallel the Gospel stories to tribal stories. These stories enrich one another and empower a person to live by both stories: Native and Christian.

In our immediate future, such a catechetical approach will present challenges. In a number of cases, textbooks, audio-visual materials and other resources do not exist which express a Native Catholic reality. So, we need to develop such materials. The Tekakwitha Conference serves as a resource in co-ordinating and producing the development of Native materials. In the meantime, materials developed for the dominant Western culture may be used with some care and caution. With such a discerning use, the Western cultural expression of Christianity can be distinguished from the underlying realities of the Christian faith.

Native Traditions view time differently than the dominant Western Tradition. While American society tends to view history as marching along in a linear fashion from point A to point E, Native Traditions view time primarily as cyclic. The chief question for Native peoples is how to maintain the harmony and balance of creation as opposed to what am I supposed to accomplish. How we view Salvation History is greatly affected by our view of time. For Natives, the Second Coming is accessible at the present time and not only at the end of time. One does not simply look forward to heaven through the passage of time but one sees the beginnings of heaven here in a life lived harmoniously with all of creation.

The role of ritual is deeply shaped by such an understanding of time. Ritual does not set out to change reality but to maintain or re-establish the harmony of life. How do these rituals fit into Roman Catholic practice? I recall being present for a liturgy which utilized the blessing of water as its penitential rite. The blessing of water is seen as a purifying ritual putting us back into harmony with creation. As we greeted the six directions, a certain centeredness was felt. Then, as we renewed our baptismal vows, I knew I was centered in creation and purified in the waters of baptism. Our task is to have our rituals reflect both our Native and Catholic Traditions.

Harmony with creation is grounded deeply in one's relationship with the land. For most Native Americans, it is impossible to speak of a personal identity apart from the land. The earth grounds us not only geographically but also psychologically. As my grandmother told me, when I lost touch with Mother

Earth, I misbehaved. When I attended to the land, however, my behaviour improved. In other words, the land itself can heal.

While this phenomenon may be difficult for a nation comprised largely of immigrants, it cannot be minimized for Native people. One is buried in the earth from which one was born. I was born from land nourished by my ancestors and in my death and burial I will nourish the land for future generations. The land becomes the means for transcending time and reaching through to other generations. Such a sense of solidarity with former and future generations can only enhance our Christian faith in the Communion of Saints. Can we appreciate the land enough to be able to appreciate other Christian generations?

A caution must be issued here not to reduce this relationship with the land to mere romanticism. The land can be harsh and exacting as well as gentle and nourishing. Do we always see the land as our Mother? I recall being present at a meeting in Hoonah in the Juneau Diocese. This wonderful woman stood up and spoke of the land and the very rocks as living beings. How can we move to such an understanding?

Finally, we need to address ourselves to our relationship with all of God's creation. Popular Western belief views humanity as the pinnacle of creation. If we were to draw this understanding, we would see a pyramid which illustrated the hierarchy of creation. Humanity is not greater than or better than any other created being. Humanity shares the life of the Creator as do all creatures.

This past winter, I spent a week at the Kisemanito Centre in Grouard, Alberta. As I spoke of our Native relationships with creatures, I could see an excited agreement appearing on the faces of the Native participants. In Scripture, we find that Jesus utilizes such an approach: look at the clouds, see the mustard seed, observe the birds of the sky. Creation reveals God to us. For Native peoples, one lives as part of the created order and not as ruler of it.

Thus, we find that a sound catechetical approach needs to be aware of the Native relationship with story, ritual, land, and all created life. These relationships can affirm the Gospel values and be deepened and transformed by the Gospel.

Third, a Native Catechesis must challenge Native peoples to examine our own Traditions and Cultures. As Jesus did thousands of years ago, the Gospel will challenge Native peoples in the areas of justice, forgiveness, and healing. Any catechetical program must be willing to live out its prophetic role.

Fourth, the experience of Native peoples takes place within the context of a tribe, clan, family. Traditions are handed down from one generation to the next. As a result, an understanding of the Church as a community of believers handing on a faith in the Lord is greatly supported by Native peoples. Can catechetics take advantage of such Traditions[?]

Fifth, as I have argued that the dominant Western culture needs to become acquainted with Native Traditions, Native peoples need to appreciate the beauty and giftedness of Western Tradition. In dialogue with one another, each will grow and develop.

We can, thus, see that a Native catechetical method has various aspects. Catechesis needs to enflesh itself in the culture. A catechetical method must support communal life and the community's life of worship and prayer. Finally, a catechetical program must challenge Native peoples to be of service to one another and to other cultures. When catechesis performs these functions, as Native people, we will remember who and where we are and manifest the life of disciples of the Lord Jesus.

Reverend P. Michael Galvan, "Native Catechesis and the Ministry of the Word," *Tekakwitha Newsletter* 6, no. 5 (May 1987): 1–3. Printed by permission.

95. Resolution and Statement by the Tekakwitha Conference, March 13, 1987

In 1985 the Vatican's Sacred Congregation of Rites recommended that Father Junipero Serra be declared venerable, a possible step toward Catholic canonization. Many Indians protested the elevation of Serra, claiming that the system of missions he founded had led to the decimation and cultural genocide of California Natives. In reply Bishop Thaddeus Shubsda of Monterey released a report in 1986 that praised not only Serra but also the entire mission enterprise. The report characterized aboriginal Indian culture in California as "doomed," with "no sense of morality," "living on the bare edge of existence," in "constant warfare," with "abortion and incest" as "common practices." The National Tekakwitha Conference aired the issue at its board meetings. With Pope John Paul scheduled to meet the annual conference in Phoenix in 1987, members of the conference signed a rebuttal to Bishop Shubsda's report.

It has been brought to the attention of the Tekakwitha Conference by Indian supporters of the Conference, that the recent report released by the Bishop and Diocese of Monterey entitled, "To the Detractors of the Serra Cause," is grossly inaccurate and totally misrepresents the native understanding of its own history and culture.

In this report about Native Indians of California, some scholars have misrepresented Indian history and culture. Those who authored this report have misinterpreted the lives of Native Americans without the Native American perspective being revealed.

Thus, at the request of the tribes of California, the Southern California Tribal Chairmen's Association, and the All-Indian organization of scholars, the American Indian Historical Society, the Tekakwitha Conference supports them in their effort to oppose the dissemination of false and misleading statements. The Tekakwitha Conference Board of Directors presents the following resolution:

Whereas, the Native Americans of California have protested the interpretation of their aboriginal society and culture by the report of Bishop Shubsda, the Diocese of Monterey, and

Whereas: It is the sense of this Board of Directors of the Tekakwitha Conference that the Indians of Southern California, as well as all aboriginal peoples, have a right to defend their history and culture;

Therefore, be it resolved: that the Tekakwitha Conference, in support of our brothers and sisters, and of the tribes of California, goes on record as fully supporting the Indians of California and all other aboriginal peoples in their efforts to protect and defend their people.

In support of this resolution, the Board of Directors asserts that In Blessed Kateri Tekakwitha, we celebrate the native people of this land. We call attention to the natural decency and order of their lives. We recognize that there were and still are peoples with their own culture, their own governing systems and laws, and their own fidelity to the laws of indigenous people and Mother Earth.

Their civilization was one that served them well. The indigenous civilization in California knew and celebrated one God. Their loyalty to one another, to their government, and to God was celebrated at every stage of their lives from birth to death.

The Tekakwitha Conference notes that many Indians are devout Catholics. Most Native Americans of Southern California are Catholic. As Catholics, they practice their ancient ways of worshipping God in a unique unity of Catholic and traditional sacred ways. The right of these Native Americans to defend their own history must be respected.

Signatures:

Fr. Patrick J. Twohy, S.J.	Sister Eva Marie Solomon, C.S.J.
Leon F. Cook	Fr. Gilbert Hemauer, O.F.M. Cap.
Msgr. Paul A. Lenz	Anthony Pico
Fr. John S. Hascall, O.F.M. Cap.	Joseph P. Savilla
Bishop Donald E. Pelotte, S.S.S.	

Marquette University, Tekakwitha Conference Archives. Printed by permission.

96. Father John Hascall, O.F.M. Cap., "President's Letter," May 3, 1988

Father John Hascall, O.F.M. Cap., has celebrated his Ojibwa religious culture in combination with his Catholicism; indeed, he has referred to himself as a "Medicine Priest." As president of the National Tekakwitha Conference in the late 1980s, he tried to foster inculturation in experimental ways, conducting sweatlodge ceremonies, healing Masses, and retreats across North America, and preaching a message of Indian self-worth. In his 1988 letter to the conference membership, Hascall enthused over the elevation of his fellow-Indian Capuchin Father Charles Chaput, O.F.M. Cap., to the bishopric of Rapid City, and he encouraged the "Native Church" of Indian Catholics to educate the non-Indian "Euro-Church" about Native ways.

Dear Brother and Sister,

As I begin to write this President's Letter, I just called ahead to Sister Eva Solomon, Native Sister and on the Board of Directors, to reserve a room at her convent in Thunder Bay. She gave me the good news that Fr. Charles Chaput, OFM Cap., Prairie Band [Potawatomi], Native priest, had been chosen to be now Bishop-Elect of the Diocese of Rapid City. This would really make the late

Bishop Dimmerling very happy. It was his desire to have Native Bishops and priests. Now Fr. Charles will succeed in his diocese, which has been vacant for six months.

We are happy for Fr. Charles in his new appointment as Bishop and will support him in prayer. We are happy for the Local Church of Rapid City and for our Native peoples in Western South Dakota.

What does it mean to have a Native Bishop? First of all it is recognition of our Native peoples in the Church today. This is our second Bishop now. In the Diocese of Rapid City, which has so many Native peoples, we are seeing a Native Spiritual Leader of the Church. Secondly, as we, as Native peoples, see leadership come from our people, we can begin to own the Church more in our lives. We can begin to see the Church as ours.

There is still a long way to go, though. We have to begin to accept ourselves as "Church," as the people. I don't mean what has been given to us from the missionaries. Yet, I am not excluding this from our lives either. I mean accept ourselves as Native peoples who are Church. There is still a reluctance and terrible fear in our people of our "traditional" way of life. I'm experiencing so much of this as I travel from place to place.

We still have a difficult time to see how Jesus speaks through the "way of our people." We tend to see the dogmas and doctrines as Church. Yet, that is not what Christ intended. The Way that Jesus gave us is a way of life that is lived. We are the peoples, we are the Church. The doctrines and dogmas clarify this Way of life. The commandments give us guidelines to follow this Way of life. In the beginning, before Ephesus, the people that followed Christ were called people of The Way. It was in Ephesus that the people were first called "Christians" — those who in their lives did what Jesus said and did. Jesus reached, as a Hebrew, into the culture of His peoples and showed how to be children of God. The way of the people spoke the messages by what they said and did.

In the Council of Jerusalem, the Church faced this same problem. Are we to make the Gentiles Jews, that is, follow all the prescriptions of the Jewish Law and Teachings? This was the first [pressure] of other cultures in relationship to Jesus. The discussions were fierce. It says in Acts that Peter and Paul almost came to blows. It was decided, and the news was taken to all the churches at the time, that the message of Jesus be what is taught and not to be, so to speak, Gentiles becoming Jews. They did not have to become Hebrew peoples, but remain themselves and live as Jesus lived and taught. This was a message of relationships and harmony.

Each of the Apostles took this message, Good News, Gospel and went to different parts of the known world. The prayer of Jesus developed within each cultural area. Today we have the nine main Rites of the Church. A few of these Rites are: Byzantine (Greek) Rite which [spread] through Greece, Eastern Europe and Russia, spoken in the many languages of the countries it inhabits; the Malabarese and Molankares Rites of India...[;] in Israel the Coptic Rite of the Middle East; the Roman Rite based on Roman Culture, mixed as it spread through Europe with the French influence, German-Irish influences.

The Roman Rite came to the Americas with the missionaries of these countries. The culture was respected in all the other peoples. They did not expect a totally different mentality of the Western Hemisphere. We were a new people who were only discovered 500 years ago. They did not know how to handle us. For many of our peoples it is a little over 100 years that Christianity has been [experienced].

How much of Christianity has been accepted by our Native peoples? We have accepted the stories and the teachings of Christ. These were told by our elders before in different words and way of teaching. We are a people of prayer so we have prayed as best we could, although many of the symbols used and concepts spoken were and are foreign to us.

We have been led to believe that the ways of prayer we were accustomed to were evil in the past. Even today, there is that extreme fear of the Traditional Ways. We learned well! Our language is, in many places, all but lost because we were forbidden to speak the language. Many parents have not taught their children the language. They did not want us to have the problems they had. They thought it would be best to learn the English and do things the "White man" way. Medicine bags were burnt or buried because of fear or because of condemnation of our prayer ways.

The people were baptized and made Christians. Where has it gone since then? Since the early 1970's and the rise of our Native Indian identity and awareness, we have seen a grand exit of external Christianity among our peoples. Our Churches, in most places, are almost empty. Some of our people have left to follow the "Traditional Way" of prayer. Many have left to follow the Fundamental Way of Scripture. This backs their fears that [the] Indian Way is evil and of the devil. They also experience community life which these churches provide. Many more, thoroughly confused, have left and a lot of these have thrown off prayer altogether. Why throw off prayer? I hear from the people, "I am not forgiveable," "I am not worthy"! Sin and guilt, which was taught so stringently to our peoples, have gripped us to such an extent that when we drink and commit other major sins of lust and excess, we feel there is no hope for us. Our concept of God taught to us, or perceived by us, is that of a strict and merciless Judge rather than the all-surrounding Creator, Mystery, who takes care of the people and provides for all. Why should we stop drinking...at least when we are drunk we can feel good and not blame ourselves. We are not ourselves when we are drunk. The alcohol is making us do it.

I'm sitting here at a park table, here at Kakabeka Falls Provincial Park in Ontario, 18 miles west of Thunder Bay. The poplar (Aspen) trees are dropping their seeds to the ground to continue their species. Only one or two of the many thousands of seeds dropped by each tree will survive to mature into a tree. The others will feed the animals, some wither up because of lack of rain and moisture. I keep thinking of our peoples. Jesus is calling each of us to a deeper relationship to ourselves, each other and especially to Himself, God. We need the proper atmosphere and love.

We are not getting that when we have missionaries who just pop in and out, like a Mass and Sacrament machine. There is never time to stop and talk. The

Church becomes a sacrament machine, doling out graces here and there, and if we are not ready, we "miss the boat," so to speak.

In many of our areas there is a language problem. We are all presumed to know English. We may speak some English but not the language of the concepts said at the altar. Those who think in their Native language and ideas, feelings and respects, have to translate what is said into concepts that are contained in our languages. Most of the ideas expressed are not translateable. There is nothing near the ideas preached. Even in using translators in different languages when I speak, the one translating tells me that some of the concepts, e.g. sweat lodge, fast, etc., can't be translated. They have to be broken down to — in our language — action words. Most of my language is verbs.

There has to be on both sides: Euro-Church and our Native People, a coming together in dialogue of how Jesus Christ speaks through the way of our people. Concepts have to be worked out together and in the language of our people.

This dialogue is where we, as Native peoples, have to sit down with the Church and tell about ourselves and the way we see things. We also have to sit down with our elders and learn. The dialogue also includes those "traditionalists" who reject the Church outright as "White Man Religion," and those who are confused.

I was talking to someone the other day and saying that we have to sit down and write a dictionary for the Church and peoples about the relationship of concepts to the Western mind, and experience in relationship **our** Native concepts and relationships.

When we do this dialogue and the Church allows us to celebrate in the way we understand God, Life, relationships and life here-after, then we will be able to own the Church more in ourselves. We must be Native Church and teach the Euro-Church who we are.

Reverend John Hascall, O.F.M. Cap., "President's Letter," *Tekakwitha Newsletter* 8, no. 1 (1988): 15–16. Printed by permission.

97. Vision Statement of the National Tekakwitha Conference, 1988

The members of the National Tekakwitha Conference produced a "Vision Statement" in 1988, addressing the needs of American Indian Catholics and the goals of the Conference.

As members of the Tekakwitha Conference, we reaffirm our faith in Christ Jesus and our appreciation for the Native communities in which the Creator has placed us. We make the following statement to call all of God's people to a life of holiness and service sustained by the Holy Spirit and inspired by Blessed Kateri Tekakwitha.

As Native Catholics, we are encouraged by the recognition of our Native cultures, traditions, and languages in the Roman Catholic Church. The beginnings of liturgical inculturation are nourishing our spiritual lives. We are supportive of the work of the Tekakwitha Conference and all ministers who help to develop and support Native ministries. The dedication of our ministers, Native and non-native, bishops, priests, deacons, women and men religious, and lay ministers strengthens our prayer, our involvement of programs for all of our people, especially our youth, that they might be able to appreciate both their Native and Catholic Traditions.

At the same time, we recognize that there are certain challenges we face. Addiction to alcohol and drugs is destroying many of our Native people. We need to develop awareness and recovery programs adapted to our Native communities. We need to address the lack of interest in, awareness of, and understanding of our Native cultures by the clergy and by the Church in certain regions of the country. This lack of understanding contributes to a lessening of efforts in inculturation and Native leadership. Our appreciation of the gifts of the women of our Native communities and their participation on all levels needs to be increased. We need to reach out to those who have fallen away from their Native and Catholic traditions. The youth among us need to feel more welcome and nourished by our Traditions. Well-developed family life and youth ministry programs will begin to address the challenge of moral and values education. A stronger Christian community will concern itself with the small numbers of Native vocations to the priesthood, diaconate, and religious life. Inadequate and insufficient adult education hinders our understanding and acceptance of the changes begun by the Second Vatican Council. Moreover, we do not always have a voice in the decision making processes in our parishes, dioceses, and the Universal Church. Finally, for many of these programs, we lack the necessary financial support.

As a result, we would perceive the following needs in our Native Communities: We need to have greater sense of pride in ourselves, in our clans, and in our tribes. A greater sense of hospitality will help in healing past wounds, in inviting our youth into the church, and in reaching out to the alienated and inactive. Our concern is for both Native people who live on our Native homelands and in our rural and urban areas of our country. Through increased inculturation and education, we will be able to participate more actively in our faith communities in roles of leadership and service. Our respect for life, the unborn, the handicapped, and our elders needs to be reinforced and supported. Finally, we need to develop our own Native ministries and leadership programs.

To address our needs we must undertake the following changes. We need more Native bishops and leaders. Our youth must be invited to a greater level of participation on all levels of community and church life. Through an increased appreciation of our Native American cultures and gifts, we will be able to help the process of inculturation as Native People become more involved in the life of the Church. With such active participation, there will...hopefully be an increase in training programs for lay and ordained ministers and an increase in Native vocations. Since many of our Native communities are experiencing a great shortage of priests, we would like dialogue within the church to develop creative solutions for ordained ministry. We appreciate the ministry of our native deacons and call for continued support and encouragement for the permanent diaconate. We need to continue and strengthen our commitment to further the work of social and economic justice, not only for our own communities, but for all people who live on Mother Earth.

We must be strengthened for this task by the many good gifts which we are experiencing in the Church: the active role of the laity, the ongoing dialogue between Native American and Catholic ways, the Tekakwitha Conference, the strong faith life which we share, and the involvement of our young people.

During the next five years, as members of the Tekakwitha Conference, we pledge to address the following problems:

1. Insufficient religious education programs, Catholic schools, and inadequate numbers of teachers

2. Alcoholism and substance abuse

3. Insufficient Youth Involvement

4. Lack of unity

5. Low Self-Esteem

During the next five years, as members of [the] Tekakwitha Conference, we pledge to develop the following five strengths:

1. Our Native Spirituality

2. Our Unity

3. Our strong family centeredness

4. Our Youth Involvement

5. Lay, Religious and Ordained Ministries in our communities

98. National Conference of Catholic Bishops, "1992: A Time for Remembering, Reconciling, and Recommitting Ourselves as a People: Pastoral Reflections on the V Centenary and Native American People," 1992

In 1992 the Tekakwitha Newsletter *printed the full text of the pastoral statement made by the National Conference of Catholic Bishops reflecting upon five centuries of contact between Europeans and American Indians. Entitled* 1992: A Time for Remembering, Reconciling, and Recommitting Ourselves as a People, *the essay built upon an earlier (1977) statement of the United States Catholic bishops on American Indians. The bishops acknowledged grievances of American Indians, called for reconciliation between Indians and non-Indians, mediated through grace and faith, and called for committed Catholic action on behalf of Indian tribes across the United States and beyond. Within the Church, the pastoral statement encouraged greater Native American inculturation, participation, and leadership.*

At their November meeting, the U.S. bishops approved a statement titled *1992: A Time for Remembering, Reconciling, and Recommitting Ourselves as a People: Pastoral Reflections on the V Centenary and Native American People.*

Bishop Elden F. Curtiss served as chairman of the ad-hoc committee that developed this statement. Committee members included Bishop Charles J. [Chaput], OFM Cap., of Rapid City, S.D.; Bishop Michael Kaniecki, SJ, of Fairbanks, Alaska; Bishop John Kinney of Bismarck, N.D.; and Bishop Donald Pelotte, SSS, of Gallup, N.M.

Consultants were Msgr. Paul Lenz, executive director of the Bureau of Catholic Indian Missions in Washington, D.C., Father Ted Zuern, SJ, Bureau of Catholic Indian Missions assistant director; and Father P. Michael Galvan of Moraga, Calif., chairman of the Tekakwitha National Conference. Also assisting was John Carr of the United States Catholic Conference's Department of Social Development and World Peace.

INTRODUCTION

The Fifth Centenary of the coming of Europeans to this land is both a challenge and an opportunity, a time for looking back at where we have been and looking ahead to where we should be as a people and a nation. No specific aspect of this observance challenges us more than the situation of Native Americans in our midst — their past treatment, their current condition and their future aspirations.

As we prepare for the historic year of 1992, with both its opportunity for dialogue and its significant controversy, the Catholic community is blessed, enriched and profoundly challenged by the faith of Native Americans in our midst. We ask the Catholic community to join us in seeking new understanding and awareness of their situation and in committing our church to new advocacy and action with our Native American brothers and sisters on issues of social justice and pastoral life which touch their lives.

In this effort, we build on our reflections of a year ago regarding the Fifth Centenary, *Heritage and Hope.*[1] In these additional comments, we do not offer a comprehensive historical perspective but rather our reflections as pastors and teachers on the successes, failures and hopes that shape the relationship between our Church and Native Americans.

We seek to speak not only to Native Americans, but to the whole Church in this land. We speak as pastors, not only about important issues but first and foremost about a people — about our brothers and sisters whose dignity, culture and faith have too often been diminished and not adequately respected and protected by our civil society or our religious institutions. We seek to recognize and respond to the strengths of traditional Native American culture and spirituality, the pastoral and human needs of Native peoples, the many pastoral efforts underway and the continuing moral challenge of pursuing justice in the face of continuing discrimination.

In our letter on the V Centenary, *Heritage and Hope,* we sought to emphasize the ongoing challenge of evangelization, calling for continuing conversion to

Jesus Christ and His values rather than emphasize a celebration of past events. We consider this historic year a time for sharing the Gospel with new energy and exploring its continuing demands. This Fifth Centenary should be a time for remembering, reconciling and recommitting ourselves as a Church to the development of the people whose ancestors were here long before the first Europeans came to these shores 500 years ago.

I. A TIME FOR REMEMBERING

In this centennial year we recall the suffering of Native peoples that followed the arrival of explorers and wave after wave of immigrants. We have spoken clearly about some of these failures in our letter on the Fifth Centenary. We repeat these strong words to remind ourselves of lessons which must be learned and commitments which must be kept as a part of this observance:

As Church, we often have been unconscious and insensitive to the mistreatment of our Native American brothers and sisters and have at times reflected the racism of the dominant culture of which we have been a part. In this quincentennial year, we extend our apology to our Native peoples and pledge ourselves to work with them to ensure their rights, their religious freedom, and the preservation of their cultural heritage.

In this letter, we point out that the coming of religious faith in this land began not 500 years ago, but centuries before in the prayers, chants, dance and other sacred celebrations of Native people.

We also acknowledge that the encounter with the Europeans was often a "harsh and painful one" for Native peoples, and we lament the diseases, death, destruction, injustices and disrespect for Native ways and traditions which came with it. We recognize that:

Often they (European Christians) failed to distinguish between what was crucial to the Gospel and what were matters of cultural preference. That failure brought with it catastrophic consequences for the Native peoples who were at times forced to become European at the same time they became Christians.

Yet that is not the whole picture. The effort to portray the history of the encounter as a totally negative experience in which only violence and exploitation of the Native peoples was present is not an accurate interpretation of the past.

Convinced of the saving truth of the Gospel and grateful for the sacrifices, care and concern of many missionaries for Native people, we point out that "the expansion of Christianity into our hemisphere brought to the peoples of this land the gift of the Christian faith with its power of humanization and salvation, dignity and fraternity, justice and love."

We bishops urge that in 1992 our nation should give renewed attention to the condition of Native Americans:

We encourage all Americans to better understand the role of Native peoples in our history and to respond to the just grievances of our Native American brothers and sisters. We hope that this will be graced time for rejecting all forms of racism.

Now in these pastoral reflections, we seek to offer some direction in realizing this hope. It is not enough for us simply to repeat strong words. The challenge of this historic year is not simply to look back, but also to look around at the current situation of Native peoples and to look ahead to future challenges for our Church and society in responding to the aspirations and needs of Native Americans.

II. A TIME FOR RECONCILIATION

We have also called for "new reconciliation in the spirit of the Gospel among all Americans and to recognize more fully our solidarity." The challenge of reconciliation in Jesus Christ requires greater awareness and understanding, increased dialogue and interaction and a commitment to mutual respect and justice among diverse peoples. Most Americans know almost nothing about the lives and history of the first Americans. Our religious organizations, schools and other educational efforts must tell the truth about how Native Americans have been treated and how they have endured in this land. History can be healing if we will face up to its lessons.

All of us need to examine our own perceptions of Native Americans — how much they are shaped by stereotypes, distorted media portrayals or ignorance. We fear that prejudice and insensitivity toward Native peoples is deeply rooted in our culture and in our local churches. Our conference has consistently condemned racism of every kind and we renew our call for increased efforts to overcome prejudice and discrimination as they touch our Native American brothers and sisters.

This reconciliation should also reflect the realities of Native American life today, in our nation and our Church. The Native American community now includes almost two million Indians, Eskimos and Aleuts, including a number of Hispanic people who also identify themselves [as] Indians. Native Americans are both citizens of the United States and members of their tribes, pueblos or nations. Native Americans are among the fastest growing populations in our country. They constitute a vital, diverse and growing community.

Native Americans are present in every state. The largest number are found in Oklahoma where many tribes were relocated. While a majority of Native Americans live in the western part of the United States, North Carolina has the fifth largest Indian population in the country. Only Oklahoma, California, Arizona and New Mexico have larger populations. Moreover, well over a third of all Native Americans now reside in large cities. Native American people are an integral part of many of our metropolitan areas, especially in the Midwest and West.

One in four Native Americans is poor. Many struggle with the realities of inadequate housing, joblessness, health problems including the disease of alcoholism. While significant numbers of Native Americans have become lawyers, doctors, artists and other professionals, many others live with dashed hopes and bleak futures as a result of discrimination, lack of opportunity and economic powerlessness.

Within our family of faith we are very blessed to have significant numbers of Native American Catholics, now numbering more than a quarter of a million. Our Church is blessed with two Native American bishops, more than two dozen priests, many deacons, 90 sisters and brothers and many lay leaders.

There are a variety of significant initiatives focused on the pastoral life and needs of Native American Catholics:

- For more than a century, the Bureau of Catholic Indian Missions has through the generosity of U.S. Catholics served the pastoral and spiritual needs of Native American Catholics providing for Native American ministries providing more than three million dollars annually;

- The Tekakwitha Conference provides an important voice and gathering place for those who serve the Native American Catholic community;

- Many dioceses have undertaken creative efforts and religious communities have established ministries to serve the needs of Native American Catholics;

- Our own National Conference of Bishops has previously developed and adopted a major statement on the Church and American Indians outlining pastoral priorities and a social justice agenda that still are valid today;[2]

- Several dioceses and state Catholic Conferences have also made justice for Native Americans a major ecclesial priority.

In this task of reconciliation, the persistence and vitality of Catholic faith in the Native American community is an irreplaceable asset. We are one family united in faith, citizenship and humanity. However, the Native American Catholic community faces three special and related challenges:

A. Inculturation

The church is called to bring the saving word of the Gospel to every people and culture. Our goal must be an authentic inculturation of Catholic faith within the Native American community through a vital liturgical life, continuing educational efforts, and creative pastoral ministry which demonstrate deep respect for Native culture and spiritualities and which enhance fidelity to the Catholic faith.

This is not an easy or simple task. Authentic inculturation moves in three integral steps: 1) the culture which the Word of God encounters is challenged and purified by that Word; 2) the best of the culture is enhanced by the truth of the Gospel; 3) the Church is enriched by respecting the culture which the Gospel embraces and which in turn embraces the Gospel.

This task of inculturation is not an unprecedented or new challenge, but it remains an essential step towards an authentic Catholic Native American Community within the structure and bonds of the Universal Church. As Pope John Paul II has said:

When the Church enters into contact with cultures, the Church must welcome all that is compatible with the Gospel in these traditions of the peoples, in order to bring the richness of Christ to them and to be enriched herself by the manifold wisdom of the nations of the earth. (Pope John Paul II, Discourse to the Pontifical Council for Cultures on January 17, 1987.)

In liturgical, pastoral, and spiritual life, we seek a genuine reconciliation between the essential traditions of Catholic faith and the best of the traditions of Native American life, each respecting, shaping, and enriching the other. Native American Catholics are called to be both true Catholic believers and authentic Native Americans. Far from being incompatible, these two traditions — the Catholic way and the Native way — enrich each other and the whole Church.

Our challenge is to make sure that a truly Catholic religious culture interfaces with truly Native American cultures. A highly secularized society can overshadow a Catholic and Native American sense of mystery when encountering God, the created world and human life.

We call on liturgists, theologians and pastoral leaders to help us address these real issues as we shape a Native American expression of faith that is authentically Catholic and deeply Native American. It is our responsibility as bishops to encourage and supervise the presentation of the faith in liturgy and catechetics which safeguard Catholic tradition and Native ways.

B. Participation

This challenge will require an ongoing effort to increase the participation of Native Americans in the life of the church. We need to hear clearly the voice of Catholic Native Americans. We need their leadership in the dialogue that can [take] place between Native American traditionalists and the Church. We welcome their gifts and contributions. We need their active participation in the ministries and life of the Church. We ask their advice about the ways the whole Catholic community can best respond to the realities of injustice and ignorance and their impact on Native peoples. We advocate full opportunities for Native people and we seek new partnerships with them in building the Body of Christ within the Native American community.

C. Pastoral Leadership

We especially need to call forth and support the leadership of Native Americans — as priests, religious and lay leaders. We are already blessed with many faithful and creative leaders, but more are needed to preach the Gospel and serve the needs of the Native American communities. We continue to welcome the generosity and commitment of many non-Native Americans who serve this community, but we look forward to the time when Native American bishops, priests, deacons, sisters, brothers and lay leaders will increasingly shape and carry out the work of the Church in the Native American community and in the larger Catholic community. All those who serve within the Native American Catholic community should be well trained in Catholic theology and Native American culture and ways.

We pray that the blessings of the past and the hard work of the present will yield an even more vibrant and faithful Catholic Native American community. We strongly support the impressive efforts underway to train and prepare Native Americans for leadership in the priesthood, diaconate, religious life and lay ministries.

In all these efforts we will build on our past and current pastoral ministries, educational commitments and spiritual care within the Native American community. We acknowledge the failure and misguided direction of some past efforts, but we also recognize the enormous contributions of Indian schools, parishes and ministries in meeting the needs of the Native American community and developing leaders from among their number. More authentic inculturation, increased participation and stronger pastoral leadership will strengthen the faith of not only our Native American sisters and brothers, but our entire family of faith in the United States.

III. A TIME FOR RECOMMITMENT

A. Public Advocacy

As we seek to respond to these ecclesial challenges, we also recommit ourselves to stand with Native peoples in their search for greater justice in our society. We seek to be advocates with Native leaders in this effort..., not simply advocates for their needs. Together, we must call our nation to greater responsiveness to the needs and rights of Native people. We recognize that there are groups working for justice and cultural recognition for Native peoples at regional and global levels. We encourage these efforts to build bridges among the indigenous people in the Americas and throughout the world.

We once again commit ourselves as the National Conference of Catholic Bishops to recognize and act upon the Native American dimensions of our ongoing advocacy regarding health, housing, employment, education, poverty and other national issues. No group is touched more directly by federal policy than Native Americans. We must be alert and active regarding federal policies which support or undermine Native American lives, dignity and rights. As a Church committed to a "preferential option for the poor and vulnerable," we recognize that Native Americans are often the most poor and vulnerable in our midst. We shall actively support initiatives to meet housing, health and employment needs of Native people, with a priority for measures that increase self-sufficiency and economic empowerment.

B. Respecting Treaty Rights

We also renew our commitment to press for justice in the prompt and fair adjudication of treaty rights. These treaties for which Native American tribes gave up their homelands, keeping only a fraction of what they originally inhabited, are of prime concern to their descendants. In some important ways they are now receiving some greater recognition of their rights, but agencies of government and courts do not always recognize the complexities of tribal autonomy within the territories of sovereign states. Native Americans have the right to be self-determining, to decide the ways their land and natural resources on those lands are used for the benefit of their people and for the broader common good.

C. Ongoing Support for Native American Communities

Our Campaign for Human Development has supported the quest for justice and self-help among Native peoples. In its brief history, CHD has provided almost $3.5 million to support more than 100 projects focused on stewardship of Indian land and resources, restoration of tribal recognition and rights, cultural preservation, and increased accountability for tribal education, welfare and legal systems. We support continued efforts to empower and assist Native Americans in their search for justice. We also renew our support for the Bureau of Catholic Indian Missions and its essential work of evangelization and pastoral care within the Native American community. The American Board of Catholic Missions and the Catholic Church Extension Society also supply valuable assistance and help to the Native American Catholic community. Their support for the Church's work is a crucial resource building a vibrant Catholic faith within our dioceses and parishes which serve Native people.

IV. A CALL TO ACTION

The Catholic community and our bishops' conference are called in this historic year to join together in renewed efforts to address several important areas which affect our Native American brothers and sisters. We call on the relevant committees of our Conference of Catholic Bishops to integrate the needs and contributions of Native Catholics into their ongoing agenda. Significant work has been done in approving translations of Eucharistic prayers, in public policy, in pastoral and social justice efforts; but more is required. Questions of Native American inculturation need to be further addressed by our Liturgy and Pastoral Practices Committees; advocacy and empowerment by our Domestic Policy and the Campaign for Human Development Committees; pastoral leadership by our Committees on Vocations, Priestly Life and Ministry, Priestly Formation and Permanent Diaconate; Indian education by our Education Committee. We also propose for consideration the establishment of an ad hoc NCCB Committee on Native American Catholics to help oversee this effort and to coordinate our Conference's response to this statement.

Finally, we ask all believers to join with us in making this centennial year a time of continuing conversion and reflection on the demands of the Gospel now as we seek to bring greater respect and justice to our ministry among Native Americans. As we said a year ago: "Evangelization is unfinished if exploitation of the weak, of minorities still exists. The Quincentenary calls us to a new commitment as Christians to right the evils of the past and the present and to be forceful advocates of the peace and justice proclaimed [by] the Gospel.... Our observances should include times of mourning over the injustices of the past and vital efforts at reconciliation with our Native American brothers and sisters through prayer and social action." This historic year calls us to both reflection and action concerning the most effective ways we

Burton Pretty on Top (Crow) from the Crow Reservation, Montana, with a sacred pipe at a Mass concelebrated by bishops, 52nd Annual Tekakwitha Conference, Norman, Oklahoma, 1991. Credit: Anne M. Scheurmann. Marquette University, Tekakwitha Conference Archives. Reproduced by permission.

can seek justice and build up the Body of Christ within the Native American community.

We recognize that Hispanic and African Americans share with Native peoples the reality of discrimination and the challenge of achieving full acceptance in our society and Church. A significant number of Hispanic people share roots and cultural ties with Native peoples, as do some African Americans. These ties of solidarity and common struggle can help these communities work together to assist the Church in recognizing diversity as a strength and gift. Native, Hispanic and African American members of our communities are called to be leaders and allies in the task of shaping a truly "Catholic" community open to all God's children.

CONCLUSION

When he came to our land four years ago, Pope John Paul II affirmed and challenged Native American Catholics as he still challenges all of us in this V Centenary year:

> I encourage you, as Native people to preserve and keep alive your cultures, your languages, the values and customs which have served you well in the past and which provide a solid foundation for the future. Your encounter with the Gospel has not only enriched you; it has enriched the

Church. We are well aware that this has not taken place without its difficulties and occasionally, its blunders. However...the Gospel does not destroy what is best in you. On the contrary, it enriches the spiritual qualities and gifts that are distinctive of your cultures.

...Here I wish to urge the local churches to be truly "catholic" in their outreaches to Native peoples and to show respect and honor for their culture and all their worthy traditions.... All consciences must be challenged. There are real injustices to be addressed and biased attitudes to be challenged.

Solidarity with the Native American community is a special challenge for our Church in this Fifth Centenary year. We ask the intercession of Blessed Kateri Tekakwitha and Blessed Juan Diego as we seek to recognize the burdens of history and meet the challenges of today. We hope and pray that 1992 will be a time for remembering, for genuine reconciliation and recommitment to work for greater justice for the descendants of the first Americans.

NOTES

1. *Heritage and Hope: Evangelization in the United States,* Pastoral Letter on the Fifth Centenary of Evangelization in the Americas, National Conference of Catholic Bishops, 1990.

2. Statement of the United States Catholic Bishops on American Indians, 1977, *Tekakwitha Newsletter* 11, no. 1 (March/April 1992): 26–28. Printed by permission.

99. Statement of the Association of Native Religious and Clergy, Distributed at the Tekakwitha Conference, Orono, Maine, August 4, 1992

Since 1971 the Association of Native Religious and Clergy (ANRC) has served as a gathering place for Catholic American Indian leadership. Often its members met in conjunction with the annual National Tekakwitha Conference meetings. In 1992 the Tekakwitha meeting was marked by dissension concerning Native leadership in the Conference and the future of inculturative programs. The ANRC issued a statement in which its members threatened to break with the National Tekakwitha Conference.

The Association of Native Religious and Clergy met this week. Saint Kateri has given us a new vision. We want to share it and our future direction with you.

Since 1971, our Association has met annually with a twofold purpose: to discern the spiritual direction of our lives and to follow God's Spirit moving among our peoples. We have had the privilege of visiting many Reservations. We have seen the spiritual power of our people and have experienced their hospitality.

In 1976, we were the only national Native organization that the Catholic hierarchy could turn to for help during the Eucharistic Congress. Our contribution: Native prayers, liturgy, and spiritual leadership was a blessing for us and all who participated. Papal Legate Cardinal Knox, serving the Congregation of Rites, was Rome's representative to that Congress. It was at this time that he and the Universal Catholic Church were introduced to the power of native spirituality.

In 1978, we became involved with the Tekakwitha Conference in Yankton, SD. There we were able to sense the Spirit at work. We could see native leadership developing. We watched the people participating. We could feel our people being healed through the ministry of our Church. Two years later in Denver, the ANRC decided to become more centrally involved in our support of the Tekakwitha Conference. Over the past 10 years, we have shared many individual and collective gifts with this Conference. Our Association has lived this Conference's low and high points, moments of frustration and faith, of struggle and success.

This past week we met at nearby Indian Island. This time our twofold purpose was to discern the direction of our Association and to clarify our relationship with this Conference.

As members of our Church, we feel the present realities in this Conference make it difficult for our membership to share the truth of our traditions. In some areas the hierarchical, ecclesiastical structures no longer hear the people's concerns nor meet their needs. Our people find this a hardship. Our Elders are not being respected or listened to as they speak. Our younger people want to hope again. We need to move in a new direction — a direction that will allow for our own spiritual growth and that of our people. We have fasted and prayed. Saint Kateri has given us a new vision. In this vision, we give our support to existing and developing Regional Conferences. We encourage more areas to create their own Regional Conferences. And, as God leads us, we will help create a new National Native Catholic Conference.

The ANRC members will no longer be reactors to the Tekakwitha Conference and its Board. Rather, we will be creative initiators and [implementers] of the Vatican II documents, developing inculturation of the Gospel of Jesus Christ in our many local Native traditions and tribal spiritualities. This is how we will serve you at the regional level. Thus, the Spirit of Jesus will become ever more fully enfleshed among our peoples.

As the Association of Native Religious and Clergy, we will continue to be available to the Tekakwitha Conference whenever such is requested of us.

Finally, we are saying, "Saint Kateri." Historically, our Church has officially canonized those whom the people have proclaimed Saints. Kateri is a Saint. Our people believe this. We believe this. We will begin calling her Saint in our prayers, in our letters, our publications and our personal conversation. We invite you to join us as we move forward, strengthening our spiritual relationship with Jesus through the intercession of Saint Kateri Tekakwitha.

Marquette University, Tekakwitha Conference Archives. Printed by permission.

100. Marvin Clifford's Recollections of Kateri Tekakwitha at a South Dakota Mission School, June 1994

Marvin Clifford retells his encounters with Kateri Tekakwitha while a student between the ages of nine and seventeen at St. Francis Mission School, Rosebud Reservation, St. Francis, South Dakota, ca. 1966–74.

Interviewed and edited by Mark G. Thiel.

One day in catechism class they handed out these little booklets and here was a story about an Indian girl from the East coast somewhere — the story of Kateri Tekakwitha. This is the first time I ever saw that they actually gave me something on paper that said, "Jesus — God loves you!" I mean this woman, Kateri Tekakwitha, got touched. She was touched. There was a miracle performed on her because I believe she was sick and she got well and then she passed away, but she was touched by God. She prayed and was religious. She got to see God's work and I thought that was something that only happened to these people, not us.

I often sat and wondered, "How does God work?" "How do these miracles come?" And the Bible — I used to always see this light and the Virgin Mary would appear or all these glorious things. Yet they never happened to me or around me. To actually read about this Indian woman made such an impact on me that for the first time I seriously believed that God could touch my life.

They built a statue of Kateri Tekakwitha in St. Francis. We had a big commemorative ceremony and for the first time there was an Indian amongst those statues in church. Those other saints always seemed to be far-off people from a far-off land but I could identify with Kateri Tekakwitha. She was an Indian. I didn't know about the Iroquois or the Mohawk because I never met an Indian from another tribe and we weren't taught about other cultures and stuff about other tribes.

So all I knew was that she was Indian and it was good enough for me because I was assured there was a place in God's heart for Native people.

Marquette University, Kateri Tekakwitha Oral History Collection. Printed by permission.

101. Jemez Pueblo Elders Joe and Juana Pecos on Saints, Prayers, and Enshrining Tekakwitha in the Southwest, July 11, 1995

Mr. and Mrs. Joe and Juana Marie Pecos of Jemez Pueblo (one of the Pueblo tribes of the upper Rio Grande region) discussed their Keresan Pueblo and Catholic prayer traditions and the events pertaining to the 1989 enshrinement of Blessed Kateri Tekakwitha at San Diego Mission, Jemez, New Mexico. Also included are references to notable events. In 1840 the survivors of Pecos Pueblo joined Jemez after suffering devastating population losses caused by Comanches, and during August 7–11, 1985, Mr. and Mrs. Pecos participated in the 45th Annual Tekakwitha Conference: "Walking in the Footsteps of Blessed Kateri," LeMoyne College, Syracuse, New York, with tours of the birthplace of

Blessed Kateri Tekakwitha (National Tekakwitha Shrine, Fonda, New York) and her tomb (St. Regis Mohawk Reserve, Kahnawake, Quebec, Canada). Interviewed and edited by Mark G. Thiel.

THIEL: What...[were] your first religious memories...as a child?

JUANA PECOS: The first one I remember was [when] I was standing next to my grandmother. She would be there...saying a prayer,...holding [up] her corn meal and...prayer feather...and...sometimes pollen from the corn...talking to the Father Spirit....I would be standing by her and...just repeat what she's saying...and...this very nice sister came to see me when I was in the Indian sanitarium. She said, "Juana, I'm going to teach you the Hail Mary" and she taught me. I was about eight years old then....[W]hen you're small, it goes up in your head and it stays there....So, that's how I got my...religion...both — Indian and Catholic....I can't live without either one of them. I'm strong with ...both....I feel very grateful....This is the only way to live. It's a good way to live, too.

[There]...are the three different things we have in our own Indian traditional way of praying....We have...retreats [for] group[s] of people [to] go... [on with]...fasting...[for] four days and four nights....[W]e're [praying] in ...thanksgiving,...and the different people...need not go into the kiva for ...their own petitions. And we go...fasting...for prayer for rain...for our crops...[so] the corn and the chili...we['ve] planted will grow....[T]hen [we pray] on the...feast days like...Our Lady of Guadalupe..., December 12th. We usually have...the matachine dance [of Spanish origin] to honor her. And ...the Lady of Presumed Loss...was brought by the Pecos Indians...[when they merged their community with Jemez in ca. 1838]. We celebrate her day on August 2nd...[with] a corn dance...in thanksgiving of our Christianity and our well-being....And...on November 12th...we honor Juan Diego. It's the feast of...Juan Diego and that's...[who] our mission church is named for, San Diego Mission.

THIEL: You mentioned...earlier that Our Lady of Guadalupe is very important to the traditions of Jemez....

JUANA PECOS: ...[S]he's honored very much in Jemez because the old folks always say, "We fell into the hand of the Lady of Guadalupe." And the two — you can see the two signs today,...in the Guadalupe Mountain and the Juan Diego Mountain...when the first Christians...and...Spaniards came, they were confused. It was the Christians — the priests [who]...thought it was the Spanish soldiers who...mistreated them [the people] before. And so, they [the people] were so frightened....[W]e used to live up there in the cliff[s], way up high and the people start[ed] jumping on the fights. Then...Juan Diego and Guadalupe made their appearance [and]...we were saved and that's how we became Christians. That's...why we honor the Lady of Guadalupe....[W]e recite our rosary, everyday — the Lady of Guadalupe rosary for the well-being of our family, our pueblo and especially all those named after her — our "Guadalupes." And... on December 12th [when] we celebrate the feast day, all the "Guadalupes" and

Joe and Juana Pecos leading the procession to enshrine Kateri Tekakwitha at San Diego Mission, Jemez, New Mexico, 1986. This was the first enshrinement of Kateri Tekakwitha among the Pueblo tribes of the Southwest. Credit: Courtesy Juana Pecos. Marquette University, Bureau of Catholic Indian Missions Records. Reproduced by permission.

... "Lupitas" and everybody have [an] open house....[W]e can go into their house[s] and have a good feast — they feed us and it's a big celebration. Then [we have]...the matachine dance...[by] two groups, the Turquoise [Clan], who do it with the violin and...the Pumpkins [Clan],...[who] do [it] with the drum. The matachine dance — It[']s beautiful, [a] beautiful dance.

THIEL: When you close your eyes when you pray, what sort of religious images do you see?

JUANA PECOS: ...I see this beautiful Indian girl, and you know who that is — that's Kateri! And way back there, it's a light....[T]he light is the Father Spirit ...a bright light. That's what I see when I...close my eyes and pray.

And Kateri is the one that's praying for me. She's the one that's laying her hands on me. And I am praying for the well-being of my family, my children, my grand-children, my people in the pueblo, all my friends and everybody... [who] asked me to pray for them, especially the National Kateri Tekakwitha group...[and] our new chief, King. Sometimes I mention all [of] their names ...so...this Kateri Tekakwitha Conference will continue on because it's doing a great job for everyone.

I'm very grateful that we have...Kateri Tekakwitha. And in the pueblos, we have...formed our own "Kateri Circles." Our...Circle here is...named...

"Awaladuwa Kateri Tekakwitha Circle" [and] what I am trying to do now is form a new group because those of us that have been members...are kind of getting old and we can't keep up with...our meetings and everything anymore. So, I'm trying to form a new group — [a] younger group...of boys and girls, ...so that this Kateri Circle in Jemez will keep going. That's what...Joe and I are doing right now...[organizing the] new group,...[with] young people as officers....

Everybody...even the non-members are very dedicated to Kateri now that we have her enshrined in the church....[There]...are...a lot of times I just sit there after mass and...watch the ladies and the different people come up to her statue and just embrace her and they'd be praying....I love that and I know Kateri loves that, too. And I would just sit back there and I would say,..."Lay your hands on her," or "Lay your hands on him," or "Pray for their patients, take them to the Lord, your holy spouse." I always tell her, "Take them to your holy spouse, please send them to Him." Because I believe that's what she told us to do.

THIEL: ...[H]ow...[was]...her statue...enshrined here in Jemez?

JUANA PECOS: ...[W]hen Joe and I went to the sacred walk...at the [Tekak-witha] Conference...in Syracuse, New York, [1985]...[w]e saw all the place[s] where she lived and...the Mohawk Indian people put on a beautiful program to show...and tell us about her....[W]e were all taken to her birthplace [Fonda, New York]...[and] then we...[went] to her tomb [Kahnawake, Quebec, Canada]. We prayed there,...and...it seems to me like I was really touched and Joe was, too....[As] we stood there in front of her tomb...it seemed like you could feel her....She was there for us, she met us, and I asked her..."Please Kateri Tekakwitha, show me how to take you back...[to] Jemez." That's when Joe and I felt the idea to bring the statue....[W]e got the idea to bring her to our Indian people, and we did. We ordered it, and it was sent to us, and then we set up a day.

The group that went with...[Joe and me],...Bernice Kachupi,...Francis Toledo,...Leonard Toledo,...[and] Mary Dodge and her son,...we [all] wanted to do...[this]...so,...[at] our next meeting...we [planned on how] to enshrine ...it here. We...talked to Father Bob [Robert Mathieu, O.F.M., our pastor], and he arranged a beautiful...[time] when to do...[this,] and in the meantime, Joe and I went and told our caciques, our governors....

JOE PECOS: Candido Armijo.

JUANA PECOS: Candido Armijo, he was...governor that year....[W]e talked to him and he told his officials...and everybody was real happy...and they all looked forward to that [meeting]....We usually have once a month [a] meeting of all the different tribes and...we...invited...[a] big group from the different pueblos and...they were all real happy to come....[I]n the meantime, my relatives and everybody [in the pueblo] got busy and cooked. They cooked,... baked bread,...all kinds of goodies,...cakes and pies, and everything....

[On the day of the enshrinement] the cacique came here to the door [of our home]....[He] got his pollen [out of a pouch] and [referring to the statue]...

said, "Lady, I am so glad you are here. I am so happy that you have come to Jemez Pueblo. We have always heard so much about you and now you are really here. . . . I want you to follow me. I want you. . . . " [T]hen he went with his corn meal [sprinkling it on the statue this way] and that way and . . . says, "Come with me, I'm going to show you where you are going to stand, taking care of you[r] Indian people in this pueblo."

So we went. . . . [W]e had a procession from here to the church. . . . I saw all that group behind me. . . . [T]hey were singing, some were carrying flowers. . . . Some were singing Indian and some were singing . . . "This is the Day the Lord has Made." . . . [W]e were in the procession carrying our statue and our pictures of her. . . . And oh, it was just beautiful—the whole procession to the church.

. . . [A]nd on the way down there, I was thinking, "Oh dear! I forgot to tell Father Melvin!" "I've got [to get] hold of him because . . . he was my favorite [priest]." And mind you, when I got to the front of the church, I looked up there, there was Father Melvin, all dressed ready! I said, "Oh Lord, you did it!" There he was!

. . . We all walked into the church and we're placed [seated] and they were blessed [by] Father Melvin and Father Bob. . . . [T]hen the churchman came up and talked to the cacique and the cacique said, "You [put a] place up there . . . for her to stand . . . [with a bag of] . . . corn meal. . . . " And they did.

. . . Father Melvin and Father Bob did the mass. It was beautiful and my brother Mike . . . was the sacristan. . . . (He's [now] passed away [but] he had been sacristan till he died.) . . . The mass went on . . . [with] the blessing of each statue and each picture. . . . [W]e stood with Kateri, the statue and then there's . . . [the] one . . . made [by] . . . my daughter . . . Esther, . . . [which] was blessed and . . . given a place . . . [in] her house.

. . . [A]fter mass, we all made a procession around the pueblo and that cacique [referring to the statue, said] . . . I've been . . . told, "Come Mother, see your children. See the Pueblo." . . . Then he walked ahead of us and everywhere he said, "This is the [Parkmans'?] house, bless it and renew the members." And over here's the cacique's house, "Renew the place." . . . [T]hen we went on. . . . "Here's our Pumpkin Kiva." . . . [T]hen we went on and he just prayed for all the different [people]. . . . [Y]ou should [have] see[n] all the people that heard us coming. They all start[ed] coming to greet her. It was just beautiful and all the men came out to greet her and to pray with their corn meal and welcome her. . . . We went all the way down to the missions . . . where we had our meeting . . . our celebration. . . . It was a big, big celebration and that's how we honor[ed] Blessed Kateri Tekakwitha . . . [in 19]89, I think.

And . . . the San Juans, . . . the Cochitis, . . . and the Lagunas [people of other Pueblo tribes] were so impressed . . . they said, "Let's enshrine her in our pueblos." And they have. We . . . had a celebration in Laguna, . . . San Juan, . . . Cochiti, and all the different places. . . . So [now] Blessed Kateri is . . . a big part in the Southwest, . . . [but] she was enshrined . . . first . . . in Jemez Pueblo. . . .

Marquette University, Kateri Tekakwitha Oral History Collection. Printed by permission.

102. Faith, Prayer, and Devotion of Mark J. Cheresposey in Laguna Pueblo, July 11, 1995

Mark J. Cheresposey (Laguna) of Laguna, New Mexico, recalls his son's life-threatening accident in 1984 and subsequent recovery amid prayers by many for Tekakwitha's intercession. Included are references to the 46th Annual Tekakwitha Conference: "A Journey of Hope," August 1–5, 1984, Phoenix Plaza Civic Center, Phoenix, Arizona.

Interviewed and edited by Mark G. Thiel.

THIEL: When did you first hear about Kateri Tekakwitha?

CHERESPOSEY: Oh,... when I went back East [as a boy]. I...[had] visit[ed] her homeland because we used to collect [solicit donations], like I said, [for] the missions....[A]lready then I knew that she was being considered for beatification....I read a short article on her and I knew that she was a great lady.

...[B]ut I think the most impressive thing that ever happened was when my son got hit by a semi [trailer truck]....[M]y brother — one of my brothers and one of my adopted sisters — were on call that night with the ambulance and they couldn't recognize who it was even though they [knew] him....[T]hey took him into Albuquerque and gave him the name John Doe.

...[W]e weren't too worried [when my son didn't call home] that night because generally they'[d] call and say they're gonna stay at...grandma's house ...[as] we used to live down in Mesita where I work. So in early morning we found out that there was an accident. Somebody was taken into the hospital so we went in. We identified him and in the meantime they'[d] given him the name of John Doe...and when...the doctors...operated on him they told us that, "I don't think your son's going to make it. If anything, we'll give him a 50–50 chance."...I think being kind to people,...knowing a lot of people, always having a kind word was repaid to us almost instantly....[W]ithin the next week we had over 500 people [had] come in and encourage[d] us and tell us they're praying for us...[and] he was in there four months....[A]bout a week...[before] that it happened...my mother had already made plans to go to Phoenix for the [1984 national] Tekakwitha Conference. And she was worried about it. She came down there and she says, "I don't think I should go. I think I should stay." I said, "No, Mom," I said. "I think you're doing more good down at the Tekakwitha Conference. Ask Kateri to help, help us. There's a lot of people who come by here and said that, further, to encourage them. Ask them to ask Kateri to intercede."

And so she left while my boy was still unconscious. He was unconscious for almost a month and a half. And he was unconscious there then. So, she left and she had arthritis and all kind of medical problems, barely got around. But she said, "I'm going to offer this to Kateri. Let's see what I can — what we can do." And it was during the conference that we were in the hospital — but I stayed with my son for two straight months. I just forgot about my job, just stayed there. And it was during the conference that we found out that he was — he actually responded. He opened his eyes and looking at us and he said, "Hi, Mom. Hi, Dad." It was — you couldn't understand quite what it was but we knew what he was talking about. And then we reminded, we said, "Grandma's down. She's in Phoenix praying for you. And she's praying to Kateri to help you up." He said, "I know, I know." And then when she came up, she — one of her first stops was going down to check. And she brought him a T-shirt, Kateri at the front. And by that time, he would say, put about three or four words together. And he put the T-shirt on. And he said, "Grandma gave me this T-shirt." "Yeah, you know who that is?" "Yeah, she made me well." Just looking at Kateri. "She made me well." And this was, you know, just the doctors even them they said, "He's going to be a vegetable. I don't know. I don't know if he'll ever be able to walk. He's lost about three or four cells out of the eight in his head. I don't know." They were giving us the — we told them to be honest with us. They said, "I don't know what else we can do." And we told them, "Well, we have faith. We have a lot of people, a lot of our friends, a lot of our relatives are praying for us. He'll pull through," I said. "Well, I sure hope your faith does something," he said, "Because I think your son's going to be a vegetable." But ever since after that somehow, he really improved. And we kept the faith.

There was another boy, a Spanish boy that was in there before him with [the] same situation, injuries and everything. And they were so surprised at how our boy started improving so quick. And they said, "You know, it just makes you wonder, it just makes you, maybe see the way the Indians are in their faith." It's so much more sincere when they come and tell you, they visit you. They tell you they're going to pray for you and all this and that. And your boy is just improving so much quicker. And I naturally had problems at work. My boss said, "Well, when are you coming back?" I said, "Well," I said, "I have sick leave and my boy comes first, my family comes first," I said. "You do what you want to but I'm going to stay here." But his other boss, the one that's higher up understood. I said, "You know that's family." He said, "You take all the time you want. It can help." They were very good about it but personalities are different in certain areas. But our arguing, I try to do what I could anyway.

So my boy was — he increased so rapidly. In fact, let's see that was July, August, September, October he went back to school four months later. And the doctors couldn't believe it. They said, "You mean you're going actually to send him back to high school?" We had a conference with the doctors, just about school and everything else. And his memory is not that great, but somehow he was ready, I don't know how he did it. He graduated from high school then in the fall, oh no, in May. But he went through the whole school year and I just can't understand it but he's very much back to normal now. And he has [married], in fact this is his...oldest daughter and his little one [referring to photograph], another little one that — he's in the hospital with right now. But to this day he still remembers Kateri. He remembers who helped him...[with] power of prayer. And although he gets discouraged a lot of times, he — he's [God?] reminding us, you're not only — you're going to hurt yourself.... All these people...prayed...[and] their prayers brought you this far. Everybody else sacrificed and that reach of spirit...helped us out.

THIEL: How often do you feel the presence of Blessed Kateri?

CHERESPOSEY: I think it's not really that frequent. Like I said we don't — we have, I think we have — yes, we do have a statue but the presence I feel is when we participate in mass, when we have our Indian mass. When I see the older people participating, getting ready for the convention or the area meetings it's just the — I don't know. It's a — looking at them, they seem weak but their spirit is so high. And they don't complain about not being able to walk. Right there they're preparing what they want to do. In fact the songs that are composed of her over in our language, it really — I think every time I hear them, I feel like a lump in my throat. And I want, I hope and I pray that she would be canonized where we could have a satisfaction of the Christian part of our upbringing-ness to see her as a saint. But in our heart as Indians, we know she's a saint. We know because we feel it and we've experienced the gifts. I think especially at Laguna. We've experienced the ministry has increased because of the lack of priests. But also because I think Kateri, she wants us to — I hate to sound like I'm bragging of the Laguna people, but I think she wants us to be an example of what faith can do. Indian, with an Indian in the Christian faith. And it's really our music has been great, music ministry, our Indian music ministry and then our, our RCIA (Rite of Christian Initiation for Adults) instructions. Oh, I saw many ministries down there that its faith has brought the people together. And somehow we don't maybe segregate and say, "Well, this is only our thing."

Somehow, I think a miracle in itself is all the people realizing that we're working for a common goal. And I think it's brought on by I would say, Kateri. Its strength, you hear at mass or we pray for the people and pray for all the saint[s] or ask her to intercede, intercession. And she's always included along with Mother Katherine Drexel who is also one of our big contributors to our faith. And I think, you know, there would be a great — I guess you might say, a great feeling to see both of those two that have influence. The Indian people hope so much to have them become saints. I think it would just, let's say, maybe being the pinnacle of what we would like to see.

Marquette University, Kateri Tekakwitha Oral History Collection. Printed by permission.

103. Sister Kateri Mitchell, S.S.A., and Reverend John Brioux, O.M.I., "In Her Footsteps," 1995

One of the most popular hymns at the National Tekakwitha Conference is "In Her Footsteps," composed by Sister Kateri Mitchell, S.S.A. (Mohawk, Turtle Clan, just like Kateri Tekakwitha), and Reverend John Brioux, O.M.I. The song compares Kateri Tekakwitha to Mother Earth and employs a Native American style of chanting and drumming, producing a combination of Catholic and American Indian spirituality. "In Her Footsteps" was performed with special power at the Tekakwitha Conference gathering at Akwesasne in 1995. Sister Kateri has translated some verses from English to Mohawk.

CHORUS: KATERI TEKAKWITHA
            NE ONKWA TATE KENHA
            ONEN KIONKINONKS
            ONWEN TSIONHAKWEKON

VERSE 3:   TEKAKWITHA
            IAKOHARKWEN
            IAKONTSENNONNI
            KWASENNAIENS

VERSE 4:   KATSITSIANORON
            KIAKORIWAIERI
            IEIATANORON
            KWASENNAIENS

VERSE 8:   TIONKISWATHETENNI
            RAOSWATHETSERA
            SATENNITERON
            TEKWANONWHERATONS

VERSE 11: KAWHATSIRAKWEKON
            TSIKIONNHE
            TETEWAIENA
            NIAWEN KOWA

Tekakwitha Conference, Potsdam, 1995. Translation provided by Sister Kateri Mitchell, S.S.A., 2000. Printed by permission.

104. Native Profession of Faith, Tekakwitha Conference, Kahnawake, Quebec, 1995

When the National Tekakwitha Conference held its annual meeting in Potsdam, New York, in 1995, members traveled to Kahnawake to visit Kateri Tekakwitha's enshrined tomb. At Mass there they made a Native Profession of Faith, affirming their belief in "the Creator, the Great Spirit, Maker of Mother Earth and Father Sky...," while participants brought offerings of corn, beans, and squash to the altar.

We believe in the Creator, the Great Spirit,
Maker of Mother Earth and Father Sky,
Creator of the seasons and of all living things.

We believe in Jesus of Nazareth, a man of God,
who lived with the courage of commitment,
who sacrificed life that the people may live,
for all people, for all ages, for us.

We believe in the Holy Spirit,
the action-love of the Great One and of Jesus,
who breaks down barriers between people
and empowers us to love one another.

In Her Footsteps - Song #8

Sr. Kateri Mitchell, SSA

Fr. John Brioux, OMI
with Sr. Kateri Mitchell, SSA

refrain

Ka-te-ri Te-kak-wi-tha   Noble Turtle, Mother Earth

Ga-thers her people   East, South West and North. (to verses)

1.	Mohawk	Algonquin	Lily	filled	wi-th	love
2.	Sister	Turtle	Cl-an	strong,	kind and	true
3.	Te-	kak-	wi-tha	hope	filled	dignity
4.	Woodland	Cross of	Life	fas-	ting and	prayer
5.	Pre-	cious	flower	vir-gin,	fair and	free
6.	Friend	with com-	passion	hel-	per and	healer

1. grate-ful   woman   we honor you. (to refrain)

2. faith-ful   woman   we honor you. (to refrain)

3. joy- ful   woman   we honor you. (to refrain)

4. mys- tical   woman   we honor you. (to refrain)

5. ho- ly   woman   we honor you. (to refrain)

6. lo- ver of   peoples   we honor you. (to refrain)

(In Her Footsteps, con't)

7.	Gift of	Nations	gen-tle and for-	giving
8.	Our_____	Sunshine	vision, bright and	keen
9.	Cre- a- tor	centered	cre- a-tion	filled
10.	Cele- brate our	gath'ring	clans, tribes,	nations
11.	Fam- 'ly u-	ni- ted	Body, blood,	life
12.	In your sac-red	journey	Blessed Ka-te-	ri

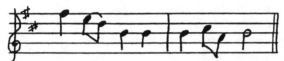

7. lo- yal witness   we thank you. (to refrain)

8. o- pen, generous we thank you. (to refrain)

9. air, sky, wa-ter   we thank you. (to refrain)

10. jus- tice, harmony we thank you. (to refrain)

11. ser- ving, sharing we thank you. (to refrain)

12. we honor you   we thank you. (to refrain)

refrain

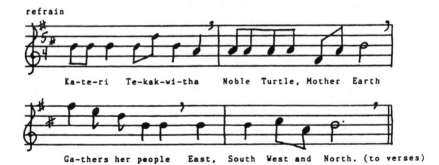

Ka-te-ri Te-kak-wi-tha   Noble Turtle, Mother Earth

Ga-thers her people   East, South West and North. (to verses)

We believe in the community
of committed and faith-filled people.
We believe it is our task
to be the salt of the earth
and the light of the world,
justice and peace-makers,
knowing that this calls us
to the sacrifice of the cross.

We believe in the power
of the Great Spirit's presence
as it fills our hearts,
helping us to reach outward
in the Four Directions
to all people in need of healing.

We believe in a just world,
in equal rights for all.
We believe in resurrection,
and in a more full life
with the Creator in the world beyond.

We believe! Help our un-belief! AMEN!

Tekakwitha Conference, Potsdam, 1995. Printed by permission.

REFERENCES AND
SUGGESTED READINGS

Adams, Eleanor B., ed. and trans. Bishop Tamarón's Visitation of New Mexico, 1760. Albuquerque: University of New Mexico Press, 1954.

Adams, Eleanor B., and (Reverend) Angelico Chavez, eds. and trans. The Missions of New Mexico, 1776: A Description by Fray Francisco Atanasio Dominguez with Other Contemporary Documents. Albuquerque: University of New Mexico Press, 1956.

Archambault, (Sister) Marie Therese, O.S.F. A Retreat with Black Elk: Living in the Sacred Hoop. Cincinnati: St. Anthony Messenger Press, 1998.

Axtell, James. "The European Failure to Convert the Indians: An Autopsy." In Papers of the Sixth Algonquian Conference, 1974, ed. William Cowan, 274–90. Ottawa: National Museums of Canada, 1975.

———. The Invasion Within: The Contest of Cultures in Colonial America. New York: Oxford University Press, 1986.

Bahr, Donald M. "Pima-Papago Christianity." Journal of the Southwest 30 (1988): 133–67.

Beaver, R. Pierce, ed. The Native American Christian Community: A Directory of Indian, Aleut, and Eskimo Churches. Monrovia, Calif.: Missions Advanced Research and Communication Center, 1979.

Béchard, Henri. The Original Caughnawaga Indians. Montreal: International Publishers, 1976.

———. Kaia'tanó:ron Kateri Tekakwitha, trans. Antoinette Kinlough. Kahnawake, Quebec: Kateri Center, 1994.

Blanchard, David. "...To the Other Side of the Sky: Catholicism at Kahnawake, 1667–1700." Anthropologica 24 (1982): 77–102.

Bolton, Herbert E. "The Mission as a Frontier Institution in the Spanish-American Colonies." American Historical Review 23 (1917): 42–61.

———. Rim of Christendom: A Biography of Eusebio Francisco Kino, Pacific Coast Pioneer. New York: Russell & Russell, 1960.

Bowden, Henry Warner. "Spanish Missions, Cultural Conflict and the Pueblo Revolt of 1680." Church History 44 (1975): 217–28.

———. American Indians and Christian Missions: Studies in Cultural Conflict. Chicago: University of Chicago Press, 1981.

Braden, Charles S. Religious Aspects of the Conquest of Mexico. Durham, N.C.: Duke University Press, 1930.

Buechner, Cecilia Bain. The Pokagons. Indianapolis: Indiana Historical Society, 1933.

Burkhart, Louise M. The Slippery Earth: Nahua-Christian Moral Dialogue in Sixteenth-Century Mexico. Tucson: University of Arizona Press, 1989.

————. "The Cult of the Virgin of Guadalupe in Mexico." In South and Meso-American Native Spirituality, ed. Gary H. Gossen, 198–227. New York: Crossroad, 1993.

Burns, (Reverend) Robert Ignatius, S.J. The Jesuits and the Indian Wars of the Northwest. New Haven: Yale University Press, 1966.

————. "Roman Catholic Missions in the Northwest." In Handbook of North American Indians. Vol. 4, History of Indian-White Relations, ed. Wilcomb E. Washburn, 494–500. Washington, D.C.: Smithsonian Institution, 1988.

Campeau, (Reverend) Lucien, S.J. La Première Mission d'Acadie (1602–1616). Monumenta Novæ Franciæ, no. 1. Québec: Presses de l'Université Laval, 1967.

————. Établissement à Québec (1616–1634). Monumenta Novæ Franciæ, no. 2. Québec: Presses de l'Université Laval, 1979.

————. Foundation de la Mission Huronne (1635–1637). Monumenta Novæ Franciæ, no. 3. Québec: Presses de l'Université Laval, 1987.

————. La Mission des Jésuites chez les Hurons, 1634–1650. Montreal: Éditions Bellarmin, 1987.

————. Les Grandes Épreuves (1638–1640). Monumenta Novæ Franciæ, no. 4. Montréal: Les Editions Bellarmin, 1989.

Castillo, Edward D. Native American Perspectives on the Hispanic Colonization of Alta California. Spanish Borderlands Sourcebooks, no. 26. New York: Garland Publishing, Inc., 1991.

Champe, Flavia Waters. The Matachines Dance of the Upper Rio Grande: History, Music, and Choreography. Lincoln: University of Nebraska, 1983.

Chittenden, Hiram Martin, and Alfred Talbot Richardson, eds. Life, Letters, and Travels of Father Pierre-Jean de Smet, S.J., 1801–1873. 4 vols. New York: Francis P. Harper, 1905.

Clifton, James A. The Pokagons, 1683–1983: Catholic Potawatomi Indians of the St. Joseph River Valley. Washington, D.C.: University Press of America, 1984.

Costello, Julia G., ed. Documentary Evidence for the Spanish Missions of Alta California. Spanish Borderlands Sourcebooks, no. 14. New York: Garland Publishing, Inc., 1991.

Costo, Jeannette Henry, and Rupert Costo. The Missions of California: A Legacy of Genocide. San Francisco: Indian Historian Press, 1987.

Delâge, Denys, and Helen Hornbeck Tanner. "The Ojibwa-Jesuit Debate at Walpole Island, 1844." Ethnohistory 41 (1994): 295–321.

Delfeld, Paula. The Indian Priest: Father Philip B. Gordon, 1885–1948. Chicago: Franciscan Herald Press, 1977.

DeMallie, Raymond J., ed. The Sixth Grandfather: Black Elk's Teachings Given to John G. Neihardt. Lincoln: University of Nebraska Press, 1984.

Dozier, Edward P. "Spanish Catholic Influences on Rio Grande Pueblo Religion." American Anthropologist 60 (1958): 441–48.

Engelhardt, (Reverend) Zephyrin, O.F.M. The Missions and Missionaries of California. 4 vols. San Francisco: James H. Barry Company, 1908–15.

————. San Diego Mission. San Francisco: James H. Barry Company, 1920.

——. San Luis Rey Mission. San Francisco: James H. Barry Company, 1921.

——. San Juan Capistrano Mission. Los Angeles: Zephyrin Engelhardt, 1922.

——. San Gabriel Mission and the Beginning of Los Angeles. San Gabriel, Calif.: Mission San Gabriel, 1927.

Enochs, Ross. *The Jesuit Mission to the Lakota Sioux: Pastoral Theology and Ministry, 1886–1945.* Kansas City: Sheed & Ward, 1996.

Espinosa, J. Manuel, trans. and ed. *The Pueblo Indian Revolt of 1696 and the Franciscan Missions in New Mexico: Letters of the Missionaries and Related Documents.* Norman: University of Oklahoma Press, 1988.

Flanagan, Thomas. *Louis "David" Riel: "Prophet of the New World."* Toronto: University of Toronto Press, 1979.

Fowler, Loretta. *Shared Symbols, Contested Meanings: Gros Ventre Culture and History, 1778–1984.* Ithaca, N.Y.: Cornell University Press, 1987.

Gagnon, François-Marc. *La Conversion par l'Image: Un Aspect de la Mission des Jésuites auprès des Indiéns du Canada au XVIIe Siècle.* Montréal: Les Editions Bellarmin, 1975.

Geiger, (Reverend) Maynard J., O.F.M., and Clement W. Meighan, eds. *As the Padres Saw Them: California Indian Life and Customs as Reported by the Franciscan Missionaries, 1813–1815.* Santa Barbara, Calif.: Santa Barbara Mission Archive Library, 1976.

Giago, Tim A., Jr. *The Aboriginal Sin.* San Francisco: Indian Historian Press, 1978.

Gómez, Arthur R., ed. *Documentary Evidence for the Spanish Missions of Texas.* Spanish Borderlands Sourcebooks, no. 22. New York: Garland Publishing, 1991.

Grant, John Webster. *Moon of Wintertime: Missionaries and the Indians of Canada in Encounter since 1534.* Toronto: University of Toronto Press, 1985.

Griffith, James S. "Franciscan Chapels on the Papagueria, 1912–1973." *Smoke Signal* 30 (1974): 234–55.

——. "The Folk-Catholic Chapels of the Papagueria." *Pioneer America* 7 (1975): 21–36.

——. *Beliefs and Holy Places: A Spiritual Geography of the Pimería Alta.* Tucson: University of Arizona Press, 1992.

Gutiérrez, Ramón A. *When Jesus Came, the Corn Mothers Went Away: Marriage, Sexuality, and Power in New Mexico, 1500–1846.* Stanford, Calif.: Stanford University Press, 1991.

Hackett, Charles W. and Charmion Clair Shelby. *Revolt of the Pueblo Indians of New Mexico and Otermín's Attempted Reconquest, 1680–1682.* 2 vols. Albuquerque: University of New Mexico Press, 1942.

Hall, (Sister) Suzanne, S.N.D., ed. *The People: Reflections of Native Peoples on the Catholic Experience in North America.* Washington, D.C.: National Catholic Educational Association, 1992.

Hann, John H., and Bonnie G. McEwan. *The Apalachee Indians and Mission San Luis.* Gainesville: University Press of Florida, 1998.

Harrod, Howard L. *Mission among the Blackfeet.* Norman: University of Oklahoma Press, 1971.

Hatcher, (Reverend) John E., S.J., and (Reverend) Patrick M. McCorkell, S.J. Builders of the New Earth: The Formation of Permanent Deacons. 3 vols. Rapid City, S.Dak.: Diocese of Rapid City, 1975–76.

Hebert, (Reverend) Donald J. South Louisiana Records: Church and Civil Records of Lafourche — Terrebonne Parishes. 12 vols. Cecilia, La.: Reverend Donald J. Hebert, 1978–85.

Hemauer, (Reverend) Gilbert F., O.F.M. The Story and Faith Journey of Seventeen Native Catechists. Great Falls, Mont.: Tekakwitha Conference National Center, 1982.

Hodge, Frederick Webb, George P. Hammond, and Agapito Rey, eds. and trans. Fray Alonso de Benavides' Revised Memorial of 1634. Albuquerque: University of New Mexico Press, 1945.

Holler, Clyde. Black Elk's Religion: The Sun Dance and Lakota Catholicism. Syracuse: Syracuse University Press, 1995.

Jackson, Robert H., and Edward Castillo. Indians, Franciscans, and Spanish Colonization: The Impact of the Mission System on California Indians. Albuquerque: University of New Mexico Press, 1995.

Kelsey, Harry. The Doctrina and Confesionario of Juan Cortés. Altadena, Calif.: Howling Coyote Press, 1979.

Kennedy, J. H. Jesuit and Savage in New France. New Haven: Yale University Press, 1950.

Kessell, John L. Mission of Sorrows: Jesuit Guevavi and the Pimas, 1691–1767. Tucson: University of Arizona Press, 1970.

———. Friars, Soldiers, and Reformers: Hispanic Arizona and the Sonora Mission Frontier, 1767–1856. Tucson: University of Arizona Press, 1976.

———. Kiva, Cross, and Crown: The Pecos Indians and New Mexico, 1540–1840. Washington, D.C.: National Park Service, U.S. Department of the Interior, 1979.

———. The Missions of New Mexico since 1776. Albuquerque: University of New Mexico Press, 1980.

Kessell, John L., and Rick Hendricks, eds. The Spanish Missions of New Mexico. Vol. 1, Before 1680. Spanish Borderlands Sourcebooks, no. 17. New York: Garland Publishing, 1991.

———. The Spanish Missions of New Mexico. Vol. 2, After 1680. Spanish Borderlands Sourcebooks, no. 18. New York: Garland Publishing, 1991.

Kidwell, Clara Sue. Choctaws and Missionaries in Mississippi, 1818–1918. Norman: University of Oklahoma Press, 1995.

Knaut, Andrew L. The Pueblo Revolt of 1680: Conquest and Resistance in Seventeenth-Century New Mexico. Norman: University of Oklahoma Press, 1995.

Lakota Inculturation Task Force. Recommendations toward the Inculturation of Lakota Catholicism. Diocese of Rapid City, S.Dak., forthcoming.

Matson, Daniel S., and Bernard L. Fontana, eds. and trans. Friar Bringas Reports to the King: Methods of Indoctrination on the Frontier of New Spain, 1796–97. Tucson: University of Arizona Press, 1977.

McGloin, (Reverend) John Bernard, S.J. Eloquent Indian: The Life of James Bouchard, California Jesuit. Stanford, Calif.: Stanford University Press, 1950.

Milanich, Jerald T., and William C. Sturtevant, eds. Francisco Pareja's 1613 Confessionario [sic]: A Documentary Source for Timucuan Ethnography. Tallahassee: Division of Archives, History, and Records Management, Florida Department of State, 1972.

Milliken, Randall. A Time of Little Choice: The Disintegration of Tribal Culture in the San Francisco Bay Area. Menlo Park, Calif.: Ballena Press, 1993.

Monthan, Guy, and Doris Monthan. Nacimientos: Nativity Scenes by Southwest Indian Artisans. Albuquerque: Avanyu Publishing, 1990.

Moore, James T. Indian and Jesuit: A Seventeenth-Century Encounter. N.P.: Loyola University Press, 1982.

Neihardt, John G. Black Elk Speaks: Being the Life Story of a Holy Man of the Ogala Sioux, as Told through John G. Neihardt (Flaming Rainbow). New York: William Morrow and Company, 1932.

Olsen, Loran, and Thomas E. Connolly, S.J. "Musical Syncretism at the Salish Missions." European Review of Native American Studies 15, no. 1 (2001): 13–17.

Painter, Muriel Thayer. With Good Heart: Yaqui Beliefs and Ceremonies in Pascua Village. Tucson: University of Arizona Press, 1986.

Painter, Muriel Thayer, Refugio Savala, and Ignacio Alvarez. A Yaqui Easter Sermon. Tucson: University of Arizona Press, 1955.

Palladino, (Reverend) Lawrence B., S.J. Indian and White in the Northwest: A History of Catholicity in Montana, 1831–1891. Lancaster, Pa.: Wickersham Publishing Company, 1922.

Parsons, Elsie Clews. "Nativity Myth at Laguna and Zuni." Journal of American Folklore 31 (1918): 256–63.

Peelman, (Reverend) Achiel, O.M.I. Christ Is a Native American. Ottawa: Novalis-Saint Paul University, 1995; Maryknoll, N.Y.: Orbis Books, 1995.

Point, (Reverend) Nicolas, S.J. Wilderness Kingdom: Indian Life in the Rocky Mountains, 1840–1847. Trans. (Reverend) Joseph P. Donnelly, S.J. New York: Holt, Rinehart and Winston, 1967.

Polzer, Charles W. Rules and Precepts of the Jesuit Missions of Northwestern New Spain. Tucson: University of Arizona Press, 1976.

The Positio of the Historical Section of the Sacred Congregation of Rites on the Introduction of the Cause for Beatification and Canonization and on the Virtues of the Servant of God, Katherine Tekakwitha, the Lily of the Mohawks. New York: Fordham University Press, 1940.

Prucha, (Reverend) Francis Paul, S.J. The Churches and the Indian Schools, 1888–1912. Lincoln: University of Nebraska Press, 1979.

Rahill, Peter J. The Catholic Indian Missions and Grant's Peace Policy, 1870–1884. Washington, D.C.: Catholic University of America Press, 1953.

Ricard, Robert. The Spiritual Conquest of Mexico. Berkeley: University of California Press, 1966.

Riel, Louis. The Diaries of Louis Riel. Ed. Thomas Flanagan. Edmonston, Alberta: Hurtig Publishers, 1976.

Rivera, Luis N. A Violent Evangelism: The Political and Religious Conquest of the Americas. Louisville, Ky.: Westminster/John Knox Press, 1992.

Rodríguez, Sylvia. The Matachines Dance: Ritual Symbolism and Interethnic Relations in the Upper Río Grande Valley. Albuquerque: University of New Mexico Press, 1996.

Rostkowski, Joëlle. La Conversion Inachavée: Les Indiens et le Christianisme. Paris: Albin Michel, 1998.

Shea, John Gilmary. History of the Catholic Missions among the Indian Tribes of the United States, 1529–1854. New York: Edward Dunigan & Brother, 1855.

Spicer, Edward H. Pascua: A Yaqui Village in Arizona. Chicago: University of Chicago Press, 1940.

———. "Spanish-Indian Acculturation in the Southwest," with comments by Florence Hawley Ellis and Edward P. Dozier. American Anthropologist 56 (1954): 663–84.

———. Cycles of Conquest. Tucson: University of Arizona Press, 1972.

———. The Yaquis: A Cultural History. Tucson: University of Arizona Press, 1980.

Starkloff, (Reverend) Carl F., S.J. "American Indian Religion and Christianity: Confrontation and Dialogue." Journal of Ecumenical Studies 8 (1971): 317–40.

———. The People of the Center: American Indian Religion and Christianity. New York: Seabury Press, 1974.

———. " 'Evangelization' and Native Americans." Studies in the International Apostolate 4 (1975): 1–37.

———. "Mission Method and the American Indian." Theological Studies 38 (1977): 621–53.

———. A Theological Reflection: The Recent Revitalization of the Tekakwitha Conference. Great Falls, Mont.: Tekakwitha Conference National Center, 1982.

———. "Keepers of Tradition: The Symbol Power of Indigenous Ministry." Kerygma 52 (1989): 3–120.

———. " 'Good Fences Make Good Neighbors' or 'The Meeting of the Two Rivers.' " Studia Missionalia 44 (1995): 367–88.

Statement of U.S. Catholic Bishops on American Indians. Washington, D.C.: United States Catholic Conference, 1977.

Steltenkamp, (Reverend) Michael F., S.J. Black Elk: Holy Man of the Oglala. Norman: University of Oklahoma Press, 1993.

Stolzman, (Reverend) William F., S.J. The Pipe and Christ. Pine Ridge, S.Dak.: Red Cloud Indian School, 1986.

Tac, Pablo. Indian Life and Customs at Mission San Luis Rey. Ed. and trans. Minna Hewes and Gordon Hewes. San Luis Rey, Calif.: Old Mission, 1958.

Thwaites, Reuben Gold, ed. The Jesuit Relations and Allied Documents. 73 vols. Cleveland: Burrows Brothers, 1896–1901.

Tinker, George. Missionary Conquest: The Gospel and Native American Cultural Genocide. Minneapolis: Fortress Press, 1993.

Treat, James, ed. Native and Christian: Indigenous Voices on Religious Identity in the United States and Canada. New York: Routledge, 1996.

Twohy, (Reverend) Patrick J., S.J. Finding a Way Home: Indian and Catholic Spiritual Paths of the Plateau Tribes. Inchelium, Wash.: St. Michaels [sic] Mission, 1984.

Usera, John J. Lakota Spiritual Life and Practice of Religion in Western South Dakota: Consultation Reports Phases I–III. Rapid City, S.Dak.: Chiesman Foundation for Democracy, 2001–2.

Vecsey, Christopher. On the Padres' Trail. American Indian Catholics, no. 1. Notre Dame, Ind.: University of Notre Dame Press, 1996.

———. The Paths of Kateri's Kin. American Indian Catholics, no. 2. Notre Dame, Ind.: University of Notre Dame Press, 1997.

———. Where the Two Roads Meet. American Indian Catholics, no. 3. Notre Dame, Ind.: University of Notre Dame Press, 1999.

Weber, (Reverend) Francis J. Documents of California Catholic History (1784–1963). Los Angeles: Dawson's Book Shop, 1965.

———. El Camino Real: A Documentary History of California's Asistencias. Hong Kong: Yee Tin Tong Printing Press, 1988.

Weiser, (Reverend) Francis X., S.J. Kateri Tekakwitha. Montreal: Kateri Center, 1972.

White, James D. Getting Sense: The Osages and Their Missionaries. Tulsa, Okla.: Sarto Press, 1997.

Wintz, (Reverend) Jack, O.F.M. "Respect Our Values." St. Anthony Messenger 83 (July 1975): 34–40.

———. "Should Junipero Serra Be Declared a Saint?" St. Anthony Messenger 95 (August 1987): 29–37.

Zuern, (Reverend) Ted, S.J. Bread and Freedom. Chamberlain, S.Dak.: St. Joseph's Indian School, 1991.

American Catholic Identities
A Documentary History
Christopher J. Kauffman, General Editor

Titles of books in the series are:

A workshop for the editors of these books was entirely funded by a generous grant from the Louisville Institute.

INDEX

Of Related Interest

Important Studies of World Christianity
Indispensable resources for understanding how Christianity has
changed from being the religion of Eur-American tribes to a world
faith.

History of the World Christian Movement
Dale T. Irvin and Scott W. Sunquist
Volume 1: Earliest Christianity to 1453 (published in 2001)
$30.00. 6X9-inches, 536 pages. Index, maps.
ISBN 1-57075-396-2

Volume 2: 1454 to the Twentieth Century (scheduled for 2005)

A study of the history of Christianity that shows how, from its earliest
beginnings, the Christian movement was vitally present in areas
outside the Mediterranean basin. Irvin and Sunquist, aided by 43
collaborating scholars, present a narrative of Christianity that puts
special emphasis on the social and cultural milieux in which the
movment has incarnated itself, the role of women, and the emergence
of a dynamic but kaleidoscopic communion.

"This corrective has long been necessary, and has been successfully
accomplished by the authors and their consultants. This is an
excellent, scholarly study which will be of great use to university
students of early Christianity."
W. H. C. Frend,
Gonville and Caius College, Cambridge University

Please support your local bookstore, or call us at 1-800-258-5838
For a free catalogue, please write us at
Orbis Books, Box 308
Maryknoll NY 1054-0302
or visit our website at www.orbisbooks.com.

Thank you for reading Orbis Books.

Readings in World Christian History
Volume 1: Earliest Christianity to 1453
Edited by John Coakley and Andrea Sterk
$30.00. 7X9 inches, two columns, 416 pages. Index
ISBN 1-57075-520-5

Destined to become the gold standard for introducing readers to the
full range of primary texts in early Christian history. The editors' task
was to include texts that everyone agrees are essential, but also to
broaden the canon by bringing into the conversation texts from Syria,
Nubia, and India.

From reviewers of the pre-publication manuscript . . .

"My impression of the whole is of a vivid and well-balanced selection."
Peter Brown,
Princeton University

"I like it. The desire to be more inclusive seems to be well realized."
Bernard McGinn,
University of Chicago

Constants in Context: A Theology of Mission for Today
Stephen B. Bevans and Roger Schroeder
$30. 6 X 9 inches, summary charts, 11 maps. Index
ISBN 1-57075-517-5

Once or twice in a generation a truly magisterial book enables the
scholarly community to gain a new perspective on the kind of dynamic
unity in diversity that Christian traditions display beneath all the
complexity of history. Bevans and Schroeder give the reader exactly
this kind of vision. Taking the theme of "mission" from its emergence
in the New Testament, they examine how it plays out historically and
theologically down to the emergence of "world Christianity" in the
twentieth century. An incredible achievement.

Thank you for reading Orbis Books.